the
COMPLETE
VEGETARIAN
COOKBOOK

the
COMPLETE
VEGETARIAN
COOKBOOK

SARAH BROWN

PUBLISHED BY THE READER'S DIGEST ASSOCIATION LIMITED

London • New York • Sydney • Montreal

A READER'S DIGEST BOOK

Published by the Reader's Digest Association Limited
11 Westferry Circus
Canary Wharf
London E14 4HE
www.readersdigest.co.uk

We are committed to both the quality of our products and the service we
provide to our customers. We value your comments, so please feel free
to contact us on 08705 113366, or via our Web site at www.readersdigest.co.uk
If you have any comments or suggestions about the content of this book, e-mail us at:
gbeditorial@readersdigest.co.uk

This book was designed and produced by
THE IVY PRESS LIMITED
The Old Candlemakers
West Street
Lewes
East Sussex BN7 2NZ

Creative Director Peter Bridgewater
Publisher Sophie Collins
Editorial Director Steve Luck
Design Manager Tony Seddon
Designer Alistair Plumb
Project Editor Caroline Earle
Photography Mary-Louise Avery, Ian Parsons
Home Economist Jacqueline Clark
Picture Research Liz Moore

A CIP catalogue record for this book is available from the British Library

ISBN 0 276 42617 7

Originated and printed by Hong Kong Graphics

Publisher's Note
To the best of the author's knowledge the recipe measurements in the book are
accurate. Both metric and Imperial measurements have been given. When making
a recipe follow one set of measurements only; do not mix them. The preparation and
cooking times given for each recipe are an approximate guide only because these
may differ according to the techniques and the type of oven used. The author cannot
be held responsible for new research or developments or individual circumstances
that may invalidate any text, advice or instructions given.

contents

Introduction   7
How to Use this Book   8

NUTRITION   10
Protein   12
Fat   13
Carbohydrate and Fibre   14
Antioxidants   15
Vitamins   16
Minerals   18
A Healthy Diet   20
Life Cycle and Different Dietary Needs   21
Lifestyle and Nutritional Needs   24
Eat Well, Stay Well   26
Different Approaches to Diet   29
Choosing Your Food   30

INGREDIENTS   32
Vegetables   34
Fruit Vegetables   54
Fruit   58
Milk and Cream Products   74
Cheese   76
Eggs   82
Non-Dairy Alternatives   83
Grains   84
Flour and Pasta   89

Pulses   90
Soya Bean Products   96
Nuts and Seeds   98
Herbs   104
Spices   108
Flavourings   112
Oil   114
Vinegar   117
Sweeteners   118

THE VEGETARIAN KITCHEN   120
The Store Cupboard   122
Equipment   126
Meal Planning   128

THE RECIPES   130
Breakfast   132
Soups and Starters   142
Light Meals   170
Main Courses   206
Side Dishes, Sauces and Relishes   282
Salads   296
Cakes, Puddings and Bread   318
Entertaining   343

Index   378
Acknowledgements   384

Introduction

Vegetarian food is food that does not include meat or fish, or any of their by-products, such as lard. From this blunt definition an inspirational and exciting cuisine has developed, which uses a vast array of ingredients and the latest cooking techniques, and encompasses a host of international influences.

This book is written for those who are vegetarian or who are thinking about becoming vegetarian and for those who like the idea of occasional meals without meat or fish. It is intended to be a comprehensive guide to the cuisine, providing information for reference and recipes for a healthy, enjoyable and practical vegetarian diet.

All over the world more people than ever before are interested in vegetarian food. There is a great variety of reasons why people decide to follow a vegetarian diet. Some do so because they feel better eating less or no meat, some because they are concerned about the quality and origin of their food. For others, their reasons focus on the plight of the animals reared for slaughter, especially by factory farming methods, and for experimentation. Many vegetarians eat eggs and dairy products, such as cheese. Those who do not eat these products or any food that involves living creatures, such as honey, are vegans.

Looking to the future, many people feel that a vegetarian diet holds the solution to modern dilemmas about our health and that of our planet, responding to environmental concerns and international food production issues.

The Complete Vegetarian Cookbook takes account of the huge changes in vegetarian food in the last few years – changes mainly brought about by an enormous increase in accessibility and choice of ingredients. Growers and producers are constantly bringing new foods to our attention. Where there used to be simply hard cheese or soft cheese, for example, there is now a rich diversity of flavours and textures on offer. Similarly, with staples such as grains, pulses and cooking oils, the variety available is greater than ever before. Gone are the days when a salad meant settling for one type of lettuce. Salad leaves alone offer a wealth of flavours from sweet to peppery, and colours ranging from white through green to ruby red. This book details more than 350 individual ingredients that can be used in snacks and meals.

Vegetarian cuisine is not bound by one style of preparation or set of ingredients. It draws inspiration from national cuisines across the world, making this way of eating both varied and flexible. Once seen as limited, bland or merely imitative of meat, vegetarian food now includes a spectrum of flavours – such as hot and spicy or aromatic and packed with herbs. Dishes range from the quick, crisp stir-fries of the Orient and the aromatic grain dishes from India and the Middle East to the gloriously coloured, garlic-rich vegetables of the Mediterranean and the fiery chillies of the Americas. Even in areas such as barbecue food, once thought exclusive to the meat eater, there is now a fund of vegetarian ideas.

If you are already vegetarian, I hope you will find inspiration among the recipes and the many cooking notes given in the ingredients section. If you are less familiar with vegetarian food, I hope that this book will help you to approach vegetarian food with more confidence. I initially enjoyed vegetarian cooking because I felt there was so much opportunity to improvise, create and be flexible. I have now been a vegetarian some 20 years and have been writing cookery books for 15 of those years. Yet in researching and developing ideas for this book, I was delighted and surprised by the number of new ingredients and techniques still to discover.

For those wanting to make changes to their diet, there is no right or wrong way to do so. Your diet needs to fit in with you, your lifestyle and your family. If you decide to give up meat and fish overnight you will be more successful if the people you cook for are willing to support you in trying a new diet. It may be that you will gradually introduce more vegetables and wholefoods into your diet. One of the best ways is to try out a couple of meat-free recipes each week until you have a good repertoire of favourites. Start by trying familiar styles of meals and then introduce the unfamiliar more gradually. Whether you are making big or small changes, remember that preparing new recipes or using new ingredients always seems to take more time initially. I hope that the ingredients and recipes in this book will inspire you and that you find a glorious and tempting array in the following pages.

How to use this book

What makes this book special is that it is not simply a collection of recipes. It covers all the techniques needed to cook vegetarian food, as well as including a wealth of detail on the many ingredients used. Underpinning this information are valuable nutritional facts and advice to reassure you that your diet is well balanced and healthy.

The book is divided into two main sections – a reference section, which covers all aspects of a vegetarian diet, and a recipe section, which includes more than 250 recipes. At the back of the book is a smaller section on menu planning and entertaining, including complete menus, as well as a comprehensive index.

The reference section is split into three parts: nutrition; ingredients; and organising a vegetarian kitchen. You can read the reference section in depth or dip into it when you need to look up a particular ingredient, nutrient or technique.

The nutrition part begins by focusing on food composition and the sources of essential nutrients. It looks at a vegetarian diet throughout the different stages in our lives, explaining what is needed and how this diet can be used to improve our health. There is also information on how you may need to vary your diet to fit in with your lifestyle. This section then goes on to consider other diets or aspects of diet that may affect your health.

The ingredients directory describes more than 350 individual ingredients, outlining everything you need to know to make the most of each. For easy reference, the ingredients are divided into several broad food groups, such as pulses or nuts and seeds. In this part you will find notes on how to select and store each ingredient, how to prepare it and which cooking techniques are the most suitable. There are also cookery notes on each ingredient, enabling you to see easily which flavours or other ingredients go well together, which will help you to develop your own creative flair.

The final part of the reference section is designed to help you use your kitchen and your time efficiently. It looks at the store cupboard, gadgets, techniques and storage, as well as offering time saving tips and advice on meal planning. All the information enables you to cook the recipes with the minimum of fuss.

The recipe section follows the reference section and is arranged in chapters. Starting with breakfast, it then moves on to soups and starters, light meals, main courses, side dishes, salads and baking. It includes many classic recipes, as well as dishes with a modern flavour and style. Every recipe is photographed and there are step-by-step photographs to help you master important techniques, such as pasta or pastry making. The book features pages on Mexican, Indian and Oriental food, as well as a section on easy meals for children. Many of the recipes are dairy-free or have options to make them so.

The final section of the book shows you how to put everything together and cook meals for your family and friends, entertaining formally and informally both at home and al fresco. There are several complete menus pictured, plus suggestions for many more.

USING THE NUTRITIONAL INFORMATION

Most of the recipes in this book indicate the nutritional content of a portion of the dish. You can use this information to help you make sure you get the major nutrients you need – but remember that other items in your diet, such as milk, cereals, bread, fruit and vegetables, make an important contribution to your balanced diet, too. If you are new to the science of nutrition, don't be too concerned about details. As a starting point, try to include as many different foods as possible in your diet.

Calcium and iron Recipes stated as being high in calcium contain no less than 250mg calcium and those high in iron contain 4g iron or more (about $\frac{1}{3}$ of the daily adult requirement). Although iron from vegetable sources is not so well absorbed as iron from animal sources, there is no reason for a vegetarian to be iron deficient for dietary reasons alone. It is a good idea to use recipes high in iron and calcium when you can, but remember that many of the other recipes do still provide valuable amounts of these nutrients. Milk, cheese and yoghurt are particularly good sources of calcium, so if you prefer to use a non-dairy product such as soya milk do ensure you choose a product that has been supplemented with calcium.

Protein Although non-vegetarians equate protein with meat, it is easy to get sufficient protein in your vegetarian diet. Try to include at least one dish which provides at least 15g protein every day, but remember that bread, rice, pasta etc will also contribute to the protein content of your diet, as will milk, cheese and yoghurt.

Fat Many of us have a high-fat diet, which is bad for health. If you are trying to control the fat content of your diet, choose main course dishes that contain not more than 15g of fat. For starters and puddings, look for 5g fat or less. Of course if you choose a low-fat main course, you could have a higher fat starter or pudding. As well as giving the total fat per portion of a recipe, I have included the amount of saturated fat. Try to choose dishes low in saturated fat when you can. The remaining fat in the dish will be either polyunsaturated or monounsaturated. These fats contain the same amount of calories as saturated fat, but are less harmful.

Kcals and kJ These are the symbols for the energy content of the dish. The SI unit for energy is the kiloJoule, written in this book as kJ. One kilocalorie is equal to approximately 4 kiloJoules.

Using the recipes

The recipes in this book are analysed per portion, except where stated otherwise – per slice or per muffin, for example.

SYMBOLS USED

Ca high in calcium (i.e. contains approximately one-third of recommended daily adult requirement)

Fe high in iron (i.e. contains approximately one-third of recommended daily adult requirement)

𝒱 suitable for vegans

Measurements are given in metric followed by imperial. Please note that you should follow only one set of measurements as they have not been converted exactly but rounded up or down to make realistic quantities. The conversions are standard, but are varied in one or two cases where the ratio of one ingredient to another is important, such as in pastry and bread making.

Standard level spoon measures are used:
1 tablespoon = one 15ml spoon
1 teaspoon = one 5ml spoon

Eggs are medium unless otherwise stated.

NUTRITION

Food provides the energy and nourishment that is needed to survive and enjoy life. This section looks at nutrition from a general and a vegetarian point of view. Nutrition is a fascinating subject and I am constantly amazed by the body's ability to get the best out of the food we eat.

Nutrition is also a modern subject and while certain facts remain undisputed, new research throws up many ideas and constantly changes our view of what we need and why. It is useful to understand a little about what your food contains and, even if you have been vegetarian for a number of years, it is worthwhile looking at some of the changes in nutritional advice.

This section starts by looking at the composition of foods to see exactly where nutrients come from, why they are needed and in what quantities. Following this is a summary of today's guidelines for a healthy diet and how this relates to a vegetarian diet. While it is useful to have an awareness of general nutrition, it is also important to think about your own specific situation. How do you make sure you are eating the right things? Are there circumstances where you need to change your diet? The influences of lifestyle and age on diet can be found on pages 21–25.

This section also looks beyond nutrition and diet at modern methods of food production and processing, which are a cause of concern for many people, and at other food issues, in order to consider their influence and their relevance to a vegetarian lifestyle.

Protein

Protein is essential during childhood and adolescence, the principal years of growth and development, but it is also needed in adulthood to help maintain the body. It has two main functions. It builds up body structures, such as cell tissues and bone matter, and is found in muscles, skin, nails and hair, as well as blood. Protein also maintains supplies of enzymes, hormones and antibodies. These regulate many of the body's most important functions, such as the ability to digest food.

Protein is made up of amino acids, which are found in many foods. Rather like building blocks, the amino acids are linked together in chain structures that give each kind of protein its specific characteristics. There are 24 known amino acids. Ten of these are called 'essential amino acids' because the body cannot survive without them, nor can it synthesise them and so they must be obtained from food.

Nuts and pulses are protein-rich ingredients that are a staple part of a well-balanced vegetarian diet.

Some foods contain all the essential amino acids in roughly the proportions that the body needs. Milk, eggs, fish and meat are good examples of these sorts of food and in the past have been defined as 'complete proteins' or 'first-class proteins'. Plant or vegetable sources of protein, apart from the soya bean, do not contain this ideal mixture. Because of this they have sometimes been known as 'incomplete proteins' or 'second-class proteins'. Do not get the impression,

however, that these foods are second rate. During digestion, protein is broken down into the component amino acids, which are then absorbed and rearranged. If essential amino acids are missing from one food, they will be extracted from another. As long as all the essential amino acids are included somewhere in the diet, the body will extract the right mixture. It is not even necessary for foods containing all the amino acids to be eaten at the same meal.

Pulses, such as red beans and lentils, which feature in this delicious main course chilli (see page 240), are a good source of protein. The recipe also contains bulgar wheat, which complements the pulses.

SOURCES OF PROTEIN

While the body can do all the processing and extracting of protein, it is still important for vegetarians to ensure that they are getting a good supply of all the essential amino acids by eating a wide variety of protein-rich foods. This is quite straightforward since, apart from dairy products, there are three staple food groups that form the main sources of protein for a non-meat eater. These are pulses (beans, peas and lentils); nuts and seeds; and grains.

What simplifies matters further is that the amino acid profiles in these food groups complement each other. When any two of the above groups are combined, they make a complete protein. It is rather like a two-piece jigsaw puzzle – each piece alone is incomplete, but together they make up the whole picture.

Fortunately, from a culinary point of view, it is easy to combine these staple foods together as they are also complementary in terms of taste and texture. Popular examples of complete protein meals include chilli beans with rice, beans on toast, corn tortilla with refried beans, pasta with pesto sauce and hummus with pitta bread. You can also make combinations of proteins in sweet dishes, for example a nut and oat crumble topping or a mixed muesli with oats, nuts and seeds.

The main point to remember is that you will get plenty of protein as long as you eat a wide range of these staple foods. If you are eating no dairy products at all, you should include food from at least two of the staple food groups every day.

Fat

Fat is a highly concentrated form of energy. Foods high in fat contain a lot of calories, so eating too many fatty foods means you are liable to put on excess weight. High-fat diets are also linked with obesity and with heart disease.

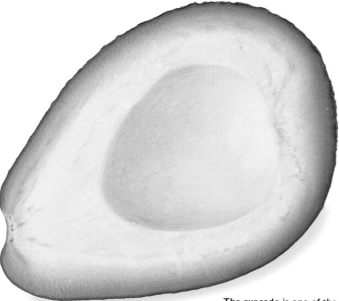

The avocado is one of the few vegetables that has a high fat content. However, it is mostly monounsaturated fat, which helps lower **LDL** cholesterol levels.

So, should you avoid fat altogether for your health? Certainly not. Fats are vital to the functioning of the body. Fatty tissues store the fat-soluble vitamins, A, D, E and K, all of which are essential for life. Fat stimulates gall bladder activity, it is needed to produce certain hormones, and it helps ensure healthy functioning of the nerves. Fat also helps keep the body warm by being stored in layers under the skin.

There are two fatty acids, linoleic and linolenic acids, which cannot be synthesised in the body and must be obtained from dietary sources. These are called essential fatty acids (EFAs).

Cholesterol is a fat-based molecule that is used as a building block for cell membranes and hormones. It is found in the blood in two forms. Low-density LDL cholesterol molecules are small enough to seep into artery walls and begin the process of hardening the arteries. High-density HDL cholesterol molecules are too large to do this and remain in the bloodstream. They help mop up the harmful LDL cholesterol. Cholesterol is produced in our bodies, and the importance of dietary sources of cholesterol is under discussion.

SOURCES OF FAT

There are three main types of fat: saturated, monounsaturated and polyunsaturated. Saturated fats are found mainly in foods of animal origin, such as butter, cream, lard and the fat that occurs in meat. This type of fat stays solid at room temperature. Plant sources of saturated fats are palm and coconut oils. Saturated fats are generally considered unhealthy, since they are thought to increase levels of LDL cholesterol in the blood.

Unsaturated (monounsaturated and polyunsaturated) fats tend to be liquid at room temperature. Monounsaturated fats are found in olive oil and avocados. They tend to be more stable and less prone to rancidity than polyunsaturated fats. They help lower LDL cholesterol levels, raise the levels of the beneficial HDL cholesterol and are a source of EFAs. Polyunsaturated fats come mainly from plant sources such as sunflower, safflower and corn oil, as well as occurring in fish oils. They also supply EFAs. However, polyunsaturates tend to be unstable; they can become rancid quickly and form carcinogenic chemicals. In the process of hydrogenation – which means making the fat solid – transfatty acids are produced, as with some margarines, for example. These are thought to interfere with the functioning of the EFAs and are associated with an increased risk of coronary heart disease.

A constant debate rages as to whether one type of fat is better than another. What is generally agreed, however, is that fat should be eaten sparingly. It is easy to calculate the fat you use in cooking. It is less easy to identify the amount of fat in ready-prepared and processed foods, which is one of the strongest arguments for doing more home cooking.

Simple ways of reducing fat intake include using natural yoghurt or silken tofu instead of cream or mayonnaise, semi-skimmed or skimmed milk instead of whole milk, and lower-fat cheeses. Choose raw vegetables or fresh fruit instead of high-fat snacks. Grill or bake food rather than fry it and use non-stick pans to cut down on the amount of cooking oil you use.

Sunflower seeds and sunflower oil are good sources of polyunsaturated fats. They also contain essential fatty acids.

Carbohydrate and fibre

Carbohydrate, a major nutrient, comes in three main types: monosaccharides, or simple sugars, which include glucose and fructose; disaccharides, which include sucrose, lactose and maltose; and complex carbohydrates, which include starch, cellulose, fibre and glycogen. Dietary fibre is the name given to a number of substances found only in plant foods, which are all constituents of complex carbohydrates. There are several types of fibre: for example, pectin, gum, cellulose, hemocellulose and lignin.

Wholemeal bread is rich in fibre and is a good source of carbohydrate.

Carbohydrate

In a healthy diet carbohydrates are our primary source of energy. Energy is measured in calories and we need calories whether we are working out in a gym or sound asleep in bed. Although all food supplies us with calories, from a nutritional point of view it is best to try and get a good percentage of your daily calorie intake from complex carbohydrate foods or starches. Complex carbohydrates not only supply energy, or calories, but also contain a package of other useful nutrients, such as proteins, vitamins and minerals. Starches are absorbed slowly into the body, giving sustained levels of energy rather than sudden boosts. They are also bulky to eat, therefore taking up room inside you and satisfying you for longer. This leaves little room for the less healthy, sugary, fatty foods.

Complex carbohydrates such as potatoes give you energy as well as other useful nutrients.

Sugar, or sucrose, is also a carbohydrate, but while it will certainly give you plenty of calories, it provides very little else. Known as 'empty calories', sugary foods lack or are very low in the vitamins, minerals and other nutrients that are needed for health and vitality. Excessive consumption of sugar has many associated health problems, such as tooth decay, diabetes and high cholesterol levels. Obesity can also

become a problem since it is very easy to consume extra calories on a high-sugar diet. Calories not used by the body are stored as fat, so avoid added sugar whenever possible.

Fibre

High-fibre diets can help to prevent or alleviate many unhealthy or life-threatening conditions. Fibre stimulates the digestive system and helps reduce the risk of digestive disorders. Soluble fibres, such as gums, act like an internal broom, sweeping away toxins. They also help to lower both blood sugar levels and cholesterol.

All fibre makes food chewy and gives it texture, and as a result you eat less and more slowly. This stimulates saliva production, neutralising acid formed on the teeth and in turn reducing dental decay. Fibre also swells up in the stomach, making you feel more satisfied, so a fibre-rich diet can help counteract obesity.

A healthy vegetarian diet tends to be naturally rich in fibre because there is so much dependence on plant foods for nutrients. To increase your fibre intake, eat more wholemeal bread and other wholegrain cereals, such as brown rice, wholewheat pasta and oats; you should also eat plenty of fresh fruit, salad ingredients and vegetables with your meals; and use lentils, beans and peas regularly in your diet.

If you are looking to increase the fibre in your diet, it is best to eat a variety of wholegrains, which contain beneficial nutrients and fibre, rather than simply adding bran. An acid in the bran called phytate combines with certain minerals in the gut, namely iron, calcium and zinc, and can prevent them from being absorbed.

SOURCES OF COMPLEX CARBOHYDRATES

In a vegetarian diet there are a wide variety of complex carbohydrates. Good examples are plant-based foods, such as potatoes; pulses, such as beans, peas and lentils; all wholegrains, such as wheat and rice, and their by-products, such as bread, flour and pasta.

Antioxidants

These compounds are produced by the body and also occur naturally in many foods, such as broccoli, tomatoes and spinach. The most common antioxidants are bioflavonoids, which occur widely in green vegetables; carotenes, found in orange and green fruit and vegetables; and vitamins **C** and **E**. The minerals copper, zinc, selenium and manganese also have an antioxidant effect as part of their function. A vegetarian diet will supply more than adequate amounts of these nutrients.

Many claims are made on behalf of antioxidants. It is thought that they may help delay or prevent the onset of cancer and heart disease, slow down the ageing process and extend life span, keep the skin young, boost fertility and reduce memory loss. Many researchers now believe that antioxidants are the medicine of the future, since the body can use antioxidants to boost its own defences and prevent diseases taking hold.

Include plenty of fruit such as grapefruit and oranges in your diet, as they are excellent sources of antioxidants and vitamin C.

One way in which antioxidants work in the body is by protecting cells from being attacked by free radicals. Free radicals are harmful substances, which are produced naturally by metabolising cells. Free radicals attack the genetic material (DNA) in the nucleus of a cell, and resulting changes may cause ageing and cancer. Antioxidants work together as a group or, more precisely, they network to mop up free radicals. When the molecules of each antioxidant absorb a free radical they become a weak free radical in the process. They then need help from other antioxidants in order to be recharged or refreshed and change back into the role of a defender. Much is still to be learnt about antioxidants but evidence of their benefits is impressive and only reinforces the advice that eating plenty of fresh fruit and vegetables is good for your health.

Green vegetables such as broccoli and cabbage contain antioxidants that are thought to boost the body's own defence system.

Vitamins

Vitamins are essential chemicals, required by the body in very small quantities for everyday functions, for its repair and development and to synthesise other nutrients. Each vitamin has a slightly different role to play and some vitamins work in conjunction with each other. Various factors influence the body's daily vitamin requirements. Growing children, pregnant women, lactating mothers, the elderly and those recovering from illness have the greatest need for vitamins. Similarly, those who smoke, drink or take regular medication also need to be sure that their food is rich in vitamins.

Apricots are a rich source of vitamin A and iron.

Vitamins fall into two distinct groups: water soluble and fat soluble. Water-soluble vitamins (**B group** vitamins, folate and vitamin **C**) dissolve in the blood and tissue fluids and cannot be stored in the body for long. Fat-soluble vitamins (vitamins **A, D, E** and **K**) are stored in the liver and fatty tissues. Vitamins can be destroyed during the storing, preparation or cooking of food. Water-soluble vitamins are vulnerable to heat; fat-soluble vitamins are generally more stable but can be sensitive to light and air.

VITAMIN A (RETINOL)

Vitamin A is essential for growth and keeps the skin and mucous membranes healthy. Deficiency in this vitamin can lead to poor night vision and gradual deterioration in sight, as well as lowering resistance to infection. Vitamin A can be stored in the body and excessive amounts can be toxic.

Beta-carotene is a retinol equivalent; in other words, the body can convert it into retinol or vitamin A. It is now thought that beta-carotene, found in orange-coloured vegetables and leafy green vegetables, is also important in its own right. Research shows that adequate intake of beta-carotene is linked with a low risk of developing certain cancers.

Good sources
carrots, milk, margarine, butter, bean-sprouts, peppers (especially red and yellow varieties)

VITAMIN B₁ (THIAMINE)

This vitamin is needed to help release energy from carbohydrates and ensure that the brain and nerves get enough glucose. A deficiency shows itself in the disease beriberi.

Good sources
germs of grains, such as brown rice, whole wheat and whole wheat derivatives (such as cereals and pasta), and also nuts, pulses, milk

VITAMIN B₂ (RIBOFLAVIN)

Vitamin B₂ helps to release energy from protein and fat, and is needed for healthy skin and mucous membranes. A deficiency can show itself in bloodshot eyes, cracked lips and sore mouth membranes.

Good sources
yeast extract, eggs, dairy products (especially milk), leafy green vegetables, mushrooms, fruit

VITAMIN B₃ (NIACIN)

Particularly involved with the release of energy within the cells, this vitamin comes from food sources or can be manufactured within the body. Deficiency is rare.

Good sources
yeast extract, nuts (especially peanuts), pulses, whole grains, milk

THE B GROUP VITAMINS

This is a group of substances involved mainly with the release of energy from food within the body. B vitamins are required for the functioning of the immune system, digestive system, brain, nervous and circulatory systems, the heart and other muscles, and for the production of new blood cells. They keep the hair, skin, eyes, mouth and liver healthy and are important in the metabolism of carbohydrates, fats and proteins in the body. Because they are water-soluble, they are not stored in the body. Most vegetables contain small quantities of the B vitamins.

While the B group vitamins work together to a certain extent, they also each have specific roles to play in the functioning of the body.

VITAMIN B₅
(PANTOTHENIC ACID)

This is required for many metabolic reactions within the body and for the synthesis of glucose and fatty acids.

Good sources
widely found, especially wholegrain products and eggs

VITAMIN B₆

Vitamin B₆ works best in conjunction with vitamin B₂ and magnesium. It is needed to metabolise protein and for the formation of the protein haemoglobin in red blood cells. Extra amounts of this vitamin are needed by women who are pregnant or taking the contraceptive pill. High alcohol consumption also increases the body's need for B₆. Deficiency can cause anaemia, fatigue and depression.

Good sources
cheese, eggs, wholegrain bread and cereals, nuts and many vegetables

Eggs and dairy products are a major source of vitamin B₆. For vegans there are plenty of non-dairy sources, such as nuts and vegetables.

VITAMIN B₁₂

Necessary for the formation of blood cells and nerves, vitamin B₁₂ is generally found in animal products (including dairy products) although there can be traces in some sea vegetables. Some soya products are fortified with B₁₂. Those who are on a vegan diet (see page 29) must take particular care to get this vitamin, usually in a supplement form. Deficiency can result in pernicious anaemia. Low intake combined with low levels of B₆ and folate (see next entry) have been linked to increased risk of coronary heart disease.

Dairy products provide vitamin B₁₂, which is vital for healthy blood cells and nerves.

Good sources
dairy products, yeast extract, fortified soya products

FOLATE *(FOLIC ACID)*

Folate is vital for the formation of new cells and therefore for the growth of the baby in the womb and normal development in children. Women wishing to conceive and those in the early stages of pregnancy should make sure they have adequate quantities of this vitamin as it can help prevent defects such as spina bifida and hydrocephalus.

Good sources
leafy vegetables, oranges, wholemeal bread, wholegrains, pulses and nuts

VITAMIN C *(ASCORBIC ACID)*

Vitamin C is necessary for healthy connective tissues, such as bone cartilage and collagen. It promotes the healing of wounds, increases the absorption of iron, helps the body fight infection and aids recovery after illness. It is an important antioxidant (see page 15). A deficiency of vitamin C may lead to a lowering of resistance to infection and slowing down of the healing process.

Good sources
citrus fruits, soft fruits (such as blackcurrants and strawberries), kiwi fruits, guavas, potatoes, green vegetables, peppers, leeks, bean-sprouts

VITAMIN D

Good sources
dairy products and fortified margarines. It is also formed by the action of sunlight on oils in the skin. Getting out for an hour or so on a sunny day should yield a reasonable amount

Vitamin D is essential for absorbing calcium and phosphorus and ensuring sound formation of bones and teeth. It is especially important for pregnant women and growing children. Deficiency can lead to rickets in children and weakened or porous bones in adults.

VITAMIN E

Good sources
vegetable oils, nuts, avocados, asparagus, wholegrains, wheatgerm

An antioxidant, vitamin E helps to protect cell membranes from oxidisation. It can help prevent the blocking-up of artery walls, and thus protect against heart disease. It also helps boost the immune system, prevents muscle inflammation and may help reduce symptoms of arthritis.

VITAMIN K

This vitamin is needed to help blood clotting and it is also essential for the formation of protein in the body.

Good sources
widely found, particularly dark green vegetables, cereals and sea vegetables

Minerals

There are a number of minerals in the body, of which about 20 are known or suspected to be essential. Some minerals, such as calcium or sodium, are needed in quite large quantities – more than 100mg per day. Other minerals, for which less than 100mg is needed each day, are referred to as trace elements. They are just as vital even though they are needed in only small quantities.

Minerals have several functions. They are part of the structural framework of the body, as components of bones and teeth; they enable muscles to contract and relax, and impulses to be transmitted through the nerves. In the form of soluble salts, they regulate the composition of body fluids. Minerals also enable many chemical reactions to take place, such as the breaking down and utilisation of food.

Plants are the main sources of minerals, which they absorb from the soil. A varied diet of wholesome foods, fresh fruit, vegetables and nuts should provide an ample supply of all the essential elements. Bear in mind that your need for minerals can be affected by your lifestyle. Living in a polluted area or taking drugs, alcohol or caffeine alters your mineral requirements. Mineral absorption can also vary according to the presence of certain vitamins. For example, vitamin C enhances the absorption of iron.

CALCIUM

A dietary deficiency of calcium, at any stage in life, may increase the risk of developing osteoporosis. Calcium is also essential for nerve function, for blood clotting, for maintenance of cell membranes and for the functioning of muscles. Calcium works closely in the body with magnesium and phosphorus.

Both vitamin D and the essential fatty acids (EFAs) can help the absorption of calcium. Equally, certain elements in foods inhibit the process, for example insoluble fibre in wholemeal bread or whole rice, tannin found in tea and oxalic acid found in some green vegetables and chocolate. It is therefore vital to eat plenty of calcium-rich foods from a variety of different sources. A deficiency is shown by stunted growth and rickets in young children and by osteoporosis, particularly in post-menopausal women.

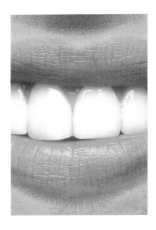

Calcium is a major component of bones and teeth. Deficiency at any stage in life may increase the risk of osteoporosis.

Good sources
dairy products (such as cheese, milk, yoghurt), tofu, nuts and seeds (such as sunflower or sesame seeds), leafy green vegetables, calcium-enriched soya milks

CHLORINE

Chlorine works in partnership with sodium. It helps remove excess sodium so may be effective in preventing high blood pressure. It is also needed for digesting proteins.

Good sources
widely found (most adults consume too much in the form of salt – sodium chloride)

MAGNESIUM

Magnesium is necessary for metabolising calcium and potassium. It is involved in energy supply, correct functioning of the nervous system and helping to regulate temperature. It works with calcium to form an integral part of bones and teeth. Low levels may be associated with increased risk of heart disease. A deficiency is shown by muscle weakness, loss of appetite and tiredness.

Good sources
nuts, cereals, green vegetables, seaweed, dairy products, soya beans

A varied diet of fruit, nuts, green vegetables and cereals provides a good supply of minerals.

PHOSPHORUS

Vital for bones and teeth, phosphorus is also important for the release of energy, working in conjunction with calcium. Deficiency is rare.

Good sources
dairy products, eggs, wholemeal bread, lentils, yeast extract

POTASSIUM

Potassium is needed for healthy cell function, and also works with sodium in regulating bodily fluids. Diets high in potassium and low in sodium are linked with lower risk of high blood pressure and stroke.

Good sources
leafy vegetables, mushrooms, potatoes, bananas, dried fruit

SODIUM

Found mainly in the blood and in fluids surrounding cells, sodium works with potassium to ensure a constant balance of bodily fluids. Deficiency is rare but excessive sodium has been linked to a susceptibility to hypertension.

Good sources
the most common source of sodium is salt

IRON

Iron is necessary for the formation of haemoglobin, which carries oxygen in the blood. Iron can also increase resistance to infection, as well as speeding up the process of healing.

Although the best source of iron is meat, it is possible to get adequate iron on a vegetarian diet, even though the type of iron found in plants is not so easily absorbed. Vitamin C enhances iron absorption and a trace of copper is needed for the correct functioning of iron in the body. Tannin-containing drinks, such as tea, decrease absorption.

Iron deficiency results in anaemia, the symptoms of which include tiredness, breathlessness and irritability. Women in particular must have adequate supplies to counteract the effect of menstruation.

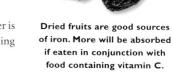

Dried fruits are good sources of iron. More will be absorbed if eaten in conjunction with food containing vitamin C.

Good sources
leafy green vegetables, pulses (particularly lentils), tofu, grains (such as wheat and millet), dried fruits (such as apricots, raisins and sultanas), cocoa powder, pumpkin seeds, nuts

MANGANESE

Manganese is a component of many enzyme systems and important in reproduction. Deficiency is rare.

Good sources
tea, nuts, grains, pulses, leafy green vegetables

MOLYBDENUM

This helps the functioning of iron in the body and works with fluoride.

Good sources
cereals, pulses, green vegetables

SELENIUM

Selenium works with vitamin E as an antioxidant (see page 15). It helps preserve the structure and functioning of membranes.

Good sources
cereals (especially wheat), cheese, eggs, walnuts, Brazil nuts

ZINC

Zinc is essential for growth and for the synthesis of proteins. It is necessary for wounds to heal; for the development of reproductive organs; the maintenance of skin, hair, nails and mucous membranes; and, it is vital for the growth of the foetus.

Good sources
dairy products, eggs, wholegrains, pumpkin seeds, pulses

TRACE ELEMENTS

The following minerals are known as trace elements and are required in very small quantities.

CHROMIUM
This is needed for normal metabolism of glucose, fatty acids, insulin and muscle growth.
Good sources wholemeal bread, wheatgerm, cheese

COPPER
Copper is needed for healthy functioning of many enzymes in the liver, brain and muscles.
Good sources nuts, dried tree fruit, pulses, green vegetables

IODINE
Very small quantities of iodine are needed for the correct functioning of the thyroid gland.
Good sources kelp and other seaweeds, iodised salt

LIQUIDS

Our bodies are made up of about two-thirds water. Water is continually lost through sweat and waste products so it is vital to drink plenty of fluids, preferably in the form of water.

Water does not contain any nutrients but its purpose is to keep the body hydrated. It helps the body eliminate toxins through waste matter. You should aim to drink between 1 and 2 litres (2 and 4 pints) of pure water a day.

A healthy diet

In the developed world access to foods has improved and conditions caused by dietary deficiency, such as scurvy or rickets, are now rare. However, the growing consumption of processed and packaged foods, together with a change in eating patterns from regular meals to snacking, has led to an increase in other ailments associated with a poor diet. A modern definition of a poor diet is one that is low in antioxidant vitamins, low in fibre and high in saturated fats.

Four Guidelines for a Healthy Diet

We have looked at the individual nutrients and their functions; it is now time to put the jigsaw together and look broadly at how to achieve a healthy, balanced diet that is also vegetarian. The most important point to remember is that it is essential to eat a wide range of foods, since no single food provides all the nutrients that are required for the body to remain healthy and function properly. Over and above that, there are four guidelines for a healthy diet. The good news for vegetarians is that all these guidelines fit very comfortably with a vegetarian diet.

Rice, featured in this Wild Rice with Hazelnuts, Carrots and Artichokes supper (see page 236), is filling but not fattening.

1 Eat plenty of foods rich in starch and fibre Foods such as brown rice, wholemeal bread and potatoes are filling but not fattening. They are rich in useful nutrients, including vitamins, minerals and dietary fibre.

2 Eat plenty of fresh fruit and vegetables These provide you with essential vitamins and minerals. There is mounting evidence to show that the biologically active substances in this food group, for example antioxidants, may combat cancer and reduce the likelihood of developing chronic diseases, such as coronary heart disease. Try to have at least five portions per day, not including potatoes, a portion being an apple or a roughly equivalent weight of 125–150g (4–5oz) in other fruit or vegetables.

3 Do not eat too many foods that contain a high proportion of fat This is one of the most important recommendations for vegetarians and would-be vegetarians. Dairy products, which are a familiar source of protein, are also high in fat. New vegetarians should be wary of cutting out meat, only to replace it with dairy products. It is important to source your protein and calcium from other food groups, such as beans, nuts and seeds, in order to have a balanced healthy diet. Nuts and seeds do contain fat but it is largely unsaturated.

4 Do not eat too many sugary foods Sugar is all calories and no nutrients. Sugary foods are easy to eat – and to over-eat. Consumption of sugar is also linked to tooth decay since the bacteria on teeth use sugar to make the acid that causes decay.

Wholegrains and cereals, together with a wide range of fresh fruit and vegetables, are essential components of a healthy diet.

Life cycle and different dietary needs

The following pages look at how our nutritional needs change throughout our lives. Although the principles for a healthy diet remain broadly the same at each stage, there are some extra factors to consider. This section begins with a look at pregnancy, including the months prior to conception, and then takes you through nutritional requirements during weaning, childhood and adolescence. It is just as important to be nutritionally aware in adulthood, and so nutritional pointers for all age groups are also given.

Pregnancy

Good diet and health are vital during pregnancy for both the mother and the growing baby. However, the months prior to pregnancy are also important and so, if you are thinking about becoming pregnant, it is a good idea to review your diet and increase nutrients as necessary. There is no reason to suggest that a diet free from meat or fish is going to leave you short of any nutrients. In fact, vegetarian foods are good sources of many of the nutrients needed at this time.

Pre-pregnancy Follow these general guidelines for good health: eat plenty of unrefined carbohydrates, such as grains and potatoes; reduce your intake of saturated fats but make sure you eat nuts and seeds to give you essential fatty acids; eat a good supply of fresh fruit and vegetables, in particular, foods to give you a good supply of folate (see page 17). This plays a vital role in protecting against birth defects such as spina bifida.

During pregnancy In addition to the basic dietary requirements outlined above, the need for certain nutrients increases during this period. Protein is required for the growth of new tissue, and iron is needed for the production of haemoglobin in both the

Stews, such as this nutritious Sweet Potato Stew (see page 241), are easy to make and freeze for days when you don't feel like cooking.

mother's and the baby's red blood cells (remember that vitamin C helps iron absorption). Calcium is essential for mineralisation of the baby's bone structure – most is required during the last three months of pregnancy. B vitamins, which are used in energy production, are also needed, as well as continuing good supplies of folate. Zinc is also important for the development of the foetus.

Take particular care over food safety during pregnancy. Don't drink unpasteurised milk; do not eat soft ripened cheese, such as Brie or Camembert; and only eat eggs that are thoroughly cooked.

While your intentions to follow a good diet during pregnancy may be good, you may be affected by morning sickness. This usually occurs only in the first few months. Skipping meals can make morning sickness worse, so try to eat little and often. When you do eat, make sure it is healthy and nutritious food.

Post-pregnancy If you are breast-feeding your baby, you will need about 500 extra calories a day because you are really feeding two. Try to eat nutrient-rich foods, following the broad dietary guidelines, and remember that this is not a time to diet.

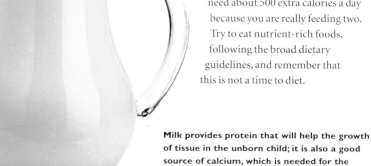

Milk provides protein that will help the growth of tissue in the unborn child; it is also a good source of calcium, which is needed for the baby's bone structure.

Babies and Toddlers

Breast milk or special infant formula contains all a baby needs in the first months of life. For vegan babies or those allergic to dairy products and who are not being breast-fed, a non-dairy formula based on soya is available.

Weaning starts at around 4 months. This is an average and much depends on the size of the baby to determine readiness for solid food. First weaning foods are usually vegetarian, for example rice (specially processed for babies), and fruit and vegetable purées, such as carrot, banana, apple and avocado.

Wheat and wheat products should be avoided for the first 6–9 months in case there is an allergy to gluten. Eggs, too, can cause allergies and are best avoided for the first 6–9 months. Do not add salt or sugar to babies' food. Nuts may cause allergies. Even if your baby does not have an allergy, do not give pieces of nut as the baby can choke. Other foods that can cause allergic reactions, even after 6 months, include citrus fruits, strawberries and egg white.

Children

Many children do not want to eat meat and there is no reason for a child brought up on a good vegetarian diet to be deficient nutritionally. Growing children need plenty of protein and calcium; their need for other nutrients is similar to adults but in smaller quantities. Young children are often very active and require

First weaning foods are vegetarian, such as purées of carrots, apples or bananas. These are easily prepared at home using a food processor.

concentrated sources of energy and a wholefood-based vegetarian diet can be bulky in relation to its energy content. To counteract this, if your child has a small appetite, you can vary the types of cereals given, occasionally choosing white rice instead of brown for example. If a high percentage of your child's food is milk, use whole milk rather than skimmed or semi-skimmed – a low-fat diet may provide too little energy for a small child who cannot eat a bulky diet.

Make sure your child eats a good selection from all the food groups. Pulses, nuts and seeds, and grains, as well as some dairy products will ensure a good supply of protein, as well as essential fatty acids. Simple food combinations, such as pasta with cheese sauce and beans on toast, appeal to children and are very nutritious. Try to make sure children have five portions of fresh fruit and vegetables a day.

Children under three should not be given whole or coarsely chopped nuts as they are a choking hazard.

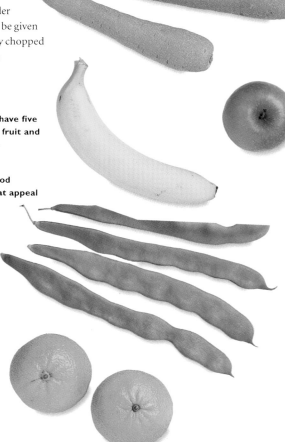

Children should have five portions of fresh fruit and vegetables a day.

Lots of simple food combinations that appeal to children are quick to cook and nutritious. Beans on toast is a classic example.

Adolescence

Adolescence is an important growth period. As well as needing protein, carbohydrates and fats, youngsters in this age group also need to increase their intake of calcium, iron, zinc and magnesium. For girls particularly, calcium is accumulated in the bones during the teenage years – adequate storage then can help prevent the onset of osteoporosis later in life. A good supply of iron is also needed at this stage, especially for girls as they begin menstruation.

Adolescence is also a time when eating patterns may become haphazard as teenagers become more independent. If meals are skipped and there is more snacking, it is important to try and make sure that whatever food is eaten, it is nutrient rich. Some teenagers choose to become vegetarian as a way to assert independence, and encouraging some self-sufficiency when it comes to cooking is a positive parental response. There are lots of basic foods, such as pasta and grains, that are not difficult to cook. This could be a good opportunity for your teenager to get involved in the kitchen.

Girls in particular may be attracted to a vegetarian diet as a way of slimming. In general, this is nothing to worry about as long as the food they eat is varied and well balanced. However, sometimes this change may be the first step in rejecting food on a wider basis, so it is important to look out for signs of eating disorders. Nine out of 10 sufferers of anorexia are women and for many this disorder starts in the teenage years.

Adulthood

For adults who are exclusively vegetarian, the broad guidelines for healthy eating outlined on page 20 should be followed within the parameters of a vegetarian diet. A vegetarian diet is as suitable for men as for women, even though their overall demand for nutrients – with the exception of iron – is slightly greater.

There are lots of basic foods that are not hard for youngsters to cook, such as this Baked Pasta Gratin on page 203.

Old Age

As we get older, we need fewer calories but we still need protein for repairing cells and tissues. It is just as important at this stage to maintain a good supply of vitamins and minerals. These boost general health as well as the ability to fight infection. If you are house-bound you may need to increase your intake of vitamin D (see page 17 for good sources). However, sitting at an open window may help the natural production of vitamin D.

If raw food is harder to eat, cook vegetables and fruit in the most nutritious way or make more use of purées by serving soup.

Many older people drink less and dehydration can become a problem, with side effects such as constipation. Try to drink plenty of liquids, especially water, fruit juices and drinks without caffeine. The recommended amount is at least eight large cups of liquid daily.

Yoghurt is a good source of calcium, a mineral that needs to accumulate in the bones during the teenage years.

Eggs are a useful source of protein and iron.

During adolescence, an important growth period, youngsters should make sure they are getting adequate calcium from nuts and seeds and plenty of iron from green vegetables.

It is vital to drink plenty of liquids to prevent conditions such as constipation.

Lifestyle and nutritional needs

Apart from age and sex, other factors influence your nutritional needs. Your lifestyle plays a significant role and dietary requirements vary according to whether you participate in sport, have a hectic business life, or have to deal with stress. Here are recommendations to ensure that you are aware of how to deal with any specific dietary needs you may have.

Sport

Exercise, even in moderate levels, alters your nutritional needs. The more you train, the more nutrients you need to maintain a good level of red blood cells so that oxygen is supplied during exercise. You also need calories to maintain muscle bulk.

Vegetarians who participate seriously in sport should consider the following:

If you take a lot of exercise you may need to boost your carbohydrate consumption, as well as increasing your fluid intake.

• Increase complex carbohydrates, such as cereals, root vegetables and fruits. These foods also contain the sort of carbohydrate that converts quickly to blood glucose.

• Maintain a good level of fluid intake, before and after exercising and during if appropriate, for example, in endurance running.

• Fat is not the best form of energy since the body takes time to mobilise and break down fatty acids. To do this a large supply of dietary carbohydrate is needed. Use monounsaturated fats, such as olive oil, and nuts and seeds for their essential fatty acids.

STRESS

Stress is a term used to describe the symptoms produced by our response to pressure. These symptoms result from high levels of adrenaline, a hormone secreted in response to stressful situations.

There are many ways to deal with stress that are not diet related, such as taking exercise and learning to relax. It is also important to become aware of the situations that cause you stress and find ways to avoid them or lessen their impact.

Vitamin C and the B group vitamins are depleted under stress. The B vitamins are further depleted by alcohol and sugary foods, which may seem comforting in times of stress. Maintain a good intake of foods rich in B vitamins, such as wholegrains. Limit caffeine drinks such as tea and coffee; try herbal teas instead. Eat plenty of fresh fruit and raw vegetables.

Business Life: Eating Out and Travel

Long hours and business travel make it more difficult to adhere to guidelines for a healthy diet, especially for anyone on a vegetarian diet. Modern working patterns are also often stressful, putting the body under pressure and raising nutritional demands.

It can be difficult to find wholesome food when away from home. Often, airline food has been standing around or is reheated, depleting the nutrients further. Many airlines do offer vegetarian fare; and it is sometimes better to ask for a dairy-free (vegan) meal, which offers a less fatty, grain or pulse main course and fresh fruit instead of a sickly-sweet dessert. Food offered on railways or at roadside restaurants varies greatly from one country to another.

In restaurants where there is no obviously suitable main course, consider ordering several vegetable side dishes and salads instead. Try to eat brown bread instead of white; look for starters, such as melon or grapefruit, to enjoy as desserts.

When travelling it is easier to maintain a regular supply of fresh fruit in your diet than vegetables, even if this does mean going shopping. On long trips away from home it is worth taking with you a few foods to supplement your diet, such as muesli or nuts and seeds.

When travelling it is not always possible to get wholesome food. However, fresh fruit is easy to find and will provide you with useful vitamins and fibre.

Drinking Habits

Whether you are very active or have a generally sedentary lifestyle, it is important to drink plenty of fluid. If you are participating in serious sports or doing a good deal of travelling, it is even more crucial to keep up your fluid intake. Water is the best choice, and there is more information on how much to drink and the benefits on page 19. Stimulants such as caffeine and alcohol have both benefits and drawbacks. The effect on your health is examined here with suggestions for alternatives.

Caffeine In small quantities caffeine, which is a stimulant, can get you up and going in the morning or give you a useful boost when you are flagging halfway through the day. However, in larger quantities, caffeine can affect your sleep, digestion and nervous system. If you have feelings of anxiety, unexplained headaches or stomach upsets, it is probably worth reducing your caffeine intake. Real coffee has more caffeine than instant coffee and tea. Tea also contains tannin, a substance that can inhibit iron absorption.

To avoid caffeine, decaffeinated coffee is not always an ideal solution, because it sometimes contains chemicals that are used in the decaffeinating process. There are caffeine-free substitutes made from grains, such as barley, but don't expect these to taste like real coffee. Herbal infusions make good hot drinks and some are believed to have additional properties, such as aiding digestion (peppermint), helping relaxation (camomile) and enhancing vitamin C (rosehip). These substitutes may not be appealing at first. However, they are worth pursuing, and within a few days your taste buds will start to appreciate their more subtle quality and the variety of flavours they offer.

Alcohol There is debate as to how alcohol fits in with a healthy diet. Small quantities of alcohol can be useful for relaxation and are also thought to help reduce the risk of heart disease. Red wine is the most beneficial to health, particularly if drunk in moderation and with meals. Red wine (and red grape juice) contain unusual antioxidants (procyanidins and phytoalexins), which may help reduce the risk of thrombosis and deposits building up inside the arteries. However, these benefits should be seen in a broader context. Alcohol is high in calories and excessive alcohol can cause serious damage to health.

Red wine, which contains rare antioxidants, may have some health benefits if drunk in moderation.

Oral Contraception

Taking the contraceptive pill for long periods may reduce levels of vitamin B_6, folate and zinc. If this applies to you, make sure that you include plenty of foods rich in these nutrients in your diet.

Coffee and tea contain caffeine which acts as a stimulant. Large quantities may affect your sleep.

Convalescence

If you have been ill or are recovering from an operation, your appetite may be reduced. What you do eat should be nutrient rich. It is often better to have 'food' in liquid form and to try to eat little and often. Make fruit or vegetable drinks from juices – freshly extracted if possible – and serve them plain or mixed with yoghurt. Use a blender or a food processor to make a good variety of soup-like meals that are easy to digest.

It is worth adding small quantities of wheatgerm to savoury or sweet meals since this is a light food but very rich in B vitamins and protein, which will help recovery.

Blenders and food processors can be used to make a good variety of easily digestible purées and soups. Food in liquid form is especially good during convalescence.

Eat well, stay well

Generally, in the developed world we are sufficiently well nourished, and many serious infectious diseases are a thing of the past. There are, however, several chronic conditions that are thought to be linked to diet. Many of these conditions are more evident in adulthood; some are general, some affect one sex more than another and some are exclusive to one sex. Although this is not a medical book as such, it is worth looking briefly at some of the more common conditions, the part that nutrients have to play and the positive benefits of a vegetarian diet.

Coronary Heart Disease

Coronary heart disease is one of the biggest killers in the Western world, accounting for at least one-third of all male deaths. Dietary advice for reducing the risk of coronary heart disease includes avoiding nutrient-poor processed food and eating wholefoods instead; and increasing intake of complex carbohydrates, such as wholemeal bread and pasta, and brown rice. These foods should account for the bulk of daily calories. In addition, increase the intake of fresh fruit and vegetables, especially raw vegetables. Try to eat roughly 500g (1lb) per day in manageable portions. Decrease the total amount of fats eaten. What fat is used should be monounsaturated or polyunsaturated. Switch to skimmed or semi-skimmed milk. Use olive oil in cooking and for salad dressings. Eat nuts and seeds as these contain essential fatty acids, which have beneficial effects on blood cholesterol. Reduce salt and sugar intake, retraining your tastebuds.

Nuts and seeds, such as pumpkin seeds, contain essential fatty acids (EFAs), which may have beneficial effects on the level of cholesterol in the blood.

Starting the day with a good breakfast based on cereal may make all the difference. Complex carbohydrates fill you up and keep you satisfied, meaning there is less room for nutrient-poor, high-fat foods such as sweets and biscuits.

High Blood Pressure

High blood pressure is a chronic condition that also affects more men than women. Particular advice for this condition is to cut back on salt consumption, remembering that a much higher percentage of salts

comes from processed and packaged food than is added in home cooking or at the table.

Eat potassium-rich foods, such as all fruit, especially bananas, dried apricots and vegetables including potatoes, mushrooms and spinach.

Bananas are rich in potassium. This mineral may help counterbalance a high-sodium diet.

Cancer

Cancer, in all its diverse forms, is one of the most common causes of death for both men and women. While many factors play a part, medical practitioners do recommend changes in diet as one way of reducing the risk of developing some forms of cancer.

Try to eat more wholegrain cereals and pulses and eat at least five portions of fresh fruit and vegetables a day. Eat food that is high in fibre, and aim for an overall diet that is low in saturated fats.

Obesity

Obesity is recognised as a modern lifestyle problem. Our tendency to become overweight is due in part to the number of high-calorie and rich snacks available, and but also to the fact that many jobs are now sedentary and a vast percentage of adults do not take exercise.

Being overweight makes you more prone to numerous problems, such as breathlessness, back pain and heartburn. It also makes you more susceptible to conditions such as high blood pressure, poor circulation, reproductive problems or certain types of cancer.

There are many approaches to slimming and the key to success is to find a diet that suits you. A vegetarian diet based around dairy products will not be slimming, nor particularly healthy. Wholemeal breads and brown rice may seem the antithesis of slimming food but in fact these do not have many calories and will keep you satisfied for a long period. The trick is not to add calories by smothering these products with butter or rich sauces.

For vegetarians trying to lose weight, cut down on fatty foods rather than cutting them out of your diet completely. Eat dairy products in moderation, switching to low-fat cheese and skimmed milk. Use nuts and seeds sparingly. Choose fresh fruit and vegetables as snacks rather than cakes, sweets or biscuits, and eat complex carbohydrates, such as brown bread, wholewheat pasta and brown rice. Always have a nourishing breakfast to sustain you through to lunch, thus eliminating the craving for mid-morning nibbles, and take plenty of exercise.

Pre-menstrual Tension

This condition affects many women and the symptoms may be physical or psychological. The problems generally occur in the second half of the cycle when a drop in the level of hormones occurs. Although evidence remains inconclusive, many women feel their wellbeing is improved by additional vitamin B_6. It is important not to have excessive quantities of this vitamin, however; it may be enough just to make sure you include foods rich in B_6 in your regular diet, rather than taking a supplement.

Osteoporosis

This is a degenerative age-related condition affecting both men and women, which begins around the age of 35 but accelerates in women after the menopause. It is vital to build up good supplies of calcium in the teenage years and 20s. A diet rich in calcium throughout adult life may slow down the progress of this condition. Doing weight-bearing exercise, such as walking, running and jumping, during your teens and 20s is also important.

In addition to a healthy diet, taking some exercise on a daily basis and enjoying active, healthy leisure pursuits, such as hiking, will help to control your weight.

Cheese is an excellent source of calcium. Adequate supplies of this mineral throughout adult life may help to prevent the onset of osteoporosis.

Food Allergies

An allergy is an overaggressive response to a substance by the body's immune system. An allergic reaction may produce a whole range of symptoms, from diarrhoea or vomiting to skin rashes and eczema.

Some allergic reactions are so severe as to be life-threatening. This is called anaphylactic shock and can be set off in some instances by having the most casual contact with the allergen. Symptoms include breathing difficulties (because the throat swells), stomach cramp, vomiting and rashes. For vegetarians, the most common foods to cause this type of reaction are peanuts, other nuts and seeds, and eggs.

Although there is evidence that the tendency to be allergic runs in families, it also seems that food allergies are on the increase. As yet, there is no answer as to why some people are allergic and others are not. Many food allergies do occur in childhood and can be outgrown. Some adverse reactions to food are not allergic reactions but a form of food intolerance. It is very hard for a lay person to distinguish between the two.

The most common ingredients to cause allergic reactions or food intolerance are listed below. Remember these may appear in many different foods and are not always readily apparent: for example, wheat is found in pasta and pastry products, and sesame seeds in hummus and burger buns; milk can be present in cereals, biscuits and sauces. It is therefore vital to check labels on food packaging.

Grains and gluten Gluten is a protein found in wheat, rye, barley and oats, and any foods that contain these ingredients, such as pastry, pasta or biscuits. However, people can be allergic to wheat without necessarily being allergic to gluten.

Milk and dairy products Lactose intolerance is where the sufferer is deficient in the enzyme lactase, which breaks down the lactose found in milk. If lactose is not broken down, it goes into the intestines, causing bloating and diarrhoea. Lactose intolerance can sometimes be just a childhood condition and is often outgrown. Some people who can't tolerate cow's milk are able to have goat's milk products.

If you have a wheat or gluten allergy, look for wheat-free breads and pasta made from corn as an alternative.

Eggs The white of the egg may cause allergic reactions. This allergy is common in toddlers and can be outgrown.

Nuts and seeds Allergy to peanuts is the most common nut allergy and can be very severe. Peanuts are also referred to as groundnuts so it is vital to avoid groundnut oil. Other common nut allergens are Brazil nuts, cashew nuts and walnuts. Sesame seeds can cause allergic reactions, too.

Fermented soya products Intolerance to products such as miso and shoyu may occur because these products contain yeast or wheat.

A childhood allergy to strawberries may be outgrown. Oranges may also trigger allergic reactions.

Strawberries and oranges Strawberries can cause a rash. This is often common in childhood and can be outgrown. Oranges have sometimes been found to be a trigger for migraine (as have eggs and chocolate).

Gluten is a protein found in the wholewheat grain and also in all wheat-based products such as pasta and flour.

Low Sperm Count

Diet is thought to be one of the many factors that can lower sperm count and affect fertility. Research findings have traced a link between low sperm count and diet by showing that 40% of sperm damage is due to the harmful effects of free radicals. Make sure you have adequate amounts of antioxidants to absorb free radicals (see page 15).

Different approaches to diet

While a vegetarian diet is strictly defined as being free from meat or fish, there are several different approaches to vegetarian food, which can influence the way that you choose and cook your food. The three most common regimes are vegan, wholefood and raw food, all of which are outlined here.

Vegan Diet

A vegan eats no animal products at all, nor anything derived from or produced by living creatures, so this diet excludes egg, dairy products and honey. Those contemplating a vegetarian diet may feel that a vegan diet is extremely restricted. However, thanks to the accessibility of an enormous choice of nuts, grains, fruit and vegetables, as well as an increasingly imaginative range of soya products, there are a good number of vegan meals possible.

From a nutritional point of view, the consumption of calories on a vegan diet is generally lower. It is also important for vegans to check they are getting vitamins and minerals such as calcium and B_{12}, which are more usually found in dairy products. For alternative sources see pages 17 and 18.

Vegan diets are usually rich in vitamin C and beta-carotene as well as being low in saturated fats and high in complex carbohydrates and fibre. If well balanced and well planned, a vegan diet can amply provide all nutrients for a healthy life.

Giant Mushrooms Stuffed with Wild Rice and Roasted Onions (see page 173) is one of the recipes suitable for vegans in this book.

A healthy vegetarian diet should include a good range of wholefood ingredients such as wholewheat bread and brown rice. Wholefoods are foods that have not been refined or processed in any way.

Wholefood Diet

Wholefoods are traditionally defined as foods that have had nothing added and nothing taken away. This is relevant to vegetarians because many wholefoods, for example brown rice and wholemeal bread, are nutrient rich, whereas their refined counterparts do not have such good nutritional value.

A healthy vegetarian diet should include a good percentage of wholefoods, although it needn't necessarily exclude refined ingredients such as white flour or white rice.

Raw Food Diet

Recognising the benefits of raw food is not a recent fad. For more than 100 years, advocates of raw food diets have researched the benefits of eating uncooked food. Arthritis, diabetes and some forms of cancer are among the serious conditions and diseases that may be helped by a diet high in raw foods. Raw foods are thought to help eliminate toxins because they contain more fibre, can restore a balanced sodium/ potassium level, help maintain balance between acidity and alkalinity and help oxygenation of cells.

Choosing your food

Turning to a vegetarian diet may well make you think more carefully about the food that you are eating, its source and its quality. Modern trends in food production have a great influence on our diet. It is useful to be aware of some of these issues so that you can make an informed choice about the best food for yourself and your family, within your lifestyle.

Some foods are now genetically altered to give enhanced resistance to disease, but the long-term effects of this process are not yet fully understood.

Organic Food

In many parts of the world over the past 50 years, farming has undergone huge changes, due to the development of machinery, pesticides and chemical fertilisers. While these developments have positive aspects, such as the eradication of pests or increased yields, there are negative factors, too, such as the worrying traces of chemicals

While research on whether organic food is healthier is not conclusive, it is thought that organic farming is beneficial to the environment.

left behind in the soil and surface water and therefore ultimately in our food. There is concern that high levels of chemical residues in our food may add to the risk of cancer. Vegetables, fruit and cereals are all crops at risk. As yet, research is inconclusive as to whether organic food is healthier, and there are arguments on both sides. However, you may well be persuaded that buying organic food is a way of limiting exposure to chemical residues.

What is more conclusive is the evidence of the value of organic farming in environmental terms. Organic farmers concentrate on conserving and enhancing the fertility of the soil by natural methods, such as crop rotation. They try to preserve natural habitats and pay

attention to environmental concerns. Organic agriculture conforms to worldwide regulations and there are many certifying organisations. In the UK, organically grown foods are regulated by the UK register of Organic Standards; in the USA, farmers may have state or independent certification.

On the whole, organic food costs more to produce than food from conventional farming, but many buyers are prepared to pay more for organic produce. Organic fruit and vegetables tend to be smaller and less regular in shape, but they should still be fresh for purchase: never accept substandard produce, even if it is organically grown.

Genetically Modified Organisms (GMOs)

Depending on where you live in the world, the introduction of genetically modified foodstuffs is either accepted as part of life or is a hotly debated subject. There are powerful lobbies on both sides of the argument.

Scientists can now identify individual genes that govern a desired trait. This gene can be extracted, copied and inserted into another organism. This process is known as genetic modification, or modern biotechnology. As well as being used as a tool in plant breeding, genetic modification is also developing in the animal world as producers look to breed cattle with better milk yields and animals with enhanced resistance to disease.

Proponents of genetic modification argue that this process can be used to make crops disease resistant, increase the amount of protein in low-protein crops, alter the fat content of foods high in saturated fats and add vitamins to fruit and vegetables. The opponents of genetic modification argue that we do not know enough about the effect of altering genes and what problems it may cause for future generations. There is also concern that copy genes could be accidentally transferred to another species with disastrous consequences, for example accidentally creating a herbicide-tolerant weed or 'super weed'. A genetic mistake is not an easy one to reverse and the effects on the body are not easy to predict. For example, a Brazil nut gene inserted into a soya bean was found to trigger allergies in people who were not previously allergic to soya.

Vegetarians in particular sometimes object to copy genes from animals being used in plant production. They are also likely to be worried about the ethics of creating animals that give higher yields or can adapt to what would normally be alien environments.

The GMO debate is not yet concluded and if any of the above statements make you pause for thought, it is probably worth trying to keep abreast of developments. This is a complex issue, involving moral and political elements.

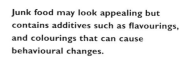

Junk food may look appealing but contains additives such as flavourings, and colourings that can cause behavioural changes.

Additives

Additives are mostly non-nutritive substances, which are added to food to prolong shelf life, assist in processing or improve the flavour and appearance of food. They are used universally and it is very hard to avoid them. Additives include flavourings and flavour enhancers, stabilisers, thickeners, emulsifiers, colourings and preservatives. Different countries have widely differing laws concerning the use of additives. The general rule is that they are supposed to be safe and not used in greater quantities than necessary. The long-term effects of many are not yet known and there is debate as to whether some additives can cause behavioural changes, particularly in children.

The best way to avoid additives is to eat as much fresh food as possible and buy unrefined products, such as wholewheat pasta and brown rice. Avoid processed and packaged foods; look out for additive-free foods.

IRRADIATION

This is a method of food preservation whereby foods are exposed to high levels of radiation. It was introduced as a solution to all our food safety problems as the irradiation process destroys harmful bacteria, such as salmonella. Concerns about irradiation, however, include worries about loss of nutrients during the process and that by making food last longer it will naturally lose more of its vitamins.

INGREDIENTS

This section of the book gives details of over 350 ingredients. For ease of reference, these ingredients are divided into the following food groups: vegetables, fruit, dairy products, grains, pulses and nuts and seeds. Fruit and vegetables are further divided into family or climate groups, such as the onion family or root vegetables. Following these sections are details of other useful ingredients, such as herbs, spices, oils and vinegars, as well as a range of further useful flavourings and sweeteners.

Each group of ingredients has a general introduction and nutritional notes, and additional ingredients within the group are also listed. There is advice on what to look for when choosing the product and how to store it, as well as notes on preparation and methods of cooking. I have also suggested ways to use the ingredients and how best to partner them with other ingredients and flavourings – I hope that experienced and enthusiastic cooks will feel confident in improvising new dishes based on these notes.

Vegetables

The success of vegetarian cookery has made everyone, from supermarket buyers to home cooks, realise that vegetables have been seriously undervalued. Vegetables are finally being appreciated for their colour and flavour, and, most importantly, for their contribution to our health.

Increasing evidence has shown how vital vegetables are to our wellbeing. Nutritionists have found strong links between diets high in vegetables and a decreased risk of many life-threatening conditions. The World Health Organization recommends that everyone eats at least five portions of fresh vegetables and fruit per day, excluding potatoes. These recommendations come at a time when, thanks to improved transportation and storage facilities, an impressive range of vegetables is available from all over the world. Freshly picked produce may be available at farmers' markets or pick-your-own outlets.

Vegetables such as winter squash can be stored for several months.

Buying and Storing Vegetables

Buying produce that is fresh is all-important – look for plumpness and a good, bright colour; avoid vegetables that are damaged, wrinkled, faded or limp. This applies equally to organic vegetables. Nutrients are lost in storage, so use vegetables as soon as possible.

Most vegetables are best stored in cool, dark places, such as the fridge, since light and heat destroy crispness and nutrients, particularly vitamin B_2 and vitamin C. Green vegetables can lose up to 50% of their vitamin C in one day if kept at room temperature.

Nutritional Value

Vegetables are good sources of antioxidants (see page 15), which protect the body by blocking or suppressing harmful substances. The most common of these are bioflavonoids, carotenes and vitamins C and E. Vegetables also provide important minerals, such as iron, calcium and potassium and other vitamins, such as vitamins of the B group. Green vegetables have magnesium, folate, vitamin C and iron, while many orange-fleshed and red varieties of vegetables, such as peppers and tomatoes, supply carotenes. Peculiar to the onion family are sulphurous compounds, which may help protect against gastric cancers; root vegetables supply starch and natural sugars for energy. In addition, vegetables bring roughage into the diet as they are a good source of dietary fibre. They are also generally low in fat (but see avocado, page 43) and cholesterol and also low in calories.

Vegetables are a good source of minerals and vitamins. They also contain antioxidants that boost the body's defence system and help to prevent diseases.

Freezing

Most vegetables – apart from salad leaves – freeze successfully. It is best to blanch them first as they will last longer. Prepare the vegetables by peeling, chopping or slicing as necessary, then plunge into a saucepan of boiling water for 1 minute. Blanch a batch of about 500g (1lb) at a time so that the water does not cool down too much. Drain the vegetables and plunge immediately into cold water to prevent further cooking. Drain again, using a salad spinner or drier. Freeze the blanched vegetables on a tray in a single layer covered with a polythene bag. Pack in boxes or bags when frozen. Some varieties will keep for 12 months. Use the vegetables straight from frozen; do not thaw them first or the vitamin content will be significantly reduced.

Most vegetables can be frozen successfully. These are good to keep on hand for emergency meals.

Preparation and Cooking

The most nutritious way to eat vegetables is in their raw state, because the more that a food is processed, the greater the loss of nutrients. Wash or scrub vegetables before use but do not soak them as water leaches out the vitamins and minerals. However, raw vegetables are not always appropriate – or even advisable, in the case of potatoes – but there are ways of cooking that minimise nutrient loss.

Steaming Steamed vegetables tend to retain their crispness, as well as more of their nutrients, and steaming is an excellent way of preparing simple side dishes. Steamed vegetables cook in the vapour produced by simmering water. You can improvise a steamer by placing a sieve over a saucepan but a stainless steel basket or a trivet with a lifting handle or a stack of bamboo steamers are more efficient and easier to use.

Steaming minimises nutritional loss. Nutrients do not leach out into the cooking water, as they do during boiling.

COOK'S TIP

Keep the water at a simmer, not a rolling boil; do not sprinkle salt over the vegetables as this draws out their juices and may discolour them; make sure the saucepan does not boil dry

Sautéing (butter steaming) Sautéing is a similar method to stir-frying in that it is a quick cooking technique done on the hob. A sauté pan is wide with high sides so that you can stir the food around without it spilling. It should have a heavy base so that ingredients don't burn. To sauté, melt a small amount of butter or oil in the pan, quickly stir in the vegetable pieces and seal them by cooking over a high heat. Reduce the heat and add just enough liquid to prevent the vegetables burning, then let them finish off cooking as the liquid evaporates.

Microwaving Vegetables cook very successfully in the microwave and retain their colour, flavour and nutrients as they are cooked quickly in a minimum amount of water. No special equipment is needed other than microwave-safe cookware.

COOK'S TIP

Cut vegetables uniformly so that they cook evenly; pierce the skin of whole vegetables so that they do not burst

Stir-frying This method is a fast, nutrient-friendly way to cook single vegetables or a colourful mixture of several varieties. Stir-frying is best done in a wok, a large rounded-base pan often made of thin metal so that it heats up very quickly and provides a large cooking surface.

COOK'S TIP

Use a small quantity (1–2 teaspoons) of oil; cut the vegetables into small, even pieces to ensure quick cooking; prepare and cook the vegetables just before serving to retain their nutrients

A stir-fry is a light, colourful and nutritious way to enjoy food.

Grilling This is a good method for cooking tender vegetables, such as tomatoes, peppers and onions. Brush the vegetables first with oil if you wish. Make sure the grill is properly heated before cooking.

Roasting At one time it seemed that only potatoes were roasted, but now roasting is a popular and delicious way of cooking a variety of vegetables. The long cooking time ensures the vegetables are really tender and the flavours can often be more intense. However, some vitamins will be lost during the cooking process.

Griddling (chargrilling) This is a nutritious way of cooking vegetables and one that uses no oil at all or a minimum amount. The best equipment is a heavy, flat, ridged griddle pan, as the vegetables are seared on the ridges, creating an attractive pattern. A large, heavy non-stick frying pan can also be used.

COOK'S TIP

Brush the pieces of vegetable with a little seasoned olive oil; arrange the pieces on the griddle pan in a single layer and don't pack them too closely together

Boiling Of the many different ways of cooking vegetables, boiling is one of the most popular. It is also one of the least desirable, since up to 45% of the minerals and 50% of vitamin C may be lost.

COOK'S TIP

Use a minimum amount of water and make sure it is boiling when you add the vegetables; never add bicarbonate of soda as it destroys vitamin C

Brassicas

This is a large family of vegetables, which includes cabbage, cauliflower and broccoli, as well as Oriental greens such as pak choi and mustard greens. They range in colour from white through shades of green to purple. As a group, brassicas are extremely beneficial nutritionally and all brassicas are good sources of vitamin C and a variety of minerals.

Cabbage heads should have a bright colour and feel heavy and solid. When cooking, discard the outer leathery leaves.

PURPLE SPROUTING BROCCOLI AND CALABRESE (*GREEN BROCCOLI*)

All brassicas are good sources of vitamin C and several valuable minerals.

Both are good partnered with dairy products; they have a strong enough flavour to counteract the blandness of a soufflé and look good in roulades. They also work well in stir-fries combined with red pepper and mushroom, or with pasta when mixed into sauces, or simply steamed and served on the side. Purple sprouting broccoli has a stronger flavour.

Buying and storing Both should have firm, compact buds or flowers, which should be dark green or dark purple, depending on the variety. Do not buy or use any that show signs of yellowing. Keep them in the fridge and use within a couple of days.

Preparation and cooking Pull off any coarse leaves and trim tough stems, peeling the skin back to the branches. Chop into florets. Steam, microwave or boil and be aware that the flower heads can break up if overcooked. Purple sprouting broccoli will leach out colour as it cooks and may discolour a dish, its purple overwhelming the colours of other vegetables. If serving in a salad, chill rapidly under cold running water.

Chop broccoli into even-sized florets. For the best results, steam, stir-fry or microwave until soft but crisp.

GREEN CABBAGE AND KALE

Although they look dissimilar, green cabbage and kale are in fact related. Green cabbage has a heart and kale has looser leaves. For cooking purposes they can be treated in roughly the same way. Cavolo nero (black cabbage) is a variety of kale.

Buying and storing Choose green cabbage and kale with outer leaves as these will help keep the main part of the vegetable fresh. There should be no hint of yellowing or limpness. Cabbage heads should be heavy and feel solid. Keep whole heads loosely wrapped in the fridge for several days or longer. Once cut, the vegetable will deteriorate more quickly and lose its nutritional value.

Preparation and cooking Discard leathery outer leaves or any that are damaged and cut out any tough ribs (kale) or core (cabbage). Chop the leaves as necessary and cook in boiling water – uncovered, or the colour dulls – for a short time in order to maximise crispness and colour. Green cabbage and kale can also be braised in a similar fashion to red cabbage, mixed with onions and spices (see page 37). They can also be stir-fried or sautéed. Young kale leaves can be used in salads; cabbage is good served with butter or cream, or used in small quantities in soups and casseroles. As a side vegetable, cabbage or kale are delicious just lightly steamed and then tossed in butter with plenty of black pepper.

WHITE CABBAGE (DUTCH)

This cabbage has a solid head with pale white to green tightly furled leaves. It is good in salads and forms the basis of traditional coleslaw, a shredded cabbage and carrot salad. There are numerous variations on that theme – the cabbage can be coated with yoghurt or crème fraîche, or mixed with grated celeriac, apple, dried fruits or fresh herbs.

Buying and storing Select firm heads that feel heavy for their size; the outer leaves should look fresh. Cabbage should keep up to 1 week in the fridge, loosely wrapped in polythene.

White cabbage has a nutty flavour with a slightly peppery aftertaste. Shred to eat raw, mixed with creamy dressings.

Preparation and cooking To shred cabbage by hand or in a food processor, cut it into quarters first and then remove the inner core if it looks woody. Cut each quarter into fine shreds using a large knife, or chop it into chunks to fit the funnel of a food processor and shred using the slicing blade. Finely shredded white cabbage makes a crunchy addition to stir-fries or can be sautéed. Whole leaves can be blanched and stuffed with a filling suitable for a vine leaf.

RED CABBAGE

Similar to white cabbage, this variety also has tight compact leaves and a firm heart. Red cabbage is delicious braised slowly; it can be eaten raw but it tends to be chewy and so is best used in small quantities and mixed with other ingredients, such as slices of orange, walnuts and wild rice for a great cold weather salad.

Buying and storing The outer leaves may look leathery but they should not be wilted. The cabbage should feel solid. Uncut, red cabbage will keep for 1–2 weeks in the fridge, loosely wrapped.

Red cabbage is a versatile vegetable that partners well with apple, dried fruits and sweet spices such as cinnamon.

Preparation and cooking Shred red cabbage as for white cabbage (see opposite). To preserve the red colour when cooking, add a little vinegar to the water. Braise slowly, with a minimum amount of water and mix with onion, grated apple, dried fruit and sweet spices, such as cinnamon. Once cooked in this way, it freezes well. Alternatively, stir-fry or sauté.

BRUSSELS SPROUTS

These look like miniature cabbages but, unlike so many baby vegetables, they don't really seem to have caught on in the cookery scene other than as an accompaniment. They are much too strongly flavoured to eat raw. Brussels sprouts are delicious lightly cooked, tossed in butter and served with roasted almonds, whole or flaked; they also work well with chestnuts.

Buying and storing Choose small ones, smaller than the size of a whole walnut, as they will be sweeter and nuttier. Keep loosely wrapped in the fridge for 3–4 days.

Preparation and cooking Trim off outer leaves and woody stalk ends. Cutting a small cross in the stem helps them to cook more quickly. It is best to leave them whole as they have more texture and are less likely to go soggy. Steam, boil, microwave or sauté. Once cooked, Brussels sprouts should be eaten immediately or they come to resemble overcooked cabbage.

Brussels sprouts have a distinctive flavour. They go well with almonds or walnuts.

Cut a small cross in the stem to help the sprouts cook through more evenly.

CHINESE LEAVES (CHINESE CABBAGE)

This is more delicately flavoured than green cabbage. Look for crisp, pale leaves when buying. Keep loosely wrapped in the fridge for 3–4 days. To prepare, discard the outer leaves and shred. Serve it stir-fried or sautéed, or use in salads.

Chinese leaves are good value as there is very little wastage in preparation. Use the shredded leaves in salads or add at the last minute to a stir-fry recipe.

CAULIFLOWER

There are many varieties other than the standard white, ranging in colour from pale green to near purple. These can be prepared and cooked in the same way. Cauliflower works well in spiced curries and as an ingredient in vegetable fritters. Classically, it is paired with dairy products, particularly cheese and cream sauces. Small pieces can be good in a chunky salad, raw or griddled.

Buying and storing Try to choose cauliflower with plenty of outer leaves as this protects the centre flower or 'curds'. Look for tight heads, which are unpitted with no brown spots. Opened-out curds are a sign that the cauliflower is old or has been exposed to the sun. Avoid outer leaves that look wilted or yellowing. Cut stalks should look moist. Keep in the fridge and use within a few days.

Look for cauliflower with plenty of outside leaves as these will keep the curds fresher.

Preparation and cooking Chop cauliflower into florets, leaving on a little of the stem. If cooking a cauliflower whole, cut a cross through the base of the stem in order to help the heat penetrate. The stems taste just as good as the flowers, with a nutty, almost sweet flavour. Slice stems thinly otherwise they will take longer to cook than the florets. Steam, boil or sauté, remembering that overcooked cauliflower goes soggy and smells unpleasant.

If cooking a whole cauliflower cut a cross in the base to help it cook quickly. Do the same for baby cauliflower too.

KOHLRABI

Not one of Nature's beauties, this vegetable is globe shaped with a purple or green skin marked with distinctive slashes where the leaf stalks have been removed. It has a hot, peppery flavour similar to turnip and can be used in a similar way.

Buying and storing Buy small specimens with smooth skins. Kohlrabi will keep in a well-ventilated polythene bag for up to 2 weeks in the fridge.

Preparation and cooking Remove the skin with a small, sharp knife rather than trying to use a vegetable peeler. The flesh discolours quickly so have to hand a bowl of water with a little lemon juice in it. Try not to leave the cut pieces in the water for too long before cooking. Add raw kohlrabi in small amounts to salads, or steam, boil or microwave.

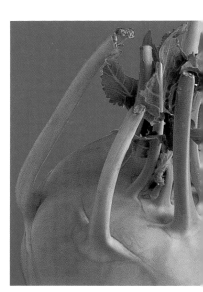

Kohlrabi may still have leaf stalks protruding from it. Cut off these and the outer skin with a sharp knife and steam, boil or microwave.

Leafy greens

Vegetables known as 'greens' are not always green, but can range in hue from a ruby red or purple through to emerald or bottle green. Many are great to steam, stir-fry or add to salad. Cooking needs to be light if you are serving greens as an accompaniment. The flavours are intense and you can take full advantage of this by making purées, which can then be used to flavour egg dishes, or used for pancake fillings.

SPINACH AND CHARD (*LEAF BEETS*)

These greens have an affinity with dairy products, and also go well with Oriental flavourings, such as chilli, ginger and shoyu, as well as with herbs such as basil and oregano.

Baby spinach is great in salads. Chard is like spinach but milder in flavour and with thicker stalks. New varieties of chard are ruby or rhubarb chard, and rainbow chard, which as the names imply are not at all green. These leafy greens contain iron, although it is a type that is not easily absorbed.

Buying and storing When buying spinach, look for richly coloured, dark leaves without traces of yellowing or slime. Chard should have glossy, dark leaves and heavy white or red stems. Keep in the fridge and eat within 2 days.

Preparation and cooking Rinse both spinach and chard in several changes of water and pat dry; shred larger leaves. Remove chard stems, slice crossways and cook separately. Steam or stir-fry. The leaves of both contain a large percentage of water so expect the quantity you cook to reduce by about half.

Chard leaves and stems need to be cooked separately.

ORIENTAL GREENS

These are mostly related to brassicas and they tend to be loose-leaved with a prominent central rib and a loosely furled heart. Some of the most common varieties are pak choi (bok choi), mustard greens and Chinese leaves. The stems and sliced leaves are good when stir-fried. Once cooked they make an alternative to spinach or chard for pancake fillings and savoury tarts. These leaves go well with Oriental flavourings, such as shoyu and ginger. The young leaves can also be eaten raw in salads.

Buying and storing Look for springy, colourful leaves without any curled or wilted edges or blemishes. Keep them in the fridge and use within a few days.

Preparation and cooking Chop or slice small leaves. With larger leaves, chop the central rib and the leaf separately. Stir-fry, steam or sauté.

Large leaves from chard or Oriental greens can be shredded and steamed or sautéed, or added to stir-fry recipes and cooked very lightly.

Stalks and buds

This is a diverse grouping of vegetables, which includes globe artichoke, asparagus, celery, fennel and chicory. Flavours range from delicate to nutty or bitter. Some of the vegetables featured here, such as globe artichoke or asparagus, demand a starring role as they are best savoured on their own. This group can be prepared and eaten in a number of ways. Stalks and buds work well served on their own or mixed with a variety of vegetables. Celery, fennel and chicory are delicious eaten raw or cooked.

GLOBE ARTICHOKE

This attractive member of the thistle family is fun and best eaten when you have plenty of time and don't mind there being a lot of mess! If you live in an area where artichokes are plentiful, it is worth cooking them and using just the hearts, which are delicious. Some of us have to settle for canned artichokes, which are perfectly satisfactory. Better still are roasted artichokes, preserved in oil, which are delightful although often expensive.

Cardoons are related to globe artichokes, but it is the stems rather than the flower heads that are eaten. They need cooking and can be treated like asparagus.

Buying and storing Choose globe artichokes with firm, tightly packed heads and a good bright colour. Brown spots at the base of the head indicate that decay has set in. Eat as soon as possible. If you have to store them uncooked, wrap in damp paper and keep in the fridge overnight.

Preparation and cooking As you work, rub all cut surfaces with lemon juice or drop in acidulated water (water with a little lemon juice added) to prevent the globe artichoke from discolouring. To prepare an artichoke for eating whole, break off the stalk and trim the base so that it will sit upright when served. Trim the pointed spines with scissors and cut off the pointed top of the artichoke with a sharp knife. Boil in salted, acidulated water for 30–40 minutes. Lift out with a slotted spoon. If one of the leaves comes away with a gentle pull, the artichoke is ready. Leave upside down to drain. To eat, pull off the leaves one at a time and dip the tiny portion of flesh at the base of the leaf in a sharp, lemony vinaigrette or plain melted butter. Eat this fleshy part and discard the main part of the leaf. When all the outer leaves have been pulled off, you are left with a cone of tiny pale leaves, the choke (a dense mat of whitish fibres) and the base, or heart. Pull off the pale leaves, then slice off or scrape away the choke with a knife to leave the heart, which can be eaten with a knife and fork.

To prepare an artichoke for stuffing, remove the stalk as before and some of the tough lower leaves. Trim as necessary and cut across the top of the artichoke, about a third of the way down. Boil as before. When cooked and cool, pull out the centre leaves until you expose the choke. Scrape this away with a teaspoon and knife, leaving a 'cup' to stuff.

To obtain artichoke hearts, the artichoke has to be dismantled, as above, before or after cooking.

Baby artichokes are becoming more widely available and can be eaten whole including the stalk and leaves. Cook for 10–15 minutes in boiling water and then serve whole with a vinaigrette, or slice and use in salads or with eggs, or bake in a rich tomato sauce. Young, fresh artichokes may also be eaten raw.

When preparing artichokes, have some fresh lemons or lemon juice handy. Rub any cut surface with a lemon or sprinkle on lemon juice to prevent discolouration.

Inside the artichoke is a dense mat of whitish fibres, the choke, which is not eaten.

ASPARAGUS

With its delicate taste, asparagus was traditionally served only with rich buttery sauces. However, it can take a range of bolder flavourings, such as chilli, ginger and sesame oil, as well as pesto and other Italian flavourings.

Buying and storing Select firm spears with tightly closed tips. Spears can be white or green and are best eaten within 24 hours.

Preparation and cooking Trim off any woody ends. Traditionally boiled upright in bunches in tall saucepans, asparagus is also excellent griddled or grilled, roasted or stir-fried.

Look for firm spears with tightly closed tips and trim off any woody ends prior to cooking. Asparagus is best cooked in bunches standing upright in a tall saucepan.

CELERY

Not generally served solo, except as crudités, celery is usually used to flavour soups and casseroles. It is also good as a crunchy addition to salads and stir-fries.

Buying and storing Choose crisp, unblemished stalks with leafy tops. Refrigerate for up to 1 week.

Preparation and cooking Separate stalks and rinse thoroughly. Trim as necessary and pull away the coarse outer 'strings'. Slice or dice to serve raw in salads, or stir-fry, grill or sauté.

Celery adds a good flavour to any slow-cooked dish such as casseroles or stews. Its texture when raw adds bite and body to salads.

FENNEL

With a distinctive hint of aniseed, this versatile vegetable goes well with all things Italian – tomatoes, basil, Parmesan – but is equally happy with citrus flavours, pears and apples, mild onion or strong salad leaves, such as watercress or radicchio. Despite its crunchy quality, it makes a smooth purée, ideal for soups and sauces.

Buying and storing Look for firm, evenly coloured, rounded bulbs with feathery, bright green fronds. Refrigerate for up to 1 week.

Preparation and cooking Trim the hard base and cut off any woody stalks. Slice finely to eat raw in salads. Grill, sauté, roast or steam.

CHICORY (*BELGIAN ENDIVE*)

This bitter-tasting, crunchy vegetable goes well with butter and cheese. It is also good flavoured with herbs and lemon juice and has an affinity with walnuts. It is a useful salad leaf.

Buying and storing Look for crisp heads with pale leaves tinged with light yellow at the tips. Refrigerate for up to 1 week.

Preparation and cooking Discard any outer leaves as necessary. For salads, slice across the vegetable or separate the leaves. For cooking, blanch the chicory whole to reduce the bitterness, then slice to grill, stir-fry or sauté.

Individual heads of chicory should look crisp with pale leaves lightly tinged at the tips. As with Chinese leaves, there is little wastage.

Fennel has a distinctive taste of aniseed. When raw, it has a crisp texture that is good in salads but it can also cook down to a smooth purée.

Salad leaves

Lettuce is available in a huge variety of shapes, textures and flavours.

Leafy green salads comprise a virtual rainbow of colours and an equally wide range of texture and flavours. There has been a huge surge of interest in salad leaves recently and consequently a blossoming of varieties.

Salads are a wonderful way to brighten any meal, and they are quick to prepare. More substance can also be added to leaf salads by using chunkier vegetables, such as tomatoes, strips of pepper, avocado, slices of fennel, and toasted nuts or seeds, or slivers of cheese. Some salad leaves, such as radicchio, rocket and sorrel, can be served warm, wilted or finely chopped and used for flavouring rather like a herb. Home-grown varieties of salad leaves are often useful, so there is always something fresh on hand.

Buying and Storing

Never choose anything that looks wilted or bruised. Remove tight polythene packaging as soon as possible and keep salad leaves in the fridge. Eat them on the day of purchase or within a day or so. Ready-mixed salad leaves are packed in special bags to keep them fresh. In this case, keep the leaves in the bag, but once you have opened the packet use the leaves as soon as possible.

Preparation

All salad leaves are fragile and need handling with care. Wash and pat dry. Use a salad spinner if you have one; otherwise heap the leaves into a clean tea towel, gather up the corners and swing around – preferably outside, unless you want an indoor shower! Tearing leaves, rather than chopping, is said to cause less cell damage and therefore preserve more nutrients and also keeps the salad crisper. Some coarser salad leaves, such as cos lettuce, however, do need to be chopped.

Only dress a salad just before serving. Leaf salads are best dressed in vinaigrette-style dressings. They should not be drowned in dressing but very lightly coated so as not to become soggy.

Varieties of Salad Leaves

Here is a list of salad leaves with descriptions of flavours and a page reference for those mentioned in other sections.

LETTUCE

The lettuce is the best known of all the salad leaves. There are many varieties – from hearted to loose-leaved and rosette types.
Butterhead lettuce: a round lettuce with soft leaves and a mild flavour.
Iceberg and crisphead: crisp texture but little flavour.
Lollo rosso: also comes in green; very curled leaves with delicate flavour.
Cos lettuce: a large-leaved, crisp and refreshing lettuce.
Little gem: a crisp, sweet, smaller version of the cos lettuce.
Lamb's lettuce (*mâche, corn salad*): succulent, mildly flavoured leaves with a pretty green hue.
Feuille de chêne (*oakleaf*): a very attractive, loose-leaved variety with maroon edges and dark insides.

CHINESE LEAVES (CHINESE CABBAGE)

More robust in flavour than lettuce but not as strong as cabbage, this has good crunchy leaves and a sweet flavour (see page 38).

ENDIVE AND CHICORY

Leaves in this family are known by a variety of names, including escarole, batavia, curly endive, frisée and radicchio. Some varieties are loosely bunched, some a jagged mass of leaves; they range in flavour from a mild tang to pronounced bitterness. Use in small quantities mixed with other leaves. Radicchio is more distinctive due to its deep red colour with contrasting white ribs. Chicory (Belgian endive) has tightly furled heads in pale white tinged with yellow (see page 41).

MISCELLANEOUS LEAVES

Mizuna: attractive, dark green, feathery leaves similar to dandelion, with a spicy, clean taste.
Sorrel: sharp-flavoured, dark green leaf. Use sparingly as the tang permeates.
Rocket: attractive, notched leaves with a peppery flavour.
Watercress: a small-leaved plant grown in fresh running water, with a spicy, pungent flavour.
Cress: hot-flavoured, delicate leaves on fine stalks.
Baby spinach: soft, dark green leaves with a clean taste (see page 39).

Other salad vegetables

A salad can be made from far more than leaves. Radish, cucumber and avocado are all wonderful ingredients to eat raw. These three are highlighted as salad vegetables as they are seldom cooked, but many other vegetables can also be eaten raw, such as the fruit vegetables and some of the stalks (see pages 40–41 and 54–57).

RADISH

Radishes have crimson red or white roots, which are either finger thick or like small globes. Characterised by a hot, peppery flavour and crisp texture, they make a perky addition to salads. They are also great eaten sliced and salted on lightly buttered bread.

Buying and storing Radishes should look 'snappy' in appearance. Refrigerate, loosely wrapped, for up to 1 week.

Radish has a distinctive hot, peppery flavour that perks up salads or sandwich fillings.

CUCUMBER

With its high water content, this is a cooling ingredient. It can be diced, sliced or cut into sticks. Cucumber is wonderful in a dip mixed with natural yoghurt, garlic and plenty of mint. For recipes like this, it is best to salt it first by sprinkling the chopped cucumber with salt and leaving it in a colander for about 1 hour. This draws out a lot of the moisture. Pat dry before using. Cucumber is good in relishes and can also be stir-fried.

Buying and storing Cucumbers should feel firm and should be kept in the fridge. Only cut as much as you need – once sliced, the pieces dry out quickly.

Cool cucumber is a refreshing salad ingredient that can be served on its own, sliced or in chunks. When adding to dips, salt first to draw out the moisture.

AVOCADO

Strictly speaking a fruit rather than a vegetable, avocado is pear shaped with knobbly or smooth skin, depending on the variety. Organic varieties are also available. Avocado is one of the few fruit vegetables with a high fat content, most of which is monounsaturated.

Buying and storing A ripe avocado will yield gently when pressed. It can be bought unripe and will ripen at home – to speed up the ripening process, place in a paper bag for a day or so. Use avocados when ripe – do not refrigerate them or they will go black. Once cut, the flesh discolours so eat straightaway or sprinkle the cut surfaces with lemon juice.

Preparation Cut lengthways through an avocado down to the large stone. Ease the two halves apart and then remove the stone using the tip of a sharp knife.

A ripe avocado will yield very slightly when pressed. They ripen well at home when left in a warm place, such as a sunny window sill.

Mushrooms

The range of edible fungi available seems to be ever increasing. Fresh mushrooms come in an array of shapes, sizes and flavours. Many species are harvested wild. Some previously wild varieties, such as the shiitake mushroom, are now cultivated, and there are several traditional varieties of cultivated mushroom. Many varieties are sold both fresh and dried.

Mushrooms are not only delicious in their own right but they are also marvellous at adding a wealth of subtle flavours as well as depth of texture to dishes as diverse as stir-fry, risotto, casserole or salads.

Each different type of mushroom has a unique flavour and texture.

Fresh Mushrooms

In recent years, there has been a growing focus on foraging for wild mushrooms, a tradition strong in Europe but less common elsewhere. If you intend picking wild mushrooms, it is vital to know exactly what to look for since many varieties that look edible are in fact poisonous. Autumn is the main season for mushrooms in Europe.

Buying and storing When buying rather than picking fresh mushrooms, look for firm and fresh-looking specimens. Avoid any that are beginning to brown in patches or those with a moist outer skin. Some mushrooms may smell strongly but it should be a pleasant smell rather than an odour. On cultivated mushrooms, pale gills are an indicator of freshness.

Store fresh mushrooms in a paper bag in the fridge. Do not keep them in polythene as they will sweat and quickly become pungent. Fresh wild mushrooms deteriorate very quickly so use them as soon as possible.

A little brush is useful for dislodging particles of earth on the cap and around the stalk.

Preparation Cultivated mushrooms need only be wiped. Even if they appear grubby, do not be tempted to wash them as the mushrooms will act like a sponge, absorbing water and becoming soggy. Trim the edges with a knife if necessary.

Fresh wild varieties do need to be thoroughly checked for earthy particles. Gently brush off the dirt and cut away any woody ends.

Dried Mushrooms

Wild mushrooms are worth buying for their exquisite flavour, which adds richness and depth to soups, stews and sauces. You need only small quantities as they should reconstitute to about four or five times their original weight.

Buying and storing dried mushrooms At first glance, dried wild mushrooms seem very expensive, but it is worth shopping around as you may be able to buy them more cheaply loose rather than pre-packed. Some dried mushrooms have surprisingly short 'sell-by' dates. Check that the contents of the packet are not dusty or, if buying loose ones, that the mushrooms are not moist. Store in a cool, dry place. They can have a pungent smell, which may infect ingredients kept nearby.

Preparation Dried mushrooms must always be soaked in liquid – boiling water, wine or lemon juice, for example – before they are used. This soaking process helps to clean the mushrooms as earthy particles will float out and be removed more easily. Soak dried mushrooms for 15–20 minutes – allow longer if you are using a cold liquid. Don't throw away the soaking liquid – it will be imbued with a rich mushroom flavour. Strain it well, preferably through a coffee filter, and then use as required. Leave the soaked mushrooms whole or chop them, depending on the recipe.

Although dried wild mushrooms can be expensive, their exquisite flavour enriches soups and stews.

Varieties of Mushroom

There are many varieties of mushroom, the most common of which are given here.

BUTTON MUSHROOM

These are the most immature cultivated mushrooms. Use them whole to make the most of their appearance. They are great in salads, marinades and stir-fries, as well as in casseroles and soups, although in these instances you may be better off using the stronger-flavoured chestnut or cremini mushroom.

CHANTERELLE (GIROLLE)

Golden-hued and concave, these dainty mushrooms have a more delicate flavour than ceps (see above right). They are available fresh or dried. Brush off grit rather than washing these mushrooms as they are quite porous, and they do exude a certain amount of water as they cook. This can be poured off if necessary and used as stock.

CHESTNUT (PARIS) AND CREMINI MUSHROOMS

Fresh chestnut mushrooms have a good dense texture, which gets darker on cooking, and are excellent in robust stews and rich sauces. They also add a distinctive flavour to nut roasts or pie fillings. Chestnut mushrooms are interchangeable with cremini mushrooms, which look similar and also have a good flavour and firm texture. Baby cremini mushrooms are also available.

ENOKI MUSHROOM

These little clusters of skinny-stemmed mushrooms with tiny heads have a crisp texture and a slight hint of lemon. They look pretty in soups and can be used in stir-fries and salads.

MOREL

Available fresh and dried, these mushrooms are an exception to the 'no washing' rule for mushrooms when fresh. The slim, conical cap of the morel has a honeycomb texture, which easily traps dirt. Leave them in salted water for

3 minutes to get rid of any insects, then rinse under cold running water and pat dry with a clean tea towel or kitchen paper. They can be used whole or finely sliced for sauces.

CEP AND PORCINI

Closely related, the cep from France and the porcini from Italy are available fresh and dried. When fresh, the mushrooms are quite chunky with a spongy underneath, which is edible. Dried ceps are sold in thin slices. They are useful for creating instant stock and for imparting a delicious, woody flavour.

SHIITAKE MUSHROOM

Available both fresh and dried, the shiitake mushroom was originally a wild mushroom native to Japan, but it is now cultivated in many parts of the world. This mushroom has a fine robust flavour and substantial chewy texture. Occasionally, you need to discard particularly woody stems. Shiitake mushrooms are good for sauces and stir-fries but need to be thinly sliced. Cut them up in larger chunks to use in casseroles. Reconstitute the dried variety in boiling water and use the liquid for stock.

STRAW MUSHROOM

This variety of small mushroom is native to China and, as you might expect, cultivated on straw. They can be used as a substitute for button mushrooms, having a similar clean taste and texture.

OYSTER MUSHROOM

Also known as pleurotte, this prettily shaped, fluted mushroom is sold fresh, sometimes in small clusters. It is usually pale grey in colour, but there are also salmon pink and pale yellow varieties. The flesh of the oyster mushroom is succulent and melting. Oyster mushrooms can be used in most recipes, but bear in mind that they release a great deal of moisture during cooking. They are particularly good in soups and sauces as well as casseroles.

OPEN, FLAT (PORTOBELLO) MUSHROOM

Treat these giants as succulent, edible plates to be served plainly grilled, roasted or stuffed and baked. Foil wrapped or well oiled, they also make a good addition to the barbecue.

Pods and sweetcorn

Encompassing a wide range of peas as well as beans, okra, corn and baby corn, these bright, succulent vegetables add a good splash of colour to a great variety of dishes and also work well as a quick accompaniment.

Fresh corn on the cob is one of the most succulent and colourful vegetables included in this group.

PEAS

Fresh peas are on sale for only a short period of the year. If the peas inside the pod are very small, they are sweet and delicious to eat raw. Shelled peas work well in spicy curry dishes, as well as with creamy pasta sauces and in stir-fries. They also make a colourful side vegetable. Organic frozen peas are sometimes available.

Buying and storing When buying fresh peas, look for pods that are full, plump and wrinkle free, and have a bright colour. All peas should have a good colour, too, and feel squeaky with life. Refrigerate for up to 3 days.

Preparation and cooking To pod fresh peas, press the base to snap open and push out the peas with your thumb. They are best lightly boiled, steamed, microwaved or added to stir-fries.

Look out for fresh peas as they are in season for only a short period. They should be firm and brightly coloured.

MANGETOUT *(SNOW PEAS)* AND SUGAR SNAPS

These are edible pods with immature peas inside. Sugar snaps are plumper than mangetout because they often have some formed peas inside but nevertheless are designed to be eaten whole. These pods are good for stir-fries and salad dishes as they add colour and texture.

Buying and storing Look for firm, crisp, bright green pods. Store in the fridge for 3–4 days.

Mangetout are slim, edible pods containing minute immature peas. Remove the fibrous strings from the pods before cooking.

Preparation and cooking String pods before cooking by breaking off the stalk and peeling off the fibrous strings from the sides of the pods. Stir-fry or lightly steam.

BEANS

There are many varieties of beans, known variously as green, French, string, runner, bobby, Italian and wax. Some are as thin as a shoelace, others finger-thick and about as long. There are also lemon-flavoured yard-long beans that are used in Asian cookery.

Fresh beans are a good way of adding colour to a stew or casserole. They go well with Mediterranean vegetables, such as tomatoes, olives and peppers; they are also great partnered with garlicky Middle Eastern dishes. When served as a side vegetable, beans should be tender yet crisp. They also work well in marinades based on olive oil or with Oriental flavours.

Buying and storing Beans should have a good colour, and all but the youngest and smallest varieties should snap in half easily if they are fresh. Yard-long beans may have patches, which will disappear on cooking. Keep beans in the fridge for 4–5 days.

Preparation and cooking String beans were originally named for the fibrous strings running the length of the bean, which were indigestible and needed to be removed before cooking. However, many stringless beans are now available. Chunky, short beans and very fine French beans need trimming but rarely stringing; runner beans are more fibrous and heavily textured, and usually do need stringing. Cut beans thinly either diagonally across the pod or lengthways. Once prepared, steam, boil, microwave or stir-fry.

Green beans come in many shapes and sizes, from finger thick to pencil fine.

BROAD BEANS

These are the heavyweights of this group. They are bigger in size, coming inevitably from larger pods, which look leathery and swollen with the plump beans inside. Broad beans are good with grain dishes, such as paella and casseroles, as well as in hearty, garlic-laden salads. They are also delicious as a simple side vegetable.

Tasty and substantial, broad beans make a good vegetable side dish but can also be served with grains or used in salads.

Buying and storing Look for plump pods, not too large, with a good colour. Store in the fridge for 3–4 days.

Preparation and cooking Open the pods and remove the beans. Really young, small beans can be cooked in boiling water for 5 minutes; older large beans may need up to 15 minutes.

OKRA *(LADIES' FINGERS, GUMBO, BHINDI)*

Okra, sometimes known as ladies' fingers, gumbo or bhindi, adds a distinctive texture and taste to soups and stews.

A distinctive, green, slim, conical vegetable, about the length of a finger, okra is used extensively in the southern states of America, as well as in Indian and African cookery. Okra pods contain a slippery, gelatinous juice, which is released when the pod is cut. This adds a distinctive quality to a soup or stew as well as thickening it.

Buying and storing Okra pods should have a good colour, be free from blemishes and firm not floppy. Keep in the fridge for up to 3 days.

Preparation and cooking Trim the ends. To release the juices the pods need to be slit. They can then be left whole or sliced and added to soups or stews. If cooking okra whole for a dry, spicy dish, typical of Indian cookery, prepare okra by trimming both ends but taking care not to split the pods. It can also be boiled and tossed in butter.

CORN *(SWEETCORN)*

Fresh corn on the cob has a delicate, sweet flavour. It is a versatile ingredient that can be eaten alone but it also adds good colour and texture to stews, grain dishes and salads. Corn is commonly used in Mexican cookery and goes well with sharp flavourings such as lime and chilli. The cobs are great to barbecue whole in the husks. Corn is gluten-free.

Buying and storing Choose cobs that are completely enclosed in green husks because these will protect the kernels and prevent the corn from drying out. If in doubt, peel back the leaves and check that the kernels are still plump. Try not to buy cobs pre-packed as you are unable to inspect them. Once harvested, sweetcorn loses its sweetness so eat as soon after buying as possible. If necessary store in a loose polythene bag in the fridge for up to 2 days.

Preparation and cooking Remove the outer leaves and the silky threads. Cook whole cobs in boiling water for 3–5 minutes, or steam them for 8–10 minutes. The individual kernels should be tender when pierced. Kernels can be stripped off the cob. Use a sharp knife and hold the cob at a slight angle, which will be safer than balancing it on one end. Scrape off a row of kernels, cutting close to the inner core and working down and away from you. Work your way in this manner around the cob. Each cob should yield about 125g (4oz) kernels.

To remove kernels from the cob, hold the cob at an angle and scrape downwards with a sharp knife.

BABY CORN COBS *(DWARF SWEETCORN)*

These are finger-length cobs with a sweet flavour and crisp texture. They are excellent in stir-fries and casseroles, or they can be steamed or sautéed for a side vegetable.

Onion family

Many varieties of onion are available, alongside other members of the onion family, such as garlic, leeks and spring onions. This group of vegetables is fundamental as a base flavouring for many recipes. The onion family can also be shown off in its own right when roasted or stir-fried.

There are many varieties of onion, which form the aromatic base of a huge number of recipes.

ONION

Revered by the Ancient Egyptians and favoured by the Greeks and Romans, the humble onion is now treated as an essential ingredient in diverse recipes. Many countries grow their own varieties, which range from deep purple-red to pure white, from sweet to pungent and from bulbous to pencil thin. Onions from colder climates tend to have stronger flavours.

Buying and storing Look for onions with firm bulbs, evenly coloured papery skin and no sprouting. Avoid any that feel spongy or look sooty; a rotting onion will also smell unpleasant. Common onions should last for several weeks, if not months, if they are stored in cool, dark, airy conditions. Red onions and sweet varieties of onion do not last so long.

Once cut, onions should be used quickly. If you have a leftover half, wrap it well before putting it in the fridge or the smell will permeate any butter or cheese. Aim to use it the following day.

Preparation and cooking Trim the ends and peel off the skin. Onions have a slippery outer surface so use a sharp knife that won't slide off. Cut the bulb in half and place each half cut-side down. Slice thinly to form crescents. To dice the onion finely, hold the sliced half firmly and cut again – at right angles to the first cuts.

To cut onion rings, trim and peel off the skin as before. Hold the onion carefully as it can be slippery and slice right through, then separate the slices into rings. To make crisp onion rings, dip them in milk and seasoned flour, then deep-fry in hot oil for 2–3 minutes.

COMMON VARIETIES OF ONION

This large family of vegetables forms the flavour base of many recipes. Apart from the common onion you may find some of the following:

Spanish onion
This is a large, juicy, white-fleshed onion, with a mild flavour.

White onion
Pure or pearl white, these onions have a paper-thin skin and crisp flesh. They are good raw or cooked.

Sweet onion
This specially developed species has a sweet flavour and is particularly good in salads. Look for specimens that are firm and shiny with a thin skin.

Red onion
Sweeter and milder than the traditional onion, red onion is good for salads and also for roasting and barbecuing as its high sugar content helps it caramelise. When selecting a red onion, make sure that its skin is not discoloured.

ONIONS WITHOUT TEARS

Cutting an onion often causes tears due to a chemical reaction that results from the onion cells being damaged. There is no universal remedy for this, although tips to combat the tears are plentiful – from wearing swimming goggles and chewing bread, to soaking the onions in ice-cold water, leaving the root intact or leaning back slightly as you chop! Remember that some varieties of onion are stronger than others.

TRANSLUCENT ONIONS

Many recipes start with onions being cooked until translucent. This stage is important since when cooked slowly and thoroughly, the onion imparts a subtle flavour to the finished dish. Other ingredients, especially tomatoes, will halt the cooking of the onion, so it is important to have the onions properly softened in the initial stages.

GARLIC

This small but pungent ingredient is used to flavour a diverse range of foods and is popular in French, Italian, Oriental and Indian dishes. Garlic has been credited with lowering blood cholesterol levels and warding off colds. However, in order to get any benefit from garlic, it needs to be eaten regularly and in large amounts.

A fresh head of garlic is firm with no slashes or slits.

Buying and storing Look for firm heads of garlic with no slashes or slits. Garlic should last for several weeks in a cool airy place – don't keep it in a steamy kitchen.

Preparation and cooking The traditional method is to chop the garlic and then crush it with the blade of a knife, adding a little salt to prevent the knife slipping. Alternatively, use a sturdy garlic press. Be careful not to burn or scorch garlic when cooking or it will become bitter. It is best to add garlic once there is another ingredient, such as onion, already cooking in the pan.

Roasted garlic is a wonderful way of adding a very subtle flavour to recipes, especially to raw salad dressing and dips where uncooked garlic might be too strong. Roast plump, firm unpeeled cloves in a preheated oven, 200°C (400°F), Gas Mark 6, for 5 minutes. Leave to cool, then peel, mash and use as required.

Garlic can be chopped, sliced or crushed. Use a sharp knife and a sprinkling of salt to prevent the knife slipping, or a sturdy garlic press.

SHALLOT

This small, brown bulb is related to the onion but has a milder, sweeter flavour. The flesh can be pink in appearance. Like onion, it is usually cooked at the beginning of the recipe to add subtle undertones of flavour.

Buying and storing Look for firm bulbs when buying and store in a cool airy place for up to a month. Prepare and cook in a similar way to onions.

Shallots can be used as background flavouring or served as an accompaniment.

LEEK

Leeks are milder in flavour than onions and develop a buttery texture when cooked slowly, which makes them excellent for pairing with cheese. Leeks also have an affinity with potatoes.

Buying and storing It is best to choose medium to small leeks since large ones sometimes have a woody core that is inedible. Look for dark green leaves, which are not dry or wilted. Store leeks in the fridge and use within 1 week.

Preparation and cooking Leeks need thorough cleaning as dirt is often trapped in the leaves. Remove the outer leaves, trim the green tops and cut off the bearded ends. Slice twice lengthways along the green part almost into the white central body of the leek. Rinse under cold running water, fanning out the leaves so that any trapped dirt is flushed away. Cut the leek into slices or chunks.

SPRING ONIONS *(SALAD ONIONS, SCALLIONS)*

These small, immature onions are usually pencil thin with a white base and green leaves. Use them in salads and stir-fries.

Buying and storing The leaves should look bright and springy with no hint of yellowing. Keep in the fridge for up to 1 week.

Preparation and cooking Trim the base and any straggly green leaves. Chop, slice or cut into lengths.

Root vegetables and tubers

This group includes familiar vegetables such as carrots and potatoes, as well as a large group of lesser-known specimens such as swede, turnip, parsnip, celeriac and Jerusalem artichoke. The poor reputation of some of these vegetables is due to perception rather than flavour. Cheap root vegetables were often served up as institutional and therefore uninspiring food; other roots were commonly used as animal fodder. But it is worth discovering their advantages.

These vegetables are all excellent ingredients to include in casseroles and stews. They work well with each other but also happily partner a broad range of other vegetables, as well as a variety of spices and herbs. They make smooth purées, which can be enriched with cream or soft cheese, and best of all they are delicious roasted, a cooking method that brings out their natural mellow flavour and sweetness. So, if you have always given them a miss, have a rethink!

Parsnips are excellent in slow-cooking dishes such as casseroles. They can also be roasted, puréed or steamed as an accompaniment.

General Advice

When buying root vegetables, look for wrinkle-free skins with no soft patches or sprouting. Some do have very knobbly exteriors but don't be put off; the vegetables should feel firm and heavy. If kept in cool, well-ventilated conditions, most root vegetables will keep for about 1 week and probably longer but they do gradually lose their vitamin C content. They should be used immediately if they start to sprout.

Fresh parsnips should look smooth and firm, with a creamy white colour. Discard any that show signs of sprouting.

CARROTS

A highly nutritious vegetable, carrots are also a great cooking mainstay, delicious both raw and cooked. Carrots can be teamed with a great variety of flavours – from the mildest dairy product to spicy Indian or Oriental flavourings.

Carrots should have a crisp texture and are great eaten raw or cooked.

Buying and storing Carrots should be crisp with a smooth surface. Avoid any that are limp or have damaged skins. Keep them in a cool airy place for about 1 week.

Preparation and cooking Peel carrots thinly to remove any chemicals, but if they are organically grown, this is not necessary. Cut off tops and root ends, and slice, dice or cut into strips. Boil, steam, microwave, roast or stir-fry.

Try not to take off more than a thin strip of peel because much of the nutritional value is just below the surface of a carrot.

POTATOES

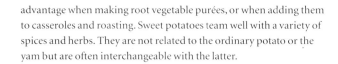

This is now one of the world's most widely grown vegetables. Potatoes fall into two categories – waxy or floury – although some all-purpose varieties are midway between the two. Waxy potatoes have a high moisture and low starch content, and are better for sautéing, boiling and salads. New potatoes tend to have a waxy character. Floury potatoes have more starch and a lighter texture and are good for baking and mashing.

Buying and storing Potatoes belong to the nightshade family, a group of plants in which all, apart from the tubers, are poisonous. Exposure to light, and sprouting, can cause a concentration of poisons, visible as a green hue, so it is vital not to buy or eat green potatoes or sprouting potatoes. A small patch of green can be cut away but discard any with a heavy green tinge.

There are two categories of potato: waxy or floury. Each suits different preparation styles.

Do not store potatoes sealed in polythene as this will create condensation and the moisture will cause them to spoil. Stored in a dry, dark place with good ventilation, potatoes will keep for at least 2 weeks, maybe longer. They are best not stored with strong-smelling foods, such as onions, as they can pick up an off-flavour.

Preparation and cooking Scrub well to remove most of the pesticides or peel thinly. Potatoes can lose up to 25% of their protein if peeled too coarsely and much of their vitamin C content is close to the skin. Boil, roast or bake whole.

SWEET POTATOES

Sweet potatoes have light brown, orange or purple skins and bright orange, or sometimes white, flesh. Their sweetness makes them less versatile than ordinary potatoes, but this quality can be used to advantage when making root vegetable purées, or when adding them to casseroles and roasting. Sweet potatoes team well with a variety of spices and herbs. They are not related to the ordinary potato or the yam but are often interchangeable with the latter.

Buying and storing Check for rotten or soft spots. Store in a cool, dry, dark place and eat within 1 week.

Preparation and cooking Scrub and bake whole, or peel and slice thinly for baking as 'crisps', or cut into chunks for casseroles. Sweet potatoes can also be boiled and mashed.

YAM

These tropical roots are more starchy than the sweet potato. They are important ingredients in recipes from West Africa, the West Indies and South East Asia.

Buying and storing Look out for rotten or soft patches. Store in a cool, dry, dark place and eat within 1 week.

Preparation and cooking Scrub, rub with oil and bake whole. Peel and slice or mash.

Yams are similar to a sweet potato but more starchy. Check carefully for soft patches before buying.

Sweet potatoes have a marvellous, cheerful colour and go well with a variety of herbs and spices.

PARSNIP

A long white root, the parsnip is similar in shape to a carrot but with creamy flesh and a strong, sweet flavour. Parsnips are not edible raw but can be cooked in a number of ways. They go well with a variety of herbs and spices, as well as flavourings such as orange and lemon. Once cooked, parsnip purées easily, making it highly suitable for soups.

Roasted parsnips make a delicious accompaniment to pies and roasts. This cooking method brings out their mellow flavour.

Buying and storing It is best to choose small smooth specimens with firm flesh; large parsnips tend to be woody in texture. Store in a cool dry place for about 1 week.

Preparation and cooking Scrub and peel parsnips thinly. Trim tops and root ends and slice or chop into lengths. Boil, steam, sauté or roast.

BEETROOT

Beetroot is cultivated for both the root and its leaves (see page 42). The roots can vary in colour from red and gold to white, although the flavour is roughly the same. The main difference is that golden beets don't bleed in the way that red beets do. The flavour of beetroot is sweet and earthy. It is great with onion or citrus flavours, as well as with soured cream, tangy goat's cheese and hot condiments, such as mustard and horseradish.

Look for turnips the size of golf balls. Their peppery flavour is great in casseroles or mashed with other root vegetables.

Buying and storing

Choose firm, smooth roots with the leaves attached. Separate the leaves before storing. Beetroot can be kept in a ventilated polythene bag in the fridge for some weeks.

Preparation and

cooking Red beets will stain everything crimson, so consider carefully what you wear, where you prepare them and what other ingredients you mix them with. Sadly, the dramatic crimson colour can turn rather easily to an unattractive pink. Beetroot is easier to peel once it has been cooked. Scrub the roots and then boil for 35–40 minutes, or until tender.

Beetroot has a sweet, earthy flavour that goes well with sour cream and tangy cheese.

Remove the skins with a sharp knife when the beetroot is cool enough to handle. Beetroot is good roasted or baked. It can be eaten raw and is then best grated or cut into thin slivers.

TURNIP

The best turnips are no bigger than a golf ball with a greenish white or purple skin. They have a slightly peppery flavour, which works well with dairy products, as well as with pungent herbs, such as thyme or tarragon.

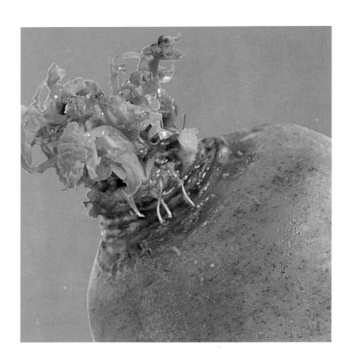

Buying and storing Look for small smooth-skinned roots with creamy flesh. Avoid shrivelled or cracked roots. Turnips will keep for up to 2 weeks in the fridge.

Preparation and cooking Small, young specimens do not need peeling – simply scrub them under running water. They can be added to casseroles, mashed with other root vegetables, steamed, sautéed or stir-fried.

JERUSALEM ARTICHOKE

These nutty tubers grow beneath yellow flowers related to the sunflower, hence the alternative name 'sunchoke'. They have a crisp flesh and a sweet flavour, a little like water chestnuts. They are great for soups and stews and can also be partnered with dairy products, such as crème fraîche or soured cream, or with spices.

Jerusalem artichokes have a nutty-flavoured, crisp flesh.

They cause flatulence due to an indigestible carbohydrate, which eventually causes a build-up of gases in the colon. It is therefore best to eat small quantities at a time.

Buying and storing Look for firm unblemished tubers. Store in the fridge for up to 2 weeks. However, you must check them and use immediately if they begin to sprout.

Preparation and cooking The knobbly surface needs a lot of scrubbing and sometimes careful peeling. Some commercially grown varieties now have much smoother skins, which are easier to deal with. Once peeled, the flesh discolours quickly so have a bowl of water containing a few drops of lemon juice handy. Try not to leave the cut pieces in the water for too long before cooking. Bake, roast, boil, steam or sauté.

Because the flesh discolours quickly after peeling, drop the cut pieces of Jerusalem artichoke into a bowl of acidulated water.

CELERIAC

The knobbly, shaggy exterior of celeriac is unattractive but do not be put off. Celeriac has a flavour and aroma akin to celery. It is delicious cooked in wine or puréed with butter, cream or soft cheese. It is also good raw in salads.

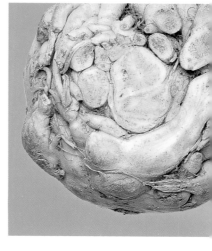

Buying and storing Buy medium varieties as older, larger specimens may have a woody texture or, worse still, may be hollow. Celeriac should feel heavy for its size.

Preparation and cooking Remove the skin with a small sharp knife, rather than trying to use a vegetable peeler. The

Celeriac has a knobbly exterior concealing a crisp celery-flavoured interior.

flesh discolours quickly so, as with Jerusalem artichokes, have a bowl of acidulated water to hand. Try not to leave the cut pieces in the water for too long before cooking. Boil or sauté.

SWEDE *(RUTABAGA)*

Once used almost exclusively for animal fodder, new varieties of swede are being grown specifically for home cooking. These tend to be smaller and not quite so hard, with orange flesh that has an attractive, warm appearance. Swede is useful in soups and casseroles and also extremely good when roasted. It goes well with ginger or nutmeg.

Buying and storing Look for smaller specimens with smooth skins, which feel firm and heavy. Store for several weeks in cool, dry conditions.

Preparation and cooking Peel thickly with a sharp knife, exposing the yellow flesh. Because it has a high water content, a simple mash can be rather tasteless. Swede is better roasted, steamed or microwaved.

The warm orange flesh of the swede and is good in casseroles or roasted with other vegetables.

Fruit vegetables

Describing vegetables as fruits may seem a contradiction in terms, but the classification distinguishes the group from flowering vegetables and from roots or shoots. This diverse group includes brightly coloured peppers, the purple-hued aubergine, tomatoes and a vast range of squashes. All members of the group are extremely versatile – many can be eaten raw as well as being roasted, grilled, fried, baked or puréed.

SWEET PEPPER (BELL PEPPER, PIMENTO)

Sweet or bell peppers are related to the chilli family, but have a mild rather than hot flavour and they sweeten as they ripen. They are marvellous vegetables, adding masses of colour to all manner of dishes. They can be eaten raw or cooked in a variety of ways and are ideal for stuffing.

Peppers come in a dazzling array of colours, the most familiar being red and green but increasingly orange, yellow and even white and purple are on sale. These are all similar but warmer colours indicate riper specimens, thus yellow is the sweetest of all while the green pepper has a fresh almost grassy flavour. Look out, too, for baby peppers, which can be used whole in a dish of marinated vegetables or stuffed for cocktail snacks. Red and yellow peppers are very good sources of carotenes and vitamin C.

Buying and storing

Choose bright, firm specimens with smooth skins, which should not be wrinkled or soft. It doesn't matter if the red ones have a touch of green, or vice versa, since this is part of the ripening process. Peppers don't have to have a regular appearance, unless you want to stuff them. Store in a cool place, preferably the fridge, and they will last for 1 week.

This slow-cooked Caponata of Roasted Vegetables (see page 176) includes many different fruit vegetables.

Preparation and cooking The easiest way to prepare peppers is to cut a slice off the top, thus removing the stalk and part of the core. Then cut a small slice off the base. (Use the flesh from these trimmings if appropriate.) This leaves you with a neat, open-ended box. Remove the core, seeds and membranes. Slice the pepper in half, and then, with the inside of the pepper uppermost (since this part is less slippery), cut the flesh into long strips or dice.

To prepare a pepper for stuffing, first slice off the top and then pull out the core. Shake out any remaining seeds and then cut out the white membranes found on the inside of pepper.

Peppers are fine to eat raw and can also be cooked in casseroles or stir-fries without being skinned. However, some people find the skin indigestible and peppers are easily skinned (see box, below).

SKINNING PEPPERS

This is done most efficiently in the oven as you don't have to stand over them. Wash and wipe the peppers and leave them plain or coat lightly with oil. Place on a baking sheet and roast in a preheated oven, 200°C (400°F), Gas Mark 6, for about 25–30 minutes, or until the skin chars and blisters. Leave to cool slightly, then peel off the skin. Don't rinse the pepper as you will lose much of the flavour. The cooking juices have a good flavour, too. Once roasted, peppers can be kept in the fridge for up to 1 week. A skinned pepper has a mellow, sweet flavour and soft texture.

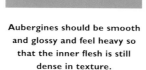

AUBERGINE (*EGGPLANT*)

The most widespread variety is the
purple-hued aubergine. It is a
versatile vegetable and features
throughout the world in many
classic dishes, such as Greek
moussaka, Turkish Imam Bayaldi (stuffed aubergine with cooked
onions, tomatoes and garlic) and Baba Ghanoush (roasted aubergine
creamed with tahini) from the Middle East.

**Aubergines should be smooth
and glossy and feel heavy so
that the inner flesh is still
dense in texture.**

Buying and storing Aubergines should look smooth and
glossy and feel heavy for their size. If they are big yet weigh little, the
insides may be spongy and past their best. Be careful when touching
the cap as it can be prickly. Store aubergines in a cool place or they
will quickly shrivel.

Preparation and cooking Wipe the aubergine and trim off
the cap. Cut into slices or dice as required, using a very sharp knife as
the outer skin can be slippery.

To roast and purée an aubergine, wipe and leave whole and place
in a roasting tin. Roast in a preheated hot oven, 200°C (400°F), Gas
Mark 6, for about 40 minutes, until the aubergine has collapsed and
is very soft. Leave to cool then scrape out the flesh. The purée can be
mixed with all manner of spices or herbs, natural yoghurt, tahini or
tofu (see page 83).

SALTING AUBERGINES

This process is used to draw out bitter juices. It is not strictly
necessary now because modern varieties of aubergines have
been developed to be less bitter. However, salting does help
prevent the aubergine from absorbing so much oil when fried.
If you have time, therefore, it is worth doing. To salt an aubergine,
cut it into slices or cubes, place in a colander and sprinkle lightly
with salt. Leave for at least 20 minutes or longer, then rinse, pat
dry with kitchen paper and use as required.

SUMMER SQUASH

This group includes courgette (zucchini), patty pan, baby patty pan
and yellow crookneck squash. Squashes are popular in America and
around the Mediterranean but, apart from the green and gold
varieties of courgette, are lesser known in Northern Europe.
Summer squashes are characterised by thinner skins and
they tend to be less watery than winter varieties.
They often have colourful flesh and roast and
purée well, making a good base for soups,
sauces and ravioli stuffing. Squash goes
well with many flavourings, including
sweet spices such as cinnamon and
nutmeg, pungent herbs such as basil
or marjoram, walnuts and some
other fruit vegetables.

The marrow is a very large
version of the courgette. It
has a thick skin and somewhat
watery flesh. Marrow is best
sautéed with spices, such as
paprika, cumin or caraway,
or pungent herbs such as
thyme. Finish off by adding
a splash of wine.

**Summer squash can
be stuffed with a variety of
flavoursome fillings and
served either hot or cold.**

Buying and storing Look for firm glossy vegetables that are
not too large – especially courgettes, which are at their best when they
are young and small. They should be heavy for their size and have
no wrinkled or brown patches. Store them in the fridge, loosely
covered, for 3–4 days.

Preparation and cooking Do not peel summer squashes as
you will lose flavour and texture. Wipe or rinse and trim the ends as
necessary. Chop large specimens.

Summer squashes are good stuffed, lightly steamed and marinated
for salads served at room temperature. They add bulk and substance
to stews and casseroles, and are useful for barbecues and griddling,
as well as stir-frying.

**Fruit vegetables range from the
tough, durable winter squashes to
the most delicate of tomatoes.
They work well in their own right,
but can also be used together or
with numerous other vegetables,
grains and pulses.**

SQUASH BLOSSOMS

Squash blossoms taste delicately of the parent vegetable and should be used the day they are picked. They can be stuffed, dipped in batter and fried, or eaten raw. Wash first, remove the stamen and trim any prickly stalk or sepals. They go well with dairy products.

WINTER SQUASH AND PUMPKIN

Don't be put off by craggy skins or monstrous-sized specimens because they will still be delicious. Winter squashes, such as pumpkin, add good colour to soups and casseroles. The purée can be used for stuffing vegetables or pasta, as well as for flavouring risotto (see pages 227 and 229). They go well with cheese, fiery spices, such as chilli or ginger, and pungent herbs and garlic.

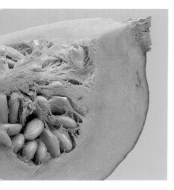

Winter squash adds a good colour to soups and casseroles and can also be puréed.

Buying and storing Avoid any with damaged skins or definite blemishes. Winter squashes can be stored whole for months in a cool, dry place with plenty of ventilation and away from frost. Once cut, use quickly or wrap and keep in the fridge for a few days only.

Preparation and cooking Some varieties, such as butternut squash, have thin skins, which can be left unpeeled in casseroles and soups, but thicker-skinned varieties will need peeling, which is hard work. Chopping large ones, such as pumpkin, into pieces can also be tricky. Use a good, large sharp knife or cleaver and don't try to cut through the stem for a perfect half. Roasted or baked halves or segments are easier to peel once cooked. This is useful to know, especially if you are making a purée.

Bake winter squash whole and unpeeled, or peel and cut into cubes, then boil, steam or bake.

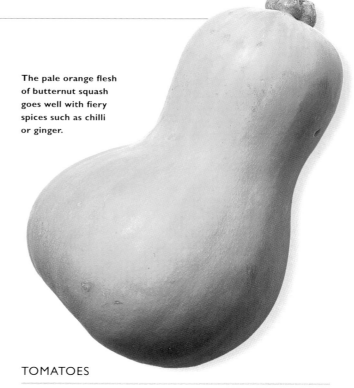

The pale orange flesh of butternut squash goes well with fiery spices such as chilli or ginger.

TOMATOES

While numerous varieties abound, tasty tomatoes are difficult to find. Many commercial varieties are grown in engineered conditions and do not have much flavour. Vine tomatoes are matured on the vine for the best flavour. There are both cherry and standard tomatoes sold in this form. If you can't buy good tomatoes locally, it is better to use good-quality canned tomatoes or sun-dried tomatoes instead.

Buying and storing Buy local varieties when you can. They should be firm but not rock hard, and have good shiny skins and a rich colour, although this isn't always an indicator of flavour. Smelling them is sometimes a better test.

Keep tomatoes at room temperature since refrigeration deadens the flavour. Keep vine tomatoes on the vine until needed. Ripe tomatoes will keep for a few days and unripe ones can take a week to develop a good flavour.

Preparation and cooking Wipe the tomato, then chop, slice or quarter, depending on the recipe. Served as a side dish, tomatoes are good grilled, griddled or baked.

SKINNING TOMATOES

Score a cross in the top of the tomato. Place in a large bowl, cover with boiling water and leave for 1 minute. You should then be able to peel away the skin easily. If the recipe requires the tomatoes to be quite juicy, leave the seeds in. Removing the seeds is a cosmetic touch and often you lose much of the flesh.

When chopping pumpkins into smaller pieces, use a large, sharp knife and don't try to cut through the stem.

VARIETIES OF TOMATO

Plum tomatoes: not so juicy as the standard tomato, these are good for pulping. Baby plum tomatoes are sometimes available, and they are good in salads and for roasting.

Cherry tomatoes: as you would expect, these are small, very sweet tomatoes, which are pretty left whole in salads or when roasted.

Beefsteak, slicing or Italian tomatoes: these giant tomatoes look impressive, thickly sliced for a simple salad. They can also be stuffed, or halved and baked, then drizzled with olive oil and balsamic vinegar.

CHILLI

Fresh chillies range in heat from mild to blisteringly hot. As a rough guide, the smaller and narrower the chilli and the darker its colour, the more powerful its heat. The hottest chillies are the habañero and tiny bird's eye; the mildest include the sweet banana and tapering green Anaheim. Red chillies are riper than green chillies and can taste slightly sweeter.

Choosing chillies is not a question of going for the burn factor! Chillies can add a wonderful dimension to your cooking, creating sensations from a rich warmth to a dramatic heat. Counteract their effects with dairy products or beer; surprisingly enough, a glass of water seems to intensify the heat rather than assuage it.

Fresh chillies, in a range of shapes and sizes, vary in heat, from being almost as mild as a bell pepper to blisteringly hot. Large green chillies are milder, while small, narrow dark-red chillies are at the hottest end of the spectrum. Choose an appropriate variety and they can add an underlying warmth rather than a dominating heat.

Buying and storing Look for bright, glossy skins and avoid any chillies that are bruised. Chillies can be stored for up to 3 weeks in the fridge. If there is any trace of mould, separate the chillies out and remove the culprit as the mould spreads quickly. If stored in oil, chillies will keep even longer.

Preparation and cooking Always treat chillies with care as they contain oils that can permeate the skin. After chopping a chilli, never touch your eyes or mouth; wash your hands thoroughly, as well as the knife and chopping board. A good precaution is to wear gloves. The skin, seeds and membrane are the hottest parts of a chilli so discard those if you wish, reserving only the flesh.

SKINNING AND ROASTING CHILLIES

This can be done in the oven or under the grill. Cook until the skin is charred. If the skin is thin and doesn't come away easily, place the chilli in a polythene bag and leave for 10 minutes to steam in its own heat. It should then be easier to peel.

Note: *if grilling chilli, do so only in a well-ventilated room as the chilli can release volatile oils that may sting your eyes.*

Rehydrating dried chillies: cover dried chillies with boiling water and leave for 30 minutes. Drain then crush with a pestle and mortar or purée in a blender. (Reserve the soaking water for adding to a stock.)

Fruit

Refreshing, colourful, versatile, aromatic, nutritious, exotic, juicy, perfumed – the adjectives that apply to fruit must be as numerous as the varieties of fruit found today in shops, markets, gardens and glasshouses around the world. Also, look out for your own local delicacies, such as Scottish raspberries or Californian peaches, as these are likely to be good quality when in season.

As with vegetables, better transportation and storage ensures that we now have access to a wider range of fruit at all times of the year. The downside of this is that many of these fruits may have to be ripened artificially or else never achieve ripeness. You are sometimes better focusing on locally grown produce bought in season and adapting recipes accordingly.

Fruit is an ingredient that fits well into any meal of the day, in both sweet and savoury recipes, as well as being delicious as a snack or drink.

Nutritional Value

Fruit has long been valued for its health-giving properties. Fruit provides energy in the form of fructose or fruit sugar; it also contains carbohydrate and fibre. Most fruits are low in fat and therefore low in calories. Fresh fruit, preferably eaten raw, is an important part of any healthy diet. Most fruit contains vitamin C, an important antioxidant which cannot be stored in the body and so needs topping up daily. Some fruits, notably orange-fleshed varieties such as apricots, mangoes and peaches, also contain carotenes. Several varieties of fruit are a rich source of many essential minerals.

Buying

If you can, choose fruit from a loose display rather than pre-packed so that you can inspect each piece. Pick fruit that is bright and fresh, avoiding any that have bruises or shrivelled skins. In general, fruit should feel heavy for its size since this is an indication of a good moisture content.

To benefit from the valuable, health-giving properties of fruit, try to eat some every day.

When choosing fragrant fruits, such as melons, peaches, nectarines, strawberries and pineapples, be guided by their aroma as this should be a good indication of their ripeness. If they have no smell at all, they may have been picked too early or have been over-refrigerated in transportation. Although some types of fruit may continue to ripen, they may never develop their full flavour.

If a piece of fruit smells almost sickly sweet and rather overpowering, it will be turning from ripeness to overripeness and may taste fermented or fizzy. Ripe fruits will spoil very quickly so handle them as little as possible. If you are allowed to taste before you buy, so much the better.

Storing

Fruits with a good protective skin, such as citrus fruit, kiwi fruit, apples, pears and bananas, can be kept at room temperature. As fruit ripens, it gives off a natural gas, ethylene, which triggers the ripening process in other fruit. This is why fruit displayed in a fruit bowl will ripen slightly more quickly. Use this effect to ripen hard fruit – for the quickest result, put the fruit inside a brown paper bag together with an apple.

If you have a ripe piece of fruit to preserve, it will need to be refrigerated to slow down the ripening process. It is also best to keep it away from other fruit.

Some fruit, such as bananas and apples, can be stored at room temperature. They will ripen slightly quicker if kept in a bowl together.

Combining a variety of ripe, raw fruits makes an enticing fruit salad.

Preparation

With the exception of a few varieties of fruit, such as gooseberries and rhubarb, which need cooking before eating, most fruit can be eaten either raw or cooked. Wash fruit if you think that it needs it and peel it only if necessary.

Once fruit is peeled or chopped it can discolour. Have ready a freshly squeezed lemon or lime or some orange juice. As soon as you peel or cut the fruit, toss it in citrus juice. When presenting individual pieces of fruit, such as a pear fan, use a pastry brush to coat each piece with citrus juice.

Fruit salads can be delicious. Keep them simple – a combination of three or four fruits at the most can show off each to advantage. Contrast tastes and textures and mix the commonplace with the exotic. Rather than swamp the fruits in a sweet syrup, add a dash of liqueur or sparkling wine. Remember to prepare fruit salads at the last moment because cutting exposes more surfaces to the harmful effects of air, and discolouration and vitamin losses result.

Cold deadens the flavour of fruit, so if you are eating fresh fruit it is best served at room temperature. Exceptions to this are very sweet melons and watermelons, which are wonderful served cold, as are segmented oranges.

Cooking and Serving Fruit

In addition to being eaten raw, fruit can be cooked in several different ways. These methods are described here.

Poaching Many varieties of fruit are delicious served lightly poached. Once cooked, the fruit can be served hot or cold with a choice of accompaniments, from natural yoghurt to luxury ice-cream. Poached fruit can be kept in the fridge for several days. Poaching is a useful way of dealing with a sudden glut of a home-grown crop. Fruit can be poached in fruit juice, wine or sugar syrup.

For a light sugar syrup, use about 125g (4oz) sugar to 500ml (17fl oz) water. Place the sugar and water in a saucepan and heat. Always make sure the sugar is completely dissolved over a very low heat before bringing the syrup to the boil. Then boil for about 1 minute. Reduce to a simmer and add the fruit. Use enough syrup to cover the fruit. Once the fruit is cooked, any remaining syrup can be reduced to a thicker consistency.

Syrups can be flavoured with vanilla pods or stem ginger, as well as spices, such as cloves or cinnamon. Lemon or orange zest also makes a good addition.

For a wine syrup, follow the method for sugar syrup, making sure that the sugar is dissolved in the alcohol before being brought to the boil. Then poach the fruit for about 15–20 minutes, depending on its size. Red wine will colour the fruit and is the classic French technique for poaching pears.

Many varieties of fruit are delicious lightly poached and this is also a good method for preserving a glut of a home-grown crop. The poaching liquid can be a light sugar syrup flavoured with vanilla or ginger.

Poached fruit can also be puréed and used in sauces or mixed with natural yoghurt, cream or soft cheese in order to make a more substantial dessert.

Grilling, griddling and barbecuing Most firm fruit grills or barbecues well in just a few minutes. These techniques can be used to make speedy simple desserts or to provide contrast to savoury ingredients. Try using apples, pears, pineapple, plums, figs, nectarines or apricots.

For grilling, cut the fruit of your choice into suitable chunks or pieces, thread on to skewers and coat well with citrus juice. Just before cooking, coat the fruit with softened, unsalted butter or a light brushing of sunflower oil. Grill for 1–2 minutes, scooping up any of the cooking juices and drizzling these over before serving. The unsalted butter can be softened and mixed with flavourings, such as maple syrup, honey or liqueurs.

Large pieces of firm fruit barbecue well, especially chunks of pineapple, bananas and mango. Brush the fruit with citrus juices or honey. Oil the barbecue first so that the fruit does not stick, then cook the fruit until slightly browned on each side.

For griddled fruit, heat a large, preferably ridged, griddle or frying pan. When hot, sear the fruit and cook for a few minutes on each side.

Baking This cooking technique brings out the natural sweetness of the fruit and cooks it to a melting texture. It is extremely easy to do and needs little preparation. The fruit can be cooking in the oven while you eat the main part of the meal. Fruit can be baked whole, in large pieces, or individually wrapped in baking parchment or foil.

Apples work well whole. Core them, then pierce the skin in a continuous line around the middle, to allow the flesh to expand during cooking. Softer fruits, such as peaches and plums, are good if halved, their stones removed, then stuffed and baked.

Baking fruit in greaseproof paper or foil is a good way of cooking mixtures of large and small fruits, for example redcurrants and pears, or cranberries with orange and apple. Butter, honey, soft cheese and flavourings such as spices can be added to the parcel. The fruit retains all its flavour and cooks in its own juices.

Baked fruits are easy to prepare and can be cooked in foil or baking parchment.

An apple corer is a useful tool for preparing baked apple or making apple rings.

Orchard, stone and vine fruit

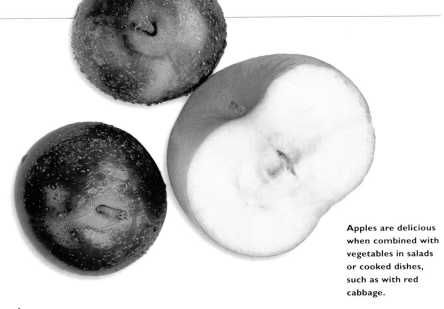

Orchard fruit (apples and pears) and stone fruit (such as apricots and peaches) are grouped here. While distinctly different in flavour, both these groups of fruit are good to eat raw and are surprisingly versatile when cooked. Many can be stewed, grilled, puréed or poached as a basis for a simple, nutritious dessert. Grapes, classed as vine fruit, are discussed at the end of the section.

Apples are delicious when combined with vegetables in salads or cooked dishes, such as with red cabbage.

APPLE

The apple has long been cherished as a health-giving, nutritious food. Despite the rise in popularity and availability of many exotic fruits, the apple still holds a special place. There are numerous varieties grown around the world with flavours that range from sweet or floral to spicy and aromatic. Apples can be eaten as a snack, are great cooked with dried fruits, used in cakes and pies or in relishes and chutney. They work well in salads, too.

Buying and storing Look for firm, unblemished fruit with smooth skins and a good colour. For long-term storage, keep apples in cool conditions, separated from other fruit and vegetables. Apples give off ethylene gas, which can turn root vegetables bitter; apples will also absorb the flavour of onions.

Preparation and cooking Wash apples just before eating. Eat them whole or chop, slice or dice for salads and fruit salads. The flesh will discolour quickly when cut so brush well with citrus juice.

There are some varieties of apple grown specifically for cooking, for example the Bramley from Britain, which reduces to a soft purée when cooked. This variety is also delicious when baked. There are lots of dessert varieties, however, that are also good to cook. On the whole, tart apples with crisp flesh work best.

Many fruits add a surprising, mellow sweetness to cooked dishes.

If fresh, ripe fruit is unavailable, dried fruit works just as well in dishes such as this Apricot Lattice (see page 328).

PEAR

Some pears are plump and bell shaped, others are slim and conical, ranging in colour from dark green to yellow. Those with a crisp flesh have a grainy texture, while others, distinctly buttery in flavour, are juicy and melt in the mouth. Pears are delicious poached or stewed for pie filling and served with natural yoghurt or cream. They work well with other fruits in fruit salads and also combine with savoury ingredients, such as blue cheese, peppery salad leaves and avocado.

Buying and storing Pears are best bought unripe since they do bruise very easily. Once ripe, however, they may last only a day or so before developing an unpleasant woolly character. If you need to ripen pears in a hurry, put them in a paper bag with apples and leave to ripen at room temperature.

Preparation and cooking Eat pears raw, washed and unpeeled. Alternatively, dice and stew, grill or poach them whole (see page 59). The flesh will discolour quickly when cut so brush with citrus juice immediately if preparing for a salad.

Because pears bruise easily once ripe, it is better to buy firm specimens and give them time to ripen at home.

APRICOT

This small, smooth-skinned, orange-coloured fruit has a good flavour only when fully ripe. It is then delicious eaten as it is or served in fruit salads. Apricots poach well, holding their shape, and once cooked can be used in pies, cakes and crumbles. They are excellent with savoury foods, especially grains and nuts, and go particularly well with Middle Eastern flavourings, such as coriander or cinnamon.

Buying and storing Choose apricots that are firm and unwrinkled with velvety, pale orange skins. When ripe, they should just yield in the palm of your hand. If you cannot buy good ripe apricots, use dried ones for both sweet and savoury recipes.

Preparation and cooking Wash apricots before eating. Slice, remove the stone and add to fruit or savoury salads. Poach, grill or stew and purée.

COOK'S TIP

An easy method for skinning apricots and peaches is to pour boiling water over them and then leave them to soak for about 1 minute. The skins can then be removed easily.

PEACH

This is an attractive, orange-yellow fruit with a downy skin. It is good served fresh, on its own or mixed with other fruit. Peaches can also be used in savoury salads mixed with vegetables or grains such as rice, nuts or cheese. They are also delicious baked or barbecued.

Buying and storing Peaches should be firm, but not rock hard, and certainly free from soft patches. They will ripen after a few days in a warm place.

Preparation and cooking Peaches can be eaten fresh, simply washed and unpeeled. Poach, barbecue, grill or stew and purée.

Peaches are delightful on their own as well as when mixed with other fruit or added to a savoury salad.

NECTARINE

This smooth-skinned member of the peach family has a sweet and juicy flesh. Nectarines are extremely easy to grill or barbecue; they can be eaten as they are, or mixed with other fruit in sweet and savoury salads.

Nectarines go well with other types of fruit. They are easy to grill or barbecue and are delicious with creamy cheese.

Buying and storing Look for firm, but not rock-hard fruit. Avoid any that are bruised or damaged. They can be left to ripen for a while in a warm place.

Preparation and cooking Nectarines can be eaten fresh, simply washed and unpeeled. Poach, barbecue, grill or stew and purée.

PLUM

This thin-skinned fruit can be large and black or small and purple, red or yellow. Some varieties of plum are grown for eating fresh while others are best cooked. Plums are often served for dessert, baked in pies or sweet crumbles. They can also be served with savouries as a chutney or relish.

Ripe plums should just yield to the touch and may have a distinctive bloom on their skin.

Damsons and greengages are other stone fruits that can be treated in a similar way to plums.

Buying and storing Plums should be quite firm and have a distinctive bloom on their skins. Unripe plums can be left to ripen in a warm place.

Preparation and cooking Dessert varieties can be eaten fresh, simply washed and unpeeled, or peeled and sliced. Plums can be grilled, poached or stewed and puréed.

CHERRY

Light to dark red in colour, cherries are a firm, succulent fruit with a sweet flavour. They can be eaten fresh, added uncooked to cakes, muffins and strudels, or cooked in a light syrup for a purée or sauce.

Buying and storing Select firm, well-coloured fruit that is not bruised or split. Store in the fridge for a few days.

Preparation and cooking Wash cherries before eating. Stone them before adding to fruit salads or sauces, or before baking.

GRAPE

Grapes range in colour from pale green to deep red. Seeded grapes contain small bitter seeds; many varieties of seedless grapes are widely available.

Buying and storing Look for plump specimens; the darker varieties will often have a natural bloom. Once grapes are ripe they do not last long. You can store them in the fridge but allow time for them to come to room temperature before eating.

Preparation Wash grapes just before eating. Eat them raw whole, or halve or chop them into sweet and savoury salads.

There is an enormous variety of grapes grown throughout the world ranging from pale green to black.

Berry fruit

This colourful group includes strawberries, raspberries, red, white and blackcurrants, blueberries, blackberries, cranberries and gooseberries. Berry fruits should be eaten within 1–2 days of purchase. Avoid any that are seeping juices or show any sign of mould. Delicate berries should be washed only just before use since water encourages them to rot.

Soft Fruit Purées

Strawberries and raspberries can be puréed without cooking. Hull and halve strawberries, but leave raspberries whole. Process in a blender or food processor then rub through a fine sieve to remove seeds. Add a fine sugar, such as icing sugar, to taste, and add a little liqueur, such as kirsch, if liked.

If making a purée with red and blackcurrants or blueberries, these need to be cooked first. Poach the fruits in a little sugar syrup (see page 59). Cool, then purée as above.

STRAWBERRY

This bright red, fleshy fruit still epitomises an English summer, although strawberries are frequently available in many countries all year round. They can be served plain or lightly dusted with sugar. Strawberries make good sauces to accompany other fruit and can be used to flavour fools, yoghurt or ice-cream. They also go well with cucumber, avocado and leafy salads.

Some people have an intolerance to strawberries, which can cause a rash or swollen fingers.

Buying and storing Look for dry berries with a good colour. Avoid any that have been squashed or show signs of mould. Keep strawberries in the fridge in a covered container or their smell will permeate other ingredients.

Preparation Remove the leaves by twisting gently and pulling or cutting out with a knife. Try to avoid washing strawberries as they will become very watery.

RASPBERRY

The raspberry is a fragile, soft fruit containing many tiny seeds. They can be served plain or with sugar, cream or yoghurt for a simple desert. They are also a great treat with morning cereal. If the fruit is damaged or beyond its best, purée with some sweetening (see above) and blend with cream or ice-cream.

Buying and storing Look for firm berries and watch out for seeping juices at the bottom of the punnet. Eat raspberries as quickly as possible. If necessary, they can be stored overnight in the fridge. Frozen raspberries are a good buy if you are intending to purée the fruit.

Preparation and cooking Avoid washing raspberries or they will turn to a mush. Pick over to remove any stalks.

Hull strawberries by gently twisting off the leaves or use a small sharp knife and cut out a conical section.

Soft berry fruit such as strawberries, raspberries and blackcurrants can easily be puréed.

Strawberries are marvellous served plain or with a sprinkling of sugar.

A few raspberries scattered over a plain cereal turn your breakfast into a real treat.

Red, white and blackcurrants are tiny fruits with a distinctive tart flavour. Look for firm, bright berries and store them in the fridge.

RED, WHITE AND BLACKCURRANTS

These tiny, round, shiny fruits have a tart flavour. They look very attractive as an uncooked garnish served with other fruit, as a topping on pavlova and cheesecake or in tiny fruit tarts. They cook down to a sauce that can be sweet or sharp-tasting.

Buying and storing Look for firm, brightly coloured berries that are moisture free. They can be stored for a day or so in the fridge.

Preparation and cooking String currants by pulling small groups through a kitchen fork. Cook them with water and a little sweetening to make the basis of a sauce. They are also good mixed with other soft fruits and stewed to make a richly coloured compote, which can be served hot or cold.

BLUEBERRY

The blueberry is the cultivated form of the wild bilberry. It is popular in America but lesser known in Europe. Blueberries can be eaten raw, sweetened with sugar or spiked with a squeeze of lemon or lime and served with yoghurt or cream. Lightly poached with sweet spices, they can be used in pies and crumbles or made into sauces for ice-cream or sorbet.

Buying and storing Select dark blue, large berries with a natural blue bloom. Blueberries keep better than other soft fruit and can be stored in the fridge for several days.

Preparation and cooking Serve as they come with a little orange or lemon juice and sweetening if preferred. Alternatively, they can be added raw to cake and muffin mixture or cooked to a sauce, sweetened with sugar and then thickened with cornflour.

A few blueberries added to a muffin mixture keeps the texture moist and adds both colour and flavour to the finished product.

BLACKBERRY

Blackberries can be eaten raw but unless they are truly ripe, they will be on the sour side. They are best cooked with a little sweetening and used for pies and sweet crumbles.

Buying and storing Blackberries do not keep very well so aim to use them as soon as possible. Store them no longer than overnight in the fridge.

Preparation and cooking Pick over blackberries and, if you have picked them wild yourself, check carefully for insect life. Avoid washing otherwise the fruit will turn to a mush. Stew with a little sugar or fruit juice.

After picking wild blackberries, check carefully for tiny spiders or grubs. Cultivated blackberries are more reliable but often have less flavour. Blackberries are best used as soon as possible.

Some soft fruits are better cooked than raw, for example, cranberries, gooseberries and blackberries. Use a little sugar to bring out their flavour.

GOOSEBERRY

Gooseberries can be pale green or deep red in colour. They need cooking and sweetening. Because they are so often watery, they are often under-rated. The trick is to cook them whole with a minimum amount of water – 200g (7oz) gooseberries with 1 tablespoon water.

Buying and storing Smaller, green gooseberries generally have the best flavour. Look for firm dry fruit. Gooseberries will keep for several days in the fridge.

Preparation and cooking Top and tail gooseberries, then cook them gently until the skin splits. Cool and sweeten with fine sugar, such as icing sugar. Sieve the cooked gooseberries if you want a smoother texture – if you are going to sieve, then you do not need to top and tail the fruit first.

CRANBERRY

Cranberries are deep red, round fruits. They can be used to make sauces and relishes, which go well with savoury dishes, such as nut roasts or root vegetables. They can also be mixed with other soft fruits to make sweet purées suitable for dessert. Commercially produced cranberry juice is tasty and widely available.

Cranberries are thought to help prevent or treat urinary tract infections and cystitis.

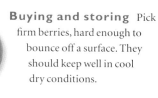

Buying and storing Pick firm berries, hard enough to bounce off a surface. They should keep well in cool dry conditions.

Preparation and cooking Place the cranberries in a little water or orange juice in a saucepan, cover and cook until the berries have popped – this takes 3–4 minutes. Sweeten to taste. The sauce can be served with savoury dishes, or used for pie and pastry fillings.

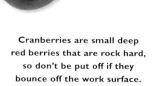

Cranberries are small deep red berries that are rock hard, so don't be put off if they bounce off the work surface.

Soft berries can be used in a number of ways. They make easy colourful garnishes, tasty purées and simple sauces to accompany other fruit.

Citrus fruit

This group includes the familiar lemon, lime, orange and grapefruit, as well as the more unusual ugli fruit and kumquat. Citrus fruits are often sprayed to give them a healthy shine. This should not affect the flesh inside, but if you are going to use the zest or eat the fruit whole, they will need to be scrubbed, or look out for unwaxed citrus fruit and for organically grown specimens instead.

The citrus family is a juicy range of fruits and a good source of vitamin C.

Juice and Zest

Citrus fruits are frequently used for their juice. To get more juice from a fruit, roll it on the work surface a few times before halving and juicing. Alternatively, place it in the microwave on HIGH (650W) for 30 seconds, as this also releases more juice.

Use citrus juice, especially lemon, when preparing apples and pears and vegetables, such as celeriac and Jerusalem artichoke, to stop them from going brown on exposure to the air. Citrus juice is delicious in vinaigrette dressings as well as in creamy dressings made with tahini or tofu (see page 317). Add the juice to soups and stews to lift earthy flavours or counteract sweetness. Oranges, lemons and grapefruit can all be cooked. Whole pieces can be added to casseroles, sauces and chutneys. Whole oranges can be baked, and oranges and grapefruit can be dusted with sugar and grilled.

Zest is the coloured part of the peel, which is full of flavour, as opposed to the white pith which is bitter. Scrub the fruit if necessary to remove any wax coating, then use a zester, a gadget designed to strip off very fine slivers of peel. Alternatively, use a potato peeler or small sharp knife. In this case, if the strips of peel are a little thick, simmer them in boiling water for 4–6 minutes to soften. Drain, refresh in cold water and use as required. For grated zest rub the fruit lightly over a grater. Brush out the grater with a pastry brush to get the maximum amount of zest.

Zest of lemon or lime can be added to cake mixes, salad dressings or sauces.

LEMON

Fragrant and acidic, lemons are used widely in vegetarian cuisine for both sweet and savoury dishes. Look out for Amalfi lemons, which are a large, richly flavoured variety.

Buying and storing
Lemons should have an even colour and be free of blemishes. With some varieties a smoother skin indicates a thinner skin. Left whole, a lemon will keep for several days. Once cut, it should be used as soon as possible.

Lemons are widely used to lift sweet and savoury dishes.

Preparation Scrub waxed lemons if adding whole pieces to a recipe or if using the zest.

LIME

This fragrant citrus fruit has a distinctive tang. Use the juice and zest to flavour salad dressings and stir-fry sauces. It goes well with other fruits, especially papaya, and is often used in cheesecakes and sorbets.

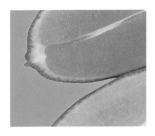

Buying and storing Look for dark green fruit, shaped like a lemon but generally smaller. As it ripens, a lime may turn more yellow in colour. Buy firm specimens and store in the fridge for up to 1 week. Once cut, use as soon as possible.

Limes have a distinctive tang. Once cut, use this fragrant fruit as soon as possible.

ORANGE

The three main varieties of orange available are the smooth, thin-skinned oranges, such as the sweet Valencia and blood oranges; thicker-skinned seedless navel oranges; and bitter oranges, like the Seville, which is used for marmalade and other cooked dishes. The blood orange, so-called because of its distinctive ruby flesh, is more strongly flavoured than a standard orange – use it in fruit salads or to make richly coloured sorbet.

Oranges can be eaten as they are, squeezed for their juice, segmented and mixed with other fruit or used in savoury salads made with leaves or pulses and grains.

Buying and storing Look for oranges with a blemish-free skin and a good orange aroma. They should keep for about 1 week in a cool place.

Preparation Scrub if necessary, peel and segment or squeeze and use the juice.

For really attractive segments, do not peel the fruit by hand. Cut the peel away using a serrated knife instead, making sure in the process that you remove the bitter white pith. Once peeled, cut down between the membrane and the flesh on both sides of each segment so that you can ease it out. Continue working around the fruit in this way. Work over a bowl to catch the juice.

Blood oranges have eye-catching ruby flesh and are slightly stronger in flavour than their orange cousins.

Relatives of the orange Tangerines, clementines, mandarins, satsumas and ortaniques are all related to the orange. These varieties tend to be easier to peel and have much thinner skins. They are not usually used for zesting or for their juice. Eat as they come, or use in fruit salads or as toppings for cheesecake.

To make attractive segments, cut away all the pith and peel as well as the membranes on either side of the orange.

GRAPEFRUIT

The grapefruit is larger than the orange with a pleasant but sour taste, which some people can only tolerate when counteracted with sugar or honey. Lightly grilled, grapefruit makes a good starter or special breakfast dish. Grapefruit can have a pale yellow flesh or delicate pink, which is sweeter but less juicy. Segmented grapefruit pieces are good in fruit salads.

Close relatives to oranges, tangerines and satsumas have thinner skins and are easier to peel.

Buying and storing When buying grapefruit choose heavy fruits and avoid any with loose or puffy skin as the flesh inside will be dry. Grapefruit should be stored in the fridge and, like the orange, still tastes good when chilled.

Preparation and cooking Cut in half, grapefruit can be eaten straight out of the peel as it is, or sweetened with honey or sugar. Grilled grapefruit works well – simply place the cut half, well sprinkled with sugar, under a preheated grill for a few minutes. Segment grapefruit as for oranges (see left).

Relatives of the grapefruit The pomelo is the largest citrus fruit and has a bitter fibrous flesh, similar to grapefruit. The tangelo is a cross between a grapefruit and a tangerine. The ugli fruit, too, is a hybrid, similar in appearance to the grapefruit but smaller and with sweeter-tasting, orange-coloured flesh.

KUMQUAT

This small, oval fruit with a sweet-flavoured, edible skin has a sharp, citrus-flavoured flesh. Beware the pips, which have an unpleasant taste. Slice kumquats and use as a garnish, with grains such as rice or couscous, and in savoury salads.

Ripe kumquats should be soft to the touch. Store in the fridge for up to 1 week. Eat them whole, including skin.

Kumquats are roughly the size of a whole pecan nut. Sliced, they make an attractive garnish.

Tropical fruit

Although these fruits are becomingly increasingly accessible, the price and quality may vary. For the purposes of making exotic fruit platters and unusual savoury salads, it is probably best to see what is on offer first, then adapt accordingly. Here are some of the best-known and most useful tropical fruits.

BANANA

Bananas are best bought unripe and then ripened at home on a hook.

Once considered exotic, bananas are now commonplace. They are usually eaten raw but are also good baked in their skins or barbecued. They make a nutritious drink or meal when blended with milk, coconut milk or tofu. Use citrus juice to stop them from going brown. Don't throw out any overripe bananas – they make great bread or cake.

The banito is like a small banana but with a sweeter flavour.

Buying and storing Bananas do not travel well and are therefore picked unripe and then ripened later or during transit. Choose those with a green to yellow skin and do not pack them at the bottom of your shopping because they bruise easily. At home, store them on a hook.

Preparation and cooking Peel and eat raw or bake with butter and honey, or bake in their skins.

PAPAYA (PAWPAW)

This is a large pear-shaped fruit with a yellow skin with a green blush. Slice one in half and you'll find orange-pink, perfumed flesh with tiny black seeds. Papaya is great served just with lime juice (or lemon as a second choice) to bring out its flavour. Use papaya with savoury ingredients, such as chilli, coriander and avocado. When chopped, it can make an unusual salsa or sauce.

Papaya contains an enzyme, papain, that helps digestion and is thought to have useful properties as a general cleanser and detoxifier.

Buying and storing Ripe papaya will feel very slightly soft to the touch. Avoid any with soft patches and look out for bruising. Store them at room temperature.

MANGO

There are many different types of mango, with skin colour ranging from green – even when ripe – to red. It is worth making a note of your favourite variety. The flesh has a wonderful flavour, and is richly perfumed and creamy. Mango is delicious eaten on its own, mixed with other fruit or used raw in savoury salads, particularly those containing rice.

Mango is highly regarded as a systemic cleanser especially for the skin and kidneys.

Buying and storing A ripe mango should be well scented and will yield slightly when pressed. Look carefully for bruising and other damage. For this reason try to buy mango that is displayed loose rather than shrink-wrapped.

Preparation Remember that the stone is oval in shape. Cut down the side of the mango, going as close to the stone as possible, using a small sharp knife. You will be left with two shallow cheeks. Score the flesh carefully with crisscross lines while it is still in its skin, then invert the skin so that the flesh stands proud and slice the cubes off. Remove the flesh left around the stone.

To create an elegant mango fan, use a fruit that is on the firm side. Peel the mango first, then holding the fruit carefully, as it can slip, make a cut down to the stone from one end to the other. Make a second cut next to this at a slight angle to give a V-shaped wedge. Ease this out with the knife, then continue to cut thin wedges around the stone.

Tropical fruits add a touch of the exotic to fruit platters and savoury salads.

Mango cubes are easy to make by scoring the flesh while it is still in the skin.

GUAVA

This small tree fruit with yellow skin and a pulpy, sweet pink flesh can be large or small in size.

Buying and storing

Ripe guavas are highly scented and yield slightly to the touch. Don't store guava near other foods as the smell may permeate. The smell of the flesh, however, is stronger than its taste. Slice in half and eat the firm flesh, or chop it and mix with soft cheese or cream. Cook guava with apples and pears to make a tasty pie or crumble filling. Guava has a particularly high vitamin C content.

This headily scented guava has a high vitamin C content. When ripe, it should just yield to the touch.

KIWI FRUIT

The kiwi fruit is an egg-sized fruit with a brown hairy exterior. Inside, the flesh is a jewel-green colour with a ring of minute black seeds. Kiwi fruit can taste like melon or gooseberry, depending on its ripeness. Its vitamin C content is higher than that of oranges.

Buying and storing When ripe, the fruit should give slightly when pressed. It can be stored in the fridge or ripened by being stored with an apple or banana. Organic varieties are usually smaller.

Preparation Cut in half and eat straight out of its skin with a teaspoon. For other uses, remove the skin with a sharp knife or vegetable peeler, then slice and use in fruit salad, as a cheesecake or pavlova topping or with savoury salads. If the skin is difficult to peel, drop the kiwi fruit in boiling water for a few seconds.

Kiwi fruit can be eaten straight from the skin as a nutritious snack. Otherwise peel first and then slice or chop.

PASSION FRUIT AND GRANADILLA

Ripe passion fruit has a hard, purple-brown wrinkled skin, inside which are hundreds of edible black seeds, which are sweet yet sharp in taste and invariably crunchy. The pulp is a golden colour and deeply perfumed.

The granadilla is similar to the passion fruit but is larger with a grey-green flesh. Its buying, storing and preparation guidelines are just as for passion fruit.

Buying and storing It is difficult to tell much about the passion fruit before buying as the exterior is hard and wrinkled. Do not buy specimens with soft patches. Use within 1 week.

With their wrinkled skin, passion fruit may not look very enticing at first glance but inside is a deeply perfumed golden flesh and hundreds of edible black seeds.

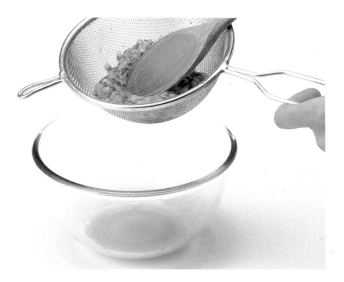

Preparation and cooking Cut the fruit in half and eat straight out of its skin with a teaspoon.

Make the most of the intense flavour by mixing the juice with other ingredients. To extract the maximum amount of juice, scrape the flesh into a small saucepan, add a little sugar – about 1 teaspoon – and heat gently. Then sieve the seeds and leave the juice to cool. A small amount of juice will flavour a fruit salad or fruit drink. It is also delicious used in sweet sauces.

Strain lightly cooked passion fruit flesh through a sieve to extract its intensely flavoured juice.

PERSIMMON (*KAKI FRUIT*) AND SHARON

A large orange-red fruit, persimmons are about the size of a slicing tomato, with a very tough skin. The sharon fruit is very closely related but is seedless and contains much less tannic acid so can be eaten when still firm.

Buying and storing The persimmon has to be eaten in a very soft condition when the jelly-like, dripping flesh is sweet and succulent. Unripe, it can taste bitter and drain the moisture from your mouth. Leave unripe fruit in a polythene bag until the flesh looks translucent and the fruit is soft to the touch. Store ripe persimmons in the fridge.

A ripe persimmon may be extremely soft to touch but it is then that it is at its best.

Preparation Slice the fruit in half and scoop out the flesh. Serve fresh or use the pulp as the basis for a sauce or fruit fool.

PINEAPPLE

One of the best-established tropical fruits, pineapple goes well with other fruit, as well as with savoury ingredients in salads or in stir-fries.

Buying and storing Pineapples do not continue to ripen once picked so select carefully. A ripe pineapple should yield to gentle pressure applied at the stem. It should be more golden than green, have a good, full scent and leaves that can be pulled off without much struggle.

Preparation and cooking Cut off the leafy plume and remove the base so that the pineapple will stand upright. Then cut down through the fruit to remove the skin but not too much of the flesh. Remove the 'eyes' with the point of a small knife. Serve pineapple in slices, cubes or quarters, removing any woody core. It is good grilled or barbecued.

Ready-to-eat pineapples should be golden with a full scent.

LYCHEE, RAMBUTAN AND MANGOSTEEN

These are three fairly similar fruits with crisp to hard skin. Not very appealing to look at, these fruits contain a translucent, pearly white flesh with a distinctive, almost grape-like flavour.

Look for firm and dry skin with no bruising, when buying these fruits. They can be cracked or cut open. Discard the brown stone.

MELON

Good in fruit salad, melon also combines with savoury ingredients, such as avocado, for starters. There are a number of varieties of melon available with different levels of sweetness, ranging in colour from amber and orange to pale green.

Buying and storing Melons need to smell ripe. Check that they feel a little soft at the stalk end. Store melon in the fridge unless it needs extra ripening.

Preparation Serve melon chilled, left in the skin in wedges or halves with the seeds removed. It can also be served in chunks, slices or balls and mixed with other fruit or salad ingredients.

Melons come in a number of different varieties from golden fleshed through to orange and green. Most have a thick skin but if you get a good specimen, it will smell ripe.

VARIETIES OF MELON

Cantaloupe: a small, round melon with salmon-coloured flesh and a craggy outer skin. Serve ripe. It is from the same family as the ogen and chanterais.

Chanterais: sweet, succulent, perfumed orange flesh and green or bluish striped skin.

Galia: straw-coloured skin with light green, fragrant flesh. A sweet flavour when ripe.

Honeydew: yellow skin with pale yellow, sometimes white flesh when ripe. It is not always easy to pick a good specimen.

Ogen: green flesh, which can be very juicy.

Piel de sapo/Emerald sugar/Frog's skin: as the names suggest, a mottled skin with succulent yellow-green flesh.

Watermelon: the giant of the melon family. Smooth, dark green outer skin, watery, pink inner flesh and a plethora of inedible black seeds.

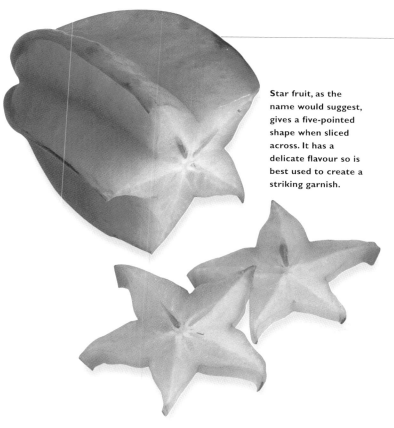

Star fruit, as the name would suggest, gives a five-pointed shape when sliced across. It has a delicate flavour so is best used to create a striking garnish.

STAR FRUIT (CARAMBOLA)

Prized more for its shape than its flavour, this angular, waxy, yellow fruit has a cross-section like a five-pointed star, hence the name.

Buying and storing Look for firm, unblemished fruit. As it ripens, a brown line develops along its ridges.

Preparation and cooking Wash, thinly slice, then use the star shapes as a garnish.

DATE

Fresh dates can be eaten as they are, or pitted and stuffed with sweet or savoury fillings. Served like this, they make tasty finger food.

Storing Keep in the fridge. Fresh dates also freeze well.

Preparation To remove the papery skin, pinch off the stalk end and then squeeze from the opposite end. To remove the stone, halve the date or pull the stone out from the stalk end.

Fresh dates served with nuts or cheese make a quick dessert or nutritious snack. Once pitted, they can be stuffed with sweet or savoury fillings.

FIG

There are many varieties of fig, ranging in colour from cream and yellow to deep purple and black. Not all varieties are available around the world. Unless you can get local or almost local types, dried figs may be a better option as you are guaranteed sweetness and flavour (see page 73).

Buying and storing A ripe fig should be unbruised and soft when pressed. Although the skin may look tough, it is edible. The inner flesh is pinkish-brown and full of edible seeds. Store figs in the fridge.

Preparation and cooking Wash before eating. Leave whole, or cut in half and macerate in alcohol or fruit syrup, or bake or stew.

Ranging in colour from deep purple to cream, ripe figs are deliciously sweet and full of flavour.

PHYSALIS (CAPE GOOSEBERRY)

This unexpected, sweet, orange berry is enclosed in an attractive lantern-like case of papery sepals. The fruit can be eaten raw – simply fold back the casing – or dipped in chocolate to serve as an after-dinner petit four.

The papery sepals of the physalis hide a sweet orange berry.

POMEGRANATE

This tough, leathery, red-skinned fruit, the size of an apple, contains tightly packed seeds enclosed in a perfumed ruby flesh. The pith and membrane are bitter and should not be eaten.

Buying and storing Look for firm fruit and store for up to a week in the fridge.

Preparation Cut through the skin to mark out four segments. Using a sharp knife, cut around the raised end so that you can lift out the hard 'button' or tuft. After peeling back the skin in sections, you can separate out the pomegranate without breaking the seeds. To extract the juice, roll the fruit over a work surface, then make a hole in the skin and squeeze out the juice.

Inside the tough leathery skin of the pomegranate is a mass of seeds surrounded by translucent ruby flesh.

Dried fruit

An extremely versatile ingredient, dried fruit can be used in sweet and savoury dishes, served hot or cold, as well as being eaten as a healthy snack. It falls into two categories – vine fruits (sultanas, raisins and currants) and tree fruits (apples, apricots, dates, figs, peaches, pears and prunes). Other dried fruit available includes cranberries, kiwi fruit, blueberries and cherries.

It takes some 2kg (4lb) of fresh fruit to produce about 500g (1lb) of sultanas, raisins or currants and nearly 3kg (6lb) of fresh fruit to produce 500g (1lb) of dried tree fruit, such as apricots and peaches. The nutritional value of these fruits is therefore highly concentrated but so, too, is their sugar content, so they should be eaten in moderation, especially when unsoaked.

Because it provides a good number of minerals and some vitamins, dried fruit makes a nutritious and tasty snack.

NUTRITIONAL VALUE

Excellent sources of many nutrients, dried fruits are also high in dietary fibre and a good source of energy. They also contain minerals, such as iron and potassium, as well as some vitamins – notably vitamins A, B_1, B_2 and C. In addition, they are rich in fruit sugars, fructose and sucrose; and they contain virtually no fat or cholesterol.

Some dried fruits are treated with sulphur dioxide – added to preserve colour and maintain water content, thereby keeping the fruit plumper. It also prevents fermentation and decay and, while it helps to preserve vitamins A and C, it does destroy the B vitamins. It is believed that this is not a harmful additive if eaten in only small quantities.

Buying and Storing

Choose good-looking dried fruit. If it is rock hard or shows any sign of crystallisation, it is old. Once the packet is open, store it in an airtight container. Keeping a piece of lemon or orange peel in the container helps keep the fruit moist. Except for apples, most varieties of dried fruit should keep for up to 1 year. As dried fruit ages it may develop a sugary coating. This can be removed by soaking in warm water for a few minutes.

Preparation and Cooking

Rinse dried fruit under warm running water to remove traces of preservative. Most fruit these days is sold ready cleaned.

To plump raisins, currants and sultanas, soak them in warm or hot liquid such as water, fruit juice or alcohol. Leave for 5–10 minutes, then drain if necessary.

Larger dried fruits, such as apricots, benefit from being soaked so that they soften and swell prior to cooking.

To reconstitute larger dried fruits, such as apricots, pears and apples, leave them to soak for several hours using plenty of liquid – water, fruit juice or wine. A quicker method is to cover the fruit with liquid and bring to the boil. Simmer, covered, for about 10–15 minutes, then leave to soak. Leftover juice can be boiled further until syrupy.

Once soaked and cooked, the fruit can be eaten as it is or easily puréed using a blender or food processor. Add a little of the soaking or cooking liquid as necessary.

Vine Fruit

All dried vine fruits are good in baking and can be added to scones, bread dough, strudels, flapjacks or cookies. They make excellent additions to breakfast cereals, such as muesli or porridge. Dried vine fruit also works extremely well with many savoury dishes, particularly with grains as a stuffing for vine leaves, peppers or courgettes, as well as in many salads.

SULTANA

Sultanas are soft, juicy, amber or golden-coloured fruits, with a sweet flavour.

RAISIN

Ranging in colour from dark brown to almost black, raisins have a wrinkled skin and a sweet mellow flavour. They are lightly oiled to prevent them sticking together once dried.

CURRANT

The smallest of the dried vine fruits, currants are dried, black seedless grapes of the Corinth variety. They are the least sweet and are used in many savoury recipes, particularly dishes from Greece and the Middle East.

Tree Fruit

These larger dried fruits can be eaten as a snack, snipped raw into cereals and salads or soaked and mixed with other dried fruits. Once reconstituted and puréed, they make great fillings for pies and tarts, or can be stirred into yoghurt, cream or tofu to make simple fruit puddings. Use a sweet purée, such as date or apricot, to replace some of the sugar required in a recipe.

Hunza apricots are smaller in size than a regular apricot and have a honey-like flavour. Here, they are shown being dried on a roof in the Hunza valley, Pakistan.

DRIED APPLE

Dried apples are sold ready-peeled, cored and sliced or in rings. They are chewy and have a mild taste with a slight tang. They are best mixed with other fruits.

DRIED APRICOT

Their rich mellow flavour is best savoured in apricots that are dried whole. For making purées, buy halves or pieces of dried apricot. Hunza apricots are beige-brown, small apricots, dried whole, and must be soaked before eating. They have a honey-like flavour once soaked and, if stewed, produce a rich liquid.

DRIED DATE

The date is an extremely sweet fruit once dried. Beware of mixing the purée into anything light-coloured as it will turn everything else very dark.

DRIED FIG

Another very sweet fruit once dried. When soaked and lightly cooked, dried figs produce a sweet, mellow liquid, which is good for flavouring fruit salads and compotes.

DRIED MANGO

Despite the difficulty of choosing fresh mangoes, the dried fruit is quite reliable in its sweetness and flavour. It is good for a snack as it is rich but not cloying.

DRIED PEACH

Dried peaches are sold in halves or slices. Some varieties can be extremely sweet; the orange-coloured ones have the most tang.

DRIED PEAR

Sold in halves, this fruit is sweet and chewy with a slightly granular texture. Dried pears have a beautiful, clear, golden-yellow colour.

PRUNE

The prune is a dried plum, which is sold either whole with a stone or pitted. It has a rich flavour and makes an excellent purée that can be used in baking or mixed with cream, yoghurt or silken tofu to make fruit fool. Prunes can also be eaten just as they come or soaked. They have a mild laxative action, due both to their high fibre content and to a substance called diphenylisatin.

Milk and cream products

Milk, cheese and eggs play an important role in a vegetarian diet since they are versatile and nutritious ingredients. If you are new to a vegetarian diet, their familiarity makes them a comforting and accessible source of protein. However, it is important to eat these delicious foods in moderation because of their high saturated fat content.

Organic Dairy Products

Recent concern about the use of growth hormones in dairy farming and how this may affect milk and milk products has raised the profile of organic milk and milk products, such as butter, yoghurt and crème fraiche. Although more expensive, these organic products may well be worth the investment. In the USA there has been widespread use of the growth hormone referred to as rBGH or rBST. However, many smaller dairies in the USA do not use this hormone and they are allowed to print that information on their cartons of milk.

Strict rules govern the production of organic milk. In general, the animals must be fed on a high percentage of organic food matter with the remainder being natural foodstuffs, rather than food concentrates or animal protein. The use of preventive antibiotics and other medicines is not allowed.

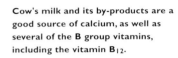

Cow's milk and its by-products are a good source of calcium, as well as several of the B group vitamins, including the vitamin B$_{12}$.

NUTRITIONAL VALUE

Cow's milk and cow's milk products are a good source of protein and calcium – 300ml (½ pint) of whole or skimmed milk provides more than half the daily calcium requirements for a child under 10. Milk is also a good source of vitamin B$_{12}$ and provides riboflavin, thiamine, niacin and folate. Whole and semi-skimmed milk contains vitamin A and a little vitamin D; skimmed milk does not. Milk also supplies zinc, potassium and phosphorus. The fat content per 100ml of cow's milk is 3.9g for whole milk, 1.6g for semi-skimmed and 0.1g for skimmed. This fat content is largely saturated.

Other milk products, such as cream, yoghurt and buttermilk, contain similar nutrients. If you are trying to eat less saturated fat, look for lower-fat versions of these products, but read labels carefully as gelatine is sometimes added to enhance the texture.

Butter, although a product of milk, contains no calcium or protein but it is a source of the fat-soluble vitamins A and D.

Goat's milk has a similar nutritional profile to cow's milk but is lower in protein and lower in calcium. It is useful for people who cannot tolerate the protein in cow's milk. For alternatives to milk and milk products see page 83.

Storage

Milk, cream, yoghurts and other milk products must be kept in the fridge and consumed by their 'use-by' date. Make sure the products smell fresh and there is no yellowing or dryness. Milk should also be kept out of the light since this destroys vitamin A.

CRÈME FRAÎCHE

This French version of soured cream has a pleasing delicate tang and tastes rich, thanks to its high fat content. It works well with hot and cold dishes, both sweet and savoury. At its simplest it can be spooned over jacket potatoes, served with

Cheese can be served as a course in its own right. Choose a combination that gives appealing contrasts in textures and flavours.

chilli or used on fruit. It can also be used with confidence when making sauces and enriching soups since its high fat content means that it can be boiled without separating. There are also low-fat versions, but low-fat crème fraîche must be used only in cold dishes as it may separate if heated.

Yoghurt makes a good base for a low-fat salad dressing, or a sweet or savoury dip.

BUTTERMILK

Once the liquid whey that was left over from the butter making process, buttermilk is now more commonly made from low-fat or no-fat milk with added cultures, which give it a tangy flavour and also thicken it slightly. It is excellent used in pancakes and soda breads and other quick breads made with bicarbonate of soda, because the acids in the buttermilk react with the baking soda in order to make the dough rise. Buttermilk provides calcium but none of the fat-soluble vitamins.

Strained or set yoghurt As the name suggests, these yoghurts have been strained so that some of the whey is removed and the yoghurt is thicker and richer. Used on their own, strained yoghurts make good salad dressings and combine well with herbs, such as chives, coriander and parsley or finely snipped spring onions. Lebneh is yoghurt cheese that is made from strained yoghurt.

YOGHURT

Yoghurt can be made from cow's, ewe's or goat's milk or even from soya beans. Whether it is thin and sharp-tasting or thick and rich depends on the individual maker. It is a matter of personal taste as to which type of yoghurt you use for various dips and dressings. Take care when cooking with yoghurt because it curdles easily. Some commercial yoghurts have vitamin D added to them.

SOURED CREAM

Soured cream has a spooning consistency and is excellent as a last-minute topping for a spicy casserole or served with potato or red cabbage. It is not of a sufficiently high fat content to be stable at a high heat so add it only to warm soups and sauces.

CLOTTED CREAM

This traditional English product is produced by heating cream to make a crust. It is generally used in sweet dishes, for example with fruit or with scones and jam for a traditional English cream tea. It is also good with waffles and pancakes.

Making your own yoghurt Commercial yoghurt makers for use at home come with useful sized containers and thermostatic controls to keep the yoghurt at the correct temperature. These are good if you want to make all your own yoghurt. For the occasional batch, however, you could simply use a wide-necked vacuum flask. Heat 600ml (1 pint) milk to 43–45°C (110–113°F). Stir in a yoghurt starter – either 2 tablespoons of natural live yoghurt or a culture powder, stir well, then pour the mixture into a clean, warmed vacuum flask. Leave overnight or until set, then transfer to a clean container and refrigerate.

BUTTER

Butter is suitable for vegetarians, and organic varieties are increasingly available. (See pages 114–116 for oils, margarine and cooking fats.)

Sour cream is ideal for enriching a baked potato or as a last-minute topping on spicy casseroles or refried lentils.

GHEE

This is a clarified butter from which the milk solids and sugars have been removed. It adds a rich flavour to cooking and has the advantage of not burning as quickly as other fats. It is widely used in Indian cookery.

Yoghurt is made by fermenting milk with bacteria, resulting in a thickened mixture with a distinctive tang.

Cheese

Some hard cheeses are encased in a protective wax coating.

Taste a fresh soft goat's cheese, a mature Parmesan or a pungent Roquefort and you get some idea of the wide range of flavours and textures within this family of ingredients. The difference between cheeses depends on many factors – the length of ageing, the manufacturing process and the type of milk used.

For everyday cooking, a standard hard cheese is fine. Choose a brand with a reasonable depth of flavour. However, it is worth gradually trying a variety of cheeses since these will add an extra dimension to your cooking. The majority of cheese is made from cow's milk. Goat's cheeses are characterised by sharp clean tastes with a pungency developing as the cheese matures. Ewe's milk cheeses are sometimes mild, the notable exceptions being Roquefort and feta.

NUTRITIONAL VALUE

Cheese provides excellent amounts of protein and is an extremely good source of calcium, which is essential for building strong bones. A quantity of 25g (1oz) Cheddar cheese provides about 20% of the daily requirements of calcium for a man and 25% of the daily requirements for a woman. Cheese is also a good source of vitamin B_{12}, as well as containing other B vitamins and zinc. The fat content varies considerably from one cheese to another, but it is usually saturated.

Goat's cheese has a similar nutritional profile to that made from cow's milk and it can be used by some people who have an intolerance to products that are made from cow's milk (see page 83 for non-dairy alternatives to cheese).

Rennet

Why aren't all varieties of cheese labelled as being suitable for vegetarians? The answer is that many cheeses, especially some traditional varieties, such as Parmesan, are made using animal rennet, an ingredient that helps to curdle the milk and separate it into curds and whey. Rennet is a substance that comes from calf's stomach and is therefore not eaten by strict vegetarians. Fortunately, increasing numbers of cheeses are made with a plant-derived alternative rennet and these are the cheeses that are labelled as suitable for vegetarians. Soft cheese on the whole does not contain any sort of rennet.

Some cheeses are labelled 'GMO-free'. This is because they do not contain a type of vegetarian rennet used by some large manufacturers that is a genetically engineered copy enzyme called chymosin. (See page 31 for more information on genetically modified food.)

Buying Cheese

It pays to choose cheese for both cooking and eating from somewhere reliable and where you can taste before you buy, especially when looking for unusual and interesting varieties. Choosing cheese for eating is a matter of flavour first. Look for contrasting tastes and textures if you are serving a number of cheeses as a course. When choosing a cheese for cooking you need to consider not only its flavour, but also whether it will melt well, can be grated and so on.

As a general rule, the longer a cheese has been matured, the stronger its flavour, the drier its texture and the longer it will keep. Mild, soft, snow-white, fresh cheeses have short 'use-by' dates and

So many varieties of cheese are now available, it is useful to shop somewhere where you can taste before you buy. Often expert advice is on hand to help you.

delicate tastes, whereas the well-aged Parmesan has a dry, hard granular texture and powerful flavour and can be kept for months.

Hard and semi-hard cheeses, such as Cheddar, should look smooth without discolouration and mould, unless of course this is part of the character of the cheese. The rind on a hard cheese should not be too dry or cracked, nor should the cheese itself be sweaty. Be guided, too, by the smell. An odourless cheese probably lacks character and flavour, while one smelling of ammonia should be avoided.

Blue cheeses are made with a culture that gives them their characteristic blue or blue-green veining. There should be no sign of pink or beige among the blue, and nor should the cheese be wet. The flavours may be strong but should not be over-salty or chalky. Try to taste before you buy.

Storing Cheese

It is best to wrap hard or semi-hard cheese and blue cheese in waxed or greaseproof paper. Do not use anything like clingfilm, as this will not let the cheese breathe. If kept well, these cheeses should remain in good condition for some time. Soft, fresh cheeses, creams and yoghurts will not keep for any length of time. Store them in the fridge and use by the recommended 'use-by' date.

Wrap a hard or semi-hard cheese in waxed or greaseproof paper to let it breathe.

On the whole, all cheeses should be kept in, and used straight from, the fridge. The exception to this rule is when serving cheese as a course during a meal – make sure that you bring the cheese out of the fridge at least 2 hours before serving. The flavours will have time to develop and will become more pronounced.

Cooking with Cheese

Always melt cheese slowly over a low heat. If you try to do this too quickly, the cheese may separate or become stringy. Cheddar, Gruyère and Gruyère-style cheeses melt very well. Mozzarella is the classic cheese for pizza toppings as it melts evenly, producing long, sinuous strands.

Goat's cheese softens and browns beautifully under the grill, while haloumi cheese is good for barbecues as it softens only slightly as it gets hot.

When melting cheese, do this slowly over a gentle heat or the result may be stringy.

For a pizza topping, choose a cheese that melts well, such as mozzarella.

It is worth experimenting with different types of cheese to appreciate the variety. Pungent blue cheese, melting Brie and nutty-tasting Cheddar are just some of the numerous tastes and textures available.

Varieties of cheese

More than 450 cheeses are made in **Britain** alone. **Add to this the many hundreds of European varieties and special American cheeses and there is an almost overwhelming selection, too numerous to mention here. The following pages detail a selection of 20 of the most readily available and the most useful cheeses. For the purposes of this book, cheeses are listed under three broad categories: hard and semi-hard cheese, such as Parmesan, Cheddar, Gruyère and feta; blue cheeses, such as Stilton, Gorgonzola and Roquefort; and soft cheeses – ripened cheeses, such as Brie and Camembert, and fresh cheeses such as goat's cheese (chèvre).**

Cheese can be used in a quick sauce to make a nutritious topping for pasta.

Hard and Semi-Hard Cheeses

These cheeses do not change in consistency once purchased (other than becoming mouldy or drying out if you leave them too long). Hard cheeses should grate or slice well, hold their shape in a salad and may melt to make toppings and sauces.

CHEDDAR

This versatile cheese is good for both eating and cooking. Dense in texture, Cheddar can range in flavour from mild to tangy, and in colour from white to deep gold. Much Cheddar is industrially produced and lacks real character, but there is a renaissance in hand-crafted Cheddar cheeses, which can be bought in good cheese shops and delicatessens.

PARMESAN

Properly aged Parmesan is labelled 'Parmigiano Reggiano' and is rigorously protected by Italian law. It is made to a strict set of standards that have not been altered for 700 years. Aged for a minimum of two years, generally longer, this cheese has a slightly gritty texture, a rich aroma and complex flavours. Strict vegetarians will not be able to use this as there is no vegetarian version of the true Parmesan, but there are now several vegetarian varieties of a Parmesan-style cheese which, although not so complex in flavour, have a reasonable taste and good texture.

EMMENTAL

Ivory-coloured, with a fairly firm, slightly oily texture, this Swiss cheese is characterised by large holes, which are the natural consequence of the cheese-making process. This type of cheese melts and grills well.

GRUYÈRE

Also from Switzerland, with a warm yellow colour, Gruyère is pockmarked with little holes and characterised by a sweet fruity flavour. It, too, melts and grills well.

FONTINA

Fontina is an ivory-coloured Italian cheese with a nutty flavour and sweet aroma. It melts well and, when mature, can be grated.

HALOUMI

This semi-hard Cypriot cheese is made from ewe's milk, and is used frequently in Turkish and Lebanese cuisine. It is delicious warmed in pitta bread. Since it softens, rather than drips or oozes when melted, it is extremely useful for making kebabs for barbecues.

FETA

Traditionally from Greece, this ewe's milk cheese is now produced in several countries. Feta should be snow-white, moist and crumbly. Its salty, sharp, almost sour tang is accentuated when cooked. In the process of making feta, the curds are salted and then covered with whey and brine. Its strong flavour marries well with hearty herbs, such as oregano and marjoram, as well as with Mediterranean dishes using olives and tomatoes.

Feta will not melt or brown in the way that other cheeses do, but it can be crumbled for use in quiches and pies. It can also be marinated in a good-quality olive oil, which acts as a preservative. Add fresh herbs, peppercorns, chillies, sun-dried tomatoes or even lemon zest to get flavoursome results. Leave refrigerated in jars for a week or so then serve as a cocktail snacks and as a filling for bread.

Blue Cheeses

These cheeses range from surprisingly mild flavours and very creamy textures to strong, salty tastes.

ROQUEFORT

Made from ewe's milk, this is a robustly flavoured, slightly crumbly cheese.

DOLCELATTE

Sweet, soft and creamy, this type of Gorgonzola is good for savoury dishes as well as partnering fruit for dessert.

STILTON

One of the few English cheeses that is manufactured under strict conditions, Stilton can be produced only in the three shires of Leicester, Nottingham and Derby. A good Stilton should be smooth and creamy, rather than dry or crumbly.

GORGONZOLA

An Italian alpine cheese made from cow's milk, Gorgonzola is blue-veined with a mild tang. It should not be too salty.

Ripened Soft Cheeses

These cheeses have a high percentage of moisture. They are easy to spread – indeed some fully ripened ones may gently spread over the plate if left at room temperature. Ripened soft cheese should be slightly springy to the touch, the outer bloom should look even and the inside should look evenly creamy. Avoid any with a firm-looking, chalky white centre.

If the cheese is overripe, a thin rind may develop or the crust may split.

The inside should not sink down or look withered. Some of these cheeses are 'washed' in brine or wine, a process that helps maintain internal moisture for fermentation. They often have a strong, piquant flavour and aroma.

BRIE

Brie is a classic French cheese that needs to be just ripe to be appreciated. Look for a pale yellow centre, which is soft but not running. It is always made as a large cheese and once cut will not ripen.

CAMEMBERT

Originally made in the small village of that name but now manufactured as far afield as America, Camembert should have a light orange-yellow rind, a pale yellow centre and be slightly springy to the touch. The cheese has a slight tang.

Fresh Soft Cheeses

These cheeses range in texture from the very creamy, with a spooning consistency, to those with firmer curds, such as ricotta. They can be between 2 and 10 days old. There should be no yellowing and the curds should look moist, not dry.

FRESH CHÈVRE

Fresh and ripened soft goat's cheeses vary greatly in appearance as they can be sold in logs, pyramids or rounds, wrapped in leaves, coated with peppercorns or ash, to name but a few varieties. What they have in common is a clean tangy taste, but nothing overpowering. The flavour will develop with age. Goat's cheese has a smooth texture and a wonderful capacity to melt.

More mature goat's cheese is firmer in texture and more powerful in flavour, with a rind or outer mould that may develop considerably. The mould is bluish-grey and, although visually off-putting, it does not mean there is anything wrong with the cheese.

COTTAGE CHEESE

Made from whole or skimmed milk curds, cottage cheese has a mild flavour and slightly coarse texture. It is good for using in salads and sandwich fillings, and for blending into low-calorie creamy dressings.

MASCARPONE

This is a high-fat, soft Italian cheese with a smooth texture. It is made from fresh cream, which is whipped to give it a very smooth texture. In Italy, mascarpone is principally used as a dessert cheese, spiked with liqueur and served with fruit. It can also be added to soups and sauces to give them a velvety texture, and can be the basis of a rich dip or dressing.

RICOTTA

This is another traditional cheese from Italy. Made from whey, it has a snow-white appearance and light texture. It is often used as a filling for ravioli, as it can be packed densely and doesn't ooze when cooked.

FROMAGE FRAIS

Made from cow's milk, this soft unripened cheese has a slightly sharp taste. It is beaten until very smooth and in some cases mixed with cream, giving it a consistency rather like a set yoghurt. The fat content of fromage frais varies from one brand to another.

MOZZARELLA

The finest mozzarella is made from buffalo's milk, which has a higher fat content than cow's milk. Since this is hard to come by, much modern mozzarella is made from cow's milk. This snow-white cheese is firm enough to cut and is sold in balls or blocks, usually packed with a little liquid, which should be drained off. When very fresh, it is delicious uncooked in salads with tomato or avocado. It is also excellent on pizzas and grilled vegetables as it melts beautifully.

QUARK

A low-fat smooth-textured soft cheese made from skimmed milk, quark can be used in the same way as cottage cheese and natural fromage frais.

Eggs

This versatile
ingredient can be
used in a multitude of
ways. Many eggs are labelled
euphemistically as 'farm fresh',
'barn' or 'hens fed on a vegetarian
diet' to hide the sorry truth of
battery production, where hens are
crammed into dark spaces and kept in
squalid conditions. Many vegetarians concerned
about animal welfare use only free-range eggs.
Free-range birds must have access to runs and a
variety of vegetation.

Nutritional Value

Eggs are an excellent source of protein, as well as vitamins A, the B group, D, E and K. They also contain iron, calcium and iodine. Eggs are high in dietary cholesterol – all of which is in the yolk – and have a low level of saturated fat. New research suggests that pre-formed dietary cholesterol has little impact on the amount of cholesterol in your blood, but it is still wise to moderate your consumption of eggs. They are fibre-free.

The size of an egg is actually its weight. There are seven grades of egg, which go up in 5g (¼oz) intervals. The largest eggs weigh around 65g (2½oz).

Salmonella

Salmonella is a particularly unpleasant bacterium, which can cause severe illness. It is endemic in chickens and is therefore fairly common in eggs.

Since bacteria are killed in the cooking process, egg dishes should be cooked thoroughly – until the white is set and the yolk has thickened and is firm. Do not eat raw egg. Salmonella also multiplies with age. Very fresh eggs, even if contaminated, will have lower levels of the bacteria. Look at the 'use-by' date and do not use eggs if you have stored them for 5 days or more. The other danger is from the egg shell itself. Do not use chipped or damaged eggs, and always wash your hands before and after handling egg shells.

Those most at risk from the effects of salmonella are children, the elderly, pregnant women and anyone whose immune system is deficient, for example when recovering from illness.

Because egg shells are porous, eggs can pick up odours from other foods stored nearby.

Buying and Storing

Avoid buying eggs with chipped, cracked or damaged shells. Store eggs in the fridge, preferably in their containers. Since their shells are porous it is best to keep them away from strong-smelling food. They should be stored pointed end downwards, which keeps the yolk roughly in the middle of the egg. Always use eggs within the 'use-by' date, preferably before. If the eggs have no date, then test them for freshness.

The basic test for freshness is to see if the egg floats or sinks. The older the egg, the lighter it will be, since it will have lost water through its shell during storage. Thus, a fresh egg will sink in a bowl of water and a stale egg will float.

Fresh eggs always sink to the bottom of a bowl of water; stale eggs will float.

The appearance of an egg once cracked is also an indication of its freshness. A fresh egg white is thick and jelly-like, supporting the yolk, which rests on top.

Separated whites and egg yolks must be kept in airtight containers. Use yolks within 2 days and whites within 1 week.

TECHNIQUES WITH EGGS

It is best to separate eggs taken straight from the fridge as the yolk is firm and less likely to run into the white.

Whisking egg whites

Egg whites should be at room temperature for whisking, so leave in a covered bowl for about 1 hour. Use only clean utensils as

any grease will prevent the whites from expanding. Whisk in a medium to large bowl, and for small quantities, use a balloon whisk. For larger quantities, use an electric whisk but start on the lowest speed setting and then increase the speed once the whites start to foam. The term 'soft peak' describes whisked egg whites that will lift in peaks but where the top of the peak will gently tip over. A 'stiff peak' is when the egg white holds its shape completely.

Non-dairy alternatives

There are many reasons why people choose not to eat dairy products, or to cut down on them. If you cannot or do not want to have milk, cheese or yoghurt, many straightforward alternatives, generally made from soya milk, are available. You may also find milk made from rice and oats. These can be used for cold drinks as well as served with cereals, but are not as suitable for cooking as they can curdle. For more information on soya alternatives, see page 96.

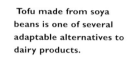

Tofu made from soya beans is one of several adaptable alternatives to dairy products.

SOYA MILK

A vegan alternative to milk, made from soya beans, soya milk does not taste like cow's milk, but is perfectly acceptable as a drink or liquid for cereals. It does have a tendency to curdle when added to hot liquids and also to separate in sauces, so it is less versatile.

Soya milk is rich in protein and low in fat. Some varieties are enriched with calcium and B_{12}. It is sold unsweetened, or sweetened with sugar or fruit juice concentrates.

SOYA CHEESE AND YOGHURT

Soya beans are used to produce milk, cheese, yoghurt and flour

Soya cheese can be firm, with the consistency of a processed cheese. It does have a flavour although it can seem rather fatty to eat. Soya yoghurt can be flavoured or natural. If you already drink soya milk, you will find these products quite acceptable.

Alternatives to Eggs

If for some reason you cannot eat eggs, there are several alternatives for use in cooking.

SOYA FLOUR

Soya flour can be used to enrich mixtures, such as a cake or a savoury bake, although it won't help lighten the mixture.

TAHINI

Tahini makes a great binding ingredient for burgers and bakes. It will thicken any moisture in the mixture prior to cooking. Even so, be sure to handle it carefully when you are cooking, as it may curdle a mixture.

TOFU

Tofu makes a good mayonnaise – blend soft or silken tofu with oil and flavourings to make a rich, creamy dressing. Silken tofu can also be scrambled to make a savoury topping for toast.

Milk, yoghurt and cheese can all be made from non-dairy sources, such as soya beans. They do not taste the same as their dairy equivalent, nor do they behave exactly the same way when heated, but they are useful sources of protein.

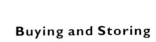

Grains

Such is the versatility of grains that they and their derivatives appear in various guises in thousands of dishes around the world – in paella, pasta, pancakes or enchiladas to name a few. Since ancient times, cereals or grains have been staple foods – wheat, rye, barley and oats in the temperate climates; rice, maize and millet in the tropics and sub-tropics.

In addition to traditional grains, there are lesser known varieties such as quinoa. Included in this group, too, are buckwheat and wild rice. Neither is strictly a grain, but they have similar nutritional properties and are interchangeable with some other grains. Grains come in many different forms besides wholegrains, which adds to their versatility as cooking ingredients. They are frequently processed as flakes or cracked grains and partially cooked, as well as being ground into flour.

NUTRITIONAL VALUE

Each wholegrain is a seed and contains many nutritional elements within its protective outer layers. These layers include the germ, which is an important source of oils and carbohydrate, and bran, a valuable source of fibre. The starches in grains are broken down during digestion to form glucose, which gives the body a sustained and steady supply of energy. It is important to chew grains thoroughly because it is an enzyme in the saliva that begins the digestion of these starches.

Grains are a rich source of many essential amino acids and should be eaten in conjunction with pulses or nuts to provide complete protein. They are also a good source of minerals, as well as vitamins, particularly the B group vitamins.

Once a wholegrain is processed for flour or flakes, the outer layer is cracked and the oil in the germ begins to oxidise and lose its nutritional value. Although flour and flakes are useful cooking ingredients, it is important to use some wholegrains in a well-balanced vegetarian diet. Refined wholegrains, such as white rice, and their products, for example white flour or white bread, are nutritionally inferior. The bran and germ have been removed and therefore many of the valuable nutrients lost.

Buying and Storing

Even though wholegrains have a long shelf life, they inevitably harden as they age and can take longer to cook. They keep indefinitely in cool dry conditions. They are best stored in airtight containers.

Processed grains, such as flakes and flour, do not keep as long, so it is best to buy them as fresh as possible. It is possible to find organically grown grains, flakes and flour but you may need to seek out a specialist outlet in order to obtain these. Flakes and flours should be kept away from any heat so that the oils they contain do not go rancid.

Cooking Wholegrains

These are general guidelines for cooking all wholegrains (rice, wheat, barley, buckwheat, millet and quinoa). The basic method remains much the same for all of them, but the water quantities and the time needed for cooking will vary with each grain (see opposite). First, rinse the wholegrains if necessary to remove surface dust.

Wholegrains can be stored for a long time in cool, dry conditions. Processed grains such as flakes or flour need to be used up more quickly.

Absorption method This is best if you work by volume, for example 1 cup of rice should be cooked in 2 cups of water. Choose a saucepan with a close-fitting lid, or use a pressure cooker. Rub a little oil around the pan to prevent the grains from sticking – this will also make the pans easier to clean. Bring the right quantity of water to the boil, quickly tip in the grains, then stir once. Bring back to the boil, reduce the heat to a simmer, cover the pan and cook for the required

Each wholegrain is a seed and contains many useful nutrients. They are a good source of amino acids, minerals and vitamins, especially the B group vitamins.

length of time until the grain is tender and all the liquid has been absorbed. Do not stir as this tends to make the grains sticky. Do not add salt as this toughens the grain.

Toasting grains before cooking helps to bring out their flavour. Use about 1 teaspoon of oil to 1 cup of grain. Heat the oil in the saucepan and gently toast the grain, then pour in the water and cook as normal. This works particularly well for millet, quinoa and buckwheat. For more flavour, spices such as cumin, coriander or chilli can be lightly toasted and cooked with the grain.

Note, a standard 250ml (8fl oz) cup filled to the brim will hold about 250g (8oz) rice or other grain. This is enough for 4 as a small side serving, or it will make a one-pot dish, such as paella or risotto, for 4 with other ingredients added. (Recipes in the book are generally based around this measurement.) If you are serving hungry adults, you may prefer to double the quantity.

Hot water or free simmer method
Bring a large quantity of water to the boil in a saucepan. Add the grain and bring back to the boil, then simmer very gently until the grain is tender. Turn into a colander or sieve and drain well.

Grains vary enormously in size and appearance, from the slender mahogany-coloured wild rice to the chunky, round risotto rice.

The advantage of this method is that the grain is unlikely to catch on the bottom of the pan. The disadvantage is that some of the nutrients will be lost as they leach into the cooking liquid and are then thrown away.

Microwave
Grains can also be cooked in the microwave but it takes virtually the same length of time. The advantage is that the grains do not stick or boil over. For microwave cooking, use an exact quantity of water as excess water increases the cooking time.

Risotto method
This method of cooking is particularly suitable for risotto rice, millet and short-grain rice. It involves patience and stirring, which gives the grain the creamy, slightly sticky quality of risotto. For 250g (8oz) grain, use about 1 litre (1¾ pints) stock. Using oil or butter, fry chopped onion and garlic, then add the grain. Add one-third of the stock and, stirring constantly, bring to the boil so that the mixture is bubbling gently. When all the stock has been absorbed, repeat the process with the next third and finally the last third of stock. The whole process will take around 20–30 minutes.

Some grains benefit from being toasted first in a little oil to bring out their flavour. Spices can also be added.

COOKING WHOLEGRAINS BY THE ABSORPTION METHOD

Type of grain in standard 250ml (8fl oz) cup	Pre-cooking instructions	Amount of liquid per 1 cup of grain	Average cooking time (minutes)
1 cup rice		2 cups	25–30
1 cup wheat	Soak overnight	3 cups	50–60
1 cup barley		3 cups	50–60
1 cup buckwheat	Toast	2–2½ cups	15–20
1 cup millet	Toast	2½–3 cups	20
1 cup quinoa	Rinse well and toast	2 cups	12–15

Wholegrains and flakes

O f all the wholegrains, barley, millet, quinoa, buckwheat, oats, rice and wheat are the most widely available. Many of these grains are also sold in flake form, which makes them more versatile. For cooking instructions see the previous page and for recipes see pages 222–39.

Many grains may be used whole, flaked or in flour.

BARLEY

Barley was popular in ancient times, but is now less widely used. Rarely served on its own, it is more commonly added to soups and casseroles, thickening and flavouring them. Once cooked, it is light and chewy. Barley flakes can be used in baking and added to breakfast cereals.

MILLET

Native to Africa and Asia, round grains of golden yellow millet can be served with stews and casseroles, or cooked with vegetables for a pilaff or risotto style of dish. Millet tends to cook unevenly so some of the grains will be crunchy while others are soft. Also, the grains will stick

together if left to stand once cooked. Millet has a milder flavour and less texture than rice. It also combines well with sweet ingredients to make a pudding similar to a rice pudding. Millet flakes and flour are available and can be used in baking, breakfast cereals and crumble mixtures. Millet is gluten-free.

QUINOA

Pronounced 'keenwa', this grain has a delicate, grassy flavour. It is somewhat similar in appearance to millet – gold in colour with minute round grains. It must be washed thoroughly before cooking because the outside is coated with bitter chemicals. It is important to keep a check on quinoa at the end of the

suggested cooking time because the grains are easily overcooked and lose their texture. In the centre of each grain is a tiny spiral thread, which is visible when cooked.

BUCKWHEAT

Buckwheat is an attractive angular seed with a distinctive strong flavour. If unroasted, the grains have a greenish tinge; once roasted, they turn a dark reddish-brown. Toasted grains are sometimes called kasha. Buckwheat goes well with cold weather vegetables, such as root vegetables, and with mushrooms and dark green vegetables. It is gluten-free.

OATS

Once the staple food of Northern Britain, oats are rarely sold as wholegrains but are used mainly when processed into meal and flakes. Use as the basis for breakfast cereals such as muesli and for porridge (see page 134).

Oat flakes are good for thickening soups or casseroles, or for adding bulk to burgers or savoury bakes. When mixed with a little flour and fat, oats make a good crumble topping – either sweet, with added sugar, or savoury, when flavoured with herbs. Oat flakes and oatmeal can also be used in bread-making and for cakes and biscuits such as flapjacks (see page 327). Oats contain a soluble dietary fibre which is thought to lower cholesterol levels in the blood.

Rice

Widely available in many different varieties, this is a popular and versatile grain. Fortunately, its long shelf life means that you can store several types and choose the most appropriate for the particular recipe.

Rice is grown in many parts of the world, such as Bali. Each variety lends a distinctive character to dishes, such as risotto or pilau.

Short-grain
This type is suitable for puddings, savoury stuffings and risotto-style dishes as it comprises plump small grains that stick together once cooked.

Glutinous rice
Also called sweet rice or sticky rice, this is a polished rice with round pearl-like grains. Although called glutinous, this grain – like all rice – is gluten-free. Once cooked, the grains tend to stick together. The rice is used for sushi (see page 281), in which cooked rice, sometimes seasoned with vinegar, is wrapped in sheets of nori.

Long-grain
The long, slender grains hold their shape once cooked. Long-grain brown rice has a nutty flavour and is good for accompanying chillies, stir-fries and curries, and makes a good base for salad. Pre-cooked white and brown rice are available – these have shorter cooking times. Pre-cooked white rice is steamed under pressure when unmilled, then milled afterwards, which helps to retain some of the vitamins and minerals.

Basmati rice
This fragrant rice with long, slender grains is native to India and Pakistan. Once cooked, the grains separate easily. Cooked plainly, it can accompany a range of dishes.

Jasmine rice (fragrant rice)
Jasmine rice is similar to basmati rice but has a slightly soft and sticky texture when cooked. It has a milder flavour than basmati rice, but still has a distinctive aromatic smell when cooking.

Risotto rice
Usually a polished grain of a medium size, risotto rice gets its creamy quality as some of the starch breaks down as it cooks. It also absorbs about five times its weight in liquid. Some superior varieties of risotto rice are sold by name – look for Arborio, Carnaroli and Vialone Nano. More nutritious risotto can be made with brown rice but the texture is less creamy.

Red Rice
This rice from the Mediterranean has medium, russet-coloured grains, which are light and chewy when cooked, with a pleasing nutty flavour. It can be mixed with ordinary rice, but also works well on its own served with simple mixtures of vegetables. Cooked in a similar manner to long grain rice. It takes about 20–25 minutes.

Wild Rice
Originally native to the Great Lakes and only found wild, this rice is now cultivated more widely. It is actually an aquatic grass with thin and slender grains coloured a dark chocolate-brown. As it cooks it

splits and curls slightly. Wild rice has a distinctive, nutty flavour and works well on its own or mixed with ordinary rice. It goes well with other nutty flavours, as well as with fruit vegetables. Cook as for long-grain rice. It takes about 35–40 minutes.

Wheat

The whole grain of wheat, known as the wheat berry, is sweet and chewy with a springy texture. It adds texture to casseroles and can also be used in savoury bakes and salads. In its other forms, wheat is used in many dishes.

Wheat is widely available and is processed in a number of ways, making it an extremely versatile ingredient.

Cracked wheat
This is made by cracking whole wheat berries between giant rollers so that the cooking time is reduced.

Bulgar
Bulgar is made from whole wheat that has been cooked, dried and then cracked. Depending on the brand, it needs little or no cooking, merely soaking in boiling water. Organic varieties can take longer to soften.

To soak bulgar, measure it into a large bowl, add a little salt and pour over twice its volume of boiling water. Leave to stand for 10–15 minutes. If still chewy, bulgar can be cooked briefly in the microwave. Bulgar can be used as a quick accompaniment, cooked like a pilaff or served cold as the basis for a salad (see pages 230 and 299).

Couscous
North African in origin, couscous is made from the inner layers of the wheat grain and is therefore slightly less nutritious than bulgar. It has the appearance of tiny golden balls. Depending on the

variety, couscous can be lightly steamed or simply soaked in boiling water for 5 minutes. Organic varieties may need more cooking. It makes a quick accompaniment for casseroles, but is also delicious as a salad base.

Semolina
Produced from the starchy part of the grain, semolina can be used for puddings or as an ingredient of gnocchi. It is also used for making commercial pasta.

Wheat flakes
Coarser in texture than oat flakes and not so creamy once cooked, these are useful for thickening soups and stews and also provide a contrasting texture to oat flakes in muesli.

Wheatgerm
This is the embryo of the grain, containing valuable nutrients such as protein, fat (mostly unsaturated), vitamin E and B group vitamins. It is important to store wheatgerm in the fridge since its high fat content means it can go rancid very easily. Even when stored properly, wheatgerm should be used within weeks rather than months. For a nutritional boost, add wheatgerm to breakfast cereal, bread or pastry dough, grain salads and savoury bakes or crumbles. Use only small quantities as it does have a distinctive flavour.

Bran
Comprising the outer layers of the whole grain, bran is a useful source of fibre, but it does need to be combined with flakes or added to savoury mixtures. It contains phytic acid, which can interfere with the absorption of certain minerals.

Flour and pasta

Flour is an essential ingredient in many dishes such as pastry, pasta, cakes and biscuits, as well as a thickening agent in sauces. All grains can be made into flour, but many are low in gluten or gluten-free, which makes them less versatile. This section concentrates on wheat and cornflour, which are probably the most widely used.

WHEAT FLOUR

Many varieties of wheat flour are widely available and it is worth stocking several types so that you can choose the most appropriate flour for the recipe.

Flour from hard wheat, often described as strong flour, has a high gluten content and is good for making bread. Flour from soft wheat, with a low gluten content, is better for cakes, pastry and baking.

Wholemeal flour can be finely ground to give a beige appearance flecked with bran.

Wholemeal flour is made from the whole wheat grain and can vary considerably according to the way in which it has been milled. Some varieties are extremely fine, while others contain visible flecks of bran. The texture of the flour will affect the end result: coarser flour absorbs more liquid.

Unbleached flour is a refined flour – it has had the bran and germ removed but has not been subjected to chemical whitening.

CORNFLOUR (*MAIZE*)

Native to America, corn appears in a variety of forms as diverse as a fresh vegetable, a sweetener and an oil.

Dried corn is ground into a distinctive yellow meal or flour. The result may be sold as maize meal, cornmeal, cornflour or polenta, the Italian name. The texture varies from fine to coarse. Once cooked, cornmeal is delicious layered with

Cornflour can be coarsely or finely milled.

OTHER TYPES OF FLOUR

Here are some types of flour that are not commonly used, but are still useful, especially the gluten-free varieties.

Buckwheat flour
This pale grey, tasty flour retains the distinctive dry taste of buckwheat. It makes excellent pancakes and is also used commercially to make Japanese soba noodles.

Rice flour
A gluten-free flour that can be used for baking and thickening sauces, or for fine batter.

Rye flour
With a pleasant tang, rye does contain gluten but it is the type that does not leaven bread. Generally rye is mixed with wheat for bread making. A spoonful or so of rye flour can add a nutty flavour to pastry.

Quinoa flour
Low in gluten, this flour needs to be mixed with wheat flour for baking because it is a soft flour.

vegetables, cheese or tomato sauce. It can also be pan-fried or griddled. (See page 222–24 for cooking instructions and recipes.)

Cornflour is found in numerous Mexican dishes, such as enchiladas and tortillas. These go well with all the foods popular in that cuisine, such as avocado, chillies and cheese.

Cornflour can be mixed with wheat flour to make a golden corn bread or a savoury topping for vegetable stews.

PASTA AND NOODLES

Dried pasta and noodles are godsends to busy cooks. Easy to have on hand because of their long shelf life, they can be served with a huge range of sauces, vegetables or even just plain olive oil or butter. Once most popular only in Italy and the Far East, their use in cooking now far exceeds these international boundaries.

Look for a range of flavours and different thicknesses. Pasta can be made from wheat, corn, buckwheat or even quinoa flour; it may be flavoured with tomato, spinach, basil, chilli, egg and a host of other flavourings.

Pasta is extremely adaptable. As a rough guideline, fine pastas are best served with lighter, smooth sauces, while larger pastas, such as shells, curls or broad noodles work better with chunky sauces, ensuring that the dish looks more balanced.

Pasta can be made with numerous different flavourings.

Pulses

Beans, peas and lentils, collectively known as pulses, are the edible seeds of leguminous plants. They are a vital group of foods for vegetarians, being both highly nutritious and extremely versatile. They also have the added advantages of being readily available and storing well, and are often cheap to buy.

Most of the world's cuisines contain a traditional dish featuring a bean or lentil – consider fiery chillies with red kidney or pinto beans from Mexico, spicy samosa from India made with mung beans, Oriental stir-fries with bean sprouts, classic baked beans in tomato sauce from America and hearty soups containing split peas from Northern Europe. These and many other recipes show the versatility of these ingredients.

Beans and lentils can be the basis for excellent soups, stews and casseroles. Puréed or mashed, they are good in dips, pâtés and burgers or savoury bakes; freshly cooked and marinated, they work well served cold in substantial salads.

While the flavour differences between varieties of pulses are small, they do come in a wide range of shapes, colours and sizes. Mixing two contrasting pulses together in the same dish is an excellent way of adding interest in terms of colour and texture.

Highly nutritious and versatile, pulses come in a variety of shapes, sizes and colours.

Pulses are a good source of protein as well as supplying useful amounts of many vitamins and minerals.

Buying and Storing

Shop for beans and lentils where you know the turnover is brisk. Although they all have a long shelf life, it is better to try to use them within a year of the harvest. Look for beans and lentils that are plump or glossy with bright colours. Avoid any that are wrinkled, chipped or cracked, as these have probably been around for some time. Keep dried pulses in a cool cupboard in an airtight jar.

NUTRITIONAL VALUE

Pulses are important in a healthy vegetarian diet because they are a good source of many of the essential amino acids, the building blocks for protein. Eaten in conjunction with grains or nuts, they provide high-quality protein.

Pulses are a good source of fibre and starch. They tend to be low in calories since, with the exception of the soya bean, they are low in fat. Rich in vitamins B_1, B_2, B_3 and calcium, they also contain some iron, phosphorus and manganese. Whole, dried pulses are easy to sprout (see page 93). Their vitamin content then increases dramatically and they become an important source of vitamins C and A.

On the minus side, pulses contain phytic acid, which can inhibit the absorption of some minerals.

Preparing Dried Pulses

It is vital to prepare pulses properly because they contain the toxin lectin, which is only rendered harmless during the soaking and cooking process.

Before using dried beans and lentils, they should be picked over for small pieces of grit, tiny sticks and ungerminated seeds. Next, put them in a sieve and rinse thoroughly to remove any surface dust or dirt. Lentils are now ready to cook (see below) but larger beans need soaking.

When using dried pulses rinse them thoroughly first. Larger pulses need soaking before cooking.

Soaking beans gives them time to swell so that the final cooking time is reduced. Immature or overdry beans, which won't cook properly, will float to the surface where they can be removed. Soaking beans before cooking also helps them become more digestible as the soaking process removes some of the complex sugars, which cause gases to build up in the gut. There are two soaking methods that you can use.

Long-soaking method Put the beans in a large bowl and cover with four times their volume of cold water. The harder the bean, the longer the soaking takes. Soya beans may need to be left for 8 hours or overnight. Chickpeas, too, take several hours; red kidney beans, pinto and black beans may well be ready after a couple of hours – you can check to see whether the beans look plump or the skin is still wrinkled.

Quick soaking method Bring the beans to the boil in a saucepan containing four times their volume of water. Boil fast for 3–5 minutes then turn off the heat and leave them to stand for 1 hour.

Cooking Beans

Once the beans are soaked by one of the above methods, drain and rinse them again. Then bring them to the boil in plenty of fresh water. Use enough water so the beans are covered and have another 2.5–5cm (1–2in) depth above them. Boil them at a fast, rolling boil for at least 10 minutes, to make sure that any toxins on the outside skins of the beans are completely destroyed. Then reduce the heat to a simmer,

COOK'S TIP

If you are soaking beans in hot conditions, they may start to ferment and you'll see the soaking water starts to look frothy. In this case, put the beans to soak in the fridge.

partially cover the pan and continue cooking the beans until soft (see table below for individual timings). Remember the timing can vary from batch to batch. During the boiling process, scum frequently forms on the surface – just skim this off. Adding a little oil to the cooking liquid can help prevent the scum forming. The beans are cooked when soft to the bite and evenly coloured all the way through – test at the end of the suggested cooking time. If the beans are not cooked, continue simmering as necessary – it is better to overcook rather than undercook pulses.

If you use a pressure cooker, the cooking time is generally reduced by at least half. Do not be tempted to cook too many beans at once because the scum that forms may clog the pressure gauge.

Beans must be fast boiled for at least 10 minutes to destroy any toxins present on the outer skin.

COOK'S TIP

Do not add salt to the cooking water as this toughens the outside skins of the beans and means they will take longer to cook.

COOKING TIMES FOR BEANS

These timings are a guideline only since length of cooking time will vary from one batch to another and may differ according to the quantity of pulses cooked. For all beans, soak them in plenty of water; drain, rinse and fast boil for 10 minutes, then cook for the following suggested times, or until tender.

Type of bean	Suggested cooking time
Mung	45–50 minutes
Flageolet	45–50 minutes
Aduki	50–60 minutes
Black-eye	50–60 minutes
Borlotti	50–60 minutes
Cannellini	50–60 minutes
Haricot	60–70 minutes
Pinto	50–60 minutes
Black	60–90 minutes
Butter	60–90 minutes
Lima	60–90 minutes
Chickpea	60–90 minutes
Ful (or foul) medames	60–90 minutes
Red kidney	60–90 minutes
Soya	up to 4 hours

Split red lentils and yellow and green split peas do not need soaking prior to cooking. Once cooked they fall to a smooth purée and are good for soups, pâtés and fillings for pasties.

Cooking Lentils

Once lentils have been picked over and rinsed, they are ready to cook. For whole lentils, bring them to the boil in plenty of water and cook until just soft. For split lentils, when trying to make a purée – for bakes, burgers and pâtés – you must measure the water exactly, otherwise it is easy to end up with a mixture that is too sloppy to use. As a rough guide, the volume of water should be double the unit of measurement of the weight of the lentils, for example 250g (8oz) lentils to 500ml (17fl oz) water.

Whole lentils need to be boiled in plenty of water. Cook until they are soft enough to bite through and then use in soups, stews or salads.

Quantities

Dried pulses will roughly double in weight once they are soaked and cooked. Generally, it is worth cooking a large batch of beans at a time and then storing them in usable quantities. Recipes in this book either use a ready-cooked weight or give clear instructions for using an uncooked weight.

Canned beans and lentils are pre-cooked by the manufacturer. The advantage is that you don't have to cook them and they are ready to use straightaway. The disadvantage is that they are generally more expensive and you do have to check the labels for additives. Be aware that many varieties will have salt or sugar added.

Freezing Beans

If you have cooked a large quantity of pulses, it is worth freezing some for future use. They can be frozen in their cooking liquid or drained and stored in a plastic container. Freeze them in shallow blocks for easy storage and fast thawing. Make your blocks of beans a suitable weight for a recipe – for example, a casserole for 4 people needs 400–500g (13–16oz) cooked weight. Beans will freeze for up to 6 months.

Leave them to thaw overnight in the fridge, or for 2–3 hours at room temperature, or defrost them in a microwave.

Beans freeze well either in their cooking liquid or drained and portioned out into suitable plastic containers or bags.

Once soaked, beans will roughly double in weight.

PREPARING AND COOKING LENTILS

Type of lentil	Soaking instructions	Cooking time
Split red	None required	20–30 minutes
Continental	Optional but recommended	30–40 minutes
Puy lentils and lentilles vertes	None required	10–25 minutes
Brown lentils	Optional but recommended	30–40 minutes
Yellow split peas	None required	30–40 minutes

MAKING BEANS MORE DIGESTIBLE

A well-known side effect of beans is flatulence and some people are worse affected than others. A golden rule is that pulses must be very thoroughly cooked. Here are a few more tips that may help to make beans more digestible:

• Change the water once or twice during the soaking process; the long-soaking method seems to work better
• Sprout the beans for a day or so before cooking
• Add a strip of kombu (seaweed) to the cooking water
• Cook the pulses with spices, such as cumin or caraway, which aid digestion
• Introduce pulses gradually into your diet
• Start by eating lentils and smaller beans, such as aduki beans, which are thought to be easier to digest

Growing Bean Sprouts

Although often categorised as bean sprouts, sprouts can be grown from grains, vegetables or pulses. Useful and nutritious ingredients for salads or stir-fries, they can be grown at any time of the year. It is easy to grow your own bean sprouts and requires very little equipment.

Mung beans and alfalfa seeds are probably the best choice for beginners as they grow quickly and have an excellent flavour. Sprouts can be grown in a variety of containers, but drainage is essential. The simplest method is to use a wide-necked jar with a porous cover, such as muslin, but colanders, fine sieves or mesh trays can be used instead.

Bean sprouts make nutritious additions to salads, sandwiches and stir-fry dishes.

1 Pick out any grit, sticks or damaged specimens and wash the beans or seeds thoroughly.

2 Put 2 tablespoons of beans or seeds into a jar, fill with lukewarm water and leave to stand overnight. This soaking process helps break down the outer shell so that the growth is quicker.

3 The next day pour off the water and leave the jar in a warm place. If bean sprouts are grown in the dark they will contain more vitamin B_2; if grown in the light, there is more vitamin C.

4 Every night and morning, until the sprouts are ready, rinse the beans or seeds in the jar with lukewarm water. Shake them gently, so as not to damage the delicate sprouts, and drain them thoroughly. It's best to turn the jar upside down so that all the excess water drains away since if too much moisture is left, the sprouts may go rancid. If the weather – or your kitchen – is warm, you may need to rinse the sprouts an extra couple of times each day to prevent them from drying out. Most sprouts take about 4 days to grow. They will keep fresh for 4–5 days in the fridge.

Grain and vegetable sprouts need no cooking but if you have particular trouble digesting pulses, it is worth cooking sprouts from peas and beans for a short time. As well as using sprouts in salads and stir-fries, you can knead them into bread dough or add them to breakfast cereals and sandwiches. For use in casseroles, don't sprout the beans fully – a couple of days should be enough.

Bean sprouts can be grown in wide-necked jars and covered with muslin or a lid pierced with several holes to make draining easy and allow air to circulate.

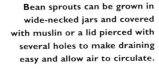

RED KIDNEY BEAN

Glossy red and named for their shape, these beans are best known for their use with chilli. They go well with hot spices and are great in casseroles and salads. Mashed and reheated for refried beans (see page 191), they are very popular in Mexican cookery.

ADUKI BEAN

Small, maroon beans from China and Japan, these are small enough to go into pie fillings and savoury bakes, and make an excellent substitute for minced meat in dishes such as lasagne or moussaka. Aduki beans go well with rice dishes, mushrooms and aubergines; for a gourmet treat, cook them with red wine. They are also good when sprouted.

CHICKPEA

Pale gold in colour with a nutty flavour and crunchy texture, the chickpea is also known as garbanzo, ceci and chana dhal. They are popular in Middle Eastern cookery, where they are served toasted and salted or puréed with garlic, oil, lemon and sesame to make hummus – a delicious soft pâté or dip (see page 167). They are also cooked and ground with spices, then deep-fried to make little savouries known as falafel (see page 174). In salads and casseroles, chickpeas make a good contrast with dark-coloured beans.

Gram flour is the powder that is made from grinding chickpeas. It makes a light batter for vegetable fritters (see page 168) and is used extensively in Indian cookery.

BLACK-EYE BEAN

This bean is similar in size to the haricot bean but with a distinctive black spot, hence its name. The beans were introduced to America from Africa and are now popular in the southern states of America, as well as in the Caribbean, as they go well with flavourings from those regions. They are particularly useful in soups and casseroles and make a good contrast with red kidney beans or chickpeas.

PINTO BEAN

Originally used in Mexican and South American cookery, pinto beans are a variety of haricot bean but speckled pink. In flavour and appearance they are similar to the Italian borlotti bean. They hold their shape well once cooked, and are good for soups, stews and salads. They can also be mashed to make refried beans (see page 191) and work well with hot and aromatic spices.

FLAGEOLET BEAN

These beans are an attractive pale green colour and have a delicate flavour. Very tender when cooked, they are quite digestible. They are good served with butter and herbs, such as chervil or chives, as well as with tomato-based sauces. They are often only available canned.

BORLOTTI BEAN

Light brown or pink with deeper red speckles, these beans cook to a soft texture and are good for pâtés or for mashing into savoury bakes or burgers. They go well with mild spices, such as nutmeg and cinnamon, and can also be served with Parmesan.

MUNG BEAN

Native to tropical Asia, mung beans are especially popular in Indian and Oriental cookery. Their small size makes them easy to mash into hot spicy snacks, such as samosas. They have a slightly sweet flavour, which is more noticeable once they are sprouted. Sprouting also means they have a very high vitamin content (see page 93). Use the sprouts in stir-fries or spring rolls, in salads and for sandwich fillings.

BUTTER BEAN AND LIMA BEAN

These are similar beans, the butter bean (top) being the larger. They are a traditional ingredient in succotash, an American stew made with corn, molasses and paprika. The smaller lima bean (bottom) also looks attractive in salads. Butter beans can be puréed with milk or cream and served as a side vegetable.

CANNELLINI BEAN

This white variety of kidney bean is used in Italian cookery and goes well with typical flavourings of the cuisine, such as basil, oregano and thyme. It also works well in soups, casseroles and salads.

SOYA BEAN

The soya bean stands alone as the only bean that provides all the essential amino acids. Although of great value nutritionally, it takes a long time to cook – up to 4 hours – and is thus rarely used as a bean in its own right. Soya products, such as tofu, tempeh, miso, soya flour and soy sauce, are more commonly used (see page 96).

FUL (OR FOUL) MEDAME

This small version of a broad bean is popular in Egypt. The beans are traditionally served boiled and mashed with garlic and spices, such as cumin and pepper, and sometimes accompanied by eggs, onion and lemon.

HARICOT BEAN

A small, oval bean with a creamy, white colour. It is most widely used in 'baked beans', but is also useful for casseroles and bean salads where it makes a good contrast with red kidney beans and chickpeas.

BLACK BEAN

These dramatically coloured beans are frequently used in central and South American dishes. They go well with cumin, chilli and tomato, as well as with citrus flavours. They are good served as refried beans (see page 191).

SPLIT RED LENTIL

Bright orange in colour, despite their name, these lentils are exceedingly versatile and highly nutritious. They disintegrate during cooking, which makes them ideal for soups and for changing the texture of casseroles. They combine well with tomatoes, eggs and cheese. Once cooked, the purée makes a good base for savoury burgers and bakes or a filling for pies.

CONTINENTAL LENTIL

These lentils, the largest of the lentil family, hold their shape once cooked. They make a textural contrast when served with larger pulses in dishes such as chilli. They also go well in salads dressed with yoghurt and plenty of garlic, parsley, coriander or mint.

PUY LENTIL AND LENTILLE VERTE

These tiny grey-green lentils are becoming increasingly easier to find. Both Puy lentils (top) and lentilles vertes (bottom) have the advantage of being very quick to cook – some varieties in about 10 minutes. Excellent in casseroles, they work well in salads mixed with creamy ingredients, such as cheese or a yoghurt dressing. They can also be used for refried bean dishes and go with both hot spices and aromatic herbs.

BROWN LENTIL

This is virtually interchangeable with the larger continental lentil or the Puy lentil. It is good for casseroles and soups as well as pie fillings.

YELLOW SPLIT PEA

This can be used in similar ways to the split red lentil, although it is slightly more robust to cook. Split peas make a good basis for soups, pâtés and purées. Their earthy flavours work well with spices and herbs and they can be made into dhal (see page 250).

Soya bean products

Soya beans are rarely cooked at home because they require a long cooking time. However, they come into their own when processed as either tofu or tempeh, or fermented to make the marvellous savoury flavourings of miso, shoyu or tamari. These forms bear very little resemblance to the original bean in either colour or flavour.

TOFU

Tofu is a nourishing food made from soya beans, which originated in the Far East. It is worth trying to introduce into your diet as it is a quick-cooking ingredient with terrific nutritional value. It contains eight essential amino acids and is low in calories, saturated fat and salt. It is particularly rich in iron and the B vitamins. Since it is a good source of calcium, it is very useful for anyone with allergies to dairy products.

Regular or firm tofu can be sliced or cubed, stir-fried and baked, despite its fairly fragile texture. Because it is virtually tasteless, it needs a chance to absorb other flavours. Do this by marinating for an hour or so – Oriental-style marinades are particularly successful – or cook the tofu in a richly flavoured casserole or sauce, such as a barbecue or chilli sauce.

In Japan, tofu is often served plain, sprinkled with shoyu or soy sauce and finely chopped spring onions.

Tofu also comes in a smooth variety known as silken tofu. This product is easy to blend into soups, sauces and drinks, giving them a creamy consistency. If you can't get silken tofu, use regular tofu but add enough water so that the tofu blends to a consistency similar to Greek yoghurt: about 75ml (3fl oz) water to 150g (6oz) regular tofu. Drain, rinse and roughly chop the tofu and place with the water in a blender or food processor. Whizz together for a minute and add more water if necessary.

Buying and storing

Tofu is generally found in chilled cabinets in stores and supermarkets or from specialist Oriental shops, sold either boxed or in polythene packets. It is worth trying different brands as they can vary in both texture and flavour. It is possible to buy tofu made from organic soya beans, as well as smoked or ready-marinated varieties.

Tofu will keep for several days in the fridge but is not suitable for freezing. Once the packet is open, any leftover tofu should be covered with fresh water, which must be changed daily. The remaining tofu should be eaten within a few days. Silken tofu will keep for months in its packet, but once opened should be eaten within 24 hours.

Firm tofu is sold in small blocks. The texture may vary from one brand to another. Flavoured or smoked tofu is sometimes available.

Regular or firm tofu can be cubed or sliced. It can be added to stir-fry dishes and casseroles, and benefits by being marinated in advance.

TEMPEH

Tempeh is another high-protein food made from soya beans, which have been cooked, fermented and mashed into blocks. It is rich in protein and fibre, a good source of the B group vitamins and low in fat. Although it can have a rather unappetising, mottled appearance, it has a slightly nutty, almost dry taste and a good capacity to absorb flavours. It is more robust than tofu and can be thinly sliced. If sold uncooked, it needs to be steamed or simmered – preferably in a marinade – for about 20 minutes. Tempeh can then be fried, crumbled or added in pieces to casseroles. When it is sold pre-cooked, it is usually ready-flavoured with other ingredients such as garlic.

Buying and storing Tempeh should be kept in the fridge and, once the packet is opened, used within a few days. It can also be frozen. Tempeh is found in chilled cabinets in stores and specialist shops.

MISO

This savoury paste is made from fermented soya beans. It comes in a variety of colours and flavours, depending on which other beans or grains it is mixed with. The most common varieties are mugi miso (soya and barley), hatcho miso (soya only) and genmai miso (soya and rice).

Miso is a living food containing bacteria, in a similar way to live yoghurt. These bacteria are destroyed by boiling so it is common to add miso at the end of cooking. Miso can be a source of vitamin B_{12}.

Miso can easily be made into a nourishing soup mixed with water or Oriental stock (see page 145), and garnished with vegetables, such as fine asparagus, roasted seaweed, thinly sliced carrots or mushrooms. Miso will add a savoury flavour to soups, stews, pie fillings or purées.

Despite its unappealing appearance, tempeh is high in protein and will absorb the flavour of other ingredients with which it is cooked.

Since it is often very dense, it is best to thin it down with water or stock to make it easier to mix. Miso can also be mixed with tahini to make a savoury spread or dip.

Buying and storing Miso is sold in jars or sturdy polythene packets and will keep for months. It is best stored in the fridge.

SHOYU, TAMARI AND SOY SAUCE

These are names for naturally fermented sauces that are made from soya beans. Shoyu can contain some wheat, whereas tamari is usually wheat-free and has a slightly stronger flavour. Both are dark black in colour and have strong, salty flavours but, unlike some other salty flavourings, they seem to enhance food rather than overpower it. Use shoyu or tamari as a flavouring in all robust savoury dishes, as a seasoning in stir-fries or sprinkle it directly over freshly cooked vegetables.

Buying and storing Try to find authentic shoyu or tamari sauce that has been made in the traditional way. These may be sold as soy sauce. Cheaper varieties of soy sauce sometimes have additional flavour enhancers and colourings, and do not have nearly such a good flavour. Keep shoyu and tamari in a cool cupboard and they will last a long time.

TEXTURED VEGETABLE PROTEIN (*TVP*)

This high-protein product is used to make meat-like sausages and mince. It is useful for imitating conventional meat meals. Personally, I find it unappealing and prefer to get protein and texture from other foods. If you are a user of TVP, you will be able to add it to many of the casseroles or savoury pie recipes featured in this book.

SOYA MILK

See 'Non-Dairy Alternatives', page 83.

Miso paste is made from fermented soya beans. Sold in jars or packets, it has a strong, savoury flavour and can be used as a spread or diluted for stocks or sauces and used in soups.

Nuts and seeds

The classic nut roast may once have been the mainstay of vegetarian cooking but the use of nuts is now more imaginative and more subtle. Nuts and seeds are an invaluable part of a balanced vegetarian diet. Highly nutritious, they can be used to great effect in both savoury and sweet dishes.

There are numerous varieties of nuts and seeds to choose from and many ways to present each type, be it whole, flaked, ground or as a milk, cream or flavoured oil. Nuts and seeds add texture, flavour and colour to many recipes. They go well with the other main food groups, particularly grains, and they also complement vegetables and fruits. They are also great for nutritious snacks, they add crunch to salads and stir-fries and can easily be cooked into soups and stews.

NUTRITIONAL VALUE

Nuts are a concentrated source of the nutrients essential to a healthy diet. They supply protein and have a reasonable fibre content. Their calorie content is high as a result of the high fat content. However, most of the fat is unsaturated and contains vital essential fatty acids (EFAs). All nuts have useful levels of iron, zinc and magnesium and many nuts contain traces of other minerals.

Seeds, too, are a good source of protein, minerals and polyunsaturated fats. Again, they have a high calorie content because of their fat content.

Buying and Storing

For everyday cooking, it is best to buy whole, shelled nuts as they are likely to have a better flavour. Look for long 'use-by' dates and check that the contents of the packet don't look dusty or broken. It is now possible to find some varieties of organically grown nuts.

If you intend to keep nuts in a bowl as a snack, it is good to buy nuts in their shells – these protect the kernels and keep them fresh. The downside is that you can't see what you are buying. It is very disappointing to crack open a shell and find nothing but a little dust. Buy from somewhere

Nuts are packed with protein and useful quantities of some minerals, although they have a high fat content.

with a good turnover so that the stock is fresh.

Seeds are generally available whole. Again, check the 'use-by' date and the appearance of the contents of the packet.

Nuts and seeds have a high oil content and can go rancid if they are exposed to warm conditions. They are best stored in a cool place, even the fridge if you have room. Keep nuts in airtight containers and try to use whole nuts within 3 months. Split, chopped or ready-ground nuts will go stale more quickly and should be eaten within 4–6 weeks. Shelled nuts will also keep in the freezer for up to 1 year.

Nuts and seeds aren't just for nibbling. They are good in salads and stir-fry recipes and can be added to risotto or crumble toppings. Store in a cool place and do not keep too long.

Roasting Nuts and Seeds

Roasting or grilling nuts brings out their flavour. Spread out the shelled nuts or seeds in a single layer on a shallow baking sheet or in a roasting tin. Leave as they are or brush with a very little oil. Place the tray in a preheated oven, 200°C (400°F), Gas Mark 6, for about 6–10 minutes, shaking the tin two or three times during cooking to ensure that the nuts brown evenly. You can also toast nuts and seeds under the grill but watch them carefully as they can burn more easily using this method.

Roasted nuts and seeds make a delicious, nutritious snack and are ideal for sprinkling over salads.

Chopping and Grinding

Many recipes call for nuts to be finely chopped or ground. For small quantities, it is best to chop nuts by hand as it is hard to get evenly sized pieces when using a food processor.

Start by chopping individual nuts roughly and then pile them together and chop as you would for quantities of herbs, using a large knife and working the blade forwards and backwards.

If you want a few flakes, cut the nuts by hand using a small sharp knife. Nuts can be ground easily with the right equipment – use an electric nut mill or food processor depending on the quantity you need. Process in bursts several times until you get an even texture.

Use a large, sharp knife for chopping nuts by hand. Keep the nuts close together in a pile, then work the blade across the nuts, cutting as you would for herbs.

Nut Creams and Milks

The best nuts for these are almonds, cashew nuts and coconut. Use the milk or cream as an alternative to dairy cream or yoghurt and serve with hot or cold fruit, cereal or waffles.

ALMOND OR CASHEW NUT MILK AND CREAM

To make the milk, blend together in a blender or food processor 1½ tablespoons ground almonds or cashews with 175ml (6fl oz) water, and sweeten to taste. To make the nut cream, start with only half the quantity of water. Blend until smooth, then add more water gradually until you get the desired consistency.

COCONUT MILK OR CREAM

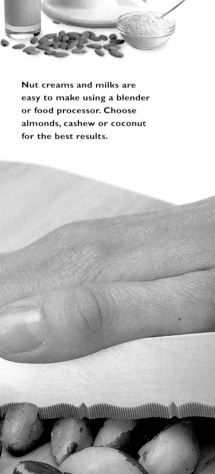

To make coconut milk, grate fresh coconut into a bowl. Cover with boiling water and leave to stand for 30 minutes. Strain through muslin or a fine sieve, extracting as much liquid as possible. Alternatively, use a block of creamed coconut. Chop roughly and then dissolve in boiling water. Add water until the mixture has the consistency you require, making it thicker for coconut cream, thinner for milk.

Nut creams and milks are easy to make using a blender or food processor. Choose almonds, cashew or coconut for the best results.

PEANUT
(GROUNDNUT)

Although grouped with nuts, strictly speaking the peanut is a legume. Because many people have an allergic reaction to them, it is vital not to serve peanuts – or any of the by-products such as groundnut oil – unless you are sure there will be no problems. For those who can eat peanuts, they are a good source of protein and go well with spices and citrus flavours. They are also an ingredient of the Indonesian salad Gado Gado (see page 306).

Serious allergic reactions to peanuts are not uncommon, so they must be used with caution.

Peanut butter This is made by puréeing peanuts with oil and salt to make a spread the consistency of butter. Always read the label as several commercial varieties also contain sugar. Peanut butter makes a nutritious sandwich spread; it can also be mixed into sauces and stews to add flavour and give a thicker consistency. Use peanut butter to make a simple pâté by mixing it with cooked lentils and seasoning with herbs, spices or citrus flavours.

Smooth or chunky, peanut butter makes a delicious spread and it can also be used for dips and sauces.

PISTACHIO

Pistachios have a brilliant green colour and slight almond flavour. Although they are often eaten roasted and salted as a cocktail snack, they work well, unsalted, in savoury grain dishes and salads, and are delicious in ice-cream.

Pick pistachio nuts with a half-open shell. If the shell is closed, the nut is not fully ripe and the shell will be very hard to remove.

To blanch and skin pistachios, put them in a bowl, cover with boiling water and leave for a few minutes. Lift out of the hot water with a slotted spoon, then pinch the softened skin. The nuts should pop out of their skins when pressed – if they don't, leave them in the hot water a little longer. Skin them while warm or the skin becomes harder to remove.

Pick pistachio nuts with a half-open shell as they are fully ripe. Unsalted nuts are good in both sweet and savoury dishes.

WALNUT

Strongly flavoured, this nut is very useful as the basis for a nut roast or burger. Walnuts work well when mixed with other milder-flavoured nuts, such as almonds or cashews, so that the walnut flavour isn't overpowering. Walnuts also combine well with grains such as bulgar, couscous, buckwheat or rice. They have an affinity with fruit, especially pears, and also with creamy cheeses such as goat's cheese and blue cheese. Use walnuts in desserts, cakes, biscuits and sweet and savoury breads.

Toasted and chopped walnuts in small quantities make substantial and nutritious garnishes. For a robust and healthy salad dressing use roasted walnuts as the basis for a vinaigrette (see page 313). See page 116 for walnut oil.

Walnuts work well with a good range of flavours in both sweet and savoury foods.

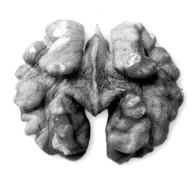

Nut roasts such as this Spiced Hazelnut and Quinoa Bake (see page 267) are delicious when well-flavoured and moist. They benefit from being served with a sauce or chutney.

PINE NUT

These slim, oval seeds have a distinctive, subtle flavour and can be eaten cooked or raw. Serve them lightly toasted in salads or with roasted vegetables. Alternatively, cook them in sauces, casseroles and grain dishes. Pine nuts have a particular affinity with many Mediterranean ingredients, such as tomatoes and peppers, and are a vital component of the classic Genoese sauce, pesto (see page 211).

The distinctive, delicate flavour of pine nuts goes well with many Mediterranean vegetables such as peppers or tomatoes.

BRAZIL NUT

Brazil nuts are delicious to eat raw, with a rich creamy quality. They are frequently sold in their shells and can be at their best when bought like this as they retain their moisture and freshness and make a nutritious snack. Paradoxically, they can be very bland once cooked and are therefore best mixed with other nuts for savoury bakes and burgers. Lightly toasted, they are delicious in salads – leave them in chunky pieces for the best effect. Skin them like hazelnuts.

Brazil nuts contrast well with the more strongly flavoured walnut or drier hazelnut.

The crunchy texture of nuts goes well with other raw ingredients in salads and provides a protein boost.

HAZELNUT

Equally good in both savoury or sweet dishes, hazelnuts go well with many varieties of grains, as well as with pasta, and are delicious in salads or stir-fries. See page 116 for hazelnut oil. They are lower in fat content than other nuts. It is worth toasting them lightly before use to bring out their flavour.

To skin hazelnuts, bake the nuts in a preheated oven, 200°C (400°F), Gas Mark 6, for 5–6 minutes. When the skins are quite brown or even slightly burnt, remove the nuts from the oven. Leave to cool slightly, then rub the nuts in your hands or in a clean tea towel. This will remove most of the skins. There may be the odd stubborn patch that remains but this shouldn't spoil the overall flavour. This method of removing the skins also roasts the nuts lightly.

Toasting hazelnuts brings out their flavour. They can then be added to salads and savoury crumbles or mixed into a breakfast cereal.

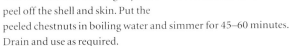

CASHEW NUT

These useful nuts, with their distinctive mild flavour, work well in both sweet and savoury dishes. They are good with many grains, particularly rice and bulgar. They are also delicious in stir-fries and are great flavoured with hot or aromatic spices.

Cashew nuts grind easily to a powder and work well as a base ingredient for nut roasts and burgers. They make very good sweet or savoury nut milks or creams (see page 99), which are useful for those allergic to, or not wishing to eat, dairy products.

PECAN

For those who find walnuts bitter, the pecan is the answer. This nut is richer and more subtle in flavour, with a more oily texture. Pecans are delicious in salads and with pasta, as well as being suitable for nut roasts. When using pecans in nut roasts, leave some whole as this highlights the flavour and creates an attractive garnish. Pecan pie is a classic sweet American pastry dish.

ALMOND

Highly versatile, almonds are sold in a variety of forms – whole, blanched, flaked, slivered and ground. They are one of the few nuts worth buying ready-processed as their sale turnover is quick, although you should still look for long 'use-by' dates.

Almonds can be used in both savoury and sweet dishes. When ground, they make a base ingredient for nut roasts and burgers (see page 99); left whole or flaked, they are good with grains, in stir-fries, salad or with pasta. Lightly salted or spiced, they make a great snack (see page 364).

Blanch and skin almonds as for pistachios (see page 100).

CHESTNUT

This nut is quite starchy compared with other nuts and has a low fat content. Chestnuts are useful for grinding into nut roasts and bakes, but also work well with vegetable mixtures, particularly leeks and mushrooms, to make savoury fillings for pies. They have a surprisingly sweet flavour; counteract this in savoury dishes by seasoning well with herbs or spices or using shoyu or soy sauce.

Chestnuts are available fresh and dried – both need preparing before use (see below). Ready-cooked chestnuts are often expensive, and some brands of chestnut purée are heavily sweetened.

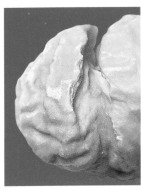

Fresh sweet chestnuts need to be peeled before use. Slit the pointed ends with a sharp knife and place them in a dish with a little water. Cook in a preheated oven, 200°C (400°F), Gas Mark 6, for about 8 minutes. Leave to cool slightly, then peel off the shell and skin. Put the peeled chestnuts in boiling water and simmer for 45–60 minutes. Drain and use as required.

To roast chestnuts in the oven, slit the pointed ends and spread out on a baking sheet. Roast in a preheated oven, 200°C (400°F), Gas Mark 6, for about 20 minutes, or until the shells split open and the chestnuts look golden brown. Leave to cool slightly, then peel off the shell and skin – they are now ready to eat.

Dried chestnuts, which can be good value, need soaking before use. Soak them in a bowl containing twice their volume of water and leave for 1–2 hours. This should give the chestnuts a chance to swell to their original size. Then cook the chestnuts in their soaking water, adding a little more water if necessary. Bring them to the boil, partially cover the pan and cook gently until just tender – about 30–40 minutes. Drain and use as required. Do not throw away the chestnut stock. It can be used instead of vegetable stock, although it has a sweet flavour. The chestnuts and their stock will keep for 3 days in the fridge or can be frozen for several months.

COCONUT

While fresh coconut is fun and a treat to eat, ready-prepared block coconut and coconut milk are more useful cooking ingredients. These add an authentic flavour to Oriental and Indian dishes. Coconut provides a velvet, creamy texture and is especially useful for those who do not want to eat dairy products.

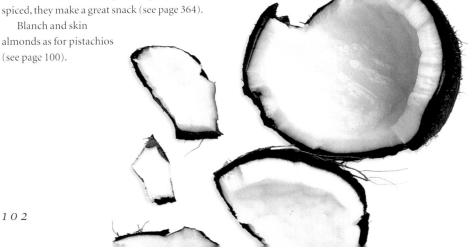

Nuts are an invaluable part of a
vegetarian diet and can be used in
many sweet and savoury dishes.

SUNFLOWER SEEDS

These highly nutritious seeds make
useful garnishes and crunchy
additions to salads especially those
with creamy dressings, such as
coleslaw. Sunflower seeds also go
well with grain dishes, particularly
those based on wheat, rice or millet.

Add the seeds to
breakfast cereals or
to cake and muffin
recipes, and a
handful of seeds
added to a basic
bread dough will
enrich the texture as
well as boosting the
nutritional content.

Toasting brings
out their flavour – do
this in the oven or use
a dry frying pan. To
make a quick snack,
roast the sunflower
seeds in a hot oven, 200°C
(400°F), Gas Mark 6, for
2–3 minutes, then toss the
hot seeds in a little soy
sauce and roast again for a further 2–3 minutes.

To make a quick, nutritious snack,
roast sunflower seeds in soy sauce.

Sunflower seeds are also made into sunflower
butter – similar to peanut butter – which
makes a nutritious spread. Sunflower oil
(see page115) is another by-product
and is a very useful, pleasantly
flavoured oil.

SESAME SEEDS

With their distinctive flavour, these
tiny seeds are an excellent source
of calcium, which is better absorbed
if the seeds are ground or made into
tahini (see below). Toasted sesame
seeds make a great topping for bread,
pizza, savoury bakes and crumbles, and
are also delicious mixed with grains
such as couscous.

Tahini This spread is made from crushed sesame seeds and has
a smooth consistency, rather similar in texture
to peanut butter, and there is usually
a layer of oil on the top,
which should be stirred in
well before use. Tahini can
be light or dark in colour,
depending on the character
of the sesame seeds used,
with the dark variety having
a slightly stronger flavour.
Use tahini to make a quick
dip – mix it with a little
water, then add some
oil, lemon juice, garlic,
shoyu or soy sauce to taste.
Once mixed, it also blends
extremely well with yoghurt.
For a sweet spread, mix tahini
with water, then clear honey or
syrup. In cooking, tahini can be mixed
with bean or lentil purées to
thicken them for burgers or patties.

Tahini will keep for several
months. It does not need to
be refrigerated.

Tahini can be used neat or
mixed with lemon juice,
garlic and other flavourings
to make delicious dips and
savoury spreads.

PUMPKIN SEEDS

These distinctive, smooth,
green seeds work well in
all kinds of salads and stir-
fries, as well as in breakfast
cereals, such as muesli.
They feature in Mexican
cookery – often ground
into pastes and sauces.
Pumpkin seeds can
be eaten straight from the packet, but they are also delicious
lightly toasted. Do this in a dry pan or in the oven,
but watch them carefully as they will colour
quite quickly. You could also toss them in
a little shoyu or soy sauce. Pumpkin
seeds contain polyunsaturated fats as
well as vitamins and iron.

Herbs

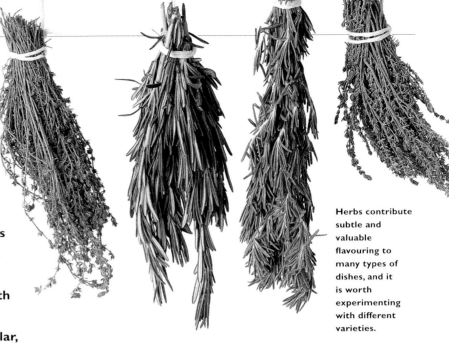

Vital to good vegetarian cooking, herbs are a small but invaluable part of many recipes, adding flavour and aroma to an enormous variety of dishes. There are no hard-and-fast rules as to which herbs to choose as a flavouring. Some clearly have a natural affinity with certain ingredients, for example basil with tomato, or marjoram with mushrooms. Many cuisines favour one herb in particular, as with the widespread use of basil in Italian cookery, parsley in many British recipes, and coriander in both Indian and Mexican dishes.

It is worth trying out a wide range of herbs and there are numerous ways to incorporate them into your cooking. Use them to highlight a flavour, give a subtle undertone or even take a leading role.

Herbs contribute subtle and valuable flavouring to many types of dishes, and it is worth experimenting with different varieties.

Buying and Storing Fresh Herbs

The cheapest way to obtain fresh herbs is to grow your own. Even if you don't have access to a garden, many herbs can be grown in pots on window sills or in tubs in courtyards or on patios. The next best source of fresh herbs is the growing pots found in garden centres and some larger shops or markets. A wide variety of cut fresh herbs is also available. Look carefully through the packets or bunches for any signs of damage or wilting, since herbs, being on the whole leafy, are generally fragile.

In the short term, cut fresh herbs should be stored in the fridge. Delicate varieties benefit from being wrapped in damp kitchen paper. The alternative is to chop their stems and stand them in water like a bunch of flowers. Either way they will last 2–4 days. For longer-term storage try the following ideas.

Growing your own herbs in pots or buying them ready potted up is an easy way to have a ready supply.

Freezing Fresh herbs are suitable for freezing, which works well for more fragile specimens. Freeze whole leaves of basil, chervil, parsley and tarragon. Wrap in polythene and store for up to 3 months.

Herb oil A good use for herbs is to put them in oil. Use a good-quality sunflower or olive oil. Lightly crush the leaves of the herbs of your choice, put them in a jar or bottle and cover with oil. Leave for a couple of weeks at room temperature, shaking the jar occasionally. Then strain into clean jars and use the oil as required. Good herbs for flavouring oil are basil, thyme, rosemary and marjoram.

Herbs imbue olive oil with their flavour. After a couple of weeks the oil will take on a delicate hint of their taste.

Herb vinegar Use the same process as for making herb oils. It takes about 3 weeks for the flavour to develop. Tarragon is a particularly good herb for flavouring vinegar but dill, bay, thyme and garlic also work well.

Home-dried herbs If you find that you have a glut of home-grown herbs, you can dry them easily. Spread out the sprigs on a rack and leave them in a dry, airy place. Once dried, strip off the leaves and store in airtight jars.

In many cases the flavour of a fresh herb is superior to the dried varieties but there are some herbs that still have a good flavour when dried. Herbs that are good when dried include bay, marjoram, oregano, rosemary, thyme and sage.

For home-dried herbs, spread out individual sprigs or leaves on a rack or hang bunches in a dry, airy place.

PARSLEY

Parsley is a splendid, versatile herb with a fresh, slightly spicy flavour. It is robust enough to be added to soups and casseroles to give a good undertone, as well as being suitable for use in large quantities for grain and pasta dishes, or with cooked vegetables and salads. Parsley also works well with mildly flavoured egg dishes.

SAGE

Sage has a powerful flavour, which can overwhelm, so use it with caution. It works well in soups, stews, risotto and pasta dishes. When dried it can have a slightly musty flavour.

ROSEMARY

This is a pungent aromatic herb with a strong flavour. It goes well with food from the Mediterranean, as well as with starchy foods like bread and potatoes. Dried rosemary needles can be quite sharp so be sure to chop them well before using.

THYME

An intensely aromatic herb that needs to be used in small quantities, thyme is useful for adding depth of flavour to soups and casseroles. It can work well with roasted vegetables and tomato-based dishes, and goes with oregano and marjoram. Add small quantities to bread dough or savoury crumbles or pastries.

MARJORAM AND OREGANO

These two herbs come from the same family and are both native to the Mediterranean and so a perfect foil to foods typical of that region, such as tomatoes, aubergines and olives. Both herbs are robust enough to stand a certain amount of cooking and can therefore be used to flavour soups, sauces and stews, as well as grain dishes.

BAY

Bay leaves add a spicy, almond flavour to food. This robust leaf does not break down during the cooking process and is therefore excellent for use in soups and stews. It is best to rub the leaf before adding it to release more flavour – remember to remove it before serving. Bay leaves are also good with grain dishes such as paella or pilaff.

BASIL

This vibrant herb is best known for its use in Italian and Mediterranean cookery. The most familiar variety is sweet basil with its fresh green appearance, soft leaves and evocative, aromatic, slightly spicy flavour. Look out, too, for the anise-flavoured and lemon-scented basils, as well as purple basil, which is good for salads.

Basil combines particularly well with tomatoes, mushrooms, beans and soft cheese. It is also a central ingredient in the classic Genoese sauce, pesto (see page 211).

MINT

A strongly flavoured herb with a clean refreshing taste, mint works well with starchy foods such as potatoes, as well as with grains like bulgar and rice. It is also delicious in yoghurt and, combined with cucumber, makes the classic tzatziki salad. Add mint only at the last minute as its flavour disappears rapidly when subjected to heat. Also look out for mint varieties, such as peppermint or spearmint.

CORIANDER

Fresh coriander is used widely in Mexican, Turkish, Indian and Asian cuisines. It is a herb that goes well with strong flavours such as garlic, ginger and chillies, as well as with milder ingredients, such as avocado. Its heady scent is released the moment you begin chopping, but despite its powerful character the flavour is ruined if subjected to prolonged cooking. It is best to add fresh coriander towards the very end of cooking, or be bold in its use as a garnish.

CHIVES

Chive blades should be springy in texture with an intense green colour. They are members of the onion family and have a very delicate flavour, which disappears on cooking. They are best snipped straight into cold soups and salads or used as a garnish. Chives are versatile, but are particularly good with potatoes, cream-based soups and sauces, eggs and cheese.

TARRAGON

This herb tastes slightly aniseed and it is much more potent when used fresh rather than dried. It works well in egg dishes, as well as with cream sauces for pasta or with creamy risotto. It is also good for herb oils and vinegars. Tarragon is also part of the classic *fines herbes* mixture where it is combined with chives, chervil and parsley.

Even if you don't have a garden, you can grow herbs in terracotta pots. If you put them by your doorstep they will reward you with their delicious aromas every time you walk past.

Herbs can be used alone, with spices or, in many instances, mixed with other herbs to give some wonderful flavours. Classic groups of herbs include bouquet garni with thyme, bay leaf, parsley and rosemary tied together, which can be added to many slow-cooking dishes such as casseroles or soups.

DILL

This feathery, fragrant herb is from the same family as fennel, caraway and anise, all of which have a delicate aniseed flavour. Dill works best if added to cooking at the last minute. It is particularly good with cucumber, and with cream cheese and other mild-tasting dairy products.

CHERVIL

This is a pretty herb with delicate leaves and a slightly aniseed flavour. As well as its affinity with eggs, chervil also acts as a refreshing foil to rich creamy sauces and soups.

SUMMER SAVORY

With its lemony tang, this pungent herb is good with green vegetables, such as French beans, broad beans and asparagus. It partners pulses well because it counteracts their earthy quality.

HERB MIXTURES

These are groups of herbs that work extremely well together.

Bouquet garni
Bouquet garni comprises bay, thyme, parsley and rosemary. These herbs can be tied together or wrapped and tied in a leek leaf. Bouquet garni is especially good in slow-cooking dishes, such as soups, casseroles and homemade stocks.

Fines herbes
This is made up of equal quantities of chives, chervil, parsley and tarragon. The mixture has a natural affinity with eggs, so is delicious in soufflés, omelettes and flan fillings.

Herbs de Provence
Herbs de Provence is a combination of thyme, rosemary, bay, basil and savory – and occasionally lavender – and, as you would expect, works well with vegetables from the Mediterranean.

Parsley mixtures
These last two herb mixtures are based around parsley. Persillade comprises garlic and parsley, which are chopped together and added at the end of cooking. It is good for pepping up a soup, stew or sauce. Gremolada, or gremolata, contains lemon zest combined with the garlic and parsley, and is used in the same way as persillade.

Spices

The bark, seeds, stems, roots and leaves of various aromatic trees and plants are used for spices. With a few exceptions, these are mostly sold dried, but unlike herbs, the drying of spices tends to concentrate, rather than diminish, their flavours. Using spices will not automatically result in hot, fiery dishes. Some spices, such as ginger and chilli, do have fiery characters, but there are also sweet, aromatic and mild spices, for example cinnamon, cumin and paprika. Don't be afraid to experiment.

Aromatic and exotic, spices are sourced from all around the world and can be bought ready ground or whole.

Buying and Storing

Increasingly, fresh spices, such as ginger, lemon grass and chillies, are now available in the shops. Dried spices, however, are more common.

Look out for whole rather than ground dried spices wherever possible. These will generally have a better and longer-lasting flavour, although they do take an extra minute or so in preparation. Although not necessarily altering in appearance over time, whole spices become stale and it is best to use them within a year. Buy spices from somewhere that has a good turnover and look for long 'use-by' dates.

If you buy ready-ground spices, do not keep them too long as their flavour diminishes over 3–6 months. It is best to have an annual clear-out of your cupboards and start again.

Store all spices, whole or ground, in airtight containers away from heat and light, which will diminish their strength.

Spices come from the seeds, roots, stems, bark and leaves of aromatic trees and shrubs.

Cooking with Spices

While some recipes in this book use only a single spice, it is more usual for spices to be used in combination. Certain blends are favoured by a national cuisine, for example lemon grass and ginger in the Orient, cumin and cinnamon in Middle Eastern cuisine and chilli and coriander in many Mexican dishes. Occasionally, a spice can be added at the last minute, such as a dusting of cinnamon, but most spices benefit from being cooked at the start of a recipe so that they release their flavours.

Spices, whole or ground, can be fried with garlic and onion at the beginning of a recipe or simply in the oil before other ingredients are added. It is important to have enough oil so that the spice doesn't scorch. An alternative is to make a spice paste by grinding and mixing the spices with 1 tablespoon of water. Add this paste to hot oil and cook gently so that the spices release their flavours.

When spices are added at the beginning of the cooking time, they blend in and release their flavours fully into the dish.

Dry-Roasting Spices

Dry-roasted spices are doubly useful as they can be added at either the beginning or the end of cooking. They can be used to flavour uncooked dishes such as salsa, which can be pepped up with a little toasted cumin, or a yoghurt sweetened with cardamom and coriander. Dry-roasting takes only a few minutes.

To dry-roast spices, heat a frying pan, add the whole spices and keep shaking the pan as the spices toast and darken. Be careful not to scorch them or they will be bitter.

If dry-roasting in the oven, you need to spread out the spices in a single layer and then shake the baking sheet frequently as they darken. Leave to cool, grind with a pestle and mortar or electric nut mill and use as required.

CUMIN

This pungent, warming spice is extremely versatile, teaming up well with coriander for mild spice combinations, but also complementing chilli for fiery hot dishes. Dry-roasted cumin makes a good addition to cooked vegetable and grain salads.

ALLSPICE

These small, round berries taste like a mixture of cloves, cinnamon and nutmeg. They can be used in savoury dishes – especially those of Caribbean origin – as well as sweet recipes, such as cakes and cookies.

CARAWAY

A strong, aromatic seed, caraway works well on its own but it is also good mixed with paprika. Cook caraway with pulses, cabbage and other brassicas because it aids digestion.

SAFFRON

These orange-red threads constitute the most expensive spice in the world. They yield a warm yellow colour to food, as well as a distinctive aroma. Saffron is used in Spanish and Mediterranean food, as well as in Middle Eastern and Indian cooking. It is good with rice dishes, such as paella and risotto, and with vegetables like fennel and onions. It can also be used to flavour bread and cakes.

FENNEL SEED

With its sweet, slightly aniseed flavour, this tiny, pale green seed can be used in curry dishes as well as in marinades for vegetables and tofu.

Whole spices keep longer than ready-ground. Store them in airtight containers away from heat and light.

CLOVES

Cloves have a penetrating flavour so the tiny buds must be used sparingly. They are mostly used in sweet dishes and with fruit, but are also good with the onion family and with sweet potato and squashes.

CAYENNE PEPPER AND CHILLI POWDER

Cayenne pepper is a very hot, powdered chilli, which needs to be used sparingly. Confusingly, chilli powder is not just ground chillies (see page 57) but contains other spices as well as cayenne pepper. It, too, is very hot.

CINNAMON

A popular and versatile spice used in both savoury and sweet cookery, cinnamon goes well with grain dishes, such as bulgar and couscous, as well as with vegetables such as aubergines and courgettes. It is also delicious with chocolate and can be used for spicing fruit dishes.

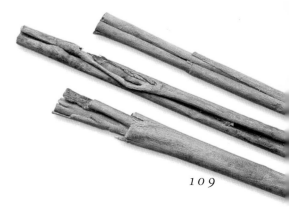

HORSERADISH

This is most readily sold creamed, although in this form it often contains a long list of unwelcome ingredients, such as emulsifiers. Look instead for flaked or dried horseradish, which can be reconstituted with a little water. It is a fiery powerful seasoning, which works well with creamy ingredients, as well as with walnuts, beetroot and onion flavours.

GALANGAL

A member of the same family as ginger, and sharing a similar form and flavour, galangal is used extensively in Indonesian and South-East Asian cookery.

GINGER

This pungent, fiery root is available fresh or ready-ground. Both fresh and dried ginger are used widely in sweet and savoury dishes, especially those from India and the Orient. Look for plump, fresh root ginger. It will keep in the fridge for at least 2 weeks and even longer, although it may begin to dry out. Peel the root before chopping or grating it. The grated pulp can also be squeezed to get drops of the fiery juice. Dried ground ginger should be used sparingly.

PAPRIKA

A brick-red, sweetish, hot spice, generally sold ground, paprika imparts both flavour and colour to food. Its mildness makes it adaptable in that it works well with numerous vegetables, as well as with pulse and grain dishes.

JUNIPER

These sweet pine-scented black berries go well with pungent flavours and can counteract oiliness. Juniper berries combine well with bay, garlic and thyme for a powerful marinade for barbecues.

CORIANDER

This spice goes well with cumin and cinnamon, creating the mild aromatic flavours of Middle Eastern and Indian dishes, including some curries. Coriander is good with both grains and pulses, as well as being an effective ingredient in marinades for vegetables.

LEMON GRASS

Lemon grass is commonly used in South-East Asian cookery. Sold fresh, it is about the size of a pencil and has a delicate hint of lemon. It should be kept in the fridge and used within 2 weeks or it becomes very dry. To use, pull off the papery outside leaves, then chop finely or pound to a paste. Lemon grass can also be used whole to add flavour and should be removed before serving.

Dried lemon grass can be substituted for fresh. If sliced, it needs to be soaked for about 1 hour before use. In powdered or flaked form, it can be used straightaway.

A pestle and mortar is the best tool for grinding single spices or mixtures. It does take a little effort but is worth it for the intense flavours.

LIME LEAVES

Lime leaves for culinary use come from the Kaffir lime, and the fresh leaves give off a citrus-like scent once bruised. Dried leaves are also available in Thai and South-East Asian grocery shops as this flavouring is used in dishes that originate from those regions. Use lime leaves like bay leaves and remove before serving.

CARDAMOM

Cardamom is a mild, perfumed seed used extensively in Indian and Middle Eastern cookery. It is an important component of garam masala, a mellow spice combination used in many savoury dishes, but can also flavour sweet dishes such as cakes and yoghurt. Whole cardamom pods are pale green. Before use, crush them with a pestle and mortar and remove the green husks to leave the black seeds, which can be ground more finely.

MACE

This spice is the outer part of the nutmeg seed and is similar in flavour to nutmeg but more powerful. Mace has an affinity with creamy dishes and is commonly used to flavour milk when making béchamel sauce.

MUSTARD

The mustard seed most commonly used as a cooking spice is brown mustard, also known as black mustard. Dry-roasted seeds are less fiery and are good with many vegetable combinations, as well as with grains. There are a huge number of prepared mustards available (see page 112).

NUTMEG

A warm, nutty flavoured kernel, nutmeg is best bought whole and grated as needed. It can be used in combination with cumin and coriander for mild savoury dishes, and with paprika and caraway for Eastern European mixtures. It is also used in sweet baking.

PEPPERCORNS

Black, white and green peppercorns are all fruits of a tropical climbing vine. Ready-ground, pepper quickly loses its flavour. It is best to keep peppercorns in a mill ready to grind freshly as a seasoning as required.

POPPY SEEDS

Poppy seeds, which can be white or blue, are used widely in Eastern European baking. They are crushed and soaked in milk or water, and add a dry nutty taste to many cakes, strudels and biscuits. Poppy seeds make a pretty decoration for bread and can also enliven a salad with a creamy dressing.

STAR ANISE

Used extensively in Oriental cookery, this attractive spice yields a distinctive aniseed flavour. It is best to dry-roast it before grinding. Star anise is one of the ingredients included in the classic Chinese five-spice powder.

TAMARIND

The dried pods produce a sour lemony-flavoured pulp, which is used in Indian, Oriental and Caribbean dishes. The pulp is often sold dried. To use, break off a walnut-sized piece and soak it in warm water for 10 minutes, then strain and use the resulting murky liquid. Ready-prepared tamarind is also available from specialist shops and large supermarkets.

FENUGREEK

A powerful, penetrating seed used widely in Indian cookery, fenugreek can also be sprouted and used in salads. Fresh fenugreek leaves are small and oval in appearance with a spicy fragrance and pungent flavour. The leaves should be used as soon as possible as they wilt quickly.

TURMERIC

Used for both its colour and flavour, turmeric imparts a yellow hue and a pungent taste. It needs to be used sparingly and is good with grains and pulses, as well as in hot, curry-style dishes.

VANILLA

This spice has a wonderful, floral spicy sweetness and is used to flavour many sweet dishes, especially those with cream or chocolate. Whole pods can be left in sugar to add flavour to the sugar. Otherwise, buy a vanilla extract – beware of vanilla flavourings, which are chemically produced.

Flavourings

Some of the major food groups that are used in a healthy vegetarian diet, particularly pulses and grains, benefit from the addition of extra flavourings. As well as the herbs and spices that have been featured on previous pages, there are a number of other miscellaneous flavourings described here that are well worth getting to know. The plus point of many of these is that you need only small quantities. Because these ingredients have a long shelf life, they are easy to keep in stock.

CAPER

Capers are the tiny, unopened green flower buds of a shrub grown in southern Europe and North Africa, which are picked and packed into jars filled with salt or wine vinegar. They have a piquant flavour, which can counteract oiliness. They go well with garlic and lemon and are great with roasted or griddled vegetables as well as with pizza.

Caper plants grow all around the Mediterranean. The buds are either preserved in vinegar or packed into jars with salt.

OLIVE PASTE

Olive paste is handy for adding to pasta, for spreading on bread, croûtons or hot toast, for mixing with roasted, grilled or griddled vegetables or for serving with mozzarella or goat's cheese.

To create a simple homemade paste, use a blender or food processor to process 250g (8oz) pitted olives with 1–2 tablespoons olive oil. Add 1 tablespoon capers, 2 crushed garlic cloves, 1 tablespoon coriander seeds, and salt and pepper to taste. Spoon into clean jars and cover with extra olive oil. The paste should keep in the fridge for 3–4 weeks.

MUSTARD

This huge range of condiments is prepared from combinations of different types of mustard seed.

English mustard
This powder has turmeric added to give it its characteristic golden colour. Quite fiery, it is useful for adding to cheese or milk-based sauces to enhance the flavour.

Dijon Mustard
Made from black mustard seeds blended with spices and white wine, Dijon mustard ranges in flavour from mild to hot and is classically used in vinaigrette dressing.

Meaux mustard
This crunchy mustard is traditionally sold in pottery jars. It is made from crushed seeds and has a fairly hot flavour. It is good with creamy dressings and sauces, and for adding to marinades and tomato sauces.

German mustard
A smooth mustard made from black seeds, it is often flavoured with tarragon. It is particularly good with green vegetables.

American mustard
A sweet, mild, yellow mustard with a sauce-like consistency, American mustard is great with grilled and roasted vegetables, as well as for barbecue marinades.

STOCK CUBES AND BOUILLON POWDER

There is a whole range of instant stock cubes and bouillon powders suitable for vegetarians. They are useful as a quick flavouring for soups, sauces and casseroles. Some are saltier or have an artificial aftertaste and it is worth trying several brands to find one you like.

YEAST EXTRACT

This highly flavoured ingredient is made from yeast broken down by its own enzymes. It is often sold under a brand name and usually comes in a screw-top jar. It will keep for several months. It can be used as a spread on crackers or bread or to flavour sauces or casseroles, but do use with a light hand as it imparts a strong, distinctive flavour which may overpower everything else. It is a useful source of B-group vitamins, including vitamin B_{12}.

GOMASIO (*GOMASHIO*)

This is made by grinding dry-roasted sesame seeds with salt. If you make your own, you may reduce the salt content to as little as 1 part salt to 10 parts sesame seeds. Gomasio has a nutty flavour and can be used to season or garnish and is especially good with grains. For a variation, add crumbled dry-roasted sea weed, such as kombu (see opposite).

Sun-dried tomatoes may be sold loose
in whole pieces. They benefit from an
hour's soaking in a warm liquid to make
them more tender.

SUN-DRIED TOMATOES AND SUN-DRIED TOMATO PURÉE

Sun-dried tomatoes, whether whole, preserved in oil or in the form of a paste have become a real boon in these days of the flavourless hothouse tomato. These products can add body to a sauce, be finely snipped for a delicious chewy mouthful in a salad or simmered slowly in a casserole.

Those sold in packets without oil are more leathery, although the flavour is the same, but they do need time and liquid to soften them so add them with the liquids at the start of a recipe. Alternatively, soak for about 1 hour in warm liquid.

TRUFFLE

This highly prized, walnut-sized fungus has an intense flavour. Truffles are often sold finely sliced or grated. Use small amounts to flavour sauces and soups, pasta and rice dishes.

Sea Vegetables

The sea's rich harvest has always played a central role in Oriental – particularly Japanese – cookery, but the use of sea vegetables is spreading as their nutritional value and flavouring quality becomes increasingly appreciated elsewhere. Today's dried seaweeds need brief soaking, little or no cooking and have a pleasant salty tang. Seaweed condiments are increasingly available. They can be used to make a quick stock or as a low-sodium alternative to salt.

ARAME

This grows in delicate black fronds and looks very appealing. Soak the arame in warm to hot water for 4–5 minutes. Arame goes well with some of the sweeter vegetables, such as peppers. It is good for stir-fries, salads, pasta and casseroles, or as a dramatic garnish.

DULSE

With purple-reddish fronds, dulse has a salty, slightly spicy flavour. It goes well with both red and green cabbage, and works well in salads and stir-fries. It can also be crumbled and dry-roasted as a condiment.

HIJIKI

Similar to arame but with thicker fronds and stronger in flavour, hijiki takes 15–20 minutes to soak and should expand to three times its original volume. Sauté or stir-fry it with vegetables.

KOMBU

Used to make clear Japanese soup, this has fairly wide black stems when fresh but can look rather grey when dried. Rinse well and use in small pieces to flavour soups, stews and casseroles. Remove it before serving as you would a bay leaf.

WAKAME

This mildly flavoured seaweed has long green fronds and a silky texture. It can be used in soups or salads or mixed with a variety of cooked vegetables. It can also be dry-roasted and crumbled, then crushed with seeds or nuts to make a condiment. Rinse wakame well then soak in cold water for 4–5 minutes before using.

NORI

Grown in tidal waters on nets, this seaweed is sold in sheets. It can be toasted until it changes colour and then crumbled and used as a seasoning or garnish. It is also wrapped around rice, to make sushi, a tasty Japanese finger food (see page 281).

AGAR AGAR

Sold in flakes or powder this can be used in virtually the same way as powdered gelatine to make jelly. Use 2 teaspoons to set approximately 600ml (1 pint) liquid. It must be boiled or it won't set. Setting recipes that contain egg white – as in a cold soufflé, for example – is more problematic as agar agar's ability to set is affected by egg white. Instead, try serving semi-frozen soufflé or versions more like a soft mousse.

NUTRITIONAL VALUE

All sea vegetables are rich sources of minerals, especially potassium and sodium. More unusually, they contain a significant amount of iodine. This mineral is important for the functioning of the thyroid gland, and is now thought to be beneficial for other glands, too.

Oil

Oil is more than just a cooking medium – it also adds flavour, acts as a seasoning and can be nutritionally beneficial. There is a huge range of culinary oils, extracted from a number of plants and seeds, now available. Unrefined, or cold-pressed, and refined, or pure, are some of the terms used to describe oils. These terms refer to the process of extraction, rather than quality.

NUTRITIONAL VALUE

Oils are fats that remain liquid at room temperature. When unrefined they contain vitamins and minerals, especially vitamin E. The fat content of most vegetable oils is polyunsaturated, or monounsaturated in the case of olive oil. Sunflower and safflower oil are high in polyunsaturated fats and are good sources of vitamin E; coconut and palm oils are saturated fats, while groundnut oil is about 50% monounsaturated and 30% saturated fat. Refined oil has the lowest nutritional value.

Unrefined Versus Refined Oils

Unrefined oils have not been subjected to any more processing than is needed to extract the oil from the nut or seed. Nor have they been subjected to chemical treatments. Consequently, they often have a stronger taste and smell. They are sometimes called cold-pressed oils, which refers to the method of extraction.

In contrast, a selection of chemicals is used to extract and produce refined oil. The resultant oil has also been bleached and deodorised and has, in effect, become a virtually tasteless, colourless product of little nutritional value. The flavouring is put back afterwards.

Buying and Storing

Oils are best stored in cool, dry places, away from heat and sunlight. Heat, light and oxygen can all oxidise oil, causing it to smell sour and taste rancid. Rancid oil should be thrown away. If you use up oil fairly quickly, it shouldn't become rancid but treat precious oils, which you won't use so frequently, with great care.

Keep a small container with your favourite cooking oils near your cooker. Refill as necessary. If you keep an oil in the fridge, it will congeal to a certain extent and then need time to warm up before it can be properly mixed into dressings.

OLIVE OIL

The versatility of olive oil makes it ideal for all sorts of culinary purposes. It heats well for frying and cooking and tastes good enough to mix into dressings and dips. Olive oil is produced in many countries and one variety can taste and look quite different from another. It is certainly worth trying several varieties as you may prefer one flavour to another. Because olive oil is monounsaturated, it is more stable and less vulnerable to rancidity than polyunsaturated oils.

A huge number of oils extracted from different sources such as olives, sunflower seeds or nuts are now available. They each have distinctive, subtle flavours and some can be used in all types of cooking; others are best used as flavourings.

Buying and storing Olive oil is commonly categorised as virgin, extra virgin or pure oil. Virgin and extra virgin olive oil have not been treated, heated or chemically processed and are graded according to acidity – the highest grade has the lowest acidity and is therefore the best oil. This is known as extra virgin. Virgin olive oil is slightly more acidic. The cheapest olive oil is called pure olive oil and is generally of a lighter colour. This is made from refined olive oil mixed with some virgin oil to give a little colour and flavour. This type of oil is suitable when you need a bland cooking oil.

You may come across very expensive estate-bottled olive oil made from olives grown on a single estate and therefore, like wine from a particular vineyard, having a unique flavour. It is certainly worth using this oil in recipes where the flavour will shine through, as in a salad or a dressing. Do not cook with it, however, because any heat will alter the flavour.

As mentioned opposite, store olive oil in cool conditions.

The seeds of the cheerful sunflower provide a good all-purpose oil that is light with a pleasant flavour. Use it for both cooking – it will stand heating to high temperatures – and for salad dressings or drizzling over food as a flavouring.

SUNFLOWER OIL

This all-purpose oil can be used for cooking, as well as for making dressings and vinaigrettes. It is good for frying as it has a high smoking point and resistance to oxidation. Refined versions of this oil have a delicate flavour, while unrefined, or cold-pressed, oils have more character but not one that will overwhelm the dish.

GROUNDNUT (PEANUT) OIL

This is commonly sold as a refined oil and therefore lacks character, although it is possible to find roasted groundnut oil, which has more flavour. It can be used rather like sesame oil and drizzled over hot vegetables as a seasoning.

It is thought that the process of refining oil removes the peanut protein believed to be responsible for triggering an allergic reaction. However, should you be allergic to peanuts, it is important to read labels carefully as peanut oil is widely used in processed foods. If in any doubt, avoid these products.

SAFFLOWER OIL

Pale in colour with a delicate nutty flavour, this is interchangeable with sunflower oil, although not widely available. It is used for frying and, unrefined, can be good as a base ingredient for salad dressings. The oil is high in polyunsaturates.

CORN OIL

Cheap to produce, corn oil is almost tasteless. Occasionally, you may find an unrefined version, which has a hint of corn. Corn oil is very popular in Mexican cookery for frying tortillas; it can be used in cooking generally, particularly where corn is one of the ingredients.

NUT OILS

Use these oils for seasoning rather than for general-purpose cooking, as they are expensive and their flavours are lost when heated to any degree. The best way to savour them is to drizzle them over fresh vegetables or mix them into dips, dressings and vinaigrette.

Nut oils are made from roasted nuts, which are pressed to release their flavour. The colour of the final oil will depend on the degree of toasting. As with most oils, it is worth experimenting to discover your favourite.

Treat nut oils as a seasoning rather than a cooking ingredient. Their flavour is shown off best when sprinkled over salads or lightly cooked vegetables.

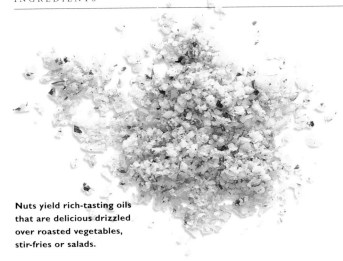

Nuts yield rich-tasting oils that are delicious drizzled over roasted vegetables, stir-fries or salads.

HAZELNUT OIL

This rich, heavy oil is gold or deep gold in colour with the sweet, strong accent of the hazelnut.

WALNUT OIL

Walnut oil has a bronze-gold colour with a rich fragrance. You can mix a small quantity of walnut oil with other oils and still get a walnut flavour coming through.

SESAME OIL

This is sold both toasted and untoasted. The untoasted has a pale colour and a delicate flavour. Toasting the sesame seeds prior to extraction intensifies the flavour and the oil is consequently darker with a stronger flavour – ranging in colour from russet to deep brown. Use sparingly as a garnish for grains and vegetable dishes. Sesame oil has a natural affinity with ginger, lime and soy sauce.

Other Oils

There are always new products to be found. Oils are no exception and you may find avocado, pumpkin seed or truffle oil. It is worth experimenting with these oils as flavourings, especially if you are able to buy them in small quantities.

MARGARINE

It is important to check labels carefully when buying margarine since many contain animal fat or fish oil. Some additives used in margarine are also not from sources acceptable to vegetarians. Margarines are generally about 80% fat, much of which is polyunsaturated but it depends on the processing and types of oil used.

There is debate about the healthiness of margarine because during its manufacture, liquid fats have to be hydrogenated to become solid. Some scientists believe this process turns relatively healthy polyunsaturates into transfats, which are thought to be as harmful as saturated fats.

INFUSED OILS

Flavoured oils are very simple to make – simply infuse oil with your chosen flavouring. The best results are achieved by using olive oil for its strong, aromatic undertones. Use a clean, preferably sterilised bottle with a cork or screw-top. The flavours will take a week or so to develop. Flavoured oils can be used, unadulterated, in your cooking where they will be noticed, for example, over freshly steamed or grilled vegetables.

Garlic oil
Mince 3–4 garlic cloves. Cover with oil and leave for 1 week. Garlic oil is good with pizza (see page 196) and pasta.

Chilli oil
Use 3–4 red or green chillies in 500ml (17fl oz) oil. You can also add whole, peeled garlic cloves and peppercorns for extra flavour. Leave for 2 weeks. Chilli-flavoured oils are great used with barbecue food or for perking up a casserole or grain dish.

Herb oil
Use 6–8 tablespoons chopped herbs to flavour 500ml (17fl oz) oil. Thyme, marjoram, oregano, parsley and bay all work well (see also page 104). Herb-flavoured oils are marvellous in salads.

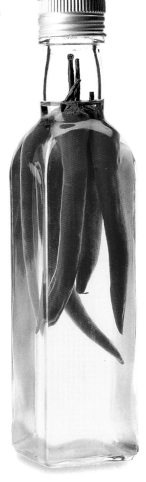

Infusing oils with different flavourings is extremely easy to do. Garlic, chilli and various herbs can be used and the process takes a week or so.

It is worth looking out for brands of margarine with a 'no hydrogenated fat' label and checking whether transfats are listed.

SOLID VEGETABLE FAT

Solid vegetable fat is a vegetarian alternative to lard. It is, however, a saturated fat and so it should be used only sparingly. It is most suitable for making pastry.

Vinegar

Vinegar works well with many vegetarian recipes. It is commonly used to counteract oil in a vinaigrette, but is also used in marinades, for enhancing sauces and for complementing the earthy flavours of beans and grains, or for sprinkling over food as a seasoning.

Vinegar is a versatile flavouring.

Nutritional Value

Vinegar contains some useful enzymes and minerals. It is also reputed to have antiseptic and antibiotic properties.

Buying and Storing

There is a wide range of vinegars to choose from and it is handy to have at least two different flavours in your store cupboard. Luckily, vinegars are designed to keep for at least 6 months, if not longer. Try to keep them away from heat and light, both of which will gradually cause the flavour to deteriorate.

RED AND WHITE WINE VINEGAR

These will vary in character depending on how they are made. Traditional methods take longer and are more expensive; faster processes usually involve heat and inevitably some of the flavours are lost. A good wine vinegar will bear some resemblance to the wine from which it comes so that you can find full-blown red wine vinegar at one end of the flavour spectrum and a delicate champagne vinegar at the other end.

APPLE CIDER VINEGAR

Low in acidity, this gentle mild vinegar should have a delicate apple undertone. It is worth looking out for organic, unfiltered varieties. These have a more lively, fruity character, which can make all the difference to a dressing. Use cider vinegar in barbecue or tomato sauces. When used with honey it is a good remedy for a sore throat.

BALSAMIC VINEGAR

Balsamic vinegar has not been allowed to ferment and therefore stays comparatively sweet. It is made from the juice of Trebbiano grapes, with a vinegar 'mother' – the technical term for a starter – and some wine vinegar added. It is then stored in wooden barrels. At the end of a year, the vinegar is moved to barrels of a different wood. It loses some of its volume but also takes on some of the flavour of the wood. This ageing process can go on for more than 20 years, the liquid gradually reducing to a thick, syrupy consistency. A good balsamic vinegar is usually aged for at least 5 years – the longer the ageing time, the more potent the flavour. Cheaper balsamic vinegar has more wine vinegar added.

Trebbiano grapes provide the basis for balsamic vinegar.

Balsamic vinegar can be mixed with oil to make a dressing, or used on its own to add a delicious sweetness to vegetables and salads. It is particularly good with the sweeter vegetables, such as tomatoes or peppers because it doesn't overwhelm them.

SHERRY VINEGAR

This is an aromatic sweet vinegar from Jerez in Spain. Like balsamic vinegar, it is mellow enough to be used neat on vegetables. It is particularly good with sautéed mushrooms, roasted peppers and courgettes. It can also be added to dressings.

RICE WINE VINEGAR

This vinegar comes in a range of colours and flavours, depending on its country of origin and whether the rice is white or brown. It is generally on the sweet side, the brown rice varieties being fuller in flavour.

Infused Vinegars

Since vinegar is an excellent medium for preserving delicate flavours, it is hardly surprising that all sorts of fruit and herb vinegars can be found, or indeed made at home. The most common are perhaps raspberry and tarragon.

RASPBERRY VINEGAR

Use roughly 500g (1lb) fruit to 500ml (17fl oz) white wine vinegar. Crush the fruit gently, pour over vinegar, then cover with a cloth. Leave to infuse for 1 week, stirring daily, then strain by allowing the mixture to drip through a muslin-lined sieve rather than pressing it, and bottle.

TARRAGON VINEGAR

Put several sprigs of tarragon in a bottle of good-quality white wine or cider vinegar and leave for 1–2 weeks. If the herbs start to look a little grey-green, strain into a clean bottle.

Sweeteners

Sweeteners are not a mainstay of a vegetarian diet but they are useful ingredients for home baking as well as being used in many desserts.

There is a whole family of sweeteners from pure white sugar to black treacle. Pure white sugar is only a sweetener and offers very little nutritionally apart from calories. Because many vegetarians are concerned about the healthiness of their diet, they tend to favour less refined sugars and also to look for sugar substitutes that have more flavour and more to offer from a nutritional point of view. These include syrups, malt extracts and fruit concentrates, all of which are described here. This section also includes a look at chocolate and carob.

NUTRITIONAL VALUE

In general, sweeteners offer mostly calories and little else. Much 'brown' sugar is merely white sugar coloured with caramel or a little molasses.

Unrefined cane sugar is between 87 and 96% sucrose and retains some useful B group vitamins and minerals. It also has a perceptible flavour. Treacle and molasses contain small amounts of some minerals and vitamins. Syrups, such as maple syrup and malt extract, also contain minerals. Honey has a slightly different composition from cane or beet sugar but is no better as a source of nutrients.

Remember, food high in sugar should make up only a small part of your overall diet. In many recipes you can cut down the quantity of sugar you use as you gradually become accustomed to a less sweet taste. You can also try sweetening with purées made from dried fruit or using fruit juice concentrates instead of sugar, although these are not appropriate in every recipe. If you like sweet cakes and desserts, try cutting down by alternating them with fresh fruit.

SUGAR

Sugar ranges from fine, powdery icing sugar to dark brown crystals. Fine sugars blend or dissolve more easily; coarse sugars can add crunch to cookies and flapjacks.

Granulated and caster sugar Granulated sugar is a light, free-flowing sugar used to sweeten sauces and cereals; golden granulated has a slightly buttery taste. Caster sugar is fine grained and free-flowing and can be used extensively in baking. Golden caster sugar has a similar taste to golden granulated sugar.

Brown sugars Demerara is a brown sugar with large crystals. It is slightly sticky and has a rich aroma. It is delicious as a sweetener and can be used in baking when the sugar is melted.

Light muscovado is a pale brown, soft sugar with a fudge-like flavour. Dark muscovado is a sugar rich in natural molasses, which gives it a sticky texture and rich flavour. It is good for strongly flavoured cakes, such as fruit cake or ginger cake, or for sweetening dark sauces, when colour is as important as taste.

Molasses is the residue from the sugar-refining process. It has a powerful flavour but is not particularly sweet.

HONEY

Honey is twice as sweet as sugar, so you should use less of it. The best honey comes from a single named flower or a small producer. The darker and more aromatic the honey, the stronger its flavour. Much commercial honey has been overheated to keep it runny, a process that can reduce the flavour and nutrients.

Honey keeps well, although it may crystallise in which case heat it gently before using.

Honey is sold in many different forms, some of which include the honeycomb as an indication that the product has not been processed.

MAPLE SYRUP

Maple syrup is a delicious sweetener, which can be used in all kinds of recipes, sweet and savoury. It comes from the sugar maple tree. It takes some 50 gallons (227 litres) of sap to make 1 gallon (4.5 litres) of syrup so it is a very concentrated form of sweetening. Make sure you get the real thing, rather than a maple-flavoured syrup, which will contain only a percentage of maple syrup. Store it in a cool place.

MALT EXTRACT

Sometimes known as barley syrup, this is not as sweet as sugar. It has a pleasant but distinctive flavour and can be used for baking and flavouring hot drinks.

PALM SUGAR (JAGGERY)

Tasting rather like a muscovado sugar, jaggery is the name given to a range of sugars used in India and South-East Asia. Many are made from sugar cane but the palm sugars are highly flavoured and quite aromatic.

Sugar-free jams and spreads are sweetened with concentrated fruit purées and contain no added sugar.

SUGAR-FREE JAMS AND SPREADS

Available in specialist shops, these are often simply highly concentrated fruit purées. They can be used in place of ordinary jam as a spread but are also used to sweeten fruit sauces, or creamed into margarine as a sugar substitute when making cakes or biscuits.

CONCENTRATED FRUIT JUICE

Apple is the most common of the fruit juice concentrates but there are several different flavours available, such as apple, strawberry or pear. Highly concentrated with a syrup-like texture, these are useful for sweetening dressings and sauces and for using in fruit salads and compotes, as well as for baking and bread making.

CHOCOLATE

Good-quality chocolate usually has a high percentage of cocoa solids and consequently less additions, such as vegetable fat. The high cocoa solids content also means there is less room for sweetening so this type of chocolate can be quite bitter.

Chocolate will vary from one brand to another. Much will depend on how it is made, how the cocoa beans are selected, dried and roasted and, finally, how they are ground and mixed to make the chocolate. The slower the final grinding and mixing, the smoother the final texture will be. There should be no powdery aftertaste.

Store chocolate in a cool dry place at about 14–16°C (57–61°F).

Dark chocolate has a higher percentage of cocoa solids and consequently less sweetening, so it may taste more bitter than milk chocolate.

CAROB POWDER

Carob powder comes from seeds contained in large pods the size of a banana. Carob is naturally sweeter than cocoa powder, has no caffeine and has a lower fat content. Carob powder can be substituted for cocoa powder – start by using about half the amount as it tends to turn mixtures very dark. Carob chocolate is also available in specialist shops, often in a variety of flavours.

Originating in the eastern Mediterranean, carob beans come from large pods. The beans are finely ground and the resulting powder can sometimes be used as a substitute for cocoa.

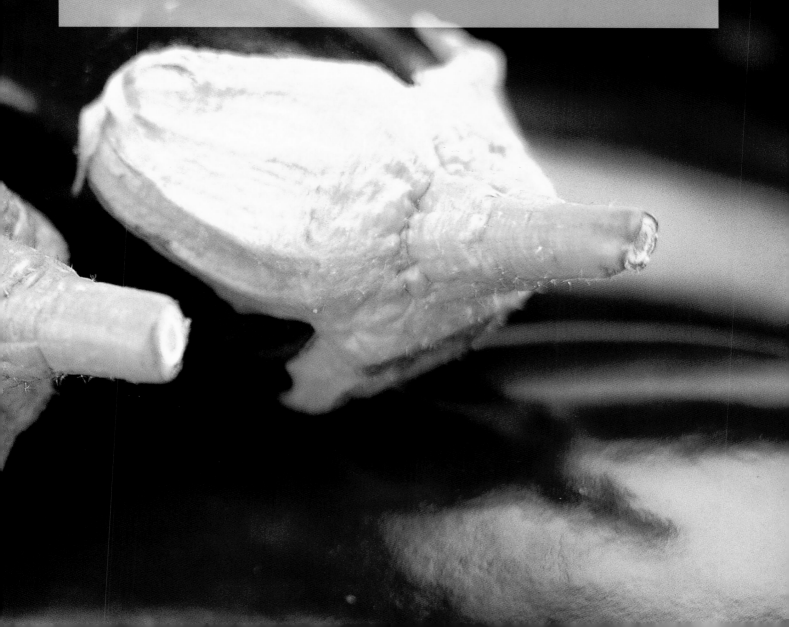

THE VEGETARIAN KITCHEN

This section looks at ways to make vegetarian cooking as simple as possible – whether on a daily or weekly basis. There are three main factors that help make organising, planning and cooking vegetarian food much easier. First, it is useful to have the right ingredients to hand, be it in your store cupboard, fridge or freezer; second, it is good to have the right equipment and, finally, it helps to have a sense of how you are going to organise a recipe, in terms of choosing a suitable technique and knowing some shortcuts. This next section covers these three points, as well as looking at specific situations you may want to cater for on a day-to-day basis.

The store cupboard

It is worth taking the trouble to build up a comprehensive store of staples, as well as some more unusual items that won't go off. If you refer to the descriptions of individual ingredients, you'll see that many of the basic foodstuffs will keep for several months.

Once you have plenty of ingredients to hand, you can choose from a wider variety of recipes, ringing the changes and improvising if necessary. This takes some of the headache out of meal planning. Basic stocks also save you from having to make frequent shopping trips.

Essentials

The following checklist of ingredients with a long shelf life is meant to give you an idea of some of the most useful items to have on hand in the kitchen, rather than being a definitive list of items to keep in stock. Remember to check on your stocks occasionally, top them up and always check the 'use-by' dates so that you use your supplies in the right order.

Wholegrains Have a choice of rice, such as a basmati and a risotto rice, and at least one other wholegrain, such as buckwheat, millet or quinoa.

Processed grain products Bulgar, couscous and polenta are all worth keeping in stock. Not only are they quick-cooking staples, but they can also be presented in numerous ways and work well with a great variety of ingredients.

Flakes These are useful for breakfast cereals, crumble toppings and baking. Oat flakes are the most versatile.

Pasta A variety of shapes and flavours is appealing, and you need only a quick sauce to make a meal.

Flour It is useful to have a strong flour for bread making and an ordinary flour for making pastry, cakes and sauces. Cornmeal is used for cobbler topping, polenta and cornbread. Buy specialist flour, such as gram flour, only when needed and then don't forget to use it up.

Pulses Quick-cooking pulses that don't need soaking, such as Puy and split red lentils, are certainly handy for last-minute meals. A selection of canned beans – chickpeas, red kidney and pinto beans – for making quick casseroles or substantial salads is useful. Dried pulses have a long shelf life and are also worth cooking in bulk and freezing (see page 92).

Many of the staples of a vegetarian diet have a long shelf life if kept appropriately.

Nuts and seeds Keep two or three of your favourite varieties in stock. Whole cashews, hazelnuts, almonds and walnuts are all good for savoury dishes, salads and in baking and desserts. Seeds, such as sunflower seeds, make good toppings and add extra protein to salads and breakfast cereals.

Dried or vacuum-packed chestnuts have long 'use-by' dates; ground almonds are useful for pâtés, sweet baking and in savoury mixtures. Nut butters, such as tahini and peanut butter, are good for dips, dressings and sauces.

Oils Keep a good-quality olive oil and a sunflower oil for general-purpose cooking and making salad dressings. Have smaller quantities of specialist oils, such as sesame or walnut oil and unusual olive oil, for flavouring for special occasions.

Tomatoes It is useful to have a choice of tomato products on hand, such as canned tomatoes, smooth passata and sun-dried tomatoes – in oil, dried or ready-prepared as a purée or paste.

Miscellaneous flavourings As well as a selection of your favourite dried herbs and spices, keep some shoyu or soy sauce, dried mushrooms, pesto, black peppercorns and at least one mild vinegar, such as red or white wine vinegar. These are all essential flavouring products.

Sweeteners Fruit juice concentrates such as concentrated apple juice are useful for both sweet and savoury recipes. Other sweeteners to keep in stock are honey, good-quality unrefined sugar, maple syrup and stem ginger.

Dried fruit and nuts are great both for nutritious nibbles and for adding to both sweet and savoury recipes.

Canned food All canned food has a long shelf life and, in addition to tomatoes, the following are particularly adaptable and can be used in numerous ways: artichoke hearts, olives, water chestnuts and sweetcorn.

Dried fruits Keep a selection of the larger dried fruits, such as apricots, peaches and pears, as well as sultanas and raisins, for use in savoury dishes, sweet baking and desserts.

Keeping a variety of fresh ingredients in the fridge will make it much easier for you to plan and produce meals.

Refrigerated Staples

Although it is best to shop regularly for fresh produce, there are still several items that have a useful shelf life in the fridge. The following checklist is of fresh food items frequently used in vegetarian cooking and useful to have in stock:

- Butter
- Eggs
- Selection of hard and soft cheese
- Crème fraîche/yoghurt/soured cream
- Regular tofu
- Margarine
- Fresh pasta
- Bean sprouts

'Fresh' Produce

Stored properly, using the guidelines in the ingredients section, the following are some useful varieties of fruit and vegetables that should keep for more than a few days:

- Onions, garlic and shallots
- Carrots and other root vegetables
- Squash
- Potatoes
- Lemons and other citrus fruit

It is best to eat many vegetables and some fruit as soon as possible after purchase, but there are exceptions and you can use this to your advantage in terms of having ingredients in stock. Plan to use ingredients such as avocado, bananas, pears, tomatoes and mango or papaya several days after you buy them to give them a chance to ripen properly.

USING THE FREEZER

When used well, a freezer can not only save you time and money but also act as an extension to your store cupboard. Below is a reminder of some ingredients that freeze well.

- Nuts – up to 1 year
- Ready-cooked pulses – up to 6 months
- Ready-cooked grains such as rice – up to 6 months
- Vegetables, such as sweetcorn, green beans and leaf spinach – up to 1 year (if blanched their freezer life is longer as certain bacteria and enzymes that cause deterioration have been destroyed)
- Fresh herbs – up to 6 months
- Fruits, such as raspberries – up to 1 year; fruit purée of apple or apricot, up to 6 months
- Double or whipping cream, frozen in small quantities – up to 3 months (the higher the fat content, the better it will freeze)
- Hard cheese – 3–6 months (best frozen grated as it becomes crumbly on thawing)
- Soft cheese, such as Brie – 3–6 months (needs plenty of time to defrost)
- Pastry, including filo pastry – up to 3 months
- Crumble toppings – up to 2 months
- Pancakes – up to 6 months
- Bread
- Fresh pasta

The following foods will not freeze: *hard-boiled eggs, single cream, salad ingredients, mayonnaise and cottage cheese. Also be guided by packet instructions on foods.*

COOKING FROM FROZEN

Vegetables and small savouries are best cooked from frozen. Sauces, soups and casseroles should be best left overnight or defrosted in the microwave. Grains such as rice need to be thawed for about 1 hour at room temperature or defrosted in the microwave.

FREEZING COOKED MEALS

In general, most vegetarian dishes are suitable for freezing as long as you bear in mind the following points about storage.

Make sure the quality of the food you are intending to freeze is good. Although freezing is a way of preserving food, it will not enhance a product so, if you have bought too many vegetables or made too much casserole, freeze it straightaway while still in peak condition.

Food to be frozen must be very well wrapped since exposure to the air will cause deterioration. Use fast freezing for the initial freezing as then only small ice crystals are formed, which are less likely to damage the structure of the food.

Fatty foods and dishes with a high fat content should not be frozen for long because they may go rancid.

The flavour of salt becomes stronger on freezing so use a light hand when seasoning foods that you know you are going to freeze. Dishes that are heavily spiced or make plentiful use of herbs may also change flavour if frozen for too long.

When stored properly some fruit and vegetables will last for more than a few days.

Equipment

Every keen cook has his or her own favourite piece of equipment or gadget, and deciding what is essential is a personal affair. It is important to have the right tools for the job, but this has to be set against the storage space you have available and your budget. This section looks at small- and large-scale equipment, as well as electrical appliances, to help you decide what is most useful and what is worth having if you have the space and finance.

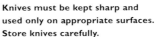

Knives must be kept sharp and used only on appropriate surfaces. Store knives carefully.

Useful Utensils

There are certain essential items in the kitchen. Good knives and a solid chopping board are invaluable. A medium-sized knife can do many jobs but knives of various lengths are better. A small, sharp knife is useful for trimming, paring and peeling. A large blade means you can chop and slice a quantity at a time. A serrated blade is useful for slicing and peeling soft fruit and vegetables such as tomatoes, and a large serrated knife slices bread.

Store knives carefully so as not to damage yourself or the blades. Sharpen them regularly with a steel. Get a large chopping board but ensure that you can lift it comfortably. If you have chopped strong-flavoured items, such as onion, garlic or chilli, make sure the board is very well washed. A second board is a good option, if you have room.

Other useful, small-scale utensils include the following:

- Measuring cups, spoons and jugs
- Nut and cheese grater
- Squeezer and zester
- Salad spinner
- Whisk
- Sturdy garlic press
- Good-sized pastry brush
- Pestle and mortar
- An effective vegetable peeler
- Kitchen scissors
- Tongs

Cookware

It is worth spending money on good cookware: a selection of saucepans – including one large enough for cooking family quantities of pasta – and large and small frying pans. A pressure cooker is useful if you intend cooking batches of beans and large quantities of soups and stews. Modern brands are easier to use than older ones.

A steamer, consisting of a purpose-built pan and steaming basket combination, is useful as it is easy to check that the pan is not boiling dry. Similarly, three-layered Oriental steamers allow you to cook several vegetables at once, adding others as necessary. A trivet or steaming basket that fits inside a saucepan is an inexpensive alternative and electric steamers are available for those with plenty of space.

A wok is great for crisp, quick stir-frying. This wide, round-based frying pan is made of thin metal, which heats up quickly and provides a good-sized cooking surface. However, you can improvise with a large frying pan.

Other useful items include a sturdy roasting tin or baking sheet and good-quality bakeware. Non-stick tins are useful, otherwise line tins with reusable baking parchment to ensure easier washing-up.

Good quality cookware is well worth the money, as it will last, even if used frequently.

Having the right tools for the job makes preparation and cooking quicker and easier.

Electrical Appliances

These appliances generally make food preparation quicker and easier. In some instances manually operated machines are a reasonable alternative.

Blender Blenders save a great deal of time, don't take up too much space and take all the hard work out of making puréed soups and smooth sauces. It is useful to have a separate small mill for grinding nuts and breadcrumbs. A hand-held electric blender is good for puréeing small quantities. Use it directly in the pan or pour the liquid to be processed into a tall jug. Non-electric alternatives include a food mill or mincer.

Food processor In some ways the food processor is the blender's big brother – both in terms of size and the number of jobs it can do. Its functions include blending, grating and slicing, rubbing in fat and making all-in-one cake mixtures. It is good for processing relatively large quantities. Some processors come with a smaller inner unit for dealing with small quantities. Make full use of your food processor by keeping it somewhere handy, otherwise just the thought of getting it out can put you off using it. Plan your jobs so that you process dry ingredients before wet ones; in this way you'll save time on dismantling, cleaning and reassembling the processor.

Electric juicer This is a costly appliance, but worth it if you have access to good supplies of fruit and vegetables. Really good fruit and vegetable juices are impossible to make any other way.

Pasta maker See pages 208–9 for instructions on making pasta by hand and by machine. Electric machines are expensive and best for pasta devotees, but manual machines are easy to use and achieve good results. They are also not too bulky to store.

Yoghurt maker Although you can make yoghurt with a vacuum flask, an electric version ensures that the temperature is constant and more consistent results are achieved.

Microwave Treat your microwave as an appliance that can speed up all sorts of stages in cooking, as well as occasionally being the best way to cook something from start to finish. When tackling a recipe you do not have to stick to conventional methods of cookery, such as the oven or the hob, or use the microwave the whole time. Choose the best method at each stage of the recipe and you will end up saving time and making better use of your kitchen equipment.

It is useful to have a microwave where you can choose a variety of temperatures, including one that is suitable for defrosting (see below).

Use your microwave for a whole range of processes. Vegetables cooked in the microwave retain a good proportion of their nutrients. You can infuse milk and make stocks and sauces in the microwave; roux-based sauces are less likely to stick or burn when cooked this way. You can toast nuts and seeds, reconstitute dried fruit, for example plumping up sultanas or raisins for a salad or cake, and processed cereals, such as bulgar and polenta, cook quickly in the microwave.

The microwave is also good for defrosting, for which most microwaves have a special setting. When freezing food that you might wish to defrost in the microwave, use straight-sided, shallow, rather than deep, dishes, so that the food gets maximum exposure. Round dishes are better than square ones. For easier defrosting of liquids, use a close-fitting container so that the outsides cannot thaw and spread out to overcook or evaporate. Remember, the greater the bulk of food and the more dense it is, the longer it will take to defrost.

Electric blenders save an enormous amount of time when making smooth soups and sauces or quick purées of fruit.

Meal planning

Curiously, the myth still persists that vegetarian food is more complicated or time-consuming to prepare. The truth is that there are just as many shortcuts with regard to techniques and ingredients as in any other cuisine. If you are not familiar with vegetarian ingredients, cooking the recipes will take longer but the more you cook with them, the quicker and easier it will become. You will start to use foods without thinking and develop an intuitive sense of what you like to serve with what. Here are lots of tips and advice for planning, preparing and cooking vegetarian meals. For planning more elaborate meals, see the section on entertaining (pages 342–377).

Efficient Cooking

There are some general principles that underlie all efficient cooking. Bear these points in mind and you will undoubtedly be more organised when you cook.

- Read the recipe. It sounds obvious but it is best to check beforehand whether anything needs soaking for a couple of hours, time to chill and so on. It is also worth finding out if any of the stages can be prepared in advance.

- Have all your ingredients within reach before you start. If you are intending to use equipment, have it to hand, not at the back of the cupboard.

- Make use of food processors and other electrical gadgets for dealing with large quantities.

A vegetarian stir-fry is one of the quickest and most nutritious meals. The possible ingredients are infinitely variable.

- If possible, use equipment in an order that saves you excess washing-up – generally, this means using dry ingredients first. Using reusable baking parchment to line roasting tins and baking sheets saves washing unwieldy tins.

- When preparing food, keep the work surface clear so that you can see what you are doing. Have a bowl or bag handy for sticking in all the vegetable peelings and trimmings as you work to minimise clearing-up time. While one thing is cooking, be preparing the next. The exception to this is a stir-fry, when you need to have everything prepared and to hand, ready to cook.

- If you double the recipe quantity this does not take double the time. If you are making a staple recipe, such as tomato sauce or a favourite casserole, make twice as much so that you can freeze or store some for another time.

Because of the quick cooking time for stir-fries, it is important to prepare all the ingredients in advance before you start to cook.

Quick Meals

Whether you plan ahead or are a spur-of-the-moment cook, it is useful to have in mind an idea of what can be put together simply and quickly, and where and how to make shortcuts.

Certain ingredients and recipe ideas are quick both to prepare and to cook. Most stir-fry vegetables fall into this category – a protein with nuts, bean sprouts or tofu, and serve with quick-cooking noodles. Couscous can be flavoured with chopped herbs and served with a quick vegetable sauté, or serve pasta with herb butter or oil or with Oriental flavourings. Cook bulgar to serve as an accompaniment or for a pilaf or salad base. Use quick-cooking lentils and serve them refried with tortillas or nachos, or spiced as a dhal with naan bread. Any omelette and basic egg dishes are quick to make, while canned pulses are ready to use and ideal in a number of quick meals.

Recipe ideas that are quick to prepare but take time to cook include most casseroles, baked potatoes, layered vegetable gratin and one-pot grain dishes, such as paella.

Bulgar wheat takes only a matter of minutes to cook.

New to Vegetarian Food

Keep in mind the points mentioned earlier and remember that it is a good idea to familiarise yourself with new ingredients gradually. It may take time to adjust to eating wholefoods so vary your diet with some refined products. Do not rely only on eggs and cheese; get into the habit of cooking grains and pulses once or twice a week. You will soon build up a repertoire of favourite dishes – some that you are able to cook without referring to the recipe!

Naan bread with lentil dhal is a vegetarian favourite.

Cooking for One or Two

Although most of the recipes in this book serve four, lots of ideas adapt easily for fewer servings. It is little trouble to cook small amounts of pasta or couscous. Stir-fry recipes can be scaled down for one or two; similarly, most of the simple savouries recipes (see pages 170–205) can be easily scaled down to serve one or two.

Salads are easy to make in small quantities. It can be trickier to reduce the quantities for dressings, but they do tend to keep long enough to be used again. Filo pastry sheets make good individual pies without the need for making lots of pastry.

Sauces, soups and casseroles are best made in large quantities and as they usually freeze well, make plenty and then store in suitable portion sizes. If you need to eat the same meal two days running, simply vary the accompaniments.

The Lone Vegetarian

Catering for one member of the family who is vegetarian while the rest are not is quite common and should not necessarily condemn the cook to a life of cooking two separate meals. There are many vegetarian meals that will be enjoyed by everyone – pies, pasta and dishes with eggs and cheese are examples which usually fall into this category.

Many recipes have a distinct point at which vegetable protein is added. This is the point to divide the meal and make part of it vegetarian and add meat or fish to the rest. Soups, stews and casseroles fall into this category. Again, don't bother to make just one portion – make plenty to freeze in suitable portion sizes.

Putting it all Together

Planning a balanced diet will be different for each individual, couple or family. Much will depend on your hours of work and proximity to shops. There are some general points to bear in mind, however, whatever your situation.

Simplicity does not equal monotony. A simple meal such as pasta with a sauce, baked potato with a warming casserole or a stir-fry with rice is nutritious, open to many variations and can be full of different flavours and textures. Build a repertoire of recipes that you and your family like so that you can make them easily. These are the ones that you'll be most happy improvising with if you haven't got every ingredient to hand.

Plan your weekly menus on firm foundations, using wholegrains and pulses for substance and carbohydrate. Add vegetables for colour and vital nutrients. Richer ingredients, such as nuts or dairy products, should be used less frequently. Serve fruit for dessert unless you have the time to make something more elaborate. Ring the changes by serving a cheese board laden with dried fruits and nuts.

THE RECIPES

The 250 recipes in the following pages contain a wide range of flavours and ingredients and I hope that you will find plenty of favourites among them. Rich in colour and texture, there are lots of recipes to choose from with something that will appeal for every meal and every occasion.

The recipes are arranged in chapters starting with ideas for breakfast, from quick and nutritious meals to deliciously lazy weekend brunches. The sections on soups and starters, followed by light meals, offer an array of tempting first courses and delicious vegetable savouries that are ideal for a lunch or supper snack. The main course recipes comprise hearty grain and pasta dishes, warming casseroles, flavoursome pies, tasty bakes and spicy stir-fries, and are divided into groups that have in common either ingredients, such as pasta or grains, or are categorised by a style of cooking, such as stir-fry or slow-cooking casseroles. Useful sauces, relishes and vegetable accompaniments are detailed in the next section, followed on by mouthwatering salads and dressings. Finally, an enticing and irresistible range of breads, cakes and puddings complete the individual recipe selections. The last part of the book focuses on entertaining, and includes another selection of recipes grouped together in menus suitable for a wide range of occasions, from buffets and barbecues to formal dinner parties.

Use the notes on ingredients and flavourings in the previous pages to help you make variations that suit your family's taste and lifestyle. I hope that the tempting photographs will encourage you to try new ideas and that you have great success with whatever you try.

Breakfast

Breakfast is an easy meal to skip and is often substituted with a quick coffee on the way to the office, but it is a time of day when your body needs an energy boost and something substantial enough to stop you feeling peckish an hour later.

Everyday breakfasts need to be nutritious, simple and fast. For quick and easy breakfasts, try a refreshing fruit juice or smoothie or create your own muesli for an energising, satisfying start to the day. Treat yourself and your guests to a lazy weekend brunch with some wholesome, quick muffins or scrumptious pancakes with fruit. There are also a number of easy savouries that can be prepared ahead during the week and look after themselves in the oven.

Straightforward and easy to create, many of the egg dishes on pages 178–85 are ideal for brunch, as are the spicy Mexican recipes on pages 190–93. You can also serve grain dishes such as risotto, Red Rice with Pan-Fried Squash, Mushrooms and Pecan Nuts (see page 229) or Paella with Many Vegetables (see page 233) for brunch. Puy lentils are quick cooking and also make an excellent breakfast dish, mixed with cooked onion and mushroom and well seasoned with shoyu or soy sauce.

fresh pear compote with apricots and prunes

This rich, spiced fruit compote is suitable for brunch as well as a winter dessert – use red wine instead of the grape juice for an alcoholic version, if preferred. The finished cooking liquid should be rich and syrupy. It can be reduced further if you wish – remove the pears after cooking, then boil the liquid until it is sufficiently reduced, before continuing with the recipe.

serves 6

preparation: 10 minutes, plus standing

cooking: about 1 hour

𝑣

300ml (½ pint) red grape juice
100ml (3½fl oz) water
75g (3oz) sugar or to taste
2 pears
1 bay leaf
1 cinnamon stick
12 peppercorns
1 sprig thyme
125g (4oz) dried apricots
125g (4oz) prunes

1 Measure the grape juice and water into a deep saucepan or flameproof casserole dish. Stir in the sugar.

2 Peel the pears and cut them into eighths. Place immediately in the grape juice and water. Add the bay leaf, cinnamon, peppercorns and thyme. Bring to the boil, then simmer for 45–60 minutes, or until the pears are just tender.

3 Add the apricots and prunes to the cooked pears and leave to soak overnight. When cold, adjust the sweetening to taste. Serve with natural yoghurt.

nutritional breakdown per serving: kcal 178, kJ 758, protein 2g, fat 0g (saturated fat 0g), carbohydrates 44g

fruit and cereals

Fresh fruit is light to eat and provides vital minerals and vitamins. Fruit platters and fruit salads sweetened with natural juice are colourful to serve. Simple combinations of one or two fruits can also make a striking display, such as a mixture of fresh apricots and figs served with white grape juice and roasted almonds, slices of fresh oranges served with passion fruit sauce, and the classic combination of papaya and lime.

Dried fruit should be soaked in plenty of liquid. Choose a mixture of peaches, apricots, pears and prunes. If you cook the fruit it will be softer and the cooking liquid more intense. You can add spices during the cooking process, if desired.

While oats and wheat are popular breakfast cereals, millet, rice and quinoa can all be served in the morning, too –

especially for cooked breakfasts and to help kickstart your body on a cold winter's day.

A creamy pudding can be made by cooking 1 part millet to 3 parts milk, bringing the mixture to the boil and then cooking over a gentle heat or in a low oven. Sweeten to taste and add spices, such as ground cinnamon or nutmeg, and dried fruit, such as raisins and sultanas.

Rice makes a good start to the day either cooked with milk, or cooked as normal (see page 87) and then served with either milk, soya milk, or natural yoghurt and chopped fruit or roasted nuts or seeds.

The soft texture of quinoa lends itself well to a type of porridge for a hearty, warming breakfast.

toasted muesli

Cereals make a wonderful start to the day, providing you with plenty of carbohydrate and fibre, while added fruit contributes essential vitamins and minerals. Many commercial cereals have a high sugar content and contain salt but it is easy to make delicious toasted cereals at home with a minimum of sweetening. The malt extract could be replaced with honey, if preferred.

serves 6

preparation: 5 minutes

cooking: 1 hour

𝑣

250g (8oz) oats
50g (2oz) blanched almonds
50g (2oz) sunflower seeds
2–3 tbsp wheatgerm
50ml (2fl oz) sunflower oil
50ml (2fl oz) malt extract
50g (2oz) raisins

1 Mix the oats, almonds, sunflower seeds and wheatgerm together in a bowl. Stir in the sunflower oil and malt extract and add a little water to moisten.

2 Spread out the mixture on a baking sheet and bake in a preheated oven, 120°C (250°F), Gas Mark ½, for 1 hour, or until lightly browned and crisp.

3 Allow to cool before stirring in the raisins.

VARIATIONS

If you prefer a raw cereal, it is a good idea to soak muesli overnight. This gives the oats a chance to soften and develop their natural creaminess. For 1 serving use about 4 tablespoons of oats and a similar amount of water. Sweeten with honey or sugar to taste and flavour with orange zest or orange juice. You can also stir in some natural yoghurt. Leave this mixture in the fridge overnight. The following day, add some fruit, such as grated apple, raspberries, sliced strawberries or seedless grapes, and nuts, such as chopped, roasted hazelnuts or almonds. This muesli is energy giving and sustaining as well as providing a good range of vital nutrients. For a family serving, simply increase the quantities.

nutritional breakdown per serving: kcal 373, kJ 1565, protein 9g, fat 19g (saturated fat 2g), carbohydrate 45g

blueberry muffins

Wholesome, moist and delicious straight from the oven, these muffins are easy to make just before breakfast.

makes 12
preparation: 5 minutes
cooking: 20 minutes
suitable for freezing

250g (8oz) wholemeal flour
125g (4oz) soft brown sugar
2 tsp baking powder
¼ tsp salt
1 tsp ground cinnamon
1 egg, beaten
250ml (8fl oz) milk
50g (2oz) melted butter or 50ml (2fl oz)
  sunflower oil
250g (8oz) blueberries

1 Mix together the flour, sugar, baking powder, salt and cinnamon in a large bowl. Then combine the egg, milk and melted butter or oil in a jug.

2 Add the wet ingredients to the bowl of dry ingredients and mix together until only just combined.

3 Stir the blueberries into the muffin mixture. Spoon into 12 paper muffin cases and bake in a preheated oven, 200°C (400°F), Gas Mark 6, for 20 minutes until risen and firm.

nutritional breakdown per muffin: kcal 159, kJ 673, protein 4g,
fat 5g (saturated fat 3g), carbohydrate 27g

VARIATIONS

Once you are familiar with the basic mixture, you can try many variations. Use ingredients such as bran or oats instead of some of the flour. Add chopped nuts or dried fruit, such as dates or sultanas instead of the blueberries. Alternatively, change the sweetening and use honey or molasses instead of the sugar. For a dairy-free version, add 1 tablespoon soya flour mixed with a little water as a substitute for the egg. Use soya milk instead of cow's milk.

american pancakes

These are great for a quick breakfast treat. An easy recipe to create, it is simply a matter of mixing together the dry and the wet ingredients. Make sure the baking powder and bicarbonate of soda are evenly distributed through the flour. When mixing the batter, simply stir until combined otherwise the pancakes won't be so light.

Many variations are possible. Try using different flour, such as rye flour or cornmeal; add spices, such as ground ginger, nutmeg or cinnamon; or sweeten with honey or molasses instead of sugar for a different flavour.

makes 12

preparation: 10 minutes

cooking: 10–15 minutes

200g (7oz) wholemeal flour
25–40g (1–1½oz) soft brown sugar
2 tbsp wheatgerm
1 tsp baking powder
2 tsp bicarbonate of soda
350ml (12fl oz) buttermilk
2 eggs, beaten
25g (1oz) butter, melted
2–3 drops vanilla extract

1 Mix the flour in a large bowl with the sugar, wheatgerm, baking powder and bicarbonate of soda.

2 In a separate bowl, beat the buttermilk with the eggs, melted butter and vanilla extract. Pour over the dry ingredients and stir until just combined.

3 Heat a large non-stick frying pan or griddle, pour in some of the pancake batter and shake the pan gently so that the mixture spreads out to a circle, about 10cm (4in) across and 5mm (¼in) thick. Cook for a few minutes then, when well risen and full of holes, flip over using a spatula and cook on the other side.

4 Repeat the process with the remaining batter to make about 12 pancakes. You can make several pancakes at a time.

nutritional breakdown per pancake: kcal 102, kJ 432, protein 4g, fat 3g (saturated fat 2g), carbohydrate 15g

layered mushroom and olive bake

This recipe can be made the day before and left overnight before cooking just prior to breakfast.

serves 4

preparation: 15 minutes and standing overnight

cooking: 35–45 minutes

25g (1oz) butter
250g (8oz) mushrooms
250g (8oz) wholemeal bread, sliced (5–6 slices)
125g (4oz) mozzarella, sliced
50g (2oz) pitted black olives, chopped
1 tsp dried oregano
4 eggs
450ml (17fl oz) milk
salt and freshly ground black pepper

1 Use a little of the butter to cook the mushrooms in a frying pan or saucepan until soft. Use the remaining butter to spread over the slices of bread and cut the slices in half.

2 Layer the slices of bread and butter in a deep, lightly greased ovenproof dish with the sliced cheeses, chopped olives and herbs, and the cooked mushrooms, seasoning each layer as you go and trimming the bread if necessary.

3 Beat the eggs with the milk in a jug and pour this over the layers of bread. Cover and refrigerate overnight.

4 The next day, cook the layered bake in a preheated oven, 200°C (400°F), Gas Mark 6, for 35–45 minutes, or until well browned and crispy on top. The middle should be soft and a little runny.

nutritional breakdown per serving: kcal 499, kJ 2092, protein 30g, fat 29g (saturated fat 11g), carbohydrate 33g

juices and drinks

It is vital for your health to drink plenty of liquids. Bodily fluids lost through perspiration and even simple activities such as breathing need continually replacing. Liquids also help flush out the system and often form the basis of cleansing and detox diets. The juice and drinks recipes here make very good alternatives to less healthy sweetened or fizzy drinks.

Freshly made juices have many benefits, being full of natural sugars and high in vitamins and minerals. Since this is already in liquid form the nutrients are easily absorbed into the bloodstream. It is best to drink freshly made juices before a meal so that they have time to be absorbed and there is less chance of feeling bloated. There are many thirst-quenching juices to try. Apple and citrus fruits make a good starting base for fruit juices and carrot, or carrot and apple, makes a good starter for a vegetable juice. Use stronger flavour vegetables such as watercress, spinach, parsley or beet in small quantities at first. The quality of the juice you make will depend on the raw ingredients. Buy organic or locally grown produce if you can.

For these juices you need an electric juicer to extract the maximum amount of juice possible from the fruit or vegetable.

carrot, apple and celery juice

serves 1–2
preparation: 5 minutes
cooking: none

v

2 large carrots
3 celery sticks
2 tart dessert apples (such as Granny Smith)

1　Wash and chop the ingredients, then juice in an electric juicer.

nutritional breakdown per serving: kcal 146, kJ 628, protein 2g, fat 1g (saturated fat 0g), carbohydrate 35g

spiced mango juice

serves 1–2
preparation: 5 minutes
cooking: none

v

fresh root ginger (small piece)
1 large orange
1 mango
lime juice to taste

1　Make the fresh ginger juice by grating a small piece of fresh root ginger. Peel the orange and mango then juice in an electric juicer. Mix in a few drops of ginger juice, then add lime juice to taste.

nutritional breakdown per serving: kcal 163, kJ 699, protein 3g, fat 1g (saturated fat 0g), carbohydrate 39g

tomato, cucumber and watercress juice

spiced mango juice
top **carrot, apple and celery juice** centre
tomato, cucumber and watercress juice bottom

serves 1–2
preparation: 5 minutes
cooking: none

300g (10oz) tomatoes
75g (3oz) cucumber
20–25g (¾–1oz) watercress

1　Wash the ingredients, then juice in an electric juicer.

nutritional breakdown per serving: kcal 80, kJ 340, protein 4g, fat 2g (saturated fat 1g), carbohydrate 14g

smoothies

These blended mixtures are more of a 'meal in a glass' than a drink, as they are based on protein-rich ingredients, such as milk, natural yoghurt, tofu and nut milk. You can interchange the base ingredient to suit your taste. The drinks are made in a blender or food processor, not an electric juicer, and are a good way of creating a light nutritious meal with little effort.

banana and almond milk

This should not be prepared in advance because, despite the lemon juice, the banana in the mixture quickly starts to go brown. Sweeten with honey instead of sugar, if preferred.

serves 1–2
preparation: 5 minutes
cooking: none
V

40g (1½ oz) ground almonds
175ml (6fl oz) water
1 banana
juice of 1 lemon
sugar to taste
1 tbsp toasted flaked almonds

1 Blend the ground almonds with the water in a blender or food processor.

2 Add the banana and lemon juice and sweeten to taste with sugar. Blend again until smooth. Serve straightaway, topped with toasted flaked almonds.

nutritional breakdown per serving: kcal 466, kJ 1944, protein 13g, fat 31g (saturated fat 3g), carbohydrate 36g

savoury smoothie

serves 1–2
preparation: 5 minutes
cooking: none
Ca

150 g (5oz) carton natural yoghurt
20g (¾ oz) spinach or watercress, chopped
1 tomato, skinned and deseeded
2–3 tsp wheatgerm
salt and freshly ground black pepper
sesame seeds, dry-roasted, to garnish

1 Place all the ingredients except the sesame seeds in a blender or food processor and blend until smooth. Season to taste and serve garnished with sesame seeds.

nutritional breakdown per serving: kcal 145, kJ 611, protein 11g, fat 5g (saturated fat 1g), carbohydrate 16g

tofu and strawberry with vanilla

As before, the sugar could be replaced with honey, if preferred.

serves 1–2

preparation: 5 minutes

cooking: none

Ⓒa 𝒱

200g (7oz) silken tofu (bean curd)
125g (4oz) strawberries
¼ tsp vanilla extract
water to thin, optional
lemon juice to taste
sugar or honey to taste

1   Put the silken tofu, strawberries and vanilla extract in a blender or food processor and blend until smooth. Add a little water if you want a runnier consistency. Add lemon juice and sugar or honey to taste, then serve.

nutritional breakdown per serving: kcal 220, kJ 920, protein 17g, fat 9g (saturated fat 1g), carbohydrate 20g

banana and almond milk left, **savoury smoothie** centre, **tofu and strawberry with vanilla** right

Soups and Starters

These soups and starters can make delicate and tempting first courses or, with a few well-chosen accompaniments, they can make substantial and easy meals, which fit in very well with today's informal style of eating. When serving a starter, choose something light if the main course is filling or rich. Remember to aim for a contrast of texture and flavour with the rest of the meal. If you are serving a soup as a starter, a smooth one is more elegant than a chunky broth.

Here you will find a range of soups and starters, with something for every occasion. For a substantial first course or supper snack try the wholesome Chowder with Sweet Potato, warming Country Vegetable Broth with Barley or Grilled Chicory with Two Cheeses. In contrast, the deliciously creamy, colourful Roasted Yellow Pepper Soup and Tamarind or Glazed Nectarines with Dolcelatte make light, elegant starters. For a quick, exotic meal, choose the spicy Oriental Mushroom Soup with Chilli and Ginger. Dips, such as Hummus and Green Olive Tapenade served with bread and crudités are always popular. And remember that soups are not just for cold weather – there is a selection of refreshing, cold soups to try on summer days, including the glorious Avocado Gazpacho.

avocado gazpacho

It is important to have ripe avocado for this delicately coloured soup. It is light enough to make a good starter for a lunch or evening party. Follow it with Artichoke and Red Pepper Gougère (see page 259) or Stuffed Italian Tomatoes with Red Pesto and Mozzarella (see page 172). For a simple meal, add finely chopped green pepper or very fresh garden peas to the soup and serve it with a good bread, feta cheese, slices of Leek and Fennel Frittata (see page 180) and a tomato salad.

serves 4

preparation: 10 minutes, plus chilling

cooking: none

2 ripe avocados
300g (10oz) natural yoghurt
300ml (½ pint) Vegetable Stock (see page 144)
juice and zest of 1 lemon
1 garlic clove
20g (¾ oz) parsley, chopped
¼ cucumber, finely chopped
2 spring onions, finely chopped
2–3 tbsp finely snipped chives

1 Peel 1 avocado, remove the stone and place the avocado flesh in a blender or food processor. Add the yoghurt, stock, lemon juice and zest, garlic and parsley. Process until smooth, then pour into a bowl.

2 Peel the remaining avocado and chop into small pieces. Stir this into the soup with the chopped cucumber, spring onions and finely snipped chives, reserving some of these for garnish.

3 Chill well before serving.

nutritional breakdown per serving: kcal 190, kJ 790, protein 6g, fat 15g (saturated fat 3g), carbohydrates 8g

stock

Making stock is not difficult – it is merely an extra stage to be considered when planning to make soup. Homemade stock can be quite sweet; to counteract this, add salt, extra herbs or some shoyu or soy sauce. If you don't have time to make your own stock, you can use the soaking water from dried mushrooms, or use a commercial stock cube or powder.

basic vegetable stock

makes 1.2 litres (2 pints)

preparation: 10 minutes

cooking: 55–70 minutes

suitable for freezing

𝑣

2 tbsp sunflower oil
1 onion, roughly chopped
2 carrots, roughly chopped
1 leek, roughly chopped
1 celery stick, roughly chopped
1.5 litres (2½ pints) water
2 sprigs parsley
1 bay leaf
6 peppercorns
1 garlic clove, left whole

1   Heat the oil in a large saucepan and fry the roughly chopped vegetables very gently. For a pale-coloured stock don't let the vegetables colour although the flavour will be less intense. For a fuller-flavoured version, allow the vegetables to brown.

2   Add the water to the vegetables, together with the parsley, bay leaf, peppercorns and garlic. Bring to the boil, then simmer for 45–60 minutes. Strain and use as required.

> minimal nutritional content

VARIATIONS

Many other ingredients may be added to basic stock. Add parsnips for a sweet nutty flavour, or celeriac and fennel for their delicate fragrance. Winter and summer squash, such as butternut squash or courgettes, may be added; another option is scrubbed potato peelings. Avoid whole pieces of potato as they will make the stock cloudy. Spices such as ginger or lemon grass are flavoursome additions, too.

Lemon Stock – add ½ a lemon to the basic vegetable stock liquid prior to simmering.

what to avoid

Some ingredients should be avoided when making stock. For example, green vegetables, such as cabbage or broccoli, can give soup a bitter taste and beetroot will turn the stock red. Very old or mouldy vegetables certainly won't do anything for the final flavour, either.

croûtons

These are made from day-old bread that is either cubed or sliced. The pieces can be fried in a mixture of olive oil and butter, or just oil. Add a little walnut oil or hazelnut oil to alter the flavour. Alternatively, the slices can be left plain and toasted or baked until crisp. For a more elaborate version make mini Bruschetta (see page 364).

dark mushroom stock

Dried mushrooms are particularly good as a base for a rich stock with complex flavours.

makes 1.2 litres (2 pints)
preparation: 10 minutes
cooking: 1¼ hours
suitable for freezing
v

50g (2oz) dried wild mushrooms
1.5 litres (2½ pints) boiling water
1 onion, roughly chopped
2 celery sticks, roughly chopped
2 leeks, roughly chopped
250g (8oz) fresh mushrooms, halved or chopped
2 tbsp olive or sunflower oil
1 bay leaf
1 sprig thyme

1 Soak the dried wild mushrooms in a bowl of the boiling water while you prepare the vegetables. Heat the oil in a large saucepan and cook the onion until well browned – this takes up to 10 minutes. Add the remaining vegetables and cook for 5 minutes.

2 Remove the soaked mushrooms from the bowl with a slotted spoon, reserving the soaking liquid. Strain the soaking liquid, preferably through a coffee filter, to remove the sediment. Then add the wild mushrooms, soaking liquid, bay leaf and thyme to the pan of vegetables.

3 Bring the stock to the boil and simmer for 1 hour, covered. Strain and use as required.

minimal nutritional content

VARIATIONS

Roast Garlic Stock – Roast 1 unpeeled head of garlic in a preheated oven, 200°C (400°F), Gas Mark 6, for about 5 minutes. Peel and mash the garlic and add to the dark mushroom stock.

Oriental Clear Stock – Add a strip of kombu (a dried seaweed) to the mushroom stock liquid prior to simmering. This stock can also be flavoured with miso, shoyu or soy sauce.

STORING SOUPS AND STOCKS

Always keep soups and stocks in the fridge. Bring to the boil to reheat. A soup will generally thicken on standing – add stock, milk or at worst water to thin down.

good soup-making tips

- Use a good stock
- Remember there are other liquids apart from stock that make a good flavour base, for example milk or coconut milk
- Make sure the onions are well cooked before adding other ingredients, otherwise they may never properly soften
- Sweat the vegetables when they are added, to improve the overall flavour. Make sure you use a big enough pan to do this; a wide pan is better than a tall pan
- Pasta, rice and dumplings add body to a thin soup
- A smooth soup need not be a chore, thanks to blenders and food processors. Always leave soup to cool before puréeing. Adding a knob of butter, a tablespoon of crème fraîche or good-quality olive oil will enrich the soup at this stage
- Many soups benefit from being made in advance and reheated

garnishes and accompaniments

It is always worth spending a minute or two thinking about and organising a garnish for a soup. A few green herbs can brighten the muted colour of a broth; a julienne of vegetables floating on a smooth purée makes a pleasing contrast in texture; a swirl of cream enhances and enriches. Here are a few ideas:

- *chopped herbs or whole herb leaves*
- *herb butter, chilled and cut into an attractive shape*
- *julienne strips of vegetables such as courgette, carrot or celery*
- *roasted nuts, chopped*
- *roughly crushed peppercorns or coriander seeds*
- *dry-roasted spice seeds such as cumin*
- *blanched zest of lemon or orange*
- *thinly sliced sautéed baby mushrooms*
- *chopped slivers of black or green olives*
- *ribbons of carrots or cucumber*
- *cooked polenta, cut into tiny shapes.*

red lentil soup with cumin

Red lentils are a great ingredient for soups as they turn so easily to a thick purée. Their earthy flavour is best counteracted with spices such as the cumin used here or with citrus fruit.

This soup could be followed by a grain dish such as Sesame Millet with Pan Fried Courgettes, Asparagus and Avocado Cream (see page 228) or the Almond Croustade with Chard (see page 268).

serves 4–6
preparation: 5 minutes
cooking: 55 minutes
suitable for freezing

Fe ♈

2 tbsp olive oil
1 large onion, finely chopped
1 garlic clove, crushed
1 tsp cumin seeds
125g (4oz) red lentils
600ml (1 pint) Vegetable Stock (see page 144)
500g (1lb) passata
salt and freshly ground black pepper
1–2 tbsp chopped coriander leaves, to garnish

1   Heat the olive oil in a large saucepan and gently fry the onion and garlic until soft. Add the cumin seeds and toast for a few minutes until just coloured.

2   Add the red lentils to the pan and stir well so they become coated with the onion mixture.

3   Next pour over the stock, bring to the boil and simmer for 15 minutes so that the lentils have a chance to soften. Then add the passata and bring to the boil. Turn down the heat and simmer, covered, for a further 30 minutes.

4   Leave to cool then, using a blender or food processor, purée the soup until very smooth. Season to taste then heat gently before serving, garnished with chopped coriander.

nutritional breakdown per serving (4 portions): kcal 196,
kJ 827, protein 10g, fat 6g (saturated fat 1g), carbohydrate 27g

chowder with sweet potato

A chowder is a traditional soup with a creamy consistency. This is a colourful version with sweetcorn, carrots and sweet potato and a stock base enriched with cream. This soup could be followed by a light savoury such as Griddled Courgette Quiche with Pine Nuts (see page 255).

serves 4
preparation: 10 minutes
cooking: about 1 hour
suitable for freezing

2 tbsp sunflower oil
1 onion, finely chopped
2 garlic cloves, crushed
125g (4oz) baby sweetcorn cobs, chopped
375g (12oz) sweet potato, finely chopped
2 carrots, peeled and finely chopped
1 red pepper, cored, deseeded and chopped
½ tsp paprika
600ml (1 pint) Vegetable Stock (see page 144)
2 tbsp finely chopped parsley
1 tsp dried thyme
100ml (3½ fl oz) double cream
salt and freshly ground black pepper

1 Heat the sunflower oil in a large saucepan and gently fry the onion and garlic until soft. Add all the prepared vegetables and stir them into the onion mixture. Cook slowly for 5 minutes so that the vegetables start to soften.

2 Sprinkle over paprika and stir it in. Pour in the stock, add the herbs and bring to the boil.

3 Remove the pan from the heat, pour in the cream and mix very well. Return the pan to the heat and simmer the mixture, partially covered, for 40–45 minutes, or until the vegetables are really soft. Season well and serve hot.

nutritional breakdown per serving: kcal 277, kJ 1154, protein 3g, fat 18g (saturated fat 8g), carbohydrate 27g

puy lentil and mushroom soup

Lentils, mushrooms and red wine are a wonderful combination, served here as a rich soup. Try to get shiitake mushrooms as they have a distinctive flavour and solid texture; second choice would be chestnut or Paris mushrooms. This soup could be followed by a simple Potato and Leek Boulangère (see page 262) or Roquefort and Celeriac Pancakes (see page 187).

serves 4–6
preparation: 10 minutes
cooking: about 1 hour
suitable for freezing

Fe 𝒱

2 tbsp olive oil
1 onion, finely chopped
1 garlic clove, crushed
1 red chilli, finely chopped
1 carrot, finely chopped
1 celery stick, finely chopped
150g (5oz) shiitake mushrooms, sliced
50ml (2fl oz) red wine
150g (5oz) Puy or brown lentils
1 litre (1¾ pints) Mushroom Stock
  (see page 145)
2 tbsp shoyu or soy sauce
salt and freshly ground black pepper

1 Heat the olive oil in a large saucepan, and gently cook the onion and garlic until fairly soft. Add the red chilli and cook for 2 minutes, then add the carrot, celery and mushrooms. Cook for 5 minutes, or until the mushrooms have begun to soften.

2 Pour in the red wine and increase the heat, then cook until most of the liquid has been driven off. Add the lentils and stir in, then pour in the mushroom stock.

3 Bring to the boil and cook for 45–50 minutes, or until the lentils and vegetables are very soft. Add the shoyu or soy sauce and season to taste. Serve hot.

nutritional breakdown per serving (4 portions): kcal 198, kJ 834, protein 11g, fat 7g (saturated fat 1g), carbohydrate 23g

roasted yellow pepper soup

This wonderfully simple soup has a good creamy texture and mellow flavour thanks to the roasted vegetable base. It could be followed by a contrasting grain dish such as the Layered Bulgar with Tomatoes and Feta (see page 231) or by a pasta dish.

serves 4
preparation: 10–15 minutes
cooking: 35 minutes
suitable for freezing
v

3 large yellow peppers, lightly brushed with oil
8 shallots, unpeeled
250g (8oz) potato, roughly chopped
600ml (1 pint) Vegetable Stock (see page 144)
freshly grated nutmeg
1–2 tbsp olive oil
salt and freshly ground black pepper

1   Place the peppers in a roasting tin and roast in a preheated oven, 200°C (400°F), Gas Mark 6, for 30 minutes. Put the shallots in the oven at the same time and roast for 20 minutes.

2   Once the vegetables are roasted, leave to cool slightly then skin the peppers and remove the seeds. Don't discard any cooking juices. Leave the shallots to cool slightly before peeling.

3   Meanwhile, cook the potato in a saucepan of boiling salted water for about 10–15 minutes, or until soft.

4   Using a blender or food processor, purée the cooked peppers, shallots and potato with the vegetable stock and any juices from the peppers. Season well and add a generous grating of nutmeg plus up to 2 tablespoons olive oil to give the finished soup a velvety texture. Pour into a large pan and heat through before serving.

nutritional breakdown per serving: kcal 118, kJ 499, protein 3g, fat 4g (saturated fat 1g), carbohydrate 18g

spiced gumbo

This is a wonderful warming meal in a bowl and is especially good when served with Savoury Cheese Corn Bread (see page 340). If you want the look of a stew rather than soup, keep all the vegetables chunky and add less liquid. This soup is best made in large quantities so that you can pack in lots of ingredients.

serves 4–6
preparation: 10 minutes
cooking: 55–65 minutes

2 tbsp sunflower oil
1 onion, finely chopped
1 garlic clove, crushed
1 red chilli, deseeded and chopped
1 green pepper, cored, deseeded and chopped
400g (13oz) potato, finely chopped
125g (4oz) okra, finely chopped
400g (13oz) can chopped tomatoes
600ml (1 pint) Vegetable Stock (see page 144)
2 bay leaves
salt and freshly ground black pepper

1 Heat the oil in a large saucepan and gently fry the onion and garlic until soft. Add the chilli and cook for 3 minutes. Add the prepared vegetables, stir well and cook for 2 minutes.

2 Pour the canned tomatoes and stock into the pan, add the bay leaves and some seasoning. Bring to the boil, then cover the pan and simmer for 45–60 minutes, or until the vegetables are very soft. Remove the bay leaves, adjust the seasoning to taste and serve hot.

nutritional breakdown per serving (4 portions): kcal 170, kJ 718, protein 5g, fat 6g (saturated fat 1g), carbohydrate 25g

carrot and parsnip soup with coconut and tamarind

Root vegetables such as carrots and parsnips make wonderful, smooth, colourful soups. They can be flavoured in many different ways – from a simple grating of nutmeg to this complex mixture of spices. The coconut milk adds a velvety quality to the finished soup, which is balanced by the slightly sour flavour of the tamarind. This soup can also be made with squash, pumpkin or sweet potato.

serves 4–6

preparation: 10 minutes

cooking: 1–1¼ hours

suitable for freezing

v

1 tsp coriander seeds
1 tsp cumin seeds
2 tbsp sunflower oil
1 onion, finely chopped
2 garlic cloves, crushed
250g (8oz) carrots, finely chopped
250g (8oz) parsnips, finely chopped
900ml (1½ pints) Vegetable Stock (see page 144)
150ml (¼ pint) coconut milk
1 tbsp tamarind (ready-prepared)
salt and freshly ground black pepper

1 In a small frying pan, dry-roast the coriander and cumin seeds until lightly roasted, then crush with a pestle and mortar and set aside.

2 Heat the oil in a large saucepan, and gently fry the onion and garlic until very soft, then add the dry-roasted spices. Add the finely chopped carrots and parsnips to the pan and cook slowly for 10 minutes, then pour in the stock and cook for 50–60 minutes.

3 Leave to cool slightly, then place the vegetable mixture in a blender or food processor with the coconut milk and tamarind and purée until smooth.

4 Season to taste, return to the pan and heat through. Serve hot.

nutritional breakdown per serving (4 portions): kcal 154, kJ 644, protein 3g, fat 7g (saturated fat 1g), carbohydrate 21g

chickpea and celery soup with gremolada

Gremolada, or gremolata, is a fresh herb flavouring made from parsley, garlic and lemon zest. It gives a definite perk to any dish and here counteracts the mellow earthy character of the chickpeas and potato.

You could use other pulses such as lima beans or black-eye beans instead of the chickpeas. Serve this soup with a good bread to make a light meal; or follow it with a simple savoury such as Giant Mushrooms stuffed with Wild Rice and Roasted Onions (see page 173) or Kuku with Spinach (see page 181).

serves 4–6

preparation: 10 minutes

cooking: about 1 hour

suitable for freezing after step 2

𝒱

2 tbsp olive oil
1 onion, finely chopped
3 celery sticks, finely chopped
200g (7oz) chickpeas (cooked weight)
1 potato, finely chopped
400g (13oz) can chopped tomatoes
900ml (1½ pints) Vegetable Stock (see page 144)
salt and freshly ground black pepper

For the gremolada:
4 tbsp chopped parsley
zest of 1 lemon
2 garlic cloves, finely chopped

1 Heat the oil in a large saucepan and gently cook the onion. Add the celery and cook for 5 minutes, then add the chickpeas and potato and cook for 5 minutes.

2 Pour in the canned tomatoes and vegetable stock and bring the mixture to the boil. Cover the pan and simmer for 45–50 minutes. Season well.

3 To make the gremolada, mix together the chopped parsley, lemon zest and garlic and stir into the soup. Leave for 1–2 minutes, then serve hot.

nutritional breakdown per serving (4 portions): kcal 170, kJ 718, protein 6g, fat 8g (saturated fat 1g), carbohydrate 21g

oriental mushroom soup with chilli and ginger

Packed with colourful vegetables, this spiced soup is virtually a meal in a bowl. If you prefer a hotter version, leave in some of the chilli seeds.

nutritional breakdown per serving (4 portions): kcal 288, kJ 1214, protein 10g, fat 9g (saturated fat 2g), carbohydrate 44g

serves 4–6

preparation: 15 minutes, plus soaking

cooking: 20 minutes

𝑣

25g (1oz) dried mushrooms (shiitake and cep)
1.2 litres (2 pints) boiling water
2 tbsp sunflower oil
150g (5oz) shallots, chopped
2 celery sticks, sliced
2 tsp grated fresh root ginger
1 red chilli, deseeded and chopped
2 carrots, cut into matchsticks
250g (8oz) shiitake and oyster mushrooms, sliced
150g (5oz) sweetcorn
3 tbsp shoyu or soy sauce
125g (4oz) medium or fine egg or rice noodles
150g (5oz) mangetout or sugar snap peas
25g (1oz) chopped coriander leaves
salt and freshly ground black pepper

1   To make the stock, soak the dried mushrooms in a bowl of the boiling water. Leave for 20 minutes, then drain, reserving the soaking liquid. Chop the soaked mushrooms roughly and set aside.

2   Heat the oil in a large saucepan and fry the shallots until soft. Add the celery, ginger and chilli and fry for a further 3–4 minutes, then add the carrots, the fresh and dried mushrooms and the sweetcorn. Stir well and cook slowly for 5–10 minutes.

3   Pour in the mushroom liquid and add the shoyu or soy sauce. Bring the soup to the boil. Meanwhile, soak the noodles in boiling water for 4 minutes, drain and add to the pan with the mangetout or sugar snap peas and half the coriander.

4   Bring the soup back to the boil and cook for 2–3 minutes, or until the mangetout is just tender. Season to taste and serve straightaway, garnished with the remaining coriander.

celeriac and emmental soup

Melted cheese gives this soup a rich texture as well as boosting the nutritional content. Follow this soup with a grain dish such as Mushroom Risotto with Tarragon (see page 226) or with the Roasted Pecan and Cashew Loaf (see page 264). Alternatively, eat on its own, served with walnut croûtons, for a light meal.

serves 4–6
preparation: 10 minutes
cooking: 1 hour
suitable for freezing (without the cheese)

25g (1oz) butter
1 onion, finely chopped
1 garlic clove, crushed
425g (14oz) celeriac (weight after peeling),
  finely chopped
750ml (1¼ pints) Vegetable Stock (see page 144)
75g (3oz) Emmental, grated
salt and freshly ground black pepper

1 Melt the butter in a large saucepan and gently cook the onion and garlic until soft. Add the finely chopped celeriac and cook slowly for about 10 minutes.

2 Pour in the stock, bring to the boil, then cover the pan and simmer for 45–50 minutes. Leave to cool then, using a blender or food processor, purée until smooth. Season to taste.

3 Return the soup to the pan, then stir in the grated cheese. Stir over a gentle heat until the cheese has melted – you need to melt the cheese slowly or it may become stringy. Serve the soup hot.

nutritional breakdown per serving (4 portions): kcal 157, kJ 647, protein 8g, fat 12g (saturated fat 7g), carbohydrate 6g

caramelised onion soup with brandy

This is a rich vegetarian version of the classic French onion soup. Use a well-flavoured dark stock as a base, but also make sure the onions are both well cooked and well browned so that the soup has a good depth of flavour and colour. This makes a great party soup followed by a pastry dish such as Chestnut and Cep Single Crust Pie (see page 257), or serve it as a warming lunch dish on a dreary day.

serves 4

preparation: 10 minutes

cooking: 45 minutes

suitable for freezing (without the cheese)

Ⓥ

50g (2oz) butter
500g (1lb) onions, chopped
3 tbsp brandy
1 litre (1¾ pints) dark Vegetable Stock
  (see page 144)
1 tsp dried thyme
1 tbsp miso, dissolved in a little stock
4 slices ciabatta or rustic bread
1 garlic clove, peeled and halved
2 tsp coarse grain mustard
125g (4oz) Gruyère or Cheddar cheese, grated
salt and freshly ground black pepper

1 Melt the butter in a large saucepan and cook the onions very gently until completely soft – this takes about 20 minutes.

2 Once soft, turn up the heat and cook the onions to a dark brown, stirring frequently. Add the brandy and cook over a high heat until reduced.

3 Pour in the stock and add the thyme and miso. Bring to the boil, then cover and simmer for 20 minutes. Season well.

4 Meanwhile, place the bread in a preheated oven, 200°C (400°F), Gas Mark 6, and bake for 3–4 minutes, until dry but not toasted. Rub with the cut side of a garlic clove, then spread with a little mustard and cover with grated cheese.

5 Pour the soup into flameproof bowls. Put a slice of bread in each bowl then place under a preheated grill until the cheese has melted. Serve immediately.

nutritional breakdown per serving: kcal 408, kJ 1699, protein 14g, fat 23g (saturated fat 14g), carbohydrate 32g

country vegetable broth with barley

Soups like this tend to be best made in large quantities so that you can include a wide selection of vegetables to give a full flavour and a good mix of colours. Easy to make and suitable for freezing, this soup makes a meal, served with a wholesome bread and cheese or a simple pâté or dip such as Oyster Mushroom and Roast Almond Pâté (see page 165) or Roasted Aubergine and Garlic Dip (see page 167). If you can, make the broth the day before you want to eat it so the flavours have plenty of time to develop. As the soup cooks, the colours will become quite muted. Counteract this by serving it with lots of fresh parsley.

serves 6–8

preparation: 10 minutes

cooking: 1–¼ hours

𝑣

1 tbsp sunflower oil
1 onion, finely chopped
1 leek, chopped
1 carrot, chopped
1 parsnip, chopped
1 bulb fennel, chopped
300g (10oz) squash or swede, chopped
50g (2oz) barley
1 litre (1¾ pints) Vegetable Stock (see page 144)
1 bouquet garni (bay leaf, 1 sprig thyme, parsley
  and rosemary tied with string – see page 107)
salt and freshly ground black pepper
2–3 tbsp finely chopped parsley, to garnish

1   Heat the oil in a large saucepan and gently cook the onion until fairly soft. Add all the prepared vegetables and the barley and cook slowly for 10 minutes, stirring occasionally, so that the vegetables sweat and start to soften.

2   Add the stock and the bouquet garni and bring to the boil. Season well, then cover the pan and simmer for 50–60 minutes.

3   Remove and discard the bouquet garni. Adjust the seasoning if necessary, then serve the broth garnished with a good sprinkling of chopped parsley.

nutritional breakdown per serving: kcal 88, kJ 370, protein 2g, fat 3g (saturated fat 0g), carbohydrate 15g

chilled bean soup

This is a delicious, refreshing soup to eat on hot days or warm evenings. The flavours will develop as it stands but it is important to use a well-flavoured stock as a base. A recipe for stock is included here but if you have stock on hand then use that instead. Follow this soup with Filo Pie with Double Mushrooms and Goat's Cheese (see page 261).

serves 4

preparation: 15 minutes, plus chilling

cooking : 15 minutes, plus making stock

For the stock:
1 tbsp olive oil
1 onion, roughly chopped
2 garlic cloves
½ bulb fennel, roughly chopped
1 carrot, roughly chopped
2 celery sticks, roughly chopped
1 litre (1¾ pints) water
1 bay leaf
sprigs of parsley and thyme

For the soup:
1 tbsp olive oil
1 onion, finely chopped
½ bulb fennel, finely chopped
100g (3½oz) green beans, sliced
100g (3½oz) peas
100g (3½oz) asparagus, sliced
100g (3½oz) mangetout or sugar snap peas
2–3 tbsp pesto (see page 211)
100g (3½oz) natural yoghurt
salt and freshly ground black pepper
basil leaves, to garnish

1 To make the stock, heat the oil in a large saucepan and gently cook all the vegetables until coated with oil and lightly browned. Add the water, bay leaf and sprigs of parsley and thyme. Bring to the boil, then simmer, covered, for 40–60 minutes. Strain and reserve.

2 To make the soup, heat the oil in a large saucepan and gently fry the onion and fennel until soft but not coloured.

3 Add 600ml (1 pint) of the vegetable stock and bring to the boil. Boil for 4–5 minutes, then add the prepared beans, peas, asparagus and mangetout or sugar snap peas. Cook for 3 minutes, or until the vegetables are just cooked but still crisp.

4 Remove the pan from the heat and leave to cool. When the soup is quite cold, stir in the pesto and yoghurt and season to taste. Chill thoroughly before serving. Garnish with fresh basil leaves.

nutritional breakdown per serving: kcal 180, kJ 749, protein 8g, fat 12g (saturated fat 3g), carbohydrate 10g

chilled melon soup with wine and honey

This fragrant chilled fruit soup is great on a hot day, perhaps served as part of an exotic picnic. The refreshing flavours also work well used as a palate cleanser between courses. Vegans can make this dish by substituting sugar for the honey. Make sure the sugar is dissolved before bringing the mixture to the boil.

serves 4

preparation: 15 minutes, plus chilling

cooking: about 5 minutes

3 tbsp honey
3 tbsp water
8 cardamom pods, husk removed and seeds
   crushed, or ½ tsp ground cardamom
75ml (3fl oz) white wine
2 small melons (Galia or Ogen)
125g (4oz) raspberries
2 passion fruit

1 Boil the honey and water in a large saucepan with the cardamom seeds. Simmer for 5 minutes, then add the wine and leave to cool.

2 Extract the juice of 1 melon with a juicer and add this to the wine and honey mixture. Scoop the remaining melon into balls or cut it into chunks and add to the melon liquid in the pan. Gently mix in the raspberries.

3 Extract the juice from the passion fruit, either by using a juicer or by adding a little sugar to the flesh and heating it in a small saucepan, then pressing it through a sieve. Add this to the melon and raspberry mixture.

4 Chill the soup thoroughly before serving.

nutritional breakdown per serving: kcal 587, kJ 2502, protein 2g, fat 0g (saturated fat 0g), carbohydrate 151g

glazed nectarines with dolcelatte

This makes an elegant starter or perhaps a light meal when augmented with a special bread and some extra green salad. Do make sure you use good-quality ripe fruit.

serves 4

preparation: 10 minutes

cooking: 3–4 minutes

2 tbsp honey
2 tbsp lime juice
2 nectarines, halved and stones removed
125g (4oz) dolcelatte, thinly sliced
zest of 1 lime
watercress or a dark green or dark red leaf
 (such as radicchio or lollo rosso), to serve

1 Combine the honey and lime juice in a small bowl.

2 Slice each nectarine half into 8 wedges. Lay the nectarine slices in a flameproof dish and pour over the lemon and honey mixture.

3 Place the dish under a preheated hot grill and grill for 3–4 minutes, or until the nectarines are lightly browned. Baste with any remaining juice.

4 Arrange slices of nectarine alternately with slices of cheese on individual serving plates. Sprinkle on a little lime zest.

5 Add some dark green or red leaves on the side. Serve at room temperature.

nutritional breakdown per serving: kcal 160, kJ 670, protein 4g, fat 10g (saturated fat 6g), carbohydrate 16g

griddled leeks and asparagus with cream cheese dressing

This simple snack or starter is quick to make. As a starter it needs no accompaniment and could be followed by Lentil Bake with Red Pepper (see page 266) or Cider Casserole with New Potatoes (see page 243). For a snack, serve with a good rustic bread.

serves 4

preparation: 5 minutes

cooking: 5 minutes

400g (13oz) baby leeks
175g (6oz) asparagus tips
2 tbsp blue poppy seeds, to garnish

For the dressing:
75g (3oz) cream cheese
2 tbsp white wine vinegar
6 tbsp olive oil
salt and freshly ground black pepper

1   To make the dressing, use a blender or food processor to blend the cream cheese with the wine vinegar. Then, with the motor running, add the oil in a thin steady stream and blend until smooth. Season to taste.

2   Heat a griddle pan or a large non-stick frying pan until very hot.

3   Slice the leeks lengthways in half if more than a finger width thick. Put the leeks and asparagus on the griddle pan and cook for 4–5 minutes, turning over once or twice during cooking.

4   Remove from the pan and arrange on individual serving plates, then pour over the cream cheese dressing and sprinkle with poppy seeds. Serve at room temperature.

nutritional breakdown per serving: kcal 264, kJ 1088, protein 5g, fat 29g (saturated fat 8g), carbohydrate 4g

grilled chicory with two cheeses

This is great for an easy lunch or supper snack with crusty bread. Try a range of different melting cheeses such as Gruyère, Emmental or fontina.

serves 4

preparation: 5 minutes

cooking: 6–8 minutes

4 heads chicory
100g (3½oz) Cheddar cheese, grated
100g (3½oz) smoked cheese, grated
salt and freshly ground black pepper

1 Quarter the heads of chicory and braise in a saucepan containing just enough stock or water to cover the vegetables for 3–4 minutes until just soft. Drain well.

2 Place the cooked chicory in a lightly greased flameproof dish and season well. Cover with both types of grated cheese and place under a preheated hot grill. Grill for 3–4 minutes, or until the cheese has melted and is well browned. Serve hot.

nutritional breakdown per serving: kcal 190, kJ 787, protein 12g, fat 15g (saturated fat 9g), carbohydrate 3g

poached vegetables with herbs and wine

This is an easy, succulent way of serving a variety of vegetables. Use a good-quality olive oil as the flavour will come through. As the colours of the cooked vegetables invariably become muted, add a handful of fresh herbs as a bright garnish, or mix in some black olives and cubes of feta cheese as a colourful contrast.

serves 4–6

preparation: 10 minutes

cooking: 10 minutes

𝑣

250g (8oz) shallots, peeled and left whole
250g (8oz) button mushrooms
250g (8oz) fennel, sliced
250ml (8fl oz) white wine
1 bay leaf
2 sprigs thyme
1 sprig rosemary
2 garlic cloves, thinly sliced
6 peppercorns
1 cinnamon stick
250g (8oz) French beans, sliced
150ml (¼ pint) olive oil
salt and freshly ground black pepper

1 Put the shallots, mushrooms, fennel and white wine in a large saucepan.

2 Add the herbs, garlic, peppercorns and cinnamon stick and bring to the boil. Simmer for 5 minutes.

3 Add the French beans, then simmer for a further 3–4 minutes.

4 Remove the pan from the heat and leave to cool slightly. Then stir in the olive oil and season to taste. Serve at room temperature.

nutritional breakdown per serving (4 portions): kcal 340, kJ 1409, protein 4g, fat 28g (saturated fat 4g), carbohydrate 9g

oranges with red onion and black olives in sherry dressing

This is a very simple but effective combination of ingredients that is both refreshing and colourful. It is quick to prepare but do leave time for chilling as the coolness of this starter is part of its charm. For a vegan alternative, substitute a concentrated fruit juice for the honey.

serves 4

preparation: 10 minutes, plus chilling

cooking: none

4 large oranges, peeled and thinly sliced
1 small red onion, thinly sliced
4 tbsp olive oil
1–2 tbsp sherry vinegar
1 tsp honey
1 tbsp chopped mint
50g (2oz) black olives
salt and freshly ground black pepper
sprigs of mint, to garnish

1 Arrange the slices of orange on a large plate with the slices of red onion.

2 Mix the olive oil, sherry vinegar, honey and chopped mint in a jug and season to taste. Pour over the oranges and leave for at least 1 hour to chill.

3 Scatter over the black olives and garnish with sprigs of mint.

COOK'S TIP

To get really attractive slices of orange, cut the peel off with a serrated knife, making sure all the white pith is removed.

nutritional breakdown per serving: kcal 204, kJ 850, protein 3g, fat 13g (saturated fat 2g), carbohydrate 21g

savoury choux with avocado and pesto

Tiny puffs of choux pastry make easy cocktail snacks. The pastry and filling can be prepared well ahead of time, leaving a quick assembly an hour or so before serving. Slightly larger buns can be filled in the same way and, served with salad, make a great light lunch or supper snack. For more on choux pastry see page 258.

makes 14–16
preparation: 15 minutes
cooking: 25–30 minutes
suitable for freezing (see note)

For the choux pastry:
125ml (4fl oz) water
50g (2oz) butter
75g (3oz) plain flour, sifted
2 eggs
50g (2oz) Cheddar cheese, grated
¼ teaspoon prepared mustard

For the filling:
1 ripe avocado
2–3 tsp pesto (see page 211)
1 tsp lemon juice
salt and freshly ground black pepper

1 To make the choux pastry, put the water and the butter in a saucepan and bring to the boil.

2 When boiling and the butter has melted, remove the pan from the heat and tip in all the flour. Beat vigorously with a wooden spoon until very glossy.

3 Beat in the eggs one at a time. Then add the grated cheese and mustard, and beat again.

4 Put dessertspoonfuls of the mixture on to a lightly greased baking sheet and bake in a preheated oven, 200°C (400°F), Gas Mark 6, for 20–25 minutes. The 'buns' should be well risen, brown and firm. It is best to over-bake them slightly so that they won't collapse. Leave to cool on a wire rack.

5 To make the filling, halve the avocado, remove the stone and scoop out the flesh. Mash with the pesto and lemon juice and season to taste.

6 To serve, make a slit in the side of each bun and fill with the avocado mixture. Serve within 2 hours otherwise the pastry may become too soft.

nutritional breakdown per choux (14 portions): kcal 99, kJ 411, protein 3g, fat 8g (saturated fat 4g), carbohydrate 4g

VARIATIONS

There are plenty of other filling options for bite-sized choux. Try mashed mild goat's cheese with lemon and chives; crumbled blue cheese with cream and chopped watercress or rocket; mascarpone cheese with finely chopped walnuts; or Green Olive Tapenade (see page 166).

FREEZING CHOUX PASTRY

Choux pastry can be frozen uncooked. Once the mixture has been spooned into the small balls in step 4, place them on non-stick baking sheets without any covering and freeze. Once they are frozen, pack the balls into bags or containers. Raw choux shapes should be cooked from frozen. Add an extra 5 minutes or so to the cooking time.

Cooked choux buns can also be frozen. Cool completely after cooking, then pack in containers, putting greaseproof or freezer paper between layers if necessary. Frozen ready-baked choux buns will need 10 minutes in a hot oven to crisp.

oyster mushroom and roast almond pâté

*This is a delicious rich pâté with a delicate blend of flavours.
It is easy to spread and goes well with crisp crackers or bread.
Alternatively, serve it with raw vegetables.*

serves 4

preparation: 10 minutes, plus cooling

cooking: 10 minutes

suitable for freezing

75g (3oz) flaked almonds
50g (2oz) butter
1 onion, finely chopped
2 garlic cloves, crushed
300g (10oz) oyster mushrooms
salt and freshly ground black pepper

1   Spread the almonds on a baking sheet and roast in
    a preheated oven, 200°C (400°F), Gas Mark 6, for
    4–5 minutes, or until light brown. Set aside a few
    flakes for garnish.

2   Melt 25g (1oz) butter in a saucepan and gently fry
    the onion and garlic until soft. Add the mushrooms
    and turn up the heat, then cook until soft and
    slightly browned. Leave to cool.

3   Place the almonds and cooked mushroom mixture
    in a blender or food processor and blend until
    smooth, adding the remaining butter. Season well.

4   Pile the mixture into an attractive bowl or
    individual ramekins and garnish with the reserved
    almond flakes.

nutritional breakdown per serving: kcal 223, kJ 923, protein 6g,
fat 21g (saturated fat 8g), carbohydrate 3g

hummus left, **green**
olive tapenade centre,
roasted aubergine
and garlic dip right

green olive tapenade

*This lusty dip has a good strong colour and flavour
to match. Serve it with crudités or with roasted peppers
and aubergine. Spread it thinly as a sandwich filling
then top with a mass of salad and sliced egg or mozzarella
for a substantial snack. Tapenade will keep in the
fridge for at least a week.*

serves 4	
preparation: 10 minutes	
cooking: none	
v	

125g (4oz) pitted green olives
2 garlic cloves, roughly chopped
2 tsp capers
25g (1oz) chopped parsley
½ tsp dried thyme
6 tbsp olive oil
salt and freshly ground black pepper

1 Put all the ingredients except the olive oil and
seasoning into a blender or food processor. Blend
for a few seconds then, with the motor running,
add the olive oil gradually in a thin steady stream
to make a thick creamy paste.

2 Check the seasoning and add extra garlic, capers or
herbs according to taste.

nutritional breakdown per serving: kcal 184, kJ 756, protein 1g,
fat 20g (saturated fat 3g), carbohydrate 0g

roasted aubergine and garlic dip

Roasted aubergine with its smoky flavour and creamy consistency makes a wonderful base for a dip or spread. Serve it with raw or grilled vegetables in pitta bread or simply add to a buffet spread. This recipe goes well with other Middle Eastern-inspired ideas such as Falafel (see page 174), Classic Tabbouleh (see page 299), Stuffed Vine Leaves with Spiced Bulgar (see page 359) and Frittatas (see page 179).

serves 4

preparation: 10 minutes

cooking: 40 minutes

V

2 aubergines
2 garlic cloves, crushed
juice of 1 lemon
½ tsp ground cumin
3 tbsp olive oil
1 small chilli, deseeded and chopped
salt and freshly ground black pepper

1 Prick the aubergines in several places and arrange in a roasting tin. Roast them in a preheated oven, 200°C (400°F), Gas Mark 6, for 40 minutes, or until they have collapsed and are completely soft.

2 Cool slightly, then cut in half and scoop out the flesh.

3 Using a blender or food processor, purée the aubergine flesh with the remaining ingredients.

4 Season to taste and pile into a small bowl. Serve at room temperature.

nutritional breakdown per serving: kcal 107, kJ 446, protein 2g, fat 9g (saturated fat 1g), carbohydrate 5g

hummus

This classic dip is not only delicious but also very easy to make. Highlight your favourite flavours by adding more of any of the ingredients. Hummus is great served with crudités or crackers as an appetiser. Use it as part of a buffet spread, especially with dishes such as Classic Tabbouleh (see page 299), Roast Peppers (see page 313) or Greek Potato Salad (see page 301). It is also useful for filling sandwiches or piling into warm pitta bread for a nutritious snack. It can be frozen for up to 1 month. For information on cooking pulses see page 90.

serves 4

preparation time: 10 minutes

cooking time: none

suitable for freezing

V

200g (7oz) cooked chickpeas
light stock or water (optional)
50g (2oz) tahini
4 tbsp lemon juice
2 garlic cloves, crushed
3 tbsp olive oil, plus extra to serve

1 tsp cumin seeds, dry-roasted, optional
2 tbsp chopped parsley or coriander leaves, optional
salt and freshly ground black pepper

1 Using a blender or food processor, purée the cooked chickpeas with enough cooking liquid (or light stock or water) to make a smooth paste.

2 Add the tahini, lemon juice, garlic and olive oil and process again until smooth. Season to taste.

3 Add dry-roasted cumin seeds and chopped parsley or coriander, if using.

4 To serve, spoon the hummus into a serving dish. Make a slight well in the centre and fill with olive oil.

nutritional breakdown per serving: kcal 210, kJ 872, protein 6g, fat 17g (saturated fat 2g), carbohydrate 9g

spiced vegetable fritters

These tasty vegetable fritters make a quick snack served with bread, salad and a yoghurt dip or Cucumber Relish with Chilli and Lemon (see page 295). Because the batter is quite thick it is best to chop the vegetables finely or even grate them so that they mix well with the batter. Don't worry if the fritters are shaped unevenly, that is part of their charm.

serves 4

preparation: 10 minutes

cooking: 5–10 minutes

𝒱

selection of vegetables (such as chopped onion, grated carrot, cauliflower florets, finely chopped red pepper), total weight 250g (8oz)
vegetable oil for frying

For the batter:
125g (4oz) chickpea flour
1 tbsp vegetable oil
1 tsp ground coriander
½ tsp ground turmeric
¼ teaspoon chilli powder
1 teaspoon salt
150ml (¼ pint) warm water

1 Mix the chickpea flour in a large bowl with the oil, spices and salt. Pour in the warm water and mix to a smooth batter, using a whisk or a wooden spoon.

2 Prepare the vegetables, grating or chopping them quite finely, and stir them into the batter.

3 Heat approximately 2.5cm (1in) vegetable oil in a deep saucepan. Drop tablespoons of the batter into the oil, cooking about 4 at a time for 2–3 minutes until the fritters are golden brown.

4 Drain on kitchen paper. The fritters are best served when freshly made but they can stand for an hour or so.

nutritional breakdown per serving: kcal 258, kJ 1075, protein 9g, fat 16g (saturated fat 2g), carbohydrate 21g

roasted peanut and coriander sambal

This spicy accompaniment is extremely easy to make. Serve it with the Spiced Vegetable Fritters (above) or use it with spiced rice and curry dishes.

serves 4

preparation time: 10 minutes

cooking time: 5 minutes

suitable for freezing

𝒱

spiced vegetable fritters with roasted peanut and coriander sambal

50g (2oz) peanuts
50g (2oz) coriander leaves, roughly chopped
1 small fresh green chilli, split and deseeded
4–6 tbsp water
2–3 tbsp lemon juice
salt

1 Spread the peanuts on a baking sheet and roast in a preheated oven, 200°C (400°F), Gas Mark 6, for 5 minutes. Leave to cool.

2 Put all the ingredients in a blender or food processor. Blend until fairly smooth, then adjust the seasoning to taste. Add more water or lemon juice if necessary.

nutritional breakdown per serving: kcal 75, kJ 310, protein 4g, fat 6g (saturated fat 1g), carbohydrate 2g

Light Meals

Eating habits have changed enormously in the last few years. Light meals and snacks, particularly in the middle of the day, are a popular alternative to more hearty fare. Generally, these lighter meals are quick and easy to make, use many fresh ingredients and can be prepared for several people without much trouble. If you are very hungry, try combining several light meals together to make a feast.

Take your pick from a delicious range of simple vegetable savouries such as succulent **Stuffed Italian Tomatoes with Red Pesto and Mozzarella**, or flavoursome **Leek and Potato Cakes with Gruyère**. There is also a selection of egg dishes that are ideal for breakfast or brunch, including the delicate **Herb Soufflé**, as well as classic omelettes, frittata, baked eggs and roulade. Mexican food is represented by a range of salsas as well as hot and spicy classics such as **Enchiladas**, **Refried Black Beans** and **Quesadillas**. Pancakes and pizzas are good for light meals and extremely straightforward to make. You'll find a choice of tempting fillings and toppings to try, such as tangy **Mushroom and Goat's Cheese Pancakes**, and **Classic Tomato Pizza Topping**, as well as a golden **Saffron Onion Pizza**. Finally, in this section there are some suggestions for simple and tasty meals for children.

herb soufflé

This is a light, simple, brilliantly coloured soufflé. It is an ideal dish when herbs are plentiful so ring the changes by using different combinations of herbs. For a slightly more substantial dish, add 50g (2oz) grated cheese in step 3. This soufflé is ideal as a starter for 4, followed by a grain or pasta dish; alternatively, serve it with a salad for a light meal for 2.

serves 2–4

preparation: 10 minutes

cooking: 30–35 minutes

25g (1oz) butter
25g (1oz) plain flour
250ml (8fl oz) milk
4 eggs, separated
50g (2oz) chopped herbs from a selection of
  parsley, basil, chives, rosemary and dill
salt and freshly ground black pepper

nutritional breakdown per serving (4 portions): kcal 174, kJ 726, protein 9g, fat 12g (saturated fat 6g), carbohydrate 8g

1 Grease a 900ml (1½ pint) soufflé dish and tie a collar of greaseproof paper around the edge of the dish.

2 Make a white sauce by melting the butter in a small saucepan. Stir in the flour to make a roux and cook for 1 minute. Add the milk gradually and, stirring constantly, bring the sauce to the boil, then simmer for 2–3 minutes – it should be very thick. Season well.

3 Stir the egg yolks and chopped herbs into the cooked white sauce.

4 Whisk the egg whites in a large bowl until stiff. Stir 1 tablespoon egg white into the white sauce. Then fold in the remaining egg white using a metal spoon.

5 Spoon the mixture into the prepared dish and bake in a preheated oven, 200°C (400°F), Gas Mark 6, for 25 minutes. If you are using a deep dish, the soufflé may take 5 minutes longer. The top should be golden brown and the soufflé well risen and firm on top. Serve hot.

stuffed italian tomatoes
with red pesto and mozzarella

Tomatoes and cheese are a timeless combination, enriched here with a heady red pesto sauce. The pesto can be made well in advance as it keeps in the fridge for at least 2 weeks. Serve this savoury with a good bread, such as focaccia, and a crisp salad. For a more substantial meal, follow with a simple pasta such as Tagliatelle with Fennel and Fresh Herbs (see page 207).

serves 4

preparation: 15 minutes

cooking: 15–20 minutes

(Ca)

4 large Italian tomatoes, halved
125g (4oz) mozzarella, sliced
salt and freshly ground black pepper

For the pesto:
2 tbsp olive oil
1 small red onion, finely chopped
2 garlic cloves, crushed

8 sun-dried tomatoes (in oil)
2 tbsp freshly grated Parmesan
4 tbsp chopped basil
25g (1oz) pine nuts

1   Put all the ingredients for the pesto in a food processor and process until finely chopped. Season to taste.

2   Lightly season the tomato halves. Divide the pesto between the 8 halves and set them on a lightly oiled baking sheet or in an ovenproof dish. Put 1 or 2 slices of mozzarella on each tomato half.

3   Bake in a preheated oven, 190°C (375°F), Gas Mark 5, for 15–20 minutes, or until the cheese is melted and the tomatoes look well cooked.

nutritional breakdown per serving: kcal 487, kJ 2017, protein 14g, fat 44g (saturated fat 10g), carbohydrate 9g

giant mushrooms stuffed with wild rice and roasted onions

Three members of the onion family roasted make a colourful and flavoursome addition to wild rice. This mixture is terrific served piled on top of succulent, roasted mushrooms. Serve these as a meal in their own right, accompanied by a moist salad, such as a tomato salad, or a side vegetable such as Butternut Squash and Carrot Purée with Nutmeg and Mascarpone (see page 286). The rice and onion mixture can be served on its own, but you should increase the quantity of rice.

nutritional breakdown per serving: kcal 396, kJ 1648, protein 7g, fat 15g (saturated fat 2g), carbohydrate 57g

VARIATIONS

For an extra gourmet snack you can top the vegetable mixture with a slice of cheese and melt quickly under a hot grill.

serves 4

preparation: 10 minutes

cooking: 50–55 minutes

suitable for freezing (rice only)

v

125g (4oz) wild rice
4–6 tbsp olive oil
2 onions, chopped
2 leeks, sliced
100g (3½oz) shallots, quartered
4 very large or 8 medium flat mushrooms
salt and freshly ground black pepper

1 Put the rice in a large saucepan and bring it to the boil in double its volume of water. Cover the pan and simmer for 35–40 minutes, or until soft.

2 While the rice is cooking, put 4 tablespoons of the olive oil in a large bowl and season well. Toss in the prepared onions, leeks and shallots, then spread out the oiled vegetables on baking sheets in one layer. Bake in a preheated oven, 200°C (400°F), Gas Mark 6, for 20 minutes, or until well browned.

3 Meanwhile, remove the stalks from the mushrooms and discard. Using the remaining oil and any residue in the bowl, coat the mushrooms and drizzle more oil on top. Season well.

4 Put the mushrooms in a shallow ovenproof dish and place in the oven with the roasting vegetables. Bake for 15 minutes, or until soft.

5 Drain the rice if necessary and toss in the roasted leeks, onions and shallots and adjust the seasoning. Pile generously on to the cooked mushroom bases and serve immediately.

falafel

This tasty snack is simple to prepare and may be served as part of a buffet meal or in pitta bread with a green salad, chopped tomatoes and a little mild onion. Falafel are traditionally deep-fried or baked but, with care, shallow-frying can produce good results. Baked falafel use less oil so are drier in texture. Counteract this by serving them with a yoghurt dip made with chopped chilli, roasted cumin and lemon juice to taste. For another yoghurt dip see page 349. Bite-sized falafel can be served as appetizers.

makes 20–24

preparation: 15 minutes, plus overnight soaking and chilling

cooking: 30–35 minutes

suitable for freezing

v

250g (8oz) chickpeas, soaked overnight
1 onion, roughly chopped
2 garlic cloves, roughly chopped
2 tsp cumin seeds
2 tsp ground coriander
2 tbsp chopped parsley
2 tbsp chopped coriander leaves
oil for frying
salt and freshly ground black pepper

1 Drain the chickpeas and rinse. Place them in a blender or food processor and grind them into a coarse powder. Scrape the powder into a large bowl.

2 Using the blender or food processor again, process the onion, garlic, spices and herbs until finely chopped. Stir into the chickpea powder and mix well with a spoon. Season well. Cover and leave to chill for up to 2 hours.

3 To make the falafel, dampen your hands and shape small amounts of the mixture between your hands to make walnut-sized balls. Flatten carefully into round cakes. (The falafel can be frozen at this point, if desired.)

4 To fry the falafel, heat the oil in a small, deep-sided frying pan. When hot, slide in the falafel, about 4 at a time. Cook for 2–3 minutes, then turn them over and cook for a further 2–3 minutes – the outside should be very crisp. Drain on kitchen paper.

VARIATION

To bake the falafel, place the cakes on a well-oiled baking sheet and brush or drizzle with oil. Bake in a preheated oven, 200°C (400°F), Gas Mark 6, for 15 minutes, then turn over and bake for a further 10–15 minutes, or until well browned.

nutritional breakdown per falafel (20 portions): kcal 57, kJ 238, protein 3g, fat 2g (saturated fat 0g), carbohydrate 7g

baked tofu and button mushrooms

This is a tasty snack that can be served on its own, with stir-fry vegetables for a light meal or with rice, noodles or buckwheat to make something more substantial. Augment the tofu with roasted shallots if you wish. Alternatively, you could spear pieces of tofu and mushrooms on cocktail sticks and serve them as miniature cocktail kebabs.

serves 4

preparation: 5 minutes, plus marinating

cooking: 10 minutes

 ⓥ

200g (7oz) tofu (bean curd)
200g (7oz) button cremini mushrooms

For the marinade:
2 tbsp lemon juice
1 tbsp shoyu or soy sauce
1 tbsp tomato purée
1 garlic clove, crushed
2 tsp chopped oregano
2 tbsp olive oil

1 Prepare the marinade by mixing all the ingredients together in a large shallow dish.

2 Chop the tofu into bite-sized pieces. Stir into the marinade with the mushrooms and leave for at least 1 hour.

3 Spread out the pieces of tofu and the mushrooms on a baking sheet and scrape over any residue of marinade. Bake in a preheated oven, 200°C (400°F), Gas Mark 6, for 10 minutes.

4 Serve hot with bread or with cooked rice, noodles or buckwheat.

nutritional breakdown per serving: kcal 100, kJ 416, protein 6g, fat 8g (saturated fat 1g), carbohydrate 2g

caponata of roasted vegetables

Caponata is a classic dish from the Mediterranean comprising sweet peppers and aubergine sharpened with capers and a dash of wine vinegar. In this version, the vegetables are roasted rather than stewed. The end result has a mellow flavour. This makes an easy lunch or snack served with good bread and a crisp green salad. Serve cubes of feta, haloumi cheese or pine nuts separately in order to boost the protein content.

serves 4

preparation: 15 minutes, plus salting

cooking: 25–30 minutes

suitable for freezing

v

2 aubergines, cubed
2 red peppers, cored, deseeded and thickly sliced
1 onion, thickly sliced
4 tomatoes, halved
8 tbsp olive oil
4 garlic cloves, left unpeeled
2 tbsp red wine vinegar
2–3 tsp capers
salt and freshly ground black pepper

1 Put the cubes of aubergine in a colander and sprinkle with salt. Leave for 30 minutes, then pat dry with kitchen paper.

2 Put the remaining vegetables in a large bowl with the salted aubergine cubes. Toss in 6 tablespoons of the olive oil and season well, then spread out in a large roasting tin.

3 Roast in a preheated oven, 200°C (400°F), Gas Mark 6, for 25–30 minutes, or until all the vegetables are well browned. Add the whole garlic cloves for the last 5 minutes of cooking time. Remove the vegetables from the oven and put everything except the garlic cloves and tomato halves in a large bowl.

4 Remove and discard the skins from the roasted tomatoes. Chop the flesh finely, then mix with any oil residue or juices from the roasting tin. Add the remaining olive oil, red wine vinegar and capers and mix well to make a dressing.

5 Crush the roasted garlic, remove the skin, and mix into the dressing. Season to taste, then mix the dressing with the roasted vegetables and serve warm or at room temperature.

nutritional breakdown per serving: kcal 268, kJ 1108, protein 3g, fat 23g (saturated fat 3g), carbohydrate 14g

leek and potato cakes with gruyère

From surprisingly humble ingredients comes this light and delicious savoury. These potato cakes are inspired by the potato gnocchi that feature in northern Italian cuisine. Baked in ramekins, they are a little more sturdy. Serve with Buttered Shallot and Wine Sauce (see page 290).

serves 4
preparation: 20 minutes
cooking: 40–45 minutes
suitable for freezing

500g (1lb) floury potatoes
25g (1oz) butter
2 leeks, finely chopped
2 garlic cloves, crushed
2 eggs, beaten
75g (3oz) Gruyère, grated
125g (4oz) crème fraîche
3 tbsp chopped parsley
salt and freshly ground black pepper
a few sprigs of parsley to garnish

nutritional breakdown per serving: kcal 385, kJ 1603, protein 12g, fat 27g (saturated fat 17g), carbohydrate 24g

1 Boil the potatoes in their skins in a large saucepan of boiling water for 15–20 minutes, or until soft. Drain well. Leave until cool enough to handle, then remove the skins and mash the potatoes.

2 Melt the butter in a small frying pan and gently fry the leeks and garlic until soft. Stir into the mashed potatoes. Remove from the heat and add the eggs, grated cheese, crème fraîche and parsley. Mix very well and season to taste.

3 Grease and line the base of 8 x 150ml (¼ pint) ramekins. Spoon the mixture into these and bake in a preheated oven, 200°C (400°F), Gas Mark 6, for 20 minutes, or until well browned. Serve hot with a sauce and garnish with parsley.

VARIATIONS

Potato cakes are popular with children and can be a good way of introducing some different vegetable flavours. Sweetcorn, carrot and finely chopped celery can be added to the mixture. You can also use Cheddar instead of Gruyère. Serve the cakes with a smooth tomato sauce or ketchup.

RAMEKINS

Ramekins are small, straight-sided dishes. Use tea cups, deep muffin tins or individual rings set on a baking sheet if you don't have any ramekin dishes.

eggs

These are genuine fast foods as they can be prepared in numerous simple ways to make a meal in minutes. Included here are all the classic ways to serve eggs, such as frittata, roulade, oven-baked egg dishes and more. First, however, there is a quick look at the many ways eggs can be prepared and served by themselves. Needless to say, with many of these recipes, variations are possible by adding simple vegetables and herbs. See page 82 for safety and storing.

fried egg

Heat a little butter or oil in a frying pan until hot but not smoking. Crack in the egg and cook for 4 minutes. Baste only the white with fat if you want to keep the yolk runny. Alternatively, baste both. Fried eggs can be turned over so as to cook evenly on both sides but take care not to break the yolk.

boiled egg

Soft-boiled Egg – Start with the egg at room temperature. Put the egg in cold water and bring to the boil. Once boiling, cook for 4 minutes, then serve. (Timing will vary according to the size of the egg – allow longer for a large egg.)

If you are worried about salmonella when making boiled eggs for children, it is a good idea to use an egg coddler. This is a traditional heavy china container with a screw-on metal lid that can withstand boiling water. The advantage is that you can look at the egg prior to cooking and check whether it is done by unscrewing the lid after a few minutes to see if the white has set. A slight disadvantage is that the egg takes a little longer to cook using this method.

Hard-boiled Egg – Start with the egg at room temperature. Put the egg in cold water and bring to the boil. Once boiling, simmer for 8–10 minutes, then plunge immediately into a bowl of cold water to prevent a black rim forming between the yolk and the white. Shell the egg once cold.

scrambled egg

Good scrambled eggs should be creamy and fluffy rather than rubbery or stringy. For perfect results, don't try to scramble the eggs too quickly over too high a heat. Stir all the time over a low heat.

serves 2

4 eggs
2 tbsp water or milk
knob of butter
salt and freshly ground black pepper

1 Break the eggs into a bowl, add the water or milk and whisk with a fork. Season well.

2 Heat the butter in a small pan until just melted. When sizzling, pour in the egg mixture. Stir constantly over a low heat for about 4–5 minutes. Once the mixture no longer has a runny quality remove the pan from the heat as the eggs will continue cooking. Keep stirring, then serve straightaway.

VARIATIONS
Mexican Scrambled Eggs – Make the eggs as in the main recipe but beat in 2–3 tablespoons of Cooked Salsa with Chilli (see page 190) as the eggs scramble.

Lots of other ingredients can be stirred into scrambled eggs. Make sure you have them ready first though. Try adding chopped herbs, such as parsley, chives or tarragon; 2–3 tablespoons grated cheese; cooked chopped onion or spring onion, cooked sliced baby mushrooms or chopped roasted pepper.

The following make good accompaniments to serve with scrambled eggs: baked tomatoes, spinach purée and roasted vegetables, such as roasted peppers, onions or shallots.

nutritional breakdown per serving: kcal 172, kJ 717, protein 13g, fat 13g (saturated fat 5g), carbohydrate 1g

poached egg

Aficionados break an egg straight into boiling water rather than cheating by cooking the eggs in a little specially designed metal dish. The texture of the white is softer if cooked straight in the water; however it can take a little practice to get right. A tip is to create a little whirlpool in the water to try to preserve an oval shape.

1 Use a wide pan, add water to a depth of about 5–7cm (2–3in) plus 1 tablespoon white wine vinegar.

2 Bring to the boil. Stir the water, crack in an egg and immediately turn the heat to low otherwise violent boiling will disperse the egg white.

3 Leave to cook for 3 minutes until the white is opaque.

nutritional breakdown per egg: kcal 75, kJ 330, protein 6g, fat 5g (saturated fat 2g), carbohydrate 0g

omelette

An omelette is a fried mixture of beaten egg. It is important to have the right size pan so that the mixture is not too thick or too thin. A 15cm (6in) frying pan works well for a 2–3 egg omelette. The eggs should not be overbeaten, otherwise the texture becomes rubbery. Simply break the eggs into a small bowl and stir with a fork until the egg yolk and white are lightly combined.

serves 1

2 eggs
knob of butter
salt and freshly ground black pepper

1 Break the eggs into a bowl, mix lightly with a fork and season to taste.

2 Melt the butter in a small frying pan. When it has stopped foaming, pour in the eggs and tip the pan so that the mixture spreads evenly around the base of the pan. Stir with a fork until the egg starts to set. As the egg sets at the edges, use a spatula to lift up the sides so that uncooked egg in the middle of the pan runs underneath.

3 When the omelette is set, add a filling if desired (see below), then fold in half in the pan and slide out.

nutritional breakdown per serving: kcal 220, kJ 915, protein 13g, fat 19g (saturated fat 9g), carbohydrate 0g

VARIATIONS

Suitable additions to omelettes include grated cheese, cooked mushrooms, roasted vegetables, such as peppers or onion and griddled asparagus, courgettes or baby leeks.

folded soufflé omelette

For this type of omelette the eggs are separated and the whites whisked until stiff, then folded into the beaten yolks. The omelette is then made as before but it turns out much lighter.

japanese omelette

These omelettes are very thin ones made with an egg and water batter for lightness. They are briefly fried then rolled up and cooked until set.

Other types of omelette

Frittata – a thick Italian omelette, partially cooked in the pan and then finished off under the grill. Can also be cooked in the oven.
Tortilla – the Spanish name for the thick omelette, usually cooked with lots of onions, potatoes and peppers, all of which are pre-fried in olive oil. The cooked mixture is flipped in the pan so that it browns and sets on both sides.
Eggah or Kuku – a traditional Persian dish where the eggs are baked omelette-style in the oven. It is served cut into wedges, hot or cold.

leek and fennel frittata

Moist and delicately flavoured, this is a straightforward savoury that can be served hot or cold. Add bread or new potatoes to make a main course of it, or serve as it is for a light lunch or supper.

serves 4

preparation: 10 minutes

cooking: 40–45 minutes

2 tbsp olive oil
1 onion, finely chopped
2 large leeks, finely chopped
1 garlic clove, crushed
300g (10oz) fennel, finely chopped
2 tbsp chopped dill
6 eggs
150g (5oz) soft goat's cheese
1–2 tbsp freshly grated Parmesan
salt and freshly ground black pepper

1 Heat the oil in a saucepan and fry the onion, leeks and garlic until soft. Add the fennel and cook for 6–8 minutes, or until lightly cooked and coloured. Add the dill and stir well, then remove the pan from the heat.

2 Mix the eggs with the goat's cheese in a large bowl and season well. Stir in the cooked vegetables, season if necessary, then pour the mixture into a lightly buttered ovenproof dish.

3 Dust with Parmesan, then bake in a preheated oven, 190°C (375°F), Gas Mark 5, for 30 minutes, or until well browned and firm in the centre.

nutritional breakdown per serving: kcal 278, kJ 1156, protein 17g, fat 21g (saturated fat 8g), carbohydrate 6g

kuku with spinach

This is one of the names given to the substantial, thick baked omelette found in many variations all over the Middle East. It is designed to be served cold so that the flavours can fully develop and is therefore ideal for warm weather suppers. This version is densely packed with spinach and has an undertone of herbs and spices, which prevents the kuku from tasting bland.

serves 4

preparation: 5 minutes

cooking: 30–35 minutes

500g (1lb) spinach
5 eggs
1 tbsp chopped mint
¼ tsp ground cumin
125g (4oz) feta (drained weight), crumbled
salt and freshly ground black pepper

1 Gently cook the washed spinach in a saucepan without adding any extra water, for 4–5 minutes, or until soft.

2 Put the spinach in a colander to drain off all the excess water, then press the spinach down with the back of a wooden spoon to squeeze out as much water as possible. Chop the spinach roughly.

3 Break the eggs into a bowl and stir lightly with a fork to combine the yolks and whites. (Stirring the eggs rather than beating them ensures that the finished texture is not rubbery.) Add the chopped spinach and mix with the mint and cumin. Stir in the crumbled feta and season well.

4 Pour the mixture into a lightly oiled ovenproof dish and bake in a preheated oven, 180°C (350°F), Gas Mark 4, for 25–30 minutes, or until just set. Leave until cold then cut the kuku into squares or wedges to serve.

nutritional breakdown per serving: kcal 202, kJ 840, protein 17g, fat 13g (saturated fat 2g), carbohydrate 5g

COOKING WITH FETA

Feta provides a salty tang but it is not a cheese that melts. To create a marbled effect in the finished dish, make sure the cheese is chopped quite small or crumbled.

baked eggs with mozzarella and fresh tomatoes

This is a simple, high-protein supper or lunch dish, which can easily be made in smaller quantities if you are cooking for fewer people. There are obviously lots of variations on this idea – add mushrooms, chopped peppers, chilli or sweetcorn to the basic sauce. This would also make a good starter for a meal such as fresh pasta with a simple sauce (see pages 208–11).

serves 4

preparation: 10 minutes

cooking: 20 minutes

2 tbsp olive oil
1 onion, finely chopped
4 tomatoes, skinned and chopped
2 tbsp chopped parsley
4 eggs
125g (4oz) mozzarella, cubed
salt and freshly ground black pepper

1 Heat the oil in a saucepan and gently fry the onion until soft. Add the tomatoes and cook for 5 minutes, then add the parsley, reserving a little for garnish, and season well.

2 Spoon the mixture into 4 lightly oiled ovenproof dishes. Make a hollow in the centre of each and break an egg into each dish. Divide the cubes of mozzarella between the dishes.

3 Bake in a preheated oven, 180°C (350°F), Gas Mark 4, for 12 minutes, or until the eggs have set. Serve straightaway, garnished with the reserved parsley.

nutritional breakdown per serving: kcal 242, kJ 1007, protein 15g, fat 18g (saturated fat 7g), carbohydrate 6g

broccoli and stilton roulade

An impressive light lunch, supper dish or starter for a special meal, a roulade is not that tricky to make. It is essentially a soufflé mixture, which is baked in a flat tray, then rolled up around a sauce or filling. You can prepare all the steps up to and including step 4 well ahead of time when entertaining guests. Cold roulades are great for buffets and picnics (see pages 354–55).

serves 4

preparation: 10 minutes

cooking: 20–25 minutes

For the sauce:
25g (1oz) butter
20g (¾oz) plain flour
150ml (¼ pint) milk
2 tbsp single cream
50g (2oz) Stilton, crumbled
salt and freshly ground black pepper

For the roulade:
250g (8oz) broccoli
15g (½oz) butter
4 eggs, separated
salt and freshly ground black pepper

1 To make the sauce, melt the butter in a small saucepan then stir in the flour to make a roux. Add the milk gradually, stirring constantly until it thickens, then bring to the boil and simmer for 3–4 minutes.

2 Stir the cream and Stilton into the sauce. Season well and keep warm.

3 Divide the broccoli into small florets and chop the stalk finely. Steam over a pan of boiling water until soft. Leave to cool, then chop finely and toss in the butter. Meanwhile, line a 20 x 30cm (8 x 12in) shallow tin with baking parchment.

4 Beat the egg yolks and mix with the cooled broccoli. Season well.

5 Whisk the egg whites in a separate large bowl until stiff. Fold into the broccoli mixture.

6 Spoon the mixture into the prepared tin. Bake in a preheated oven, 200°C (400°F), Gas Mark 6, for 10–15 minutes, or until just browned and firm.

7 When the roulade is cooked, remove from the oven and turn out on to a piece of greaseproof paper.

8 Quickly spread the warm sauce over the roulade, then roll it up by folding in one end of the oblong, then, using the underneath sheet of greaseproof paper to help you, ease it into a roll. Transfer to a serving dish and serve straightaway.

nutritional breakdown per serving: kcal 320, kJ 1330, protein 14g, fat 26g (saturated fat 15g), carbohydrate 7g

strata

This colourful dish comprises layers of buttered bread, chopped peppers and tomatoes all doused with a seasoned egg and milk mixture. The strata can be baked straightaway or refrigerated for several hours, therefore making it a good dish for a special breakfast as it can all be assembled the day before, then baked in the morning.

Richer versions of this recipe can be made using extra cheese and vegetables.

serves 4

preparation: 10 minutes, plus chilling

cooking: 35–45 minutes

 Ca Fe

250g (8oz) wholemeal bread, sliced
25g (1oz) butter
1 red pepper, cored, deseeded and sliced
1 yellow pepper, cored, deseeded and sliced
8 sun-dried tomatoes, finely chopped
3 tbsp chopped parsley
2 tbsp chopped basil
4 eggs
500ml (17fl oz) milk
4 tbsp freshly grated pecorino
salt and freshly ground black pepper

1   Spread the slices of bread with the butter and cut the slices in half. Layer the slices of bread and butter with the sliced peppers, chopped tomatoes and fresh herbs in a buttered deep ovenproof dish, seasoning each layer as you go and trimming the bread if necessary.

2   Beat the eggs in a jug with the milk and pour the mixture over the layers of bread. Cover and refrigerate for 4–5 hours, or overnight if you wish.

3   Sprinkle with grated cheese and bake in a preheated oven, 200°C (400°F), Gas Mark 6, for 35–45 minutes, or until well browned and crispy on top – the middle should be soft but not runny.

nutritional breakdown per serving: kcal 628, kJ 2618, protein 23g, fat 43g (saturated fat 12g), carbohydrate 40g

asparagus and pea fricassee with eggs

This fresh-looking dish with shades of green is particularly good with new potatoes and a deeper green salad made from watercress and feuille de chêne. Small portions would make an elegant hot starter, ideally followed by a simple pasta dish such as Tagliatelle with Fennel and Fresh Herbs (see page 207) or a risotto.

serves 4

preparation: 15 minutes

cooking: 25 minutes

250g (8oz) asparagus, halved
4 tbsp water, optional
250g (8oz) peas (shelled weight)
1–2 tbsp lemon juice
6 eggs
1–2 tbsp finely chopped mint, to garnish

For the sauce:
50g (2oz) butter
250g (8oz) shallots, finely chopped
3 tbsp plain flour
200ml (7fl oz) white wine
200–300ml (7–10fl oz) Vegetable Stock
  (see page 144)
salt and freshly ground black pepper

1 To make the sauce, melt the butter in a medium saucepan and gently cook the shallots until soft. Stir in the flour to make a soft roux. Gradually add the white wine and 200ml (7fl oz) of the stock, stirring constantly, and bring to the boil, stirring quickly as the sauce thickens. Add more stock if the sauce is too thick. Season well and keep warm.

2 Microwave the asparagus with 2 tablespoons water on 800W for 2 minutes or steam over a saucepan of boiling water for 5 minutes, or until tender. Drain and stir into the shallot sauce.

3 Similarly, microwave the peas with 2 tablespoons water on 800W for 2 minutes, or steam for 3 minutes until just tender. Again, drain and stir into the shallot sauce. Adjust the seasoning and add lemon juice to taste.

4 Bring the eggs to the boil in a large saucepan of water and boil for 8 minutes. Run the hard-boiled eggs under cold water, then shell while still warm. Cut lengthways into quarters and reserve 4 quarters for garnish.

5 Stir the eggs into the vegetable fricassee and spoon into a warmed serving dish. Garnish with the reserved egg quarters and sprinkle with the chopped mint.

nutritional breakdown per serving: kcal 377, kJ 1567, protein 18g, fat 20g (saturated fat 9g), carbohydrate 25g

pancakes

Pancakes turn up throughout the world in many guises – from the tiny yeasted blinis made with buckwheat flour, to the golden Mexican tortilla. In whatever form, pancakes are an attractive way of serving a variety of fillings. Below are the standard wheat and buckwheat batter pancakes that are traditional in Northern Europe.

Pancakes are quick and easy to make and, thanks to food processors, there should no longer be a problem with lumpy batter. It is important to have the right pan, however, which you should keep solely for pancakes and omelettes so that it develops a good non-stick surface. A good pancake pan should be about 18cm (7in) in diameter and have curved sides so that the pancakes can be easily flipped or turned over and removed from the pan. Traditional Breton galettes or lace pancakes are much larger and for these you need a griddle or completely flat cooking area on which to spread the batter.

Cooked pancakes can be kept for 3 days in the fridge when stored on a plate, interleaved with, and then wrapped in grease-proof paper or clingfilm. For freezing, place freezer wrap or clingfilm between each pancake then wrap in foil or use a freezer bag. Filled pancakes (if the filling is suitable for freezing) should be kept in rigid containers. Allow the filling to cool before adding.

Unfilled pancakes can be frozen for 6 months; filled pancakes for up to 2 months. To thaw, separate out and leave at room temperature for 30 minutes. To reheat, stack in a lightly greased ovenproof dish and heat through in a preheated oven, 180°C (350°F), Gas Mark 4, for 15–20 minutes, depending on the number of pancakes. Filled pancakes take longer to reheat.

wholemeal pancakes

makes 8

preparation: 10 minutes, plus standing

cooking: 30–35 minutes

suitable for freezing

300ml (½ pint) milk
1 egg
pinch of salt
1 tsp vegetable oil, plus extra for frying
100–125g (3½–4oz) wholemeal flour

1 To make the batter using a blender or food processor, put the milk, egg, salt and oil into the goblet or bowl and blend thoroughly. Then add the flour and blend again for about 30 seconds.

2 To make the batter by hand, put the flour and salt in a bowl. Using a balloon whisk, beat the egg in a jug with the milk and oil, then pour this into the flour and whisk in until the batter is smooth.

3 Let the batter stand for 30 minutes if possible.

4 To cook the pancakes, heat a little oil in a suitable pancake pan and, when hot, pour in about 2 tablespoons of batter. Tilt the pan so that the batter coats the base of the pan evenly.

5 Cook for about 2–3 minutes, then loosen the edge and either toss or flip the pancake over with a spatula, then cook the other side for 1 minute.

6 Keep the cooked pancakes warm while you make more in the same way until all the batter is used. If not eating immediately, cool the pancakes on a flat surface, then wrap and store (see above).

nutritional breakdown per pancake: kcal 69, kJ 290, protein 4g, fat 2g (saturated fat 1g), carbohydrate 10g

buckwheat pancakes

makes 8

preparation: 10 minutes, plus standing

cooking: 30–35 minutes

suitable for freezing

300ml (½ pint) milk
2 eggs
pinch of salt
1 tsp vegetable oil, plus extra for frying
50g (2oz) wholemeal flour
50g (2oz) buckwheat flour

1 To make the batter using a blender or food processor, put the milk, eggs, salt and oil into the goblet or bowl and blend thoroughly. Then add both flours and blend again for about 30 seconds.

2 Alternatively, to make the batter by hand, put both types of flour and salt in a bowl. Using a balloon whisk, beat the egg in a jug with the milk and oil, then pour this into the flour and whisk in until the batter is smooth. Leave to stand for 30 minutes if possible.

3 To cook the pancakes, heat a little oil in a suitable pancake pan and, when hot, pour in about 2 tablespoons of batter. Tilt the pan so that the batter coats the base of the pan evenly.

4 Cook for about 2–3 minutes, then loosen the edge and either toss or flip the pancake over with a spatula, then cook the other side for 1 minute.

5 Keep the cooked pancakes warm while you make more in the same way until all the batter is used. If not eating immediately, cool the pancakes on a flat surface then wrap and store (see page 186).

nutritional breakdown per pancake: kcal 80, kJ 340, protein 4g, fat 3g (saturated fat 1g), carbohydrate 9g

RICH MIXTURE

For an enriched mixture, use an extra egg. If you make the enriched batter by hand, beat the egg well with the flour to a smooth consistency, then add the milk slowly. This should ensure a lump-free batter.

roquefort and celeriac pancakes

This heavenly filling with a rich taste and texture can be prepared well in advance, as can the pancakes, leaving you with just a last-minute assembly job. Serve with a crisp side salad of endive and watercress.

serves 4

preparation: 10 minutes, plus pancake making

cooking: 15–20 minutes, plus pancakes

1 quantity Wholemeal or Buckwheat pancake batter (see page 186 and above)
250g (8oz) celeriac (weight after peeling)
100g (3½oz) mascarpone cheese
100g (3½oz) Roquefort
3 tbsp chopped parsley
25g (1oz) butter, melted
salt and freshly ground black pepper
50g (2oz) chopped walnuts, toasted, to garnish

1 Make 8 pancakes according to the instructions on page 186.

2 Cook the celeriac in a saucepan of boiling water for 8–10 minutes. Leave to cool.

3 Using a blender or food processor, purée the celeriac with the mascarpone and Roquefort until smooth. Stir in the parsley and season to taste.

4 Spoon the filling on to the prepared pancakes and fold or roll them up and place in a lightly greased ovenproof dish. Brush each pancake with melted butter.

5 Cover the dish with foil and heat through in a preheated oven, 180°C (350°F), Gas Mark 4, for 8–10 minutes. Serve the pancakes hot, garnished with toasted chopped walnuts.

nutritional breakdown per serving: kcal 504, kJ 2093, protein 16g, fat 39g (saturated fat 20g), carbohydrate 23g

mushroom and goat's cheese pancakes

Goat's cheese and mushrooms are a great combination, being both tangy and succulent, and this straightforward tasty filling is very quick to create. The pancakes make an easy supper dish, or serve with extra salads for a special meal.

serves 4

preparation: 5 minutes, plus pancake making

cooking: 15 minutes, plus pancakes

suitable for freezing

1 quantity Wholemeal or Buckwheat pancake
  batter (see pages 186–87)
75g (3oz) butter
2 shallots, finely chopped
1 garlic clove, crushed
250g (8oz) oyster mushrooms, thinly sliced
250g (8oz) button mushrooms, thinly sliced
125g (4oz) soft goat's cheese, crumbled
3–4 tbsp water
3 tbsp chopped coriander leaves
salt and freshly ground black pepper
sprigs of coriander, to garnish

1 Make 8 pancakes following the instructions on page 186.

2 Melt 50g (2oz) of the butter in a large frying pan, add the shallots and garlic and cook gently until soft. Add the mushrooms and season well. Cook over a high heat for about 2 minutes. Then reduce the heat, cover the pan and cook for 5 minutes, or until the mushrooms are soft and juicy.

3 Add the goat's cheese and stir in as it melts; add 3–4 tablespoons of water if the mixture is too thick. It should have the consistency of pouring cream. Season to taste. Stir in the chopped coriander leaves.

4 Spoon the filling on to the prepared pancakes and fold or roll up and place in an ovenproof dish. Melt the remaining butter and brush it liberally over each pancake.

5 Cover the dish with foil and heat through in a preheated oven, 180°C (350°F), Gas Mark 4, for 8–10 minutes. Serve the pancakes hot, garnished with coriander.

nutritional breakdown per serving: kcal 360, kJ 1503, protein 14g, fat 25g (saturated fat 15g), carbohydrate 12g

crespelles

These are pancakes stuffed with chard, cream and smoked cheese, then baked in the oven smothered with creamy tomato sauce. The end result is a warming main course suitable for a family meal or, dressed up, for a special occasion. The pancakes themselves can be prepared some time ahead or frozen, as can the tomato sauce, but prepare the filling fresh. Serve as they come, or add a contrasting side vegetable or crisp salad.

serves 4

preparation: 5 minutes, plus pancake making

cooking: 65 minutes

suitable for freezing

1 quantity Wholemeal or Buckwheat pancake
  batter (see pages 186–87)

For the filling:
500g (1lb) chard, shredded
75ml (3fl oz) double cream
125g (4oz) smoked cheese, grated
salt and freshly ground black pepper

For the sauce:
2 tbsp olive oil
1 onion, finely chopped
1 garlic clove, crushed
1 bay leaf
500g (1lb) passata
½ tsp sugar
50ml (2fl oz) double cream
50g (2oz) smoked cheese, grated
salt and freshly ground black pepper

1 Make 8 pancakes according to the instructions on page 186.

2 To make the filling, place the chard in a saucepan and cook without adding extra water, for about 5 minutes. Remove from the heat, then stir in the cream and grated smoked cheese. Season well.

3 To make the sauce, heat the oil in a saucepan and cook the onion until soft. Add the garlic and cook for a few minutes, then add the bay leaf, passata, sugar and ½ teaspoon of salt.

4 Bring to the boil, then simmer, covered, for 30–40 minutes. Remove the bay leaf, adjust the seasoning and stir in the double cream.

5 To assemble the dish, put a spoonful of filling on each pancake and roll up. Place the filled pancakes in a lightly greased ovenproof dish.

6 Cover with the tomato sauce, then sprinkle over the grated cheese. Bake in a preheated oven, 200°C (400°F), Gas Mark 6, for 15 minutes, or until heated through. Serve hot.

nutritional breakdown per serving: kcal 523, kJ 2184, protein 21g, fat 36g (saturated fat 18g), carbohydrates 32g

mexican food — tortillas and fillings

Mexican food has a lot to offer vegetarians, with its strong flavours and liberal use of spices and herbs. You can create plenty of variety with a few simple recipes, mixing and matching to make platters to suit everyone. If you are entertaining, highlight these tasty dishes by using brightly coloured crockery and tableware to recreate the striking colours of Mexican culture.

OTHER MEXICAN RECIPES

Green Rice with Chilli
(see page 232)
Pinto Bean Salsa
(see page 292)

cooked salsa with chilli

serves 4

preparation: 10 minutes, plus soaking

cooking: 25 minutes

suitable for freezing

𝑣

3 chillies, soaked in hot water for 15 minutes
1 onion, finely chopped
1 garlic clove, finely chopped
1–2 tbsp olive oil
6–8 fresh tomatoes, chopped
salt

1 Lift the chillies out of the soaking water and remove the seeds and the veins. Sprinkle the chillies with salt and pound to a paste, using a pestle and mortar.

2 Add a little of the chopped onion and garlic and pound again to get a rough paste.

3 To make the salsa, heat the oil in a saucepan and fry the remaining onion until soft. Add the remaining garlic and fry a little longer, then add the tomatoes and fry to soften.

4 Add the 1–2 teaspoons of pounded chilli mixture and the chilli soaking water. Cover the pan and simmer for 20 minutes.

5 Cool slightly then, using a blender or food processor, process until smooth. Season with salt.

nutritional breakdown per total recipe: kcal 285, kJ 1189, protein 5g, fat 18g (saturated fat 3g), carbohydrate 28g

black beans

serves 4

preparation: 5 minutes, plus overnight soaking

cooking: 50–60 minutes

suitable for freezing

250g (8oz) black beans, soaked overnight
1 onion, quartered
1 garlic clove, chopped
salt and freshly ground black pepper

1 Drain the beans, then bring to the boil in a large saucepan of fresh water. Add the onion quarters and garlic and boil fast for 10 minutes, then cover the pan and simmer for 45–60 minutes, or until the beans are soft. Season to taste.

2 At this stage the beans are often served drained as an accompaniment to scrambled egg or with Enchiladas (see page 191).

nutritional breakdown per serving: kcal 184, kJ 783, protein 13g, fat 0g (saturated fat 0g), carbohydrate 34g

refried black beans

This is an extension of the previous recipe. It is easier to make refried beans while the beans are warm and freshly cooked.

1 Complete step 1 of the previous recipe. Leave the beans in the saucepan in their cooking water.

2 To make refried beans, heat 1 tablespoon olive oil in a large frying pan.

3 Remove several tablespoons of beans at a time from the saucepan using a slotted spoon.

4 Mash into the hot oil, add a little more olive oil if necessary and, if the mixture gets too dry, add some of the beans' cooking liquid to get a soft paste rather than a floury mixture. Gradually mash in the rest of the beans. Add more liquid if necessary. Season with salt.

nutritional breakdown per serving: kcal 217, kJ 917, protein 14g, fat 3g (saturated fat 0g), carbohydrate 36g

enchiladas

serves 4

preparation: 5 minutes

cooking: 5 minutes

 Ca Fe

2–3 tbsp corn oil
12 corn tortillas
1 quantity Cooked Salsa with Chilli
  (see page 190)
1 quantity Refried Black Beans (see above)
1 iceberg lettuce, shredded
125ml (4fl oz) soured cream
125g (4oz) Cheshire cheese, crumbled

1 To assemble the enchiladas, heat the corn oil in a large frying pan and quickly fry the tortillas, one at a time, to soften them.

2 Remove the tortillas with a slotted spoon, then dip them, one at a time, in the pan of cooked salsa.

3 Lift out on to a work surface and place a generous tablespoon of refried beans on each tortilla. Fold the tortillas in half and arrange singly or grouped together on plates.

4 Top the tortillas with shredded lettuce, soured cream and crumbled cheese. Serve straightaway.

nutritional breakdown per serving: kcal 774, kJ 3246, protein 29g, fat 36g (saturated fat 13g), carbohydrate 89g

salsa mexicana

This is the classic salsa or relish, so called because the ingredients echo the colours of the Mexican flag. The onion, tomatoes and coriander should be chopped to approximately the same size.

serves 4

preparation: 5 minutes

cooking: none

𝒱

1 onion, finely chopped
1 garlic clove, finely chopped
4 tomatoes, finely chopped
20g (¾oz) chopped
   coriander leaves
salt

1 Mix all the ingredients together in a bowl, then season with salt.

nutritional breakdown per total recipe: kcal 119, kJ 502, protein 5g, fat 2g (saturated fat 0g), carbohydrate 23g

VARIATIONS

Salsa with Chilli – Add a fresh green chilli (a serrano chilli if possible) to create a hotter version. Quarter the chilli lengthways, remove the veins and seeds and chop finely. Stir into the salsa.

Salsa with Lime – For a more piquant flavour add the juice of ¼ of a lime to the basic salsa.

Chunky Guacamole – This variation is excellent served with Quesadillas (see below). Make the basic salsa and add a finely chopped avocado, 1–2 tablespoons lemon juice and extra finely chopped garlic to taste.

quesadillas

These easy snacks comprise folded tortillas filled with melted cheese.

serves 4

preparation: 5 minutes

cooking: 10 minutes

Ⓒₐ

2–3 tbsp corn oil
12 corn tortillas
125–175g (4–6oz) cheese, crumbled
1 quantity Chunky Guacamole (see above)

1 Heat the corn oil in a large frying pan and quickly fry the tortillas, one at a time, to soften them.

2 Lift out with a slotted spoon and place some crumbled cheese on top. Fold each tortilla in half then return it to the frying pan, pressing it down until the cheese melts.

3 Top with Chunky Guacamole and serve hot.

nutritional breakdown per serving: kcal 485, kJ 2029, protein 15g, fat 26g (saturated fat 9g), carbohydrate 51g

huevos rancheros

An easy, colourful egg dish which makes a great snack at any time of day.

serves 4

preparation: 5 minutes

cooking: 10 minutes

2–3 tbsp corn oil, plus extra for frying eggs
4 corn tortillas
4 eggs
1 quantity Cooked Salsa with Chilli
  (see page 190)
1 yellow and 1 red pepper, sliced, then grilled
  or fried

1   Heat the corn oil in a large frying pan and quickly fry the tortillas, one at a time, to soften them. Lift out with a slotted spoon and keep warm.

2   Heat a little oil in the pan for frying the eggs. Break the eggs into the pan, 2 or more at a time depending on the size of your pan. Cook for 4 minutes, basting the white, and the yolk too if desired, with fat.

3   When cooked, put 1 egg on top of each tortilla, cover with cooked salsa and slices of cooked peppers. Serve hot.

nutritional breakdown per serving: kcal 273, kJ 1140, protein 10g, fat 17g (saturated fat 3g), carbohydrate 22g

pizzas

Modern, fast-acting yeast and strong flour mean you can put together a pizza base in just 10 minutes. It then has to be left to rest for about 15 minutes, but that time can be used to make the topping. Toppings are simple to make, and you can include a selection of your favourite ingredients, which can be as unusual as you like. For those who don't like tomato, I've created a succulent onion pizza, which makes a great savoury or easy snack when served in small pieces.

basic pizza bases

Pizza dough is straightforward to make. It is essentially a bread dough, but because it is rolled into a thin crust it needs less time to rise. The dough takes about 10 minutes to make, less than half an hour to rest, 5 minutes to cook and is then ready for the topping.

makes 2 × 25cm (10in) pizza bases; serves 4–6	
preparation: 10 minutes, plus resting	
cooking: 5 minutes	
suitable for freezing	
ⓖ 𝑣	

350g (12oz) strong white flour, plus extra for dusting
7g (¼oz) sachet easy-blend yeast
1 tsp sugar
1 tsp salt
200ml (7fl oz) warm water
2 tbsp olive oil, plus extra for brushing

1 Mix the flour in a large bowl with the yeast, sugar and salt. Pour in the warm water and add the olive oil.

2 Draw the mixture into a dough and knead well. Add more flour if necessary. Return the dough to a clean bowl and cover with clingfilm. Leave to rest for 15 minutes or longer.

3 Turn out the dough on to a lightly floured work surface and knead again. Divide in half. Roll out each piece into a round, about 25cm (10in) in diameter. Place on a baking sheet and prick with a fork. Leave to rest for 10 minutes.

4 Part-bake in a preheated oven, 220°C (425°F), Gas Mark 7, for 5 minutes. Brush with olive oil or Garlic Oil (see page 196), before adding topping.

nutritional breakdown per pizza base: kcal 1432, kJ 6063, protein 38g, fat 27g (saturated fat 4g), carbohydrate 277g

three-flour pizza bases

This pizza dough combines three different flours. The wholemeal flour adds a nutty flavour and the rye flour has a distinctive tang. Depending on your personal taste you can alter the ratios of the flours. The technique for making this dough, known as the sponge or batter method, is slightly different from the earlier basic recipe. Initially, only a small quantity of flour (without salt) is mixed with the water and stirred to make a batter similar to a pancake batter. The advantage of this method is that the yeast gets started very easily with the absence of salt and, as the sponge starts to rise, gluten is formed, thus making the dough more elastic. This method is most appropriate when using heavier flours or flours that are lower in gluten, such as rye.

makes 2 x 25cm (10in) pizza bases; serves 4–6
preparation: 15 minutes, plus resting
cooking: 5 minutes
suitable for freezing
(Fe) *v*

175g (6oz) strong white flour, plus extra
  for dusting
125g (4oz) wholemeal flour
50g (2oz) rye flour
7g (¼oz) sachet easy-blend yeast
200ml (7fl oz) warm water
1 tsp sugar
1 tsp salt
2 tbsp olive oil, plus extra for brushing

1 Measure the 3 flours into a bowl. Spoon about one-third of the flour mixture into a separate bowl and sprinkle in the yeast. Add the warm water and mix very thoroughly to form a batter. Cover the bowl with a damp tea towel and leave the batter for about 30 minutes or until it looks frothy.

2 Mix the sugar and salt with the reserved flour, then tip this into the batter. Stir well and add the olive oil.

3 Draw up into a dough and knead well. Add more flour if necessary. Return the dough to a clean bowl and cover with clingfilm. Leave for 15 minutes or longer.

4 Turn out the dough on to a lightly floured work surface and knead again. Divide in half. Roll out each piece into a round, about 25cm (10in) in diameter. Place on a baking sheet and prick with a fork. Leave to rest for 10 minutes.

5 Part-bake in a preheated oven, 220°C (425°F), Gas Mark 7, for 5 minutes. Brush with olive oil or Garlic Oil (see page 196), before adding topping.

> nutritional breakdown per pizza base: kcal 689, kJ 2918, protein 19g, fat 14g (saturated fat 2g), carbohydrate 129g

Step 1 Add the oil to the flour and water mixture.
Step 2 Knead the dough until smooth using the heel of the hand.
Step 3 Roll the dough thinly into a large round and place on a baking sheet.
Step 4 Prick well and leave to rest, then bake for about 5 minutes.

classic tomato pizza topping

This simple pizza topping is redolent with aromatic herbs and comprises a tomato mixture that is cooked down to a thick pulp.

makes sufficient for 2 x 25cm (10in) pizza bases

serves 4–6

preparation: 5 minutes

cooking: 15–20 minutes

suitable for freezing

𝑣

1–2 tbsp olive oil
1 onion, finely chopped
1 garlic clove, crushed
400g (13oz) can chopped tomatoes
1 tsp dried oregano
1 tsp dried thyme
1 bay leaf
salt and freshly ground black pepper

1 Heat the oil in a saucepan and gently fry the onion and garlic until soft.

2 Add the can of chopped tomatoes, oregano, thyme and bay leaf and stir well. Bring the mixture to the boil, then simmer, uncovered, over a moderate heat for 15–20 minutes, stirring frequently until some of the liquid has evaporated to leave a rich tomato pulp. Remove the bay leaf and season to taste.

nutritional breakdown per serving (4 portions): kcal 69, kJ 287, protein 2g, fat 5g (saturated fat 1g), carbohydrate 6g

garlic oil

This is a useful infusion to have handy when making pizza or bruschetta.

makes 150ml (¼ pint)

preparation: 5 minutes

cooking: none

𝑣

4 garlic cloves
150ml (¼ pint) olive oil

1 Crush the garlic or chop it finely and put in a screw-top jar.

2 Cover with olive oil and leave for 2 days at room temperature, during which time the oil will take on a subtle hint of garlic. This oil can be kept for 2–3 weeks in a cool place.

nutritional breakdown: kcal 999, kJ 4107, protein 1g, fat 110g (saturated fat 15g), carbohydrate 2g

pesto, plum tomato and black olive pizza

makes 2 × 25cm (10in) pizzas; serves 4–6

preparation time: 10 minutes, plus pizza base making

cooking time: 15–20 minutes, plus pizza bases

suitable for freezing

2 tbsp pesto (see page 211)

2 precooked Basic or Three-Flour Pizza Bases (see pages 194–95)

1 quantity Classic Tomato Pizza Topping (see page 196)

250g (8oz) plum tomatoes, sliced

12 basil leaves

125g (4oz) mozzarella, sliced

25g (1oz) pitted black olives

1 Spread the pesto over the precooked pizza bases, then cover with the tomato topping.

2 Arrange the sliced fresh tomatoes on top of the tomato sauce and tuck the basil leaves in between. Cover with the cheese and black olives.

3 Bake in a preheated oven, 200°C (400°F), Gas Mark 6, for 15–20 minutes.

nutritional breakdown per serving (4 portions): kcal 622, kJ 2610, protein 22g, fat 21g (saturated fat 8g), carbohydrate 76g

VARIATIONS

Other additions to pizza toppings could include artichoke hearts, sliced peppers, sweetcorn, green olives, mild or hot chillies (with care!), different cheeses and pine nuts.

cheese and tomato pizza

makes 2 x 25cm (10in) pizzas; serves 4–6

preparation time: 5 minutes, plus pizza base making

cooking time: 15–20 minutes, plus pizza base

suitable for freezing

(Ca)

2 precooked Basic or Three-Flour Pizza Bases
  (see pages 194–95)
1 quantity Classic Tomato Pizza Topping (see
  page 196)
125g (4oz) mozzarella, sliced
1 tbsp olive oil

1 Cover the precooked pizza bases with the tomato topping. Cover with the sliced cheese, then drizzle the olive oil over the top.

2 Bake in a preheated oven, 200°C (400°F), Gas Mark 6, for 15–20 minutes.

nutritional breakdown per serving (4 portions): kcal 586, kJ 2387, protein 18g, fat 23g (saturated fat 7g), carbohydrate 77g

mushroom pizza

makes 2 x 25cm (10in) pizzas; serves 4–6

preparation time: 10 minutes, plus pizza base making

cooking time: 20 minutes, plus pizza bases

suitable for freezing

(Fe) (Ca)

2 precooked Basic or Three-Flour Pizza Bases
  (see pages 194–95)
1 quantity Classic Tomato Pizza Topping (see
  page 196)
1 tbsp olive oil
400g (13oz) button mushrooms, very thinly sliced
125g (4oz) mozzarella, sliced, optional

1 Cover the precooked pizza bases with the tomato topping.

2 Heat the olive oil in a frying pan and fry the mushrooms until soft.

3 Arrange the mushrooms on top of the tomato sauce, then cover with cheese, if desired. Bake in a preheated oven, 200°C (400°F), Gas Mark 6, for 15–20 minutes.

nutritional breakdown per serving (based on 4 portions): kcal 578, kJ 2427, protein 21g, fat 24g (saturated fat 24g), carbohydrate 76g

saffron onion pizza

makes 2 x 25cm (10in) pizzas; serves 4–6

preparation: 10 minutes, plus pizza base making

cooking: 30 minutes, plus pizza bases

suitable for freezing

2–3 onions, about 450g (14–15oz)
  total weight
2–3 tbsp olive oil
1/4 tsp saffron, infused in 3 tbsp water
2 precooked Basic or Three-Flour Pizza Bases
  (see pages 194–95)
1 tsp green peppercorns or capers, roughly
  chopped
salt and freshly ground black pepper

cheese and tomato pizza (foreground), **mushroom pizza** and **saffron onion pizza**

1 Slice the onions into thin rings. Heat 2 tablespoons of the oil in a saucepan and gently cook the onions for about 10 minutes, or until very soft and translucent.

2 Add the infused saffron and water and cook until the liquid has evaporated. Season well.

3 Brush the pizza bases with a little of the remaining oil, spread on the onion mixture, then scatter over the peppercorns. Drizzle the rest of the oil on top.

4 Bake in a preheated oven, 200°C (400°F), Gas Mark 6, for 15–20 minutes. Serve hot or at room temperature.

nutritional breakdown per serving (4 portions): kcal 463, kJ 1949, protein 11g, fat 14g (saturated fat 2g), carbohydrate 79g

spinach and chilli calzone

Calzone is the term for a folded pizza, a little like a turnover. The advantage of this style of pizza is that you can cook moist fillings without them drying out. The end result is quite substantial but you can always cut the calzone in half once cooked to serve more people. Serving the calzone with the filling exposed looks very appetising.

makes 6

preparation: 15 minutes, plus pizza dough making

cooking: 25 minutes

suitable for freezing

(Ca) (Fe) *v*

1 tbsp olive oil
1 onion, finely chopped
1 garlic clove, crushed
1 chilli, deseeded and chopped
25g (1oz) pine nuts
400g (13oz) spinach, shredded
50g (2oz) currants
125g (4oz) mozzarella or smoked tofu (bean curd), cubed
1 quantity uncooked Basic Pizza Base dough (see page 195)
flour for dusting
salt and freshly ground black pepper

1 Heat the oil in a saucepan and gently fry the onion, garlic and chilli until soft. Add the pine nuts and fry until just lightly browned.

2 Add the shredded spinach and stir-fry until the leaves have wilted – about 3–4 minutes. Remove from the heat, season well, stir in the currants and leave to cool.

3 When cool, mix in the pieces of mozzarella or tofu.

4 Divide the pizza dough into 6 equal pieces. On a lightly floured work surface roll out each piece to a small circle, about 15–18cm (6–7in) in diameter.

5 Divide the filling between the 6 circles. Moisten the edges with cold water, fold over each piece of dough to make a semicircle, then press the edges together.

6 Place on a baking sheet and bake in a preheated oven, 220°C (425°F), Gas Mark 7, for 15 minutes. Serve hot or allow to cool on a wire rack and serve warm.

nutritional breakdown per circle: kcal 392, kJ 1648, protein 15g, fat 14g (saturated fat 4g), carbohydrate 57g

quick scone pizza with grilled vegetables and gruyère

This scone base covered with a topping of lightly grilled vegetables and melted cheese makes a quick tasty meal. You could cut the dough into small circles and make individual pizzas as substantial snacks, if preferred.

serves 4
preparation: 10 minutes
cooking: 20–25 minutes
suitable for freezing: base only

For the scone base:

40g (1½oz) butter or margarine

250g (8oz) self-raising flour (wholemeal or white), plus extra for dusting

1 egg, beaten, mixed with milk to make up to 150ml (¼ pint)

For the topping:

1 onion, sliced into rings

1 yellow or red pepper, cored, deseeded and sliced

1 courgette, sliced

1–2 tbsp olive oil

2–3 tbsp passata or ready-made tomato sauce

125g (4oz) Gruyère or other hard cheese suitable for melting, grated

1 To make the scone base, rub the fat into the flour until the mixture resembles fine breadcrumbs. This can be done by hand or in a food processor. Add the egg and milk and mix quickly to a dough.

2 Turn out the dough on to a lightly floured surface and press it into a round, about 20cm (8in) in diameter. Place on a greased baking sheet and bake in a preheated oven, 220°C (425°F), Gas Mark 7, for 15–20 minutes.

3 To make the topping, spread out the onion, pepper and courgette on a grill pan. Drizzle with the olive oil and season well. Place under a preheated grill and grill for 4–5 minutes, or until well browned, turning them over once during the cooking.

4 Spread the passata or tomato sauce over the cooked scone base, arrange the grilled vegetables on top and cover with the grated cheese. Cook under the grill until the cheese has melted. Serve hot.

IN A HURRY

Use a scone dough for a classic pizza base when you are in a hurry.

nutritional breakdown per serving: kcal 514, kJ 2156, protein 18g, fat 26g (saturated fat 14g), carbohydrate 55g

easy meals for children

The inclusion of a special section on children's food is not to imply that they cannot manage to eat the majority of recipes in this book. Children do enjoy sophisticated and sometimes strong flavours, proved by the number of children who like spiced foods from India, as well as from South America.

I've used this section to highlight some simple ideas for quick meals that you might wish to make on occasions when the whole family cannot eat together. Also included is a list of ideas from the book that make good family meals.

I have added a couple of fried recipes, such as Quick Nut Nuggets, which are on a par with popular fast food. There is also a wheat-free burger and a dairy-free burger, as well as some low-sugar baked beans. These recipes all offer a healthy option when you need fast food.

quick baked beans

Many commercial brands of baked beans have a lot of sugar added. By making your own, you are more in control of what your children are eating. The final taste will be different, but by juggling around with ingredients you can highlight a favourite flavour.

serves 4

preparation: 5 minutes

cooking: 40 minutes

suitable for freezing

𝒱

1 tbsp olive oil
1 onion, finely chopped
1 garlic clove, crushed
125g (4oz) haricot or black-eye beans (cooked)
  or 400g (13oz) can beans, rinsed and drained
1 dessert apple, grated
400g (13oz) can chopped tomatoes
2 tbsp tomato ketchup
2 tbsp concentrated apple juice
sugar to taste
salt and freshly ground black pepper

1 Heat the oil in a large saucepan and gently cook the onion and garlic until very soft. Add the cooked beans and stir well, then cook for 3 minutes.

2 Add the apple, tomatoes, tomato ketchup and concentrated apple juice. If necessary, sweeten a little more with sugar and season well.

3 Cook for 30 minutes, stirring occasionally. Serve hot.

nutritional breakdown per serving: kcal 203, kJ 860, protein 9g, fat 4g (saturated fat 1g), carbohydrate 36g

baked potatoes

These are straightforward to make and can easily be filled to suit everyone's taste.

1 Scrub and prick the potato or slash through to make an attractive pattern or hedgehog effect. Bake in a preheated oven, 200°C (400°F), Gas Mark 6, for 1–1½ hours. To keep the skin soft, wrap the potato in foil before cooking.

2 Fill with dips, such as Hummus (see page 167); cottage cheese, soft cheese or grated cheese; cooked mushrooms; simple stir-fry vegetables; or Chunky Guacamole (see page 192).

nutritional breakdown per medium potato including skin: kcal 136, kJ 580, protein 4g, fat 0g (saturated fat 0g), carbohydrate 32g

baked pasta gratin with fresh sweetcorn

This makes a simple but colourful supper dish, which appeals equally to grown-ups and children. Go easy on the herbs if your children's taste buds are quite conservative. It is best made with fresh sweetcorn, but canned will do.

serves 4

preparation: 10 minutes

cooking: about 1 hour

suitable for freezing

250g (8oz) wholewheat pasta shells or spirals
2 sweetcorn cobs

For the sauce:
2 tbsp olive oil
1 onion, finely chopped
1 garlic clove, crushed
500ml (17fl oz) passata
½ tsp dried thyme, optional
½ tsp dried oregano, optional
1 bay leaf
150g (5oz) hard cheese, grated, or mozzarella, sliced
salt and freshly ground black pepper

1 Cook the pasta in a large saucepan of boiling water for 8–10 minutes, or until just cooked. Drain and set aside.

2 Meanwhile, strip the kernels off the sweetcorn using a sharp knife. Steam for 6–8 minutes over a pan of boiling water or microwave with 3 tablespoons water at 650W for 3–4 minutes. Drain and set aside.

3 To make the sauce, heat the oil in a large saucepan and gently cook the onion and garlic until soft. Add the passata and herbs, if desired, and bring to the boil. Cover the pan and simmer for 30–35 minutes. Remove the bay leaf and season to taste.

4 Mix the cooked pasta and sweetcorn with the sauce and spoon the mixture into a lightly oiled ovenproof dish. Cover with grated or sliced cheese.

5 Bake in a preheated oven, 180°C (350°F), Gas Mark 4, for 15–20 minutes, or until the cheese has melted and the pasta heated through. Serve hot.

nutritional breakdown per serving: kcal 436, kJ 1836, protein 20g, fat 15g (saturated fat 6g), carbohydrate 58g

tofu fritters

This is a dairy-free recipe for children who cannot tolerate eggs or cheese.

makes 8 small fritters

preparation: 10 minutes

cooking: 12 minutes

𝒱

200g (7oz) tofu (bean curd), drained and grated

150g (5oz) short-grain or risotto rice (cooked weight)

50g (2oz) carrot, grated

50g (2oz) spring onion, finely chopped or mild onion, grated

1 tbsp Gomasio (see page 112)

1 tbsp shoyu or soy sauce

1–2 tbsp sunflower oil

1 tbsp plain flour, optional

salt and freshly ground black pepper

1 Mix all the ingredients except the oil and flour together in a large bowl and season well.

2 Shape into 8 small balls, between 2 spoons or using your hands. Keep them damp and the fritter mixture will be less likely to stick. The mixture will only lightly hold together – for something less fragile add the tablespoon of flour.

3 Heat the oil in a frying pan and fry the fritters, 2 or 3 at a time, for about 3 minutes, then turn over and fry the other side for about 3 minutes. Serve hot.

nutritional breakdown per fritter: kcal 110, kJ 460, protein 4g, fat 3g (saturated fat 0g), carbohydrate 18g

quick nut nuggets

This is a very simple idea for children that you can make in a real hurry but you do need a food processor. The mixture is quite soft and needs cooking carefully, which is why I suggest making nuggets rather than larger burgers. Many variations with additional ingredients are possible, such as adding herbs or grated carrot.

makes 10

preparation: 5 minutes

cooking: 15 minutes

suitable for freezing

1 onion, roughly chopped
2 leeks, roughly chopped
1 red pepper, cored, deseeded and
  roughly chopped
125g (4oz) walnuts
125g (4oz) almonds
150g (5oz) fresh wholemeal breadcrumbs
2 tbsp shoyu or soy sauce
2 eggs, beaten
vegetable or sunflower oil for shallow-frying
salt and freshly ground black pepper

1 Put the vegetables, nuts and breadcrumbs in a food processor and process until finely ground. Add the shoyu or soy sauce and blend again, adding more sauce if you like a salty flavour.

2 Add the eggs and blend again so that they are evenly mixed in. Season to taste. Divide the mixture into walnut-sized nuggets.

3 Heat a little oil in a frying pan and shallow-fry nuggets of the mixture. Once the outsides are crisp, turn down the heat and cook slowly for a further 10 minutes so that the nuggets are cooked through to the centre. Serve hot.

nutritional breakdown per nugget: kcal 244, kJ 1011, protein 8g, fat 19g (saturated fat 2g), carbohydrate 10g

other meal suggestions for children

Pizza (see page 194)

Pasta with sauce (see page 210)

Egg dishes such as Strata (see page 184) or Baked Eggs with Mozzarella and Fresh Tomatoes (see page 182)

Polenta with sauces, as well as Polenta Cheese Squares (see page 222)

Grain dishes such as Layered Bulgar with Tomatoes and Feta (see page 231), Risotto (see pages 226–27) or Paella with Many Vegetables (see page 233)

Small savouries such as Baked Tofu and Button Mushrooms (see page 175), Falafel (see page 174) or Enchiladas (see page 191)

Bakes and casseroles such as Almond Croustade with Chard (see page 268), or Country Casserole with Spiced Cheese Dumplings (see page 244)

Main Courses

Whatever the taste, occasion or season, here you'll find a wealth of delicious, hearty recipes for a wide range of main courses from original recipes to mouthwatering variations of traditional dishes, all rich in flavour, texture and visual appeal. Try the fresh, simple Pasta with Sauté Vegetables and Mascarpone or fabulously colourful Bulgar with Roasted Aubergine, Yellow Pepper and Red Onion to experience some of this wonderful variety.

Each section is either centred around a family of ingredients, such as pasta and polenta or rice and grains, or takes as a focus a style of cookery, such as casseroles, bakes or stir-fries. Nutritious and substantial recipes such as Broccoli and Mushroom Lasagne with Almonds, Baked Polenta with Rich Tomato and Mascarpone Sauce, or Paella with Many Vegetables, are meals in their own right. Where main courses need accompaniments, such as warming Sweet Potato Stew or spicy Red Bean and Lentil Chilli, the recipe introductions give suggestions for complementary side dishes. There are plenty of quick-to-cook ideas here, especially within the pasta, rice and stir-fry sections – for a tasty supper try Layered Bulgar with Tomatoes and Feta, which takes only about 15 minutes! Some main courses take longer to prepare, especially the pastry dishes, but many steps can be prepared in advance and the delicious results are well worth it.

tagliatelle with fennel and fresh herbs

Fresh and delicate, this simple pasta makes an easy supper dish or light lunch. A vegan version can easily be made without butter. A mixture of olive oil and walnut oil instead adds an extra dimension to the flavour.

serves 4
preparation: 10 minutes
cooking: 10 minutes

25g (1oz) butter
6 tbsp olive oil
2 garlic cloves, crushed
250g (8oz) fennel, finely chopped
1 tsp lemon zest
4 tbsp chopped parsley
4 tbsp chopped basil
2 tsp snipped fennel tops
250g (8oz) peas
500g (1lb) fresh tagliatelle, or 350g (12oz) dried
salt and freshly ground black pepper
freshly grated Parmesan, optional, to serve.

1 Melt the butter in a small saucepan with the olive oil and gently cook the garlic, fennel and lemon zest for 5 minutes. Stir in the herbs, remove from the heat and season well.

2 Cook the peas in a saucepan of boiling water for 3–4 minutes, until just tender. Drain well.

3 Meanwhile, cook the pasta in a large saucepan of boiling salted water until al dente, then drain.

4 Quickly mix together the fennel and herb sauce with the cooked peas and pasta. Serve immediately, sprinkled with Parmesan, if desired.

nutritional breakdown per serving: kcal 636, kJ 2562, protein 20g, fat 25g (saturated fat 6g), carbohydrate 83g

pasta

Making your own pasta may appear rather daunting, but it is not tricky to do and nor is it necessary to purchase special equipment either. As with other cookery techniques, such as bread-making or pastry-making, you'll find you get more confident and achieve better results after a little practice.

Once you have learned how to make plain pasta, you can experiment with flavouring the basic dough with lots of different ingredients. You can also make delicious, but simple ravioli and mezza luna (large circles of pasta stuffed and folded), which can be hard to find in the shops.

Use a strong plain flour, preferably one that is recommended for bread-making. The gluten in it will make the dough more elastic and stretchy, so that it roll outs easily. Strong wholemeal flour can also be used to make pasta. The fibre in this type of flour absorbs more liquid so it is best to add an extra egg initially. The texture of wholewheat pasta will be robust, rather than melting, so always serve plenty of sauce with it.

To store homemade pasta, keep it in the fridge and aim to use it within 24 hours. Homemade pasta will also freeze and can be cooked from frozen.

basic pasta

makes sufficient for 3–4 for a light main course

preparation: 40 minutes, plus resting

cooking: none

suitable for freezing

350g (12oz) strong plain white flour, plus extra
 for dusting
1 tsp salt
3 large eggs, lightly beaten
1–2 tbsp olive oil
1–2 tbsp water

1 Sift the flour and salt into a large bowl. Make a well in the centre and add the eggs. Mix with a rounded knife to make a dough, then add 1 tablespoon of olive oil and 1 tablespoon of water. Knead again and if the mixture seems too dry, then gradually add equal quantities of olive oil and water 1 teaspoon at a time until you have a smooth but firm dough. If the dough seems sticky, sprinkle on a little more flour. Knead the dough until it is smooth and elastic – this can take 5–10 minutes.

2 Cover the bowl with clingfilm and leave the dough to rest for 30–60 minutes. It is then ready to roll out and cut (see below). (If you have a food processor, you can use it to make the pasta dough, then do the final kneading by hand.)

nutritional breakdown per serving (4 portions): kcal 379, kJ 1603, protein 14g, fat 9g (saturated fat 2g), carbohydrate 66g

quantities

For fresh pasta, either bought or homemade, allow 125g (4oz) per person for a reasonable main course helping. Obviously, allow less for a starter and adjust quantities if you are feeding children. For dried pasta, allow about 75g (3oz) per person for a good portion.

Cooking Pasta

Both fresh and dried pasta need to be cooked in plenty of salted water. Use a large saucepan and allow 4 litres (7 pints) per 500g (1lb) pasta. If your pan is too crowded, the pasta will stick together. You can also add 1 tablespoon of olive oil to the water to prevent the pasta from sticking together.

Once cooked, pasta should be eaten straightaway. It cools very quickly so have warmed plates and your sauce ready before you start cooking the pasta. Some fresh pasta takes only minutes to cook. Filled ravioli take 8–10 minutes; dried wholemeal pasta takes the longest – up to 10–12 minutes.

To check pasta is cooked, remove a piece of pasta from the pan. It should be al dente – firm to the bite but not hard in the centre.

rolling out

A pasta machine will make excellent evenly thin dough. Small hand-operated machines work on the principle of a mangle. Changing the settings each time the pasta dough is passed through makes it thinner. This is most useful when you want to make long strands of pasta, such as tagliatelle.

If rolling by hand, use a good sturdy rolling pin. Working on a lightly floured surface, use one-quarter or half the dough at a time so that it will be more manageable, and roll it into oblongs (top picture). Cut the dough with a pastry wheel or large chef's knife (bottom picture) so that you don't drag it out of shape. Once the strands are cut, leave them to dry hanging over a floured broom handle or similar for 15 minutes.

For lasagne and ravioli, roll the dough into large squares or oblongs and cut appropriately sized sheets for lasagne or cut out circles 10–15cm (4–6 in) in diameter for mezza luna. Keep the cut pieces of pasta on a lightly floured surface otherwise they will stick. For ravioli you can cut small circles or use a raviolamp (a special ravioli tray divided into sections). Leave to dry for 15 minutes.

Step 1 Make a well in the flour and add the beaten eggs.
Step 2 Mix with a rounded knife.
Step 3 Add the oil and water, then knead the mixture.
Step 4 Leave the dough to rest for 30–60 minutes. Then roll out and cut.

flavoured and coloured pasta

Practise making a basic dough before trying variations. Additions will invariably alter the look and texture of the pasta so you must be sure you are going to get it right in the first place. Add dry ingredients, such as herbs, with the sifted flour. Ingredients that contain moisture, such as sun-dried tomato purée or cooked spinach, should be added with the eggs.

The following ingredients can be added to pasta dough:

- 3–4 tablespoons very finely chopped herbs, such as parsley, rosemary or basil
- Substitute walnut or hazelnut oil for the olive oil
- 50g (2oz) very finely chopped raw baby spinach
- For a red pasta, add 50g (2oz) finely chopped sun-dried tomatoes, or sun-dried tomato purée to taste
- For green pasta, add 50g (2oz) cooked spinach or chard
- For golden pasta, add a few strands of saffron – grind the strands with a pestle and mortar, then infuse in 1 tablespoon boiling water. Leave the liquid to cool, then add to the dough with the eggs.

savoury butters

Savoury butters are one of the easiest additions to plain pasta, adding both richness and a subtle flavour. Always start with a butter that has been out of the fridge for a while so that it is slightly soft but still cool. Allow time for the butter to firm up again once you have added the flavouring. As well as serving with pasta, savoury butters can be tossed into freshly cooked vegetables or dotted over vegetables prior to grilling. Use small cutters to create interesting shapes for garnish. A non-dairy alternative to savoury butter is to make infusions of herbs and garlic in a good-quality olive oil.

sage butter

serves 4

preparation: 5 minutes

cooking: none

suitable for freezing

75g (3oz) butter
2 tbsp sage leaves, finely chopped
2 tsp lemon juice
salt and freshly ground black pepper

1 Soften the butter in a bowl. Add the finely chopped sage leaves and mix into the softened butter.

2 When creamy, stir in the lemon juice and season to taste. Chill until required.

nutritional breakdown per serving: kcal 140, kJ 580, protein 0g, fat 15g (saturated fat 10g), carbohydrate 0g

lightly spiced tomato sauce

PEP IT UP

For extra zip add a finely chopped chilli to the oil, with the garlic and shallots.

This is based on the classic Italian sauce, puttanesca. It is a combination of bold flavours and has a thick and pulpy texture. Quick to make, it is ideal with spaghetti or tagliatelle.

serves 4

preparation: 10 minutes

cooking: 30 minutes

suitable for freezing

𝑣

2 tbsp olive oil
2 garlic cloves, crushed
2 shallots, finely chopped
1 tsp fennel seeds
400g (13oz) can chopped tomatoes
50g (2oz) capers
50g (2oz) olives, roughly chopped
salt and freshly ground black pepper
1 tbsp snipped fennel tops, to garnish

1 Heat the oil in a saucepan and cook the garlic and shallots very gently so that they infuse the oil rather than scorch.

2 Stir in the fennel seeds and cook for 1 minute. Add the tomatoes, capers and olives and mix well.

3 Bring to the boil, then simmer, semi-covered, over a medium heat for 25 minutes.

4 Season to taste, garnish with the fennel tops and serve hot over your chosen pasta.

nutritional breakdown per total recipe: kcal 61, kJ 252, protein 1g, fat 5g (saturated fat 1g), carbohydrate 3g

pesto

Pesto is the classic Genoese sauce, made with basil, olive oil, Parmesan and garlic. Its colour is vibrant and its consistency like that of a thick but smooth vinaigrette. Make this basic pesto and you'll see opportunities for a multitude of variations by changing the type of nuts or cheese used. Pesto goes brilliantly with pasta, making fully flavoured but light dishes – simply stir 1–2 tablespoons pesto into freshly cooked pasta. It is also wonderful drizzled over new potatoes, mixed into roasted peppers or added as a flavouring to tomato sauces. The possibilities are endless.

makes 200–250g (7–8oz)

preparation: 10 minutes

cooking: none

50g (2oz) basil
2 garlic cloves, roughly chopped
50g (2oz) pine nuts
4–6 tbsp olive oil
50g (2oz) Parmesan, grated
salt and freshly ground black pepper

1 Using a blender or food processor, blend together the basil, garlic and pine nuts to make a rough paste.

2 With the motor running, gradually add the olive oil in a thin steady stream and blend until quite smooth.

3 Add the grated cheese and process briefly. Season to taste.

4 Store the pesto in a screw-top jar in the fridge for up to 2 weeks. Cover with a little extra olive oil if necessary.

nutritional breakdown per whole recipe: kcal 519, kJ 2142, protein 14g, fat 51g (saturated fat 10g), carbohydrate 3g

roast garlic butter

serves 4

preparation: 10 minutes

cooking: 5–6 minutes

suitable for freezing

6 garlic cloves, unpeeled
75g (3oz) butter
1 tbsp lemon juice
salt and freshly ground black pepper

1 Roast the unpeeled garlic cloves in a preheated oven, 200°C (400°F), Gas Mark 6, for 5–6 minutes. Allow to cool, then squeeze out of their skins and mash the flesh.

2 Soften the butter in a bowl and mash in the roasted garlic and lemon juice. Season well and chill until required.

nutritional breakdown per serving: kcal 140, kJ 582, protein 0g, fat 15g (saturated fat 10g), carbohydrate 1g

mushroom sauce with wine and herbs

Richly flavoured with wine and herbs, this dark mushroom sauce is good with both wholewheat and plain pasta. If you can, prepare it well ahead so the flavours have time to develop.

serves 4	
preparation: 10 minutes	
cooking: 35 minutes	
suitable for freezing	
𝒱	

1 tbsp olive oil
1 onion, finely chopped
1 garlic clove, crushed
500g (1lb) mushrooms, thinly sliced
50ml (2fl oz) red wine
300ml (½ pint) passata
125ml (4fl oz) water
1 tsp dried oregano
1 tsp dried thyme
salt and freshly ground black pepper

1 Heat the oil in a large saucepan and gently fry the onion and garlic until soft. Add the mushrooms and cook for 5 minutes until quite soft.

2 Pour in the wine, then cook over a high heat for 3–4 minutes to reduce the liquid.

3 Reduce the heat and add the passata and water. Stir well, mix in the dried herbs and season to taste.

4 Bring to the boil, then simmer, semi-covered, for 20–25 minutes. Adjust the seasoning and serve hot with your chosen pasta.

nutritional breakdown per serving: kcal 75, kJ 314, protein 4g, fat 4g (saturated fat 1g), carbohydrate 6g

gorgonzola sauce with walnuts

A very rich but easy sauce for serving with a pasta such as shells, bows or twists. The walnuts can be toasted in advance but the wine sauce needs to be made just prior to eating.

serves 4	
preparation: 5 minutes	
cooking: 10 minutes	
Ⓒₐ	

25g (1oz) butter
2 garlic cloves, finely chopped
100g (3½oz) walnut pieces
200ml (7fl oz) white wine
200g (7oz) gorgonzola, finely cubed
salt and freshly ground black pepper
2–3 tbsp finely chopped sorrel, to garnish

1 Melt the butter in a frying pan and gently fry the garlic. Then add the walnuts and fry until slightly toasted and well coated with the butter. Set aside.

2 Heat the wine in a small saucepan and, when warm, add the gorgonzola and melt it gently, stirring constantly. Season to taste.

3 To serve, toss the walnut pieces and sauce into your chosen pasta. Serve straightaway, garnished with chopped sorrel.

nutritional breakdown per serving: kcal 426, kJ 1760, protein 14g, fat 37g (saturated fat 14g), carbohydrate 1g

mushroom and olive ravioli

makes 48–60 pasta circles or 16–20 mezza luna; serves 4

preparation: 20 minutes, plus pasta making

cooking: 20 minutes

suitable for freezing

1 quantity Basic Pasta (see page 208)
flour for dusting

For the filling:
2 tbsp olive oil
1 onion, finely chopped
2 garlic cloves, chopped
250g (8oz) chestnut or cremini mushrooms, sliced
50ml (2fl oz) red wine
100g (3½oz) pitted black olives
salt and freshly ground black pepper
25g (1oz) butter or Very Easy Tomato Sauce
  (see page 292) and freshly grated Parmesan,
  to serve

1 To make the filling, heat the oil in a saucepan and gently fry the onion and garlic until very soft.

2 Add the mushrooms and cook until soft, then pour over the red wine and increase the heat. Simmer the mixture until most of the water has evaporated.

3 Leave to cool slightly, then process the cooked mushroom mixture with the olives in a food processor until finely chopped. If you prefer a smoother texture, process the mixture to a coarse paste. Season well.

4 Roll out the pasta thinly on a lightly floured surface, following the instructions on page 209. Using a 6cm (2½in) cutter, cut 48–60 rounds of pasta or, using a 10cm (4in) cutter, cut out 16–20 circles.

5 Fill the small circles with 1 teaspoon filling or the large circles with about 1 tablespoon filling.

6 Moisten half the edge of each circle with water, fold over to make a semicircle and seal the edges well. Leave on a lightly floured plate.

7 Bring a large pan of salted water to the boil and cook the pasta for 8–10 minutes, or until al dente. Drain and serve either tossed in butter or with a sauce. Hand out the Parmesan separately.

nutritional breakdown per serving: kcal 530, kJ 2232, protein 16g, fat 22g (saturated fat 6g), carbohydrate 69g

pasta with sauté vegetables and mascarpone

This delightful tangle of fresh vegetables enriched with melting cheese makes a very simple supper dish. Brown the leeks before adding the other vegetables as this adds to the quality of the sauce.

serves 4

preparation: 10 minutes

cooking: 15 minutes

2 tbsp olive oil
1 garlic clove, crushed
2 leeks, sliced
250g (8oz) oyster mushrooms, sliced if large
1 red pepper, cored, deseeded and sliced
4–6 tbsp mascarpone cheese
300g (10oz) dried pasta or 500g (1lb) fresh pasta
salt and freshly ground black pepper

1 Heat the oil in a saucepan and gently fry the garlic for 2 minutes.

2 Add the leeks and increase the heat so that they start to brown. Cook for 4–5 minutes.

3 Add the oyster mushrooms and red pepper. Stir well and cook over a moderate heat, until the mushrooms are soft and the red pepper browned.

4 Season well and stir in the mascarpone, reduce the heat and keep the sauce warm.

5 Meanwhile, have ready a saucepan of boiling salted water. Add the pasta, bring to the boil and cook according to packet instructions, or until tender. Drain, toss into the vegetables, adjust the seasoning and serve immediately.

nutritional breakdown per serving: kcal 597, kJ 2399, protein 19g, fat 22g (saturated fat 11g), carbohydrate 81g

ricotta, pesto and herb ravioli

makes 48–60 pasta circles or 16–20 mezza
luna; serves 4

preparation: 15 minutes, plus pasta making

cooking: 10 minutes

suitable for freezing

 (Ca) (Fe)

1 quantity Basic Pasta (see page 208)
flour for dusting

For the filling:
300g (10oz) ricotta cheese
50g (2oz) chopped herbs (such as basil, parsley,
    marjoram, oregano, thyme)
2–3 tbsp pesto (see page 211)
salt and freshly ground black pepper
25g (1oz) butter or Very Easy Tomato Sauce
    (see page 292) and freshly grated Parmesan,
    to serve

1 Mix the ricotta in a bowl with the herbs and pesto
    and season well.

2 Roll out the pasta thinly on a lightly floured surface,
    following the instructions on page 209. Using a

6cm (2½in) cutter, cut 48–60 rounds of pasta or,
using a 10cm (4in) cutter, cut out 16–20 circles.

3 Fill the small circles with 1 teaspoon filling or the
    large circles with about 1 tablespoon filling.

4 Moisten half the edge of each circle with water,
    fold over to make a semicircle and seal the edges
    well. Leave on a lightly floured plate.

5 Bring a large saucepan of salted water to the boil
    and cook the pasta for 8–10 minutes, or until
    al dente. Drain and serve either tossed in butter
    or with the tomato sauce, with the Parmesan
    handed out separately.

VARIATION

An alternative easy
filling for ravioli is to
mix ricotta cheese
with pesto and an
equal quantity of
mashed potato.
Season well. This
makes a creamy but
less rich filling.

nutritional breakdown per serving (without butter or
tomato sauce to serve): kcal 602, kJ 2526, protein 24g, fat 28g
(saturated fat 12g), carbohydrate 68g

pasta with roasted fennel and patty pans

If you can't get patty pan squash, try to find golden courgettes instead.

serves 4

preparation: 15 minutes

cooking: 30 minutes

(Fe)

250g (8oz) fennel, chopped
500g (1lb) patty pan squash, kept whole or
  golden courgettes, chopped
2 onions, sliced
3 tbsp olive oil
350g (12oz) dried pasta or 500g (1lb) fresh pasta
salt and freshly ground black pepper
freshly grated Parmesan, to serve

For the walnut pesto:
50g (2oz) walnuts
50g (2oz) basil
1–2 garlic cloves, roughly chopped
25g (1oz) Parmesan, freshly grated
6–8 tbsp olive oil

1 Toss the prepared vegetables in a bowl with the olive oil and season well. Spread out on 1 or 2 large roasting tins or baking sheets and roast in a preheated oven, 200°C (400°F), Gas Mark 6, for 20 minutes, or until well browned.

2 Meanwhile, to make the pesto, blend together the walnuts, basil, garlic and Parmesan in a blender or food processor. Then, with the motor running, add the oil gradually in a thin steady stream to produce a sauce-like consistency.

3 When the vegetables are roasted, toss them in 2–3 tablespoons pesto and keep warm.

4 Cook the pasta in a saucepan of boiling salted water until just tender. Drain and toss into the cooked vegetables. Serve immediately with extra Parmesan handed out separately.

nutritional breakdown per serving: kcal 900, kJ 3656, protein 27g, fat 49g (saturated fat 8g), carbohydrate 90g

pasta with spinach, shiitake mushrooms and tofu

This Oriental-style dish is a departure from Italian flavourings but is a combination that works very well and produces a robust sauce which goes perfectly with either wholewheat or buckwheat pasta. Tofu boosts the protein content, making this a complete meal, which is quick and simple to make. This recipe also works very well with smoked or ready-marinated tofu.

serves 4

preparation: 10 minutes

cooking: 20 minutes

 Ca Fe 𝑣

2 tbsp sunflower oil
1 onion, finely chopped
2 garlic cloves, crushed
200g (7oz) tofu (bean curd), thinly sliced
300g (10oz) shiitake mushrooms, thinly sliced
2 tbsp shoyu or soy sauce
750g (1½lb) spinach, shredded
1 tsp sesame oil
350g (12oz) dried wholewheat or
  buckwheat pasta
salt and freshly ground black pepper
2–3 tbsp sesame seeds, dry-roasted, to garnish

1 Heat the oil in a large saucepan or lidded frying pan, and gently fry the onion and garlic until soft.

2 Add the slices of tofu and the mushrooms and stir well. Cook slowly until the mushrooms are soft, then add the shoyu or soy sauce. Cover the pan and cook for 4 minutes so that the mushrooms release their juices.

3 Add the spinach in handfuls and stir until it wilts and reduces in size. Cook until soft, then sprinkle over the sesame oil and season well.

4 Meanwhile, cook the pasta in a large saucepan of boiling salted water until tender. Drain well.

5 Pile the cooked vegetables over the cooked pasta, then serve immediately, garnished with dry-roasted sesame seeds.

nutritional breakdown per serving: kcal 420, kJ 1775, protein 23g, fat 12g (saturated fat 2g), carbohydrate 61g

lentil lasagne

Lentils make a hearty bolognese-style filling for lasagne. Puy lentils or brown lentils work best since their small size means that they blend well into the sauce. You can also use larger Continental green lentils or aduki beans for this recipe. The crème fraiche in the white sauce adds a good tang to counterbalance the earthy quality of the lentils. As with any lasagne, try to get as much as possible prepared in advance.

serves 4–6

preparation: 15 minutes, plus standing

cooking: about 1½ hours

suitable for freezing

6–8 sheets lasagne (or enough to make 3 layers)
1–2 tbsp freshly grated Parmesan

For the filling:
250g (8oz) green or brown lentils
2 tbsp olive oil
1 onion, finely chopped
2 garlic cloves, crushed
2 celery sticks, finely chopped
2 red peppers, cored, deseeded and
  finely chopped
250g (8oz) mushrooms, chopped
2 tbsp chopped sun-dried tomatoes
3–4 tbsp chopped basil
500ml (17fl oz) passata
salt and freshly ground black pepper

For the béchamel sauce:
450ml (¾ pint) milk
6 black peppercorns
½ onion
1 bay leaf
1 sprig thyme
40g (1½oz) butter
25g (1oz) plain flour
200g (7oz) crème fraîche
salt and freshly ground black pepper

1 To make the filling, cook the lentils in a large saucepan of boiling water for 15–25 minutes, or until quite soft. Drain and set aside.

2 Heat the oil in a large saucepan and gently fry the onion and garlic until soft. Add the celery and cook for a few minutes, then add the red peppers and mushrooms and cook until soft. Stir in the cooked lentils with the sun-dried tomatoes and basil and mix well.

3 Pour in the passata and season well. Bring the sauce to the boil, then simmer, covered, for 10–15 minutes. Season well.

4 Meanwhile, to make the white sauce, warm the milk in a small saucepan and add the peppercorns, onion, bay leaf and thyme. Leave to stand for 15 minutes.

5 Next, melt the butter in a small saucepan. Add the flour to make a roux and cook over a gentle heat for 2 minutes. Gradually strain the infused milk into the roux and bring the sauce to the boil, stirring constantly. Simmer for 2–3 minutes, until the sauce thickens. Then stir in the crème fraîche and season well with salt and pepper.

6 Unless using quick-cook lasagne, prepare the lasagne by covering with boiling water, or following the packet instructions. Drain and separate the sheets.

7 To assemble the dish, place 2–3 spoonfuls of the lentil and tomato sauce in the bottom of a large ovenproof dish, cover with 2 or 3 sheets of lasagne. Cover with half the lentil sauce and spoon over a little of the white sauce. Cover with 2 or 3 more sheets of lasagne, then cover with the remaining lentil and tomato sauce and a little more white sauce. Finish with sheets of lasagne. Cover these with the remainder of the white sauce and top with grated Parmesan.

8 Bake in a preheated oven, 190°C (375°F), Gas Mark 5, for 35–40 minutes, or until browned on the top.

nutritional breakdown per serving (4 portions): kcal 665, kJ 2800, protein 30g, fat 25g (saturated fat 22g), carbohydrate 87g

broccoli and mushroom lasagne with almonds

Lasagne is a splendid complete meal in itself and here almonds add texture and protein. Try to make the main sauces, generally tomato and white sauce, well ahead of time. Both of these can be frozen.

serves 4–6

preparation: 15 minutes

cooking: 1½ hours

suitable for freezing

(Ca) (Fe)

500g (1lb) broccoli, divided into florets
40g (1½oz) butter
50g (2oz) flaked almonds
500g (1lb) mushrooms, sliced if large
9 sheets of lasagne (or enough to make 3 layers)
freshly grated Parmesan
salt and freshly ground black pepper

For the tomato sauce:
1 tbsp olive oil
1 onion, chopped
1 garlic clove, crushed
400g (13oz) can chopped tomatoes
½ tsp sugar
½ tsp salt

For the white sauce:
50g (2oz) butter
50g (2oz) plain flour
600ml (1 pint) milk (semi-skimmed used for
  nutrient content)
salt and freshly ground black pepper

1 Steam the broccoli over a saucepan of boiling water for 2 minutes. Drain and set aside.

2 Melt the butter in a large frying pan, add the almonds and cook until brown, then add the mushrooms and cook until quite soft. Stir in the broccoli with the mushrooms, then remove the pan from the heat.

3 To make the tomato sauce, heat the oil in a saucepan and gently fry the onion and garlic until soft. Add the chopped tomatoes, sugar and salt. Bring to the boil, then cover the pan and simmer for 35 minutes.

4 Mix the tomato sauce with the broccoli and mushroom mixture and season well.

5 To make the white sauce, melt the butter in a saucepan and stir in the flour to make a roux. Cook for 2 minutes, then gradually pour in the milk and bring to the boil, stirring constantly. Cook for 2 minutes, then season to taste.

6 Before assembling the dish, prepare the lasagne according to the packet instructions.

7 Lightly oil a large ovenproof dish, put in a little of the broccoli mixture, then cover with 3 sheets lasagne, cover with half the remaining broccoli mixture and cover with lasagne. Repeat this layer with the remaining broccoli and lasagne, then pour over the white sauce.

8 Sprinkle the Parmesan over the top and bake in a preheated oven, 190°C (375°F), Gas Mark 5, for 35 minutes, or until golden brown. Serve hot.

nutritional breakdown per serving (4 portions): kcal 670, kJ 2809, protein 26g, fat 35g (saturated fat 16g), carbohydrate 68g

polenta

Polenta can be served plainly boiled, but cooked like this it tastes fairly bland and is somewhat lacking in texture. If this doesn't appeal, it is worth trying polenta baked or grilled. This type of polenta can then be eaten with any of the sauces featured earlier in this chapter (see pages 210–17).

Polenta can also be layered and baked with sauces in a similar fashion to lasagne. This type of recipe makes a substantial but appealing supper dish, and it is easy to make vegan versions.

Polenta is also good served as a quick snack fried with a cheese filling. This 'sandwich' has a crisp outside with a succulent melting centre.

Brands of polenta vary in texture and consequently may absorb differing amounts of water. Be guided by the instructions on the packet. The amount you need will also vary depending on whether it is to be the main part of a meal or a snack – 150–350g (5–12oz) should serve 4 people. Serve the smaller quantity for a light meal and the larger amount as a more substantial dish.

polenta cheese squares

These succulent squares can be a snack or light meal for 4 people or a main course for 2. Serve them plainly or with a simple tomato sauce, roasted vegetables, grilled tomatoes or a green salad.

serves 4

preparation: 15 minutes

cooking: 30 minutes

600ml (1 pint) water
150g (5oz) polenta, plus a little extra for dusting
½ tsp salt
2 tbsp finely chopped sun-dried tomatoes
175g (6oz) fontina or Gruyère, sliced
2 eggs, lightly beaten
125g (4oz) fresh breadcrumbs
sunflower oil for shallow-frying

1   To make the polenta, bring the water to the boil in a large saucepan. Stir in the polenta, salt and sun-dried tomatoes. Stir constantly until the mixture thickens, then continue stirring over a medium heat for 5 minutes, or according to the packet instructions.

2   Spoon out the cooked polenta on to a large board and flatten with the back of a spoon or a palette knife into a rough oblong about 20 x 30cm (8 x 12in). The polenta should be slightly less than 1cm (½in) thick. Leave to cool.

3   Cut the polenta into 5cm (2in) squares. Sandwich a slice of cheese between a pair of polenta squares. Dust with a little extra polenta flour, then dip in lightly beaten egg and coat with breadcrumbs.

4   Heat the oil in a large frying pan until it will sizzle a piece of bread dropped in. Fry the polenta squares for about 3–4 minutes on each side. Drain on kitchen paper towel. Serve immediately.

nutritional breakdown per serving: kcal 533, kJ 2220, protein 22g, fat 31g (saturated fat 11g), carbohydrate 43g

baked polenta with rich tomato and mascarpone sauce

Both the sauce and polenta can be cooked well in advance, leaving you an easy assembly and a dish that is ready in 20 minutes. This makes a good family supper served with green beans, broccoli or a colourful salad.

serves 4
preparation: 15 minutes
cooking: 1–1 ¼ hours
suitable for freezing
Ⓒa

750ml–1 litre (1¼–1¾ pints) water
200g (7oz) polenta
2 tbsp freshly grated Parmesan
salt and freshly ground black pepper

For the sauce:
2 tbsp olive oil
1 onion, chopped
2 garlic cloves, crushed
1 red pepper, cored, deseeded and chopped
500ml (17fl oz) passata or creamed tomatoes
6 sun-dried tomatoes, finely chopped
2 tbsp chopped basil
½ tsp ground cinnamon
125g (4oz) mascarpone cheese

1   Bring the water to the boil in a large saucepan, add the polenta with ½ teaspoon salt and stir well for 5–10 minutes, until the mixture has thickened. Alternatively, follow the packet instructions.

2   Pour the polenta into a greased dish and leave to cool before cutting into bite-sized squares.

3   To make the sauce, heat the oil in a saucepan and fry the onion and garlic until soft but not coloured.

4   Using a blender or food processor, purée the red pepper with the passata, or creamed tomatoes, sun-dried tomatoes and the basil. Add this purée to the pan of onions, add the cinnamon and stir well.

5   Bring the mixture to the boil, then simmer, partially covered, for 30–40 minutes over a low heat. Cool slightly, then stir in the mascarpone. Season to taste.

6   To assemble the dish, spoon a thin layer of sauce into a lightly greased shallow gratin dish. Cover with squares of polenta, add another layer of sauce and more polenta, finishing with the sauce.

7   Sprinkle over the grated Parmesan and bake in a preheated oven, 200°C (400°F), Gas Mark 6, for 20 minutes, or until the Parmesan is well browned and the sauce heated through. Serve hot.

nutritional breakdown per serving: kcal 598, kJ 2483, protein 11g, fat 41g (saturated fat 13g), carbohydrate 49g

rosemary polenta with aubergine and dolcelatte

Fresh rosemary makes a fragrant addition to the polenta, leaving it attractively flecked with green. Serve it on its own as an elegant light snack or with Fennel and Red Pepper Salad with Lemon and Oregano Dressing (see page 308) for a main meal.

Although there are quite a number of stages when making this recipe, each step is very simple. The polenta, tomato concasse and aubergine slices can be prepared in advance, leaving just the task of assembling and last-minute grilling. If you can't get all the portions under the grill at once have the oven preheated and keep half warm in the oven while grilling the second batch.

serves 4

preparation: 20 minutes, plus salting

cooking: 30 minutes

nutritional breakdown per serving: kcal 400, kJ 1664, protein 10g, fat 26g (saturated fat 11g), carbohydrate 33g

1 aubergine, thickly sliced
1 tbsp finely chopped rosemary
150g (5oz) polenta
600ml (1 pint) water
1 tbsp olive oil, plus extra for frying
1 small onion, chopped
1 garlic clove, crushed
4 tomatoes, skinned and chopped
1 tbsp tomato purée
200g (7oz) dolcelatte, sliced
salt and freshly ground black pepper

1 Put the aubergine slices in a large colander and sprinkle with salt. Leave for 20–30 minutes. Mix the finely chopped rosemary with the polenta.

2 Bring the water to the boil in a large saucepan, add the polenta with ½ teaspoon salt and stir well for 5–10 minutes, until the mixture has thickened. Alternatively, follow the packet instructions. Pour the polenta into a greased dish and leave to cool.

3 To make the tomato concasse, heat the oil in a saucepan and fry the onion and garlic until soft. Add the skinned chopped tomatoes and tomato purée. Cook for 5 minutes.

4 Cool the tomato concasse slightly then, using a blender or food processor, purée until smooth. Sieve for an extra smooth finish and season to taste.

5 Pat the aubergine slices dry with kitchen towel, then fry the slices in olive oil until well browned and soft.

6 To assemble the dish, cut the cooled polenta into large circles using a 7cm (3in) cutter, allowing for 2 circles per person for a main course or 1 for a light snack.

7 Top each polenta round with a spoonful of the tomato concasse and 1–2 slices aubergine. Divide the dolcelatte between the portions and place them under a preheated hot grill to cook until the cheese is thoroughly melted.

8 Transfer the polenta rounds to serving plates, using a spatula, then spoon over any residue of melted cheese. Serve straightaway.

potato gnocchi

Popular in Northern Italy, gnocchi are a type of dumpling made from a plain potato or semolina base and flavoured with spinach, chard or ricotta cheese. Gnocchi can be served with flavoured butters, pesto or a rich tomato sauce. They can be a light meal in themselves, especially if accompanied by a salad, or can be served as a starter followed by Strata (see page 184) or Mediterranean Galette (see page 358). A vegan version can be made without eggs but the mixture is more fragile.

Gnocchi are very quick to cook, but you must allow time for chilling the mixture and about 30 minutes for making it. It is worth getting the preparation done well ahead of time.

serves 4

preparation: 15 minutes, plus chilling

cooking: 25–30 minutes

suitable for freezing (after step 4)

800g (1lb 10oz) floury potatoes
1 egg, beaten
175–200g (6–7oz) strong plain flour
1 tbsp olive oil
salt
flavoured melted butter, pesto or a tomato sauce
 and freshly grated Parmesan, to serve

1 Cook the potatoes in their skins in a large saucepan of boiling salted water for about 20 minutes, or until soft. Drain. When cool enough to handle, peel them, then mash or sieve until smooth.

2 Beat in the egg and half the flour. Turn out on to a floured board and gradually add more flour, kneading lightly until you have a soft but not sticky dough.

3 Keep the board well floured while you roll pieces of the dough into long thick sausage shapes about 2.5cm (1in) thick. Cut each 'rope' into pieces about 2.5cm (1in) long to make gnocchi.

4 Press the gnocchi against the back of a fork to make the traditional indentations, then place on a floured tray. Cover with a floured cloth and leave for at least 30 minutes to chill.

5 To cook the gnocchi, bring a large pan of salted water to the boil. Add the olive oil and reduce the heat to a gentle simmer since fast boiling will destroy the shape of the gnocchi.

6 Add the gnocchi to the water in batches, cooking them for 2–3 minutes. They should float to the surface when they are almost cooked. Remove from the water with a slotted spoon and keep warm in a buttered serving dish while you cook the remainder.

7 Have ready a flavoured melted butter or sauce. When all the gnocchi are cooked, pour over the melted butter or sauce and sprinkle with grated Parmesan. Serve hot.

nutritional breakdown per serving (gnocchi only): kcal 342, kJ 1449, protein 11g, fat 5g (saturated fat 1g), carbohydrate 67g

risotto

A good risotto should be creamy but not sticky. This is achieved by cooking the rice slowly and stirring in the wine and stock almost continually until the liquid is absorbed. It is best to use risotto rice (see page 87), which is a plump robust grain that can withstand a good deal of stirring without breaking down. Although it is possible to make risotto-style dishes using short-grain brown rice, the end result is well flavoured but lacks the silky characteristic of classic risotto.

mushroom risotto with tarragon

LEFTOVERS

Left over risotto is perfect for making into little croquettes. The neatest way to do this is to gather up portions of rice in a little square of clingfilm and press them into an oval shape between your hands. Alternatively, dampen your hands and shape the rice between your palms. Tuck a small piece of mozzarella inside each croquette, if desired. Roll the croquette in plain flour, then beaten egg, then breadcrumbs and shallow-fry for 4–5 minutes, or until crisp all over.

Dried mushrooms add an intense underlying flavour to this simple risotto, while the tarragon cuts through the richness with a clean tang – a great combination. Serve this as a main course with side vegetables, such as fresh peas, broad beans or courgettes.

serves 4
preparation: 15 minutes, plus soaking
cooking: 35 minutes
suitable for freezing

15g (½oz) dried mushrooms
600ml (1 pint) boiling water
50g (2oz) butter
2 shallots, finely chopped
1 garlic clove, crushed
175g (6oz) chestnut mushrooms, thinly sliced
250g (8oz) arborio rice
150ml (¼ pint) white wine
1 tbsp chopped tarragon
2 tbsp freshly grated Parmesan
salt and freshly ground black pepper

1 Soak the dried mushrooms in a bowl of the boiling water for at least 30 minutes. Drain through a fine sieve or coffee filter to remove any sediment and reserve the liquid as stock. Rinse the mushrooms and chop finely.

2 Melt 40g (1½ oz) butter in a large saucepan or frying pan and gently fry the shallots and garlic until soft but not coloured. Add the sliced fresh mushrooms and fry until softened.

3 Add the rice and chopped dried mushrooms and stir until well coated with the butter. Pour in the wine and cook over a low heat, stirring continuously until the liquid has been absorbed.

4 Add a third of the reserved mushroom stock. Keep stirring and cook until the stock has been absorbed, then add a further third of the stock and repeat this process, before adding the remaining stock. The rice should become thick and creamy but not sticky and should take 20–25 minutes to cook in total.

5 Season well and add the remaining butter, the chopped tarragon and grated Parmesan.

nutritional breakdown per serving: kcal 383, kJ 1614, protein 7g, fat 12g (saturated fat 8g), carbohydrate 59g

risotto with roasted squash

The melting flesh of squash combines brilliantly with creamy rice for a warmly coloured risotto. Roasting the squash first brings out a very mellow flavour. This recipe could also be made with other winter squashes or with pumpkin. Serve with buttered leeks or steamed broccoli.

serves 4
preparation: 10 minutes
cooking: 1¼ hours
suitable for freezing

1kg (2lb) onion squash, cut into large chunks
  and deseeded
3 tbsp olive oil
25g (1oz) butter
1 onion, finely chopped
1 garlic clove, crushed
250g (8oz) arborio rice
150ml (¼ pint) white wine
450ml (¾ pint) hot Vegetable Stock (see page 144)
salt and freshly ground black pepper
1 tbsp finely chopped flat leaf parsley, to garnish
freshly grated Parmesan, to serve

1 Measure 1 tablespoon of the olive oil into a bowl and season well. Add the squash to the bowl and mix well to coat the squash lightly with oil. Keep back one-quarter of the squash flesh to cook as a garnish.

2 Place the remaining squash in a roasting tin or on a baking sheet and cook in a preheated oven, 200°C (400°F), Gas Mark 6, for 40 minutes, or until the outer skin looks brown and the flesh is soft. Leave to cool, remove any tough skin and chop roughly.

3 To cook the risotto, heat the remaining olive oil with the butter in a large saucepan or frying pan and gently cook the onion and garlic until translucent.

4 Add the rice, stir well until coated with the butter and oil, then pour in the white wine and cook gently until all the liquid has been absorbed.

5 Add the cooked squash and about one-third of the hot stock. Keep stirring and cook until the stock has been absorbed, then add a further one-third of the stock and repeat the process. Finally, add the remaining stock and stir less frequently. The whole process takes about 20–25 minutes and the rice should become thick and creamy. Season well.

6 While the risotto is cooking, roast the remaining squash. Cut into fairly thin slices and coat with extra seasoned oil if necessary. Place in a roasting tin or on a baking sheet and roast at 200°C (400°F), Gas Mark 6, for 25 minutes.

7 Use the slices to garnish the risotto and sprinkle with chopped parsley. Serve grated Parmesan separately.

nutritional breakdown per serving: kcal 478, kJ 2016, protein 8g, fat 15g (saturated fat 5g), carbohydrate 78g

sesame millet with pan-fried courgettes, asparagus and avocado cream

This is a dish of wonderful contrasts, with lightly textured millet, succulent vegetables and creamy avocado topping. It stands on its own as a main course but could be served with a starter of Oyster Mushroom and Roast Almond Pâté (see page 165). Millet does not cook evenly so expect some crunchy grains when tasting to see if it is cooked.

serves 4

preparation: 15 minutes

cooking: 25 minutes

(Fe)

1 tsp sunflower oil
1 tsp cumin seeds
200g (7oz) millet
2 tbsp sesame seeds
750ml (1¼ pints) boiling water

For the pan-fried vegetables:
2 tbsp sunflower oil
6 spring onions, chopped
1 red pepper, cored, deseeded and thinly sliced
250g (8oz) asparagus, chopped
4 courgettes, sliced
salt and freshly ground black pepper

For the topping:
1 ripe avocado
3–4 tbsp crème fraîche
2 tbsp chopped parsley
salt and freshly ground black pepper

1 Heat the oil in a large saucepan and lightly toast the cumin seeds. Add the millet and sesame seeds and toast for 2 minutes.

2 Pour in the boiling water. Bring back to the boil, then cover the pan and simmer for 20 minutes. Season well.

3 Meanwhile, to cook the vegetables, heat the oil in a large frying pan and gently fry the spring onions. Add the red pepper, asparagus and courgettes and, stirring frequently, fry over a medium heat for 5–10 minutes, or until soft and browned. Season well.

4 To make the topping, halve the avocado, remove the stone and scoop the flesh into a bowl. Mash with the crème fraîche and mix in the parsley. Season well.

5 When the millet is cooked, spoon it out on to warmed plates and cover with the pan-fried vegetables. Top with the avocado cream or serve it separately.

nutritional breakdown per serving: kcal 373, kJ 1553, protein 8g, fat 17g (saturated fat 8g), carbohydrate 45g

red rice with pan-fried squash, mushrooms and pecan nuts

Warm russet colours and nutty flavours dominate this dish. Serve it on its own for a light meal or serve it with a contrasting green vegetable or leafy salad. For a more substantial meal start with a creamy soup such as Celeriac and Emmental (see page 154).

serves 4
preparation: 10 minutes	
cooking: 20 minutes	
V	

250g (8oz) red rice
2 tbsp sunflower oil
1 onion, chopped
500g (1lb) butternut squash, chopped
500g (1lb) mushrooms, quartered
125g (4oz) pecan nuts
salt and freshly ground black pepper

1 Place the rice in a large saucepan and bring it to the boil in double its volume of water. Cover the pan and simmer for 20 minutes or until soft.

2 Meanwhile, heat the oil in a large frying pan and cook the onion until soft. Add the squash, mushrooms and pecan nuts and increase the heat.

3 Cook the vegetables for 5–10 minutes, or until the squash is lightly coloured and the mushrooms softened, then turn down the heat and cook until the vegetables are quite tender. Season well.

4 Once the rice is cooked, drain well, then toss the pan-fried mixture with the rice and serve while hot.

nutritional breakdown per serving: kcal 553, kJ 2302, protein 11g, fat 29g (saturated fat 3g), carbohydrate 61g

VARIATION

This recipe could also be made with brown rice but the colour is less intense.

bulgar with roasted aubergine, yellow pepper and red onion

SALTING

Up until the last decade or so, most aubergines were salted before use to draw out bitter juices. Less bitter strains have now been developed but a salted aubergine seems to absorb less oil when cooked. So if you have time, it's a step worth doing.

This easy supper dish can inspire many variations. Ring the changes with different vegetables such as red pepper, fennel or courgette. Bulgar needs a sauce or dressing to counterbalance the dry texture of the grains. In this recipe I've created a quick but nutritious sauce using tahini. You could use Chunky Guacamole (see page 192) or Salsa Mexicana (see page 192), instead.

serves 4

preparation: 15 minutes, plus salting

cooking: 20–25 minutes

Fe 𝒱

2 aubergines, cubed
4–6 tbsp olive oil
2 yellow peppers, cored, deseeded and sliced
1 red onion, sliced
200g (7oz) bulgar

400ml (14fl oz) boiling water
2 tbsp finely chopped coriander leaves
salt and freshly ground black pepper

For the sauce:
4 tbsp tahini
4 tbsp water
juice of 1 lemon
1–2 tbsp olive oil
1 garlic clove, crushed
1 tsp ground coriander, dry-roasted
1 tbsp shoyu or soy sauce
salt and freshly ground black pepper

1 Place the cubes of aubergine in a large colander and sprinkle with salt, then leave for 20–30 minutes. Pat dry with kitchen paper.

2 Pour the oil into a large bowl and season well. Mix the salted aubergine cubes, yellow peppers and onion in the seasoned oil and spread on a baking sheet. Roast the vegetables in a preheated oven, 200°C (400°F), Gas Mark 6, for 20–25 minutes, or until well browned. Turn the vegetables over once or twice during cooking.

3 Meanwhile, place the bulgar in a large bowl, add ½ teaspoon salt and pour over the boiling water. Leave to soak for 15–20 minutes. Drain if necessary. Stir in the coriander and adjust the seasoning to taste.

4 To make the sauce, mix the tahini in a bowl with the water until well blended. Add the lemon juice, olive oil, crushed garlic, dry-roasted coriander and shoyu or soy sauce and mix well. Season to taste.

5 Spoon the bulgar into a large shallow serving dish and pile all the vegetables on top. Serve immediately with the tahini sauce.

nutritional breakdown per serving: kcal 550, kJ 2292, protein 13g, fat 35g (saturated fat 5g), carbohydrate 49g

layered bulgar with tomatoes and feta

This is an extremely easy meal that takes only a matter of minutes to prepare. Serve together with a green salad or steamed green vegetables.

serves 4

preparation: 10 minutes

cooking: 10 minutes

(Fe)

250g (8oz) bulgar
4–5 plum tomatoes, skinned and thickly sliced
1 small red chilli, deseeded and finely chopped
1–2 tbsp olive oil
200g (7oz) feta (drained weight)
6 pitted black olives, chopped
salt and freshly ground black pepper

1 Place the bulgar in a large bowl with ½ teaspoon salt. Cover with boiling water and leave for 5 minutes, then drain.

2 Spoon the bulgar into a lightly oiled flameproof dish. Cover with the tomato slices and season well.

3 Sprinkle over the red chilli, then drizzle over the olive oil. Cook under a preheated grill for 5 minutes.

4 Crumble the feta on top and sprinkle over the chopped olives. Return the dish to the grill for a further 5 minutes, or until the feta is well browned. Serve hot.

SKINNING TOMATOES

To skin tomatoes, cut a cross in the end of each tomato and drop them in a bowl of boiling water. Leave for 1 minute, then remove with a slotted spoon and peel off the skins.

nutritional breakdown per serving: kcal 409, kJ 1708, protein 15g, fat 11g (saturated fat 1g), carbohydrate 51g

green rice with chilli

This is a spiced rice with a delicate green colour, inspired by Mexican cuisine. It is great as an accompaniment for casseroles such as Red Bean and Lentil Chilli (see page 240). Leftovers can be stuffed into green peppers and baked with tomato sauce.

serves 4

preparation: 20 minutes

cooking: 55 minutes

suitable for freezing

𝓋

1 large green pepper
2 mild green chillies
3 garlic cloves, crushed
25g (1oz) coriander leaves
2 tbsp olive oil
1 onion, finely chopped
250g (8oz) brown rice
475ml (16fl oz) hot Vegetable Stock
  (see page 144)
salt and freshly ground black pepper

1 Place the pepper on a baking sheet or in a roasting tin and roast in a preheated oven, 200°C (400°F), Gas Mark 6, for 25 minutes, or until well blistered and soft. Place in a polythene bag, seal and leave for 10 minutes, then peel and remove the seeds.

2 Roast the chillies for 10 minutes at 200°C (400°F), Gas Mark 6. Place in a polythene bag and leave for 10 minutes, then peel and remove the seeds.

3 Using a blender or food processor, process the roasted pepper, chillies, garlic and coriander leaves to make a coarse green paste.

4 Heat the oil in a large saucepan and gently cook the onion until soft. Add the rice and stir to coat well with the oil. Mix in the green pepper paste and pour in the boiling stock.

5 Stir once or twice and bring to the boil, then cover the pan and simmer for 25 minutes, or until the rice is cooked and all the stock has been absorbed. Season towards the end of cooking.

nutritional breakdown per serving: kcal 290, kJ 1232, protein 5g, fat 8g (saturated fat 1g), carbohydrate 54g

paella with many vegetables

This may seem a long list of ingredients but this dish is straightforward to make. Do use a range of vegetables as they give the paella plenty of texture, colour and flavour. Saffron, tomato and paprika create warm undertones. You can, of course, use a number of other vegetables, such as broad beans, fine beans or coloured peppers, as well as adding cashew nuts or sliced egg for extra protein. This dish needs serving with nothing more than a crisp salad.

serves 4

preparation: 15 minutes

cooking: 50 minutes

𝑣

2 tbsp olive oil
1 onion, finely chopped
2 garlic cloves, crushed
1 tsp fennel seeds
3 celery sticks, finely chopped
100ml (3½fl oz) white wine
250g (8oz) short-grain rice
pinch of saffron, infused in 2 tbsp hot water for 5 minutes
1 tsp paprika
600ml (1 pint) hot Vegetable Stock (see page 144) or water
3 tbsp tomato purée
6 plum tomatoes, skinned and chopped
150g (5oz) peas, fresh or frozen
150g (5oz) asparagus, roughly chopped
150g (5oz) baby sweetcorn cobs, roughly chopped
2 tbsp chopped parsley
black olives, to garnish
wedges of lemon, to serve

1 Heat the olive oil in a large saucepan or frying pan and gently fry the onion and garlic until soft.

2 Add the fennel seeds and celery and cook for 4–5 minutes. Pour in the white wine and simmer until most of the liquid has evaporated.

3 Add the rice and stir well. Add the infused saffron water to the rice with the paprika, stock, tomato purée and fresh tomatoes. Bring the mixture to the boil, then season well and simmer for 30 minutes, or until the rice is cooked.

4 About 5 minutes before the end of cooking add the peas, asparagus, sweetcorn and parsley.

5 Just before serving, stir in black olives and serve with wedges of lemon.

nutritional breakdown per serving: kcal 390, kJ 1650, protein 11g, fat 8g (saturated fat 1g), carbohydrate 70g

almond and lemon pilaf

USING SPICES

When using a quantity of spices, mix them to a paste with a little water, then fry. The water prevents the spices from scorching and allows the aroma of the spices to develop.

A simple rice dish that can be a meal in itself, accompanied by steamed green beans or peas and a bowl of plain or seasoned yoghurt. Alternatively, add extra vegetables to the pilaf itself if you want to keep it a meal in one pan. Mushrooms, peppers or celery could all be added. This recipe also makes a good accompaniment to Mixed Lentil Dhal (see page 250) and Spiced Vegetable Fritters (see page 168).

Although this dish is suitable for freezing, it should not be frozen for more than 1 month because of the quantity of spices, which can deteriorate in flavour.

serves 4

preparation: 10 minutes

cooking: 40 minutes

suitable for freezing

2 tbsp olive oil
1 onion, finely chopped
2 garlic cloves, crushed
75g (3oz) blanched almonds, roughly chopped
1 tsp paprika
1 tsp ground cumin
1 tsp ground coriander
½ tsp ground cinnamon
2 tbsp water
2 tsp grated fresh root ginger
3 carrots, finely chopped
250g (8oz) basmati rice
600ml (1 pint) boiling water
juice and zest of 1 lemon
salt and freshly ground black pepper
lemon rind, cut into thin strips, to garnish

1 Heat the oil in a large saucepan or frying pan and gently fry the onion and garlic. Add the chopped almonds and cook until lightly toasted.

2 Mix the paprika, cumin, coriander and cinnamon to a paste with the 2 tablespoons of water. Add the paste to the pan with the root ginger and stir well. Cook for 2–3 minutes.

3 Add the carrots and cook for a further 2–3 minutes, stirring well. Then add the rice and stir in.

4 Pour in the boiling water and the lemon juice and zest. Bring to the boil, stirring once or twice. Cover the pan and cook over a low heat for 25–30 minutes.

5 At the end of the cooking time the water should have been absorbed and the rice soft. Season to taste and fluff with a fork before serving. Garnish with a few strips of lemon rind, if desired.

nutritional breakdown per serving: kcal 415, kJ 1727, protein 10g, fat 17g (saturated fat 2g), carbohydrate 56g

spiced mushroom rice

Warm and spicy, this easy rice dish needs little attention once the spices have been cooked. Soaking rice not only shortens the cooking time but also reduces the amount of water needed. Varieties of basmati may differ so you may need to adjust quantities slightly.

Serve on its own with a few simple accompaniments such as natural yoghurt with cucumber or Spiced Vegetable Fritters (see page 168).

serves 4

preparation: 10 minutes, plus soaking

cooking: 35–40 minutes

40g (1½oz) clarified butter
1 onion, finely chopped
2 garlic cloves, crushed
½ chilli, finely chopped
2.5cm (1in) piece of fresh root ginger, grated
125g (4oz) mushrooms, chopped
250g (8oz) brown basmati rice, soaked
  for 2 hours
300ml (½ pint) boiling water
salt and freshly ground black pepper

1 Melt the butter in a large saucepan or frying pan and fry the onion, garlic, chilli and ginger together, stirring well.

2 Add the mushrooms, ½ teaspoon salt and the drained, soaked rice. Cook for 5 minutes.

3 Add the water and bring to the boil. Cover the pan with a close-fitting lid, turn down the heat and simmer for 25 minutes without stirring. At the end of this time all the water should have been absorbed and the rice cooked. If necessary, cook for a few minutes without the lid if there is excess water.

4 Stir with a fork, adjust the seasoning to taste and serve immediately.

PAN LIDS

If your pan doesn't have a close-fitting lid, try tying a tea towel around the outside of a lid as this can make it fit more snugly.

nutritional breakdown per serving: kcal 308, kJ 1300, protein 5g, fat 10g (saturated fat 6g), carbohydrate 52g

wild rice with hazelnuts, carrots and artichokes

This slender mahogany-coloured grain with its faintly salty tang combines well with the sweet nutty flavours of hazelnuts and artichokes. Carrots add a splash of colour and the end result is a lightly textured dish, great on its own or served with a frittata for a more substantial meal. Use fresh artichoke hearts if you can. Otherwise, buy good-quality canned or marinated ones and use a few more if they are small.

serves 4

preparation: 10 minutes

cooking: 50–55 minutes

𝑣

250g (8oz) wild rice
2 tbsp olive oil
1 red onion, finely chopped
1 garlic clove, crushed
6–8 artichoke hearts, halved, or 10–12 canned
  artichoke hearts
50g (2oz) roasted hazelnuts, roughly chopped
4 carrots, cut into julienne strips
2 tbsp shoyu or soy sauce
2 tbsp lemon juice
2 tbsp chopped coriander leaves
salt and freshly ground black pepper

1 Cook the rice in a large saucepan of boiling salted water for 35–40 minutes, or until cooked. Drain and keep warm.

2 Heat the oil in a large frying pan and gently cook the onion and garlic until soft.

3 Add the artichoke hearts, hazelnuts and carrot juliennes and cook over a high heat until lightly browned. Then reduce the heat and cook for 5–6 minutes, or until the carrots are slightly soft.

4 Stir in the shoyu or soy sauce and lemon juice and season well. Stir in the warm rice and coriander. Adjust the seasoning to taste and serve the rice hot or warm.

nutritional breakdown per serving: kcal 397, kJ 1655, protein 10g, fat 15g (saturated fat 2g), carbohydrate 57g

couscous with spiced tofu and mixed pepper sauce

Couscous is a delicate grain that needs a sauce or moist dressing otherwise it can seem dry. Here it is served with a mildly spiced mix of peppers and tofu. A big advantage of tofu is that it will soak up flavours quickly, as well as giving a nutritional boost to a dish. Put the tofu in at the beginning so that it can absorb the flavours and always mix it in carefully or the pieces may break up. Serve this couscous dish with a simple contrasting vegetable or salad, such as steamed green beans or a cucumber salad.

serves 4

preparation: 10 minutes

cooking: 55 minutes

(Ca) (Fe) 𝑣

2 tbsp sunflower oil
1 onion, finely chopped
2 garlic cloves, crushed
½ tsp cumin seeds
½ tsp ground coriander
¼ tsp ground cinnamon
200g (7oz) tofu (bean curd), cut into bite-sized pieces
2 red peppers, cored, deseeded and finely chopped
2 green peppers, cored, deseeded and finely chopped
4 carrots, chopped
500ml (17fl oz) passata
50g (2oz) currants
250g (8oz) couscous
450ml (¾ pint) boiling water
salt and freshly ground black pepper

1 Heat the oil in a large saucepan and gently fry the onion, then add the garlic and spices and cook for a few minutes.

2 Add the tofu to the pan and mix it in carefully but well. Add the peppers and carrots and cook slowly for 10 minutes.

3 Pour in the passata, add the currants and bring the mixture to the boil. Cover the pan and simmer for 35–40 minutes. Season to taste.

4 Just before serving, tip the couscous into a large bowl, add ½ teaspoon salt and the boiling water. Leave to soak for 5 minutes, then fluff with a fork and spoon out on to individual plates or a large serving platter. Top with the spiced tofu and pepper sauce and serve hot.

nutritional breakdown per serving: kcal 356, kJ 1490, protein 13g, fat 10g (saturated fat 1g), carbohydrate 56g

buckwheat with leeks and wild mushrooms

Buckwheat has a distinctive earthy flavour and pleasant character, and this dark robust dish is great on colder evenings. Contrasting vegetables such as steamed carrots or other roots such as beets and parsnips or Butternut Squash and Carrot Purée with Nutmeg and Mascarpone (see page 286) are ideal accompaniments.

serves 4
preparation: 15 minutes, plus soaking
cooking: 35 minutes
suitable for freezing
v

15g (½oz) dried mushrooms
300ml (½ pint) boiling water
300ml (½ pint) hot water or Vegetable Stock (see page 144)
2 tbsp sunflower oil
1 onion, finely chopped
2 garlic cloves, crushed
1 tsp grated fresh root ginger
2 leeks, sliced
175g (6oz) buckwheat
salt and freshly ground black pepper

1 Soak the dried mushrooms in a bowl of the boiling water for 15 minutes. Drain, reserving the soaking liquid, then chop the mushrooms finely.

2 Heat the oil in a large saucepan and gently fry the onion and garlic until soft.

3 Add the ginger and fry for 2–3 minutes, then add the leeks and chopped mushrooms. Cook for 5 minutes, or until the leeks are beginning to soften. Add the buckwheat and stir well.

4 Add hot water or vegetable stock to the reserved mushroom liquid to make 600ml (1 pint) stock. Pour this over the buckwheat and bring to the boil, then cover the pan and simmer for 20 minutes, or until the buckwheat is cooked and the water has been absorbed.

5 Season well and serve hot.

nutritional breakdown per serving: kcal 243, kJ 1013, protein 5g, fat 7g (saturated fat 1g), carbohydrate 44g

millet pilaf with pine nuts

Millet works well in pilaf-style dishes although you should eat it as soon as it is cooked since it tends to become rather solid on standing. The grains do not always cook evenly but a light crunchy texture is quite pleasant. Serve this on its own or with a casserole such as Chickpea Curry (see page 247) or with a stir-fry of contrasting vegetables.

serves 4

preparation: 10 minutes

cooking: 35–40 minutes

v

2 tbsp sunflower oil
200g (7oz) millet
50g (2oz) pine nuts
1 tsp coriander seeds, lightly crushed
½ tsp cardamom seeds, lightly crushed
1 onion, finely chopped
1 garlic clove, crushed
½ tsp finely grated fresh root ginger
400g (13oz) carrots, finely chopped
750ml (1¼ pints) boiling water
1 red pepper, cored, deseeded and
  finely chopped
250g (8oz) green beans, chopped
salt and freshly ground black pepper

1 Using 1 teaspoon of oil, toast the millet and pine nuts in a large saucepan for 2–3 minutes, then remove from the pan.

2 Add the remaining oil to the pan, and fry the coriander and cardamom seeds until just toasted. Add the onion, garlic and ginger and cook until soft, then add the carrot and cook for 2–3 minutes.

3 Return the millet and pine nuts to the pan and stir well. Pour in the boiling water and bring back to the boil. Cover the pan and cook for 15 minutes over a low heat.

4 Add the red pepper and green beans to the pan, but do not stir in. Cover the pan and cook for a further 10 minutes.

5 Season well and fluff the millet with a fork, mixing in the red pepper and green beans, which should have steamed on the top. Serve immediately.

nutritional breakdown per serving: kcal 382, kJ 1588, protein 7g, fat 16g (saturated fat 1g), carbohydrate 52g

red bean and lentil chilli

Chilli bean casseroles, with their warm flavours and rich hues, have deservedly become a classic vegetarian staple. The secret is to include many different textures by using a variety of beans and lentils – use more than two types if you wish – and a range of vegetables. I add bulgar as it absorbs the liquid and thickens the dish without making it heavy. Be sure to cook the spices well at the beginning otherwise the casserole will have a raw finish. Add more chilli to suit your temperament! Serve this chilli with a choice of the suggested toppings, as well as rice, baked potato, corn bread or soft tortillas.

| serves 4 |
| preparation: 10 minutes |
| cooking: about 1¼ hours |
| suitable for freezing |
| (Fe) 𝒱 |

3 tbsp olive oil
1 onion, roughly chopped
2 garlic cloves, crushed
½–1 tsp chilli powder
2 tsp cumin seeds
1 cinnamon stick
2 celery sticks, sliced
3 carrots, chopped
1 red pepper, cored, deseeded and chopped
250g (8oz) brown lentils (cooked weight)
250g (8oz) red kidney beans (cooked weight)
500ml (17fl oz) passata
300ml (½ pint) Vegetable Stock (see page 144)
50g (2oz) bulgar
salt and freshly ground black pepper

To serve:
soured cream, crème fraîche or silken tofu
  mixed with lemon juice
1–2 tbsp chopped coriander leaves
grated cheese

1 Heat the oil in a large saucepan or flameproof casserole and gently fry the onion and garlic until soft but not coloured.

2 Add the chilli powder, cumin seeds and cinnamon to the pan and fry for 2 minutes. Add the celery, carrots and red pepper and cook slowly for 7–10 minutes.

3 Then add the lentils and beans and mix in well. Pour in the passata and stock and bring the mixture to the boil. Season well, cover the pan and simmer for 40–50 minutes, stirring occasionally.

4 Add the bulgar and cook for a further 10 minutes, or until the bulgar is soft. Adjust the seasoning and serve hot topped with crème fraîche or silken tofu mixed with lemon juice and a sprinkling of coriander and grated cheese.

nutritional breakdown per serving: kcal 310, kJ 1303, protein 14g, fat 10g (saturated fat 1g), carbohydrate 43g

cooking pulses

A 400g (13oz) can contains approximately 250g (8oz) beans, lentils or chickpeas. To produce approximately 250g (8oz) cooked weight of beans, chickpeas or lentils, you will need 125g (4oz) of the dried pulse. Dried beans and chickpeas need to be soaked in a bowl of cold water for at least 4 hours, then drained and boiled fiercely in a saucepan of fresh water for 10 minutes, before being cooked over a reduced heat until soft. Lentils do not need soaking but should be boiled in plenty of water for 10 minutes then simmered until soft. It is probably worth cooking a larger quantity of pulses and freezing them for use in other recipes. See pages 90–91 for more information on cooking pulses.

sweet potato stew

This is a warming stew, both in flavour and colour. It is enriched with peanut butter, which rounds out the overall taste and means that the cooking time is quite short. This stew could be served with corn bread, rice or wholemeal bread. Other quick-cooking vegetables could be added, such as green beans, courgettes, fresh peas or coloured peppers.

serves 4
preparation: 15 minutes
cooking: 35–40 minutes
𝑣

2 tbsp sunflower oil
1 onion, finely chopped
1 garlic clove, crushed
1 tsp caraway seeds
1 green chilli, deseeded and chopped
2 celery sticks, sliced
300g (10oz) sweet potato or orange-fleshed
  squash, cubed
2 red peppers, cored, deseeded and chopped
175g (6oz) baby sweetcorn cobs, chopped
500ml (17fl oz) passata
200ml (7fl oz) Vegetable Stock (see page 144)
1–2 tbsp smooth peanut butter
salt and freshly ground black pepper

1 Heat the oil in a large saucepan or flameproof casserole and gently fry the onion and garlic until soft.

2 Add the caraway seeds and green chilli and cook for 2–3 minutes.

3 Add all the vegetables and cook for 5 minutes, stirring occasionally, so as to coat all the vegetables well with the chilli and onion mixture.

4 Pour over the passata and stock and bring to the boil. Cover the pan and cook for 20 minutes. If you are using oranged-flesh squash instead of sweet potato, cook for longer.

5 Remove 1–2 tablespoons of liquid from the pan and mix in a small bowl with the peanut butter, then return this to the stew. Season to taste and serve hot.

NUT BUTTER

Nut and seed butters, such as peanut butter, can be used to enrich and thicken stews, sauces or dressings. Always mix them first into a runny consistency with a little of the cooking liquid, otherwise they are quite tricky to blend in thoroughly.

nutritional breakdown per serving: kcal 245, kJ 1030, protein 7g, fat 7g (saturated fat 2g), carbohydrate 34g

broad bean and chickpea tagine

Tagine is the North African word for a slowly simmered stew or casserole and this recipe uses the aromatic spices characteristic of that cuisine. You can add extra vegetables, such as okra, cauliflower or green beans, or even a handful of slivered dried apricots or dark raisins if you like a fruit and vegetable combination. Use fresh broad beans, which are delicious, if you can; otherwise frozen or canned are perfectly acceptable. Serve this dish with couscous or bulgar.

serves 4	
preparation: 15 minutes	
cooking: 1 hour 15 minutes	
suitable for freezing	
(Fe) 𝑣	

2 tbsp sunflower oil
1 onion, finely chopped
3 garlic cloves, crushed
2 tsp grated fresh root ginger
2 tsp ground cumin
2 tsp ground coriander
½ tsp ground cinnamon
2 red peppers, cored, deseeded and finely chopped
400g (13oz) broad beans
250g (8oz) chickpeas (cooked weight)
500ml (17fl oz) passata
150ml (¼ pint) Vegetable Stock (see page 144)
2 tbsp tomato purée
2 bay leaves
salt and freshly ground black pepper
chopped coriander leaves or parsley, to garnish

1 Heat the oil in a large saucepan or flameproof casserole and fry the onion and garlic gently for 4–5 minutes, or until soft.

2 Add the ginger, cumin, coriander and cinnamon and fry for a few minutes. Then add the peppers, broad beans and chickpeas and cook very slowly for about 5–10 minutes, until just beginning to soften.

3 Pour in the passata and vegetable stock and stir in the tomato purée. Add the bay leaves and season well.

4 Bring the mixture to the boil, then cover the pan and simmer gently for at least 1 hour. Remove the bay leaves, adjust the seasoning and serve hot, garnished with chopped coriander or parsley.

nutritional breakdown per serving: kcal 238, kJ 1000, protein 13g, fat 9g (saturated fat 1g), carbohydrate 28g

cider casserole with new potatoes

Tart apple and cider impart a clean flavour to this light vegetable casserole. New potatoes add a distinct bite, but you can use chunks of ordinary potato when new potatoes are out of season. This casserole is great served with chunks of rustic bread and perhaps a glass of cider.

serves 4
preparation: 15 minutes
cooking: about 1¼ hours
suitable for freezing

2 tbsp sunflower oil
1 onion, chopped
1 leek, sliced
2 celery sticks, sliced
4 carrots, finely chopped
4 courgettes, finely chopped
500g (1lb) new potatoes
1 tart dessert or cooking apple, cored and
 finely chopped
250ml (8fl oz) cider
250ml (8fl oz) Vegetable Stock (see page 144)
250ml (8fl oz) double cream
2 tbsp chopped parsley
salt and freshly ground black pepper

1 Heat the oil in a large saucepan or flameproof casserole and gently cook the onion until soft.

2 Add the leek and celery and cook for a further 4–5 minutes. Add the carrots, courgettes and new potatoes and cook over a low heat until just beginning to soften – this takes about 10 minutes.

3 Add the apple and pour in the cider, stock and cream. Season well and bring to the boil, then simmer for 45–50 minutes, or until all the vegetables are tender.

4 Stir in the parsley and adjust the seasoning to taste.

nutritional breakdown per serving: kcal 503, kJ 2090, protein 6g, fat 37g (saturated fat 20g), carbohydrate 36g

country casserole with spiced cheese dumplings

This tasty casserole is made from simple ingredients, which benefit from slow cooking. The leeks added late on in the cooking process accentuate the onion flavour. Dumplings add extra nutrients and substance and are easy to make at the last minute. Garnish with extra grated cheese. The casserole is a meal in itself but you could serve a simple green side vegetable with it if you like.

serves 4
preparation: 15–20 minutes
cooking: 1½ hours
suitable for freezing (without dumplings)

2 tbsp sunflower oil
1 onion, finely chopped
2 celery sticks, finely chopped
2–3 carrots, chopped
1 turnip, chopped
1 small swede or sweet potato, chopped
500ml (17fl oz) passata
300ml (½ pint) Vegetable Stock (see page 144)
   or water
2 leeks, finely chopped
2–3 tbsp chopped parsley, to garnish

For the dumplings:
125g (4oz) wholemeal self-raising flour
25g (1oz) vegetable margarine
50g (2oz) cheese, grated
½ tsp dried mustard powder
½ tsp paprika
4 tbsp semi-skimmed milk
salt and freshly ground black pepper

1 Heat the oil in a large saucepan or flameproof casserole and gently fry the onion until soft.

2 Add all the remaining vegetables, except the leeks, to the pan. Cook slowly for about 10 minutes, stirring well.

3 Pour in the passata and stock. Bring to the boil and season well, then cover the pan and simmer gently for 50 minutes.

4 To make the dumplings, tip the flour into a large bowl and rub in the fat until the mixture resembles fine breadcrumbs. Stir in the grated cheese, mustard powder, paprika and seasoning, then pour in the milk and mix quickly into a soft dough. (The dumplings could also be made in a food processor, if preferred.)

5 Add the leeks to the casserole then add spoonfuls of dumpling mixture, making about 8 dumplings. Leave the casserole to simmer, uncovered, for about 20 minutes, basting the dumplings occasionally.

6 Adjust the seasoning and serve, garnished with chopped parsley.

nutritional breakdown per serving: kcal 328, kJ 1373, protein 11g, fat 17g (saturated fat 6g), carbohydrate 35g

tofu goulash with aubergines and mushrooms

This is a well-flavoured supper dish with a good colour. Tofu is an ideal ingredient for casseroles and stews. It adds to the nutritional value of the dish, as well as absorbing flavours from the cooking liquid – in this case the classic goulash spices of paprika and caraway. Top the goulash with soured cream or extra silken tofu blended with lemon juice if you want to avoid dairy products, and serve with baked potatoes, rice or millet.

serves 4
preparation: 15 minutes
cooking: 1–1¼ hours
Ⓒ 𝒱

2 tbsp olive oil
2 leeks, chopped
2 garlic cloves, crushed
250g (8oz) tofu (bean curd), cubed
2 tbsp paprika
1 tsp caraway seeds
1 aubergine, cubed
250g (8oz) mushrooms, sliced
2 red peppers, cored, deseeded and finely chopped
500ml (17fl oz) passata

200ml (7fl oz) Vegetable Stock (see page 144)
  or water
1–2 tsp chopped dill
salt and freshly ground black pepper

1 Heat the oil in a large saucepan or flameproof casserole and gently cook the leeks and garlic until soft.

2 Add the tofu and sprinkle in the paprika and caraway seeds. Cook for 3–4 minutes. Add the remaining vegetables and stir well; cook over a low heat for 10–15 minutes, or until just softened.

3 Pour in the passata and add the stock or water. Bring to the boil and season well, then simmer for 35–45 minutes, or until everything is well cooked.

4 Add the chopped dill and cook for a further 5 minutes. Adjust the seasoning and serve hot.

nutritional breakdown per serving: kcal 176, kJ 736, protein 10g, fat 10g (saturated fat 1g), carbohydrate 13g

chickpea curry

Pulses make a good addition to curry dishes as they add texture and colour, while also absorbing the spice flavours and giving a nutritional boost to the dish. This recipe is based on an aromatic spice paste made from cumin, coriander and chilli. The paste is made in a blender or food processor and cooked thoroughly so that the spices develop in character. Serve this curry with some cooling natural yoghurt and a plain or spiced rice such as Spiced Mushroom Rice (see page 235). You could also serve some Vegetable Fritters (see page 168) as an appetiser.

serves 4
preparation: 10 minutes
cooking: 35 minutes
suitable for freezing
(Fe)

2 onions, finely chopped
2 chillies (see right)
1 garlic clove, roughly chopped
1 tbsp ground cumin
1 tbsp ground coriander
4 tbsp sunflower oil
400g (13oz) can tomatoes
250g (8oz) chickpeas (cooked weight)

250ml (8fl oz) Vegetable Stock (see page 144)
  or liquid from cooking the chickpeas
2 tbsp chopped coriander leaves
juice of 1 lemon
salt and freshly ground black pepper

1 Place the onions, chillies, garlic, salt, black pepper, ground cumin and coriander in a blender or food processor and blend to a paste, adding a little water if necessary.

2 Heat the oil in a large frying pan and cook the paste for 10 minutes, allowing it to brown slightly.

3 Add the canned tomatoes, cooked chickpeas and stock or liquid. Bring the mixture to the boil and simmer, uncovered, for 20 minutes.

4 Adjust the seasoning if necessary and stir in the chopped coriander and lemon juice just before serving.

nutritional breakdown per serving: kcal 232, kJ 969, protein 7g, fat 14g (saturated fat 2g), carbohydrate 21g

CHILLI POWER

This dish will be very hot if you use the whole chillies, since much of the fire power is in the seeds and skin. To make a milder curry, remove the seeds. For a milder version still, roast and peel the chilli. Although suitable for freezing, highly spiced dishes should not be frozen for longer than a month or the spices can develop unpleasant flavours.

spinach and new potato curry with coconut

Coconut adds an underlying velvety texture to this tasty, colourful curry. Use main crop potatoes when new ones are no longer in season. Serve this curry with spiced bread or rice or, for a more substantial meal, with Mixed Lentil Dhal (see page 250) or Chickpea Curry (see page 247).

serves 4
preparation: 15 minutes
cooking: 30–35 minutes
(Fe) 𝑣

250g (8oz) new potatoes
250g (8oz) spinach
2 tbsp sunflower oil
1 onion, halved then finely sliced
2 garlic cloves, crushed
1 tsp ground turmeric
1 chilli, finely chopped
1 tbsp ground coriander
1 tsp freshly ground black pepper
75g (3oz) coconut block, dissolved in 200ml (7fl oz) water
juice of ½ lemon
salt

1 Parboil the new potatoes in their skins for 8–10 minutes. Drain and cut in half.

2 Meanwhile, cook the spinach in a saucepan for 3–4 minutes. Drain and chop roughly.

3 Heat the oil in a large frying pan, and fry the onion with the garlic, turmeric, chilli, ground coriander and black pepper until soft.

4 Add the cooked potatoes and cook until slightly brown, about 6–8 minutes. Add the cooked spinach and coconut milk. Bring to the boil, then simmer for 7 minutes.

5 Season and add lemon juice to taste, and serve hot.

nutritional breakdown per serving: kcal 249, kJ 1036, protein 5g, fat 19g (saturated fat 12g), carbohydrate 16g

spinach and new potato curry with coconut opposite

tomato raita with cumin

A rosy-coloured accompaniment with an aromatic taste.

serves 4
preparation: 5 minutes, plus chilling
cooking: none

250g (8oz) natural yoghurt
1 tomato, skinned and chopped
1 spring onion, finely chopped
2 tsp dry-roasted cumin seeds
salt and freshly ground black pepper

1 Tip the yoghurt into a bowl and stir in the chopped tomato, spring onion and cumin seeds. Season well and chill before serving.

nutritional breakdown per serving: kcal 45, kJ 189, protein 4g, fat 0g (saturated fat 0g), carbohydrate 6g

mixed lentil dhal

Dhal is a pulse-based Indian dish made with either lentils or split peas. Its consistency can be sloppy like soup or slightly drier so that it can be scooped up and eaten with bread. My version combines two types of lentils – the red fall to a purée to give an underlying texture, while the green keep their shape and give the dhal a little bite. As with all spice dishes, cook the spices well before moving on to the next stage of the recipe. Serve the dhal with bread or Spinach and New Potato Curry with Coconut (see page 249) and a plain or spiced rice.

serves 4
preparation: 10 minutes
cooking: 35 minutes
suitable for freezing
(Fe) 𝑣

3 tbsp sunflower oil
1 onion, finely chopped
2 garlic cloves, crushed
2 tsp grated fresh root ginger
1 tsp chilli powder
½ tsp ground turmeric
125g (4oz) Puy or green lentils

mixed lentil dhal left.
tomato raita with
cucumber and **spiced**
cauliflower and green
beans right

125g (4oz) red lentils
450ml (¾ pint) water
salt and freshly ground black pepper

1 Heat the oil in a large saucepan and gently cook the onion and garlic until quite soft.

2 Mix the root ginger, chilli powder and turmeric in a small bowl with 1 tablespoon water to make a thin paste. Add this to the pan and cook for 2 minutes.

3 Add the lentils and the measured water and bring to the boil. Cover the pan and cook on a low heat for 20–25 minutes, or until the red lentils have fallen to a purée and the green lentils are soft.

4 Season to taste then leave to cool a little before serving.

nutritional breakdown per serving: kcal 282, kJ 1187, protein 16g, fat 9g (saturated fat 1g), carbohydrate 36g

spiced cauliflower and green beans

This is a light vegetable dish that can be part of a spicy meal. It has a dry finished texture which goes well with more moist dishes, such as the Spinach and New Potato Curry with Coconut (see page 249). Make sure the vegetables don't catch on the bottom.

serves 4

preparation: 15 minutes

cooking: 30–40 minutes

(Fe) *v*

40–50g (2oz) gram flour
4–6 tbsp sunflower oil
1 garlic clove, finely chopped
1–2 fresh red chillies, deseeded and
  finely chopped
250g (8oz) green beans, halved
500g (1lb) cauliflower, divided into florets
1 tbsp sesame seeds
25g (1oz) cashew nuts, ground
1 tsp garam masala
¼ tsp ground turmeric
1–2 tbsp lemon juice
salt and freshly ground black pepper

1 Dry roast the gram flour in a small pan until it looks light brown and smells toasted.

2 Heat the oil in a large saucepan and gently fry the garlic and chillies for 3–4 minutes.

3 Add the green beans and cauliflower and cook gently, stirring frequently until they begin to soften, for about 5–10 minutes.

4 Mix together the gram flour, sesame seeds, ground cashew nuts, spices and ¼ teaspoon salt in a bowl. Sprinkle this mixture over the slightly softened vegetables. Mix well, pour in just enough water to cover the vegetables, and cook over a medium heat for 5–10 minutes or until the vegetables are soft.

5 Just before serving, sprinkle over the lemon juice and adjust the seasoning to taste. Serve hot or at room temperature.

nutritional breakdown per serving: kcal 273, kJ 1133, protein 11g, fat 20g (saturated fat 3g), carbohydrate 14g

wholemeal shortcrust pastry

It is not difficult to make a good, crisp light pastry with wholemeal flour. Bear in mind the following points and you should have success every time. First, work with cool ingredients – the fats and water you are using must be well chilled. Second, use a fine milled flour and add a little baking powder as this makes the end result lighter and crisper. Wholemeal flour absorbs more water, not just initially but while the dough is resting so make the dough wetter than a white flour pastry. Adding a little oil helps to create moisture without making the pastry tough. Sugar is used by many caterers in savoury pastry as it makes the dough more elastic. If using brown sugar, you need to dissolve it first or it will show up as brown flecks.

makes approximately 450–500g (15oz–1lb) dough

preparation: 10 minutes, plus chilling

cooking: none

suitable for freezing

v

250g (8oz) wholemeal flour, plus extra for dusting

pinch of salt

½ tsp baking powder

125g (4oz) chilled butter, solid vegetable fat or a mixture

1 tsp caster sugar

4–6 tbsp ice-cold water

1 tbsp sunflower or olive oil

1 Place the flour, salt and baking powder in a large bowl and cut in the fat. Rub the fat into the flour, using your fingertips, until the mixture resembles fine breadcrumbs. Shake the bowl occasionally so that the larger lumps of fat come to the surface and ensure that the fat is evenly rubbed in. Alternatively, use a blender or food processor to achieve the same result.

2 Dissolve the sugar in the water and mix in the oil. Sprinkle most of the mixture over the flour and stir with a rounded knife. Only add as much water as is necessary to draw the mixture together.

3 Turn the dough on to a lightly floured board and knead gently until the surface of the dough is smooth.

4 Chill for 15–20 minutes, or while you prepare a filling.

nutritional breakdown per total recipe: kcal 1739, kJ 7262, protein 32g, fat 111g (saturated fat 27g), carbohydrate 164g

Step 1 Sift the flour into a large bowl, add the salt and baking powder, then rub in the fat. **Step 2** Add the oil to the sugar and water mixture. **Step 3** Stir in with a rounded knife. **Step 4** Turn the dough out on to a floured surface.

spinach and lentil turnovers

Spinach and lentils, peppered with warm spices, make a good moist filling for a pastry turnover. They make a meal on their own but could easily be accompanied by a choice of simple salads. Make sure the pastry is made entirely with vegetable fats if cooking for a vegan. Serve tiny versions as appetisers.

makes 6

preparation: 15 minutes, plus pastry making

cooking: 45 minutes

suitable for freezing

(Fe)

1 quantity Wholemeal Shortcrust Pastry (see page 252) or Quick Flaky Pastry (see page 256)
flour for dusting

For the filling:
2 tbsp sunflower oil
1 onion, finely chopped
1 garlic clove, chopped
1 chilli, deseeded and finely chopped
1 tsp cumin seeds
1 tsp coriander seeds
125g (4oz) red lentils
250ml (8fl oz) boiling water
250g (8oz) spinach
1 tbsp lemon juice

1 To make the filling, heat the oil in a large saucepan and cook the onion, garlic and chilli until soft. Add the spices and fry for 2–3 minutes, or until lightly toasted.

2 Add the red lentils and stir in, then pour in the boiling water. Bring back to the boil, cover the pan and cook for 10–15 minutes, or until all the water has been absorbed and the lentils have fallen to a purée.

3 Meanwhile, cook the washed spinach in a large pan, without adding any extra water, for 6–8 minutes. Drain if necessary and chop finely.

4 Stir the spinach into the cooked lentils and add the lemon juice. Season to taste and set aside.

5 Roll out the pastry on a lightly floured surface and cut into six rounds 15cm (6in) in diameter. Spoon a little filling on to each round, then fold the pastry over to make a semicircle and seal the edges with cold water.

6 Prick each turnover and bake in a preheated oven, 200°C (400°F), Gas Mark 6, for 20–25 minutes. Serve hot or warm.

nutritional breakdown per turnover: kcal 408, kJ 1707, protein 12g, fat 23g (saturated fat 12g), carbohydrate 42g

enriched shortcrust pastry (pâte brisée)

makes approximately 350–450g (12oz–15oz) dough

preparation: 10 minutes, plus chilling

cooking: none

suitable for freezing

200g (7oz) plain flour
½ tsp salt
100g (3½oz) chilled butter
1 egg, lightly beaten
up to 2 tsp cold water

troubleshooting with pastry

- pastry shrinks during baking – not enough resting time
- pastry is tough – too much liquid, overhandling when drawing up to a dough
- pastry cracks when rolling out – too dry

1 Sift the flour and salt into a large bowl and cut in the butter. Rub the butter into the flour, using your fingertips, until the mixture resembles fine breadcrumbs. Make a well in the centre.

2 Pour the beaten egg into the well and work the pastry with a scraper or rounded knife until the mixture draws into a dough. Add the cold water, a teaspoon at a time, if necessary.

3 Bring the dough together and shape into a rough ball. Wrap in greaseproof paper or clingfilm that is suitable for fatty foods, and chill for 30 minutes. If the dough is very cold, leave for a few minutes before rolling out.

nutritional breakdown per total recipe: kcal 1493, kJ 6237, protein 26g, fat 90g (saturated fat 56g), carbohydrate 155g

Step 1 Sift the flour and salt and cut in the butter.
Step 2 Rub the butter into the flour using your fingertips.
Step 3 Pour in the egg and work the pastry with a rounded knife until the mixture draws into a dough.
Step 4 Shape into a rough ball, wrap in suitable clingfilm and chill for 30 minutes.

griddled courgette quiche with pine nuts

serves 4–6

preparation: 15 minutes, plus pastry making

cooking: 50 minutes

suitable for freezing

(Fe)

1 quantity Enriched Shortcrust Pastry
  (see page 254)
flour for dusting
2 tbsp freshly grated Parmesan

For the filling:
400g (13oz) courgettes, sliced
125g (4oz) shallots, sliced
50g (2oz) pine nuts
2 tsp chopped rosemary
3 eggs
150ml (¼ pint) double cream
3 tsp pesto (see page 211)
salt and freshly ground black pepper

1 Roll out the pastry on a lightly floured surface to fill a 23cm (9in) flan ring. Line with baking parchment and weigh down with baking beans. Bake in a preheated oven, 200°C (400°F), Gas Mark 6, for 15 minutes.

2 Meanwhile, to make the filling, heat a griddle pan or large non-stick frying pan and griddle the courgettes and shallots until quite brown and softened, turning them over several times during cooking.

3 Add the pine nuts and cook until toasted. Remove from the heat and add the rosemary.

4 Beat the eggs in a bowl with the cream and add the pesto and plenty of seasoning.

5 Combine the griddled courgettes and shallots mixture with the egg and pour into the cooked flan case. Dust with the grated Parmesan and bake in a preheated oven, 200°C (400°F), Gas Mark 6, for 35 minutes. Serve warm.

nutritional breakdown per serving: kcal 769, kJ 3198, protein 18g, fat 58g (saturated fat 29g), carbohydrate 48g

quick flaky pastry

Do remember to start with cold ingredients and have the fats frozen solid beforehand as this makes them easier to grate in.

makes approximately 550g (1lb 2oz) dough
preparation: 15 minutes, plus chilling
cooking: none
suitable for freezing
𝒱 (optional)

below **Follow these easy stages for perfect flaky pastry. The rolling and folding will give the dough the characteristic flaky texture.**

250g (8oz) plain flour, plus extra for dusting
½ tsp salt
150g (5oz) butter, solid vegetable fat or a
  mixture, frozen for 30 minutes before using
1 tbsp lemon juice
125–150ml (4–5fl oz) ice-cold water

1 Sift the flour and salt into a large bowl. Grate in the frozen fat.

2 Add the lemon juice and just enough water to draw the mixture into a dough, using a rounded knife. Draw up to a ball and knead very lightly.

3 Wrap the dough in greaseproof paper or clingfilm suitable for fatty foods, and chill for 30 minutes.

4 If the dough is very cold, leave for a few minutes before rolling out. On a lightly floured surface, roll it out to a long oblong. Lightly mark the pastry into thirds. Fold in one end third on top of the middle third, then fold the remaining third over the top. Seal the edges and give it a quarter turn on the work surface. Repeat this process once more to trap air in the pastry and chill again for 30 minutes.

nutritional breakdown per total recipe: kcal 1962, kJ 8188, protein 24g, fat 126g (saturated fat 54g), carbohydrate 196g

chestnut and cep single crust pie

This is a moist flavoursome pie, which uses the classic combination of mushrooms, walnuts and chestnuts. The sweetness of the chestnuts with their dry texture combines well with the rich intense walnuts and woody mushrooms. Serve this pie as the hot centrepiece for a special meal on a cool evening, with a mushroom or onion sauce, Roasted Root Vegetables with Caraway (see page 283) and a green vegetable. For a midweek meal, you could top the pie filling with a savoury crumble topping (see page 271).

serves 4–6

preparation: 15 minutes, plus soaking

cooking: 45 minutes

suitable for freezing

𝒱

½ quantity Quick Flaky Pastry (see page 256)
flour for dusting
egg yolk and water, for brushing (optional)

For the filling:
15g (½oz) dried ceps
100ml (3½fl oz) boiling water
2–3 tbsp sunflower oil
2 onions, finely chopped
2 garlic cloves, crushed
2 leeks, sliced
2 carrots, finely chopped
3–4 tbsp red wine
125g (4oz) walnuts, chopped
200g (7oz) chestnuts (cooked weight), roughly chopped
4 tbsp chopped parsley
2–3 tbsp shoyu or soy sauce
salt and freshly ground black pepper

1 To make the filling, place the ceps in a bowl with the boiling water and leave to soak for 30 minutes.

2 Heat the oil in a large saucepan and gently cook the onions and garlic until very soft. Add the leeks and carrots and cook for 3–4 minutes, or until just beginning to soften. Add the red wine and cook gently to reduce the liquid.

3 Drain the ceps, reserving the soaking liquid. Chop if necessary, then add to the vegetables with the walnuts, chestnuts, parsley and soaking liquid from the ceps. Cook for 2–3 minutes, then remove the pan from the heat. Stir in the shoyu or soy sauce, season well and leave to cool.

4 Roll out the pastry on a lightly floured surface to a size at least 2.5–5cm (1–2in) larger than the 20cm (8in) deep ovenproof dish you will need to use. Place the dish in the centre of the pastry. Cut out the exact shape of the dish, then cut a collar about 2.5cm (1in) wide from the remaining pastry.

5 Spoon the cool pie filling into the dish. Moisten the edge of the dish with water, then press on the pastry collar. Brush with cold water.

6 Place the pastry lid on top, using a rolling pin to help lift it into place, then press it on to the collar. Trim the pastry with a sharp knife. Crimp the collar and the lid together, using a fork or fingertips.

7 Cut a small hole in the top of the pie to allow steam from the pie filling to escape. If you wish, give the pastry a golden finish by brushing with egg yolk beaten with a little water and salt.

8 Bake in a preheated oven, 220°C (425°F), Gas Mark 7, for 30 minutes, or until golden brown.

nutritional breakdown per serving (4 portions): kcal 660, kJ 2748, protein 11g, fat 46g (saturated fat 10g), carbohydrate 52g

USING DRIED CHESTNUTS

If you are using dried chestnuts, soak 125g (4oz) dried chestnuts in plenty of water for 30 minutes. Then bring to the boil in the same water and simmer for 30 minutes, or until quite tender. Drain, reserving the stock for other uses. This should provide you with at least 200g (7oz) cooked chestnuts.

choux pastry

Step 1 Bring the mixture to the boil and tip in the flour.
Step 2 Beat well with a wooden spoon.
Step 3 Cook until the mixture forms a ball.
Step 4 Beat in the egg.
Step 5 The dough should look smooth and glossy.
Step 6 Stir in the grated cheese.

preparation: 5 minutes
cooking: 5 minutes
suitable for freezing

250ml (8fl oz) water
100g (3½oz) butter
150g (5oz) plain flour
1 tsp salt
4 eggs, beaten
50g (2oz) Cheddar cheese, grated
egg yolk and water for brushing

1 Bring the water and butter to the boil in a saucepan.

2 When the butter has melted and the liquid is boiling, tip in all the flour and the salt. Remove the pan from the heat and beat well using a wooden spoon. Return briefly to the heat and cook until the flour forms a ball.

3 Take off the heat, add 1 egg and beat in until completely absorbed.

4 Add the remaining eggs in the same way, beating until the dough is smooth and glossy with a soft but not runny consistency. It should drop off the spoon when shaken.

5 Stir in the grated cheese. The choux pastry can now be used in a variety of ways depending on the recipe.

VARIATIONS

For cocktail snacks and appetisers, make 30–40 'buns' by spooning out 30–40 small mounds or piping them using a 1cm (½in) piping nozzle. Brush the tops with a little beaten egg yolk and water and bake in a preheated oven, 200°C (400°F), Gas Mark 6, for 20 minutes, or until crisp and golden.

For gougère, spoon or pipe walnut-sized amounts of the mixture around a greased ovenproof dish. Bake in a preheated oven, 200°C (400°F), Gas Mark 6, for 25–30 minutes.

nutritional breakdown per total recipe: kcal 1749, kJ 7284, protein 52g, fat 122g (saturated fat 71g), carbohydrate 117g

artichoke and red pepper gougère

Elegant enough for a dinner party, this is a glorious colourful dish that is light but satisfying. This version focuses on the summer flavours of roasted peppers and artichokes. Use fresh artichokes if you can, otherwise splash out on good-quality marinated artichoke halves.

It is easy to make a simpler gougère for suppertime treats – just fill the cooked gougère with a vegetable stir-fry or sauté, and moisten it with tomato sauce or white sauce.

serves 4–6

preparation: 20 minutes, plus choux pastry making

cooking: 1 hour 10 minutes

suitable for freezing (gougère only)

(Fe)

1 quantity Choux Pastry (see page 258)
freshly grated Parmesan for sprinkling

For the sauce:
4 red peppers
6 tbsp olive oil
2 tbsp white wine vinegar
salt and freshly ground black pepper

For the filling:
2 tbsp olive oil
1 onion, finely chopped
2 garlic cloves, crushed
8 artichoke hearts, halved
300g (10oz) cherry tomatoes
salt and freshly ground black pepper

1 To make the sauce, place the peppers on a baking sheet or in a roasting tin and roast in a preheated oven, 200°C (400°F), Gas Mark 6, for 25 minutes. Leave until cool enough to handle then remove the skins and seeds. Chop the flesh roughly.

2 Using a blender or food processor, purée the red peppers with the olive oil until smooth. Add the vinegar and purée again. Season well.

3 To make the filling, heat the oil in a saucepan and gently fry the onion and garlic until soft. Add the artichoke hearts and cook until lightly browned, then add the cherry tomatoes. Cook until these are quite soft. Pour the red pepper sauce over the artichokes and mix in well. Adjust the seasoning to taste.

4 To make the gougère, spoon or pipe walnut-sized amounts of the choux pastry around a greased ovenproof dish. Bake at 200°C (400°F), Gas Mark 6, for 25–30 minutes.

5 When the gougère is cooked, pile the filling into the centre of the dish and sprinkle with grated Parmesan. Bake for a further 5 minutes. Serve hot.

nutritional breakdown per serving (4 portions): kcal 733, kJ 3045, protein 18g, fat 54g (saturated fat 21g), carbohydrate 48g

leek and feta parcels

These well-flavoured light parcels make great party food. This version is shaped like an individual strudel, but it is just as easy to make triangles.

makes 24
preparation: 25 minutes
cooking: 25–30 minutes
suitable for freezing

For the filling:
25g (1oz) butter
2 tbsp olive oil
1kg (2lb) leeks, shredded
2 garlic cloves, crushed
freshly grated nutmeg
200g (7oz) feta (drained weight), crumbled
salt and freshly ground black pepper

For the pastry:
50g (2oz) butter
3 tbsp olive oil
24 sheets filo pastry

1　To make the filling, melt the butter and oil together in a large frying pan, then gently cook the shredded leeks with the garlic until soft.

2　Leave to cool, then add a grating of nutmeg and the crumbled feta. Season well.

3　To assemble the parcels, melt the butter and oil for the pastry together. Use 1 sheet of filo pastry at a time and brush well with melted butter and oil.

4　Spoon a tablespoon or so of filling in the central third of the sheet, leaving a margin at the top. Fold over the top edge to cover the filling then fold in the sides. Brush the folded pastry with melted fat.

5　Roll up the pastry to make a cigar shape. Brush well with more melted fat.

6　Repeat with the remaining sheets of pastry and the filling. Bake the parcels in a preheated oven, 200°C (400°F), Gas Mark 6, for 15–20 minutes, or until crisp. Serve warm or at room temperature.

nutritional breakdown per parcel: kcal 153, kJ 642, protein 5g, fat 6g (saturated fat 1g), carbohydrate 20g

filo pie with double mushrooms and goat's cheese

Mushrooms and goat's cheese are a good combination and form a rich filling for this feather-light pie. This could easily be part of a meal suitable for entertaining, served with new potatoes, a green vegetable or salad. Begin the meal with a contrasting soup or refreshing Oranges with Red Onion and Black Olives (see page 163).

serves 4–6

preparation time: 20 minutes

cooking time: 40–45 minutes

suitable for freezing

(Fe)

For the filling:
50g (2oz) butter
500g (1lb) oyster mushrooms, roughly chopped
300g (10oz) chestnut mushrooms, sliced
1 tsp dried marjoram
75ml (3fl oz) white wine
150g (5oz) goat's cheese, roughly chopped
3 eggs
salt and freshly ground black pepper

For the pastry:
50g (2oz) butter
2–3 tbsp olive oil
12 sheets filo pastry

1 To make the filling, melt the butter in a large frying pan and cook the mushrooms over a medium heat so that they colour slightly. When fairly soft, add the marjoram and white wine and season well, then cook over a high heat until the liquid has reduced. Set aside.

2 Using a blender or food processor, blend the goat's cheese and eggs to make a smooth sauce. Pour this over the cooked mushrooms and mix well. Season well.

3 To assemble the pie, melt the butter with the olive oil for the pastry. Brush the melted butter mixture over the base of a square ovenproof dish.

4 Take 1 sheet of filo and use it to line the base and sides of the dish. Brush with the melted butter mixture.

5 Place another sheet of filo on top, at an angle to the first, and brush with more of the melted butter. Continue layering filo in the same way until you have a base of 6 sheets, with each successive sheet at a slightly different angle.

6 Spoon the mushroom filling on top and fold over any filo pastry edges.

7 Cover the filling with a sheet of filo brushed with more of the melted butter mixture and tuck in the edges. Repeat this using the remaining sheets. Mark a cross through the centre of the pastry with a sharp knife.

8 Bake in a preheated oven, 200°C (400°F), Gas Mark 6, for 35–40 minutes, or until the pastry is crisp and golden. Turn the oven down a little for the last 10 minutes if the pastry is becoming too brown. Serve hot.

nutritional breakdown per serving (4 portions): kcal 695, kJ 2905, protein 22g, fat 39g (saturated fat 20g), carbohydrate 59g

potato and leek boulangère

This fabulous dish makes a wonderful meal for family or company. It is easy to make enormous quantities if you are having an informal supper party. The recipe is very quick to prepare and the dish is then slowly cooked in the oven. When ready, it needs little accompaniment other than a light salad.

serves 4–6
preparation: 15 minutes
cooking: 1 hour
suitable for freezing
(Ca)

25g (1oz) butter
500g (1lb) leeks, sliced
2 garlic cloves, chopped
875g (1 ¾lb) potatoes, scrubbed and thinly sliced
4 tomatoes, sliced
300ml (½ pint) double cream
300ml (½ pint) milk
125g (4oz) smoked cheese, grated
salt and freshly ground black pepper

1 Use the butter to grease a large, deep 30 x 30cm (12 x 12in) ovenproof dish. Put in half of the chopped leeks and garlic, cover with half of the slices of potato and season well.

2 Cover with a layer of the remaining leeks and garlic, then the remaining potato slices and season well again. Cover with the slices of tomato.

3 Mix the cream with the milk and pour over the top. Don't worry if it settles on the top as it will melt through during the cooking process.

4 Cover with grated cheese and bake in a preheated oven, 180°C (350°F), Gas Mark 4, for 1 hour, or until the potatoes are cooked and the cheese well browned.

nutritional breakdown per serving (4 portions): kcal 719, kJ 2996, protein 18g, fat 51g (saturated fat 32g), carbohydrate 50g

sweet potato and courgette gratin

This is similar in concept to the boulangère (see page 262), but with a very different look and distinctive delicious flavour. The sweet potato and golden courgettes add warm autumnal tones. This dish is good enough for a dinner party, served with a simple salad.

serves 4–6
preparation: 15 minutes
cooking: 1 hour
suitable for freezing
(Ca) (Fe)

25g (1oz) butter
500g (1lb) golden courgettes, sliced
250g (8oz) shallots, sliced
875g (1¾lb) sweet potatoes, scrubbed and
  thinly sliced
300ml (½ pint) double cream
300ml (½ pint) milk
125g (4oz) Emmental, grated
salt and freshly ground black pepper

1 Use the butter to grease a large, deep 30 x 30cm (12 x 12in) ovenproof dish. Put in half of the sliced courgettes and shallots, cover with half of the slices of sweet potato and season well.

2 Cover with a layer of the remaining courgettes and shallots, then the remaining sweet potato slices and season well again.

3 Mix the cream with the milk and pour over the top. Don't worry if it settles on the top as it will melt through during the cooking process.

4 Cover with grated cheese and bake in a preheated oven, 180°C (350°F), Gas Mark 4, for 1 hour, or until the sweet potatoes are cooked and the cheese well browned.

nutritional breakdown per serving (4 portions): kcal 840, kJ 3511, protein 19g, fat 53g (saturated fat 33g), carbohydrate 78g

roasted pecan and cashew loaf

This rich nut loaf, encrusted with roasted nuts and seeds, makes a good centrepiece for an evening or weekend meal. Serve it with a mushroom, onion or tomato sauce (see pages 291–92), roast or baked potatoes or root vegetables and a green vegetable or salad. Nut roasts are rich so you need serve only small portions. Leftovers will keep well and can be reheated successfully or served cold.

This recipe can be made with soya flour for a vegan alternative. Mix 2 tablespoons soya flour with water to a runny consistency and use in place of the eggs. While just as tasty, it will not hold together quite so well and is therefore better baked in a larger shallower dish. Consequently, it will cook in a shorter time so check it after 35 minutes.

serves 4–6
preparation: 10 minutes
cooking: 1 hour 10 minutes
suitable for freezing
Ⓕ 𝒱

150g (5oz) pecan nuts
150g (5oz) cashew nuts
50g (2oz) sunflower seeds
15g (½oz) dried mushrooms
150ml (¼ pint) boiling water
2 tbsp sunflower oil
1 onion, finely chopped
2 garlic cloves, crushed
2 celery sticks, finely chopped
250g (8oz) chestnut mushrooms, finely chopped
6 tbsp red wine
1 tbsp plain flour
2 tbsp chopped parsley
1 tbsp shoyu or soy sauce
2 eggs, beaten
salt and freshly ground black pepper

1 Put the nuts and seeds on a large baking sheet and roast in a preheated oven, 200°C (400°F), Gas Mark 6, for 5 minutes, or until lightly browned. Set aside enough to garnish the top of the roast.

2 Soak the dried mushrooms in a bowl of the boiling water to make a simple stock. Drain the mushrooms and chop finely, reserving the mushroom stock.

3 Heat the oil in a large frying pan and cook the onion and garlic until soft. Add the celery, fresh mushrooms and dried mushrooms and cook until quite soft.

4 Add the red wine and increase the heat, then cook until most of the liquid has evaporated.

5 Sprinkle in the flour, stir and cook for 2 minutes. Pour in the mushroom stock, bring the mixture to the boil, then simmer for 2 minutes. Remove from the heat and season well.

6 Using a food processor, process the roasted nuts and seeds, the mushroom sauce, parsley and shoyu or soy sauce together until fairly smooth.

7 Add the beaten eggs to the mixture and process again. (Alternatively, add the mixed soya flour and water.)

8 Adjust the seasoning, then spoon the mixture into a greased and lined 1.2 litre (2 pint) loaf tin. Arrange the reserved nuts and seeds over the top, pressing in lightly.

9 Bake in a preheated oven, 190°C (375°F), Gas Mark 5, for 45–55 minutes, or until quite firm to the touch. Leave in the tin for 10 minutes, before turning out to serve.

nutritional breakdown per serving (4 portions): kcal 695, kJ 2877, protein 18g, fat 59g (saturated fat 8g), carbohydrate 20g

cooking with nuts

Nut roasts have become a humorous cliché in a vegetarian diet and are seen as a poor alternative to meat. The truth is they are not like meat, nor meant to be, but are delicious in their own right. Here are a few tips on making a great nut roast.

- A nut roast must have a moist base, made with a thin sauce or a well-flavoured stock or wine, otherwise the end result will be dry.

- Roasting the nuts first highlights their flavour.
- Be bold with your use of herbs and spices since, although rich in themselves, nuts do benefit from extra flavourings.
- Mixtures of nuts often work better than using just a single variety as their different flavours complement each other.
- Make a loaf or roast look more attractive by layering the mixture with cooked vegetables, such as sliced mushrooms, thick tomato sauce or spinach purée.

lentil bake with red pepper

Red lentils make a great basis for a savoury bake as they cook to a soft but well-textured purée. Season the dish well and don't skimp on the parsley. If it isn't to hand then flavour the bake with lemon juice and zest instead. This can be served as an easy supper or lunch dish with a simple tomato or mushroom sauce and a selection of roasted vegetables.

serves 4

preparation: 15 minutes

cooking: 1 hour 10 minutes

suitable for freezing

(Fe)

125g (4oz) red lentils
300ml (½ pint) water
2 tbsp sunflower oil
1 onion, finely chopped
2 celery sticks, finely chopped
1 tsp paprika
1 large red pepper
6 tbsp finely chopped parsley
3 eggs, separated
salt and freshly ground black pepper

1 Place the lentils in a saucepan with the water and bring to the boil. Cover the pan and simmer very gently for 25–30 minutes, or until all the water has been absorbed and the lentils are tender. Beat in the pan until smooth and set aside.

2 Heat the oil in a frying pan and gently fry the onion until soft. Add the celery and paprika and cook for 3–4 minutes.

3 Cut the stalk end from the red pepper and slice off 4 rings. Reserve for garnish. Finely chop the remainder of the pepper and add to the onion and celery mixture. Cook for 2–3 minutes. Stir the cooked vegetables and the parsley into the lentil purée and season well.

4 Stir the egg yolks into the lentil mixture. Beat the egg whites in a bowl until stiff, then fold into the lentil mixture.

5 Spoon the mixture into a lightly oiled ovenproof dish and garnish with the red pepper rings. Bake in a preheated oven, 200°C (400°F), Gas Mark 6, for 30–35 minutes, or until golden brown and firm to the touch. Serve hot.

nutritional breakdown per serving: kcal 226, kJ 949, protein 13g, fat 10g (saturated fat 2g) carbohydrate 22g

spiced hazelnut and quinoa bake

Although nuts are a rich ingredient, they can seem dry in a bake. I've used coconut milk in this recipe to add moisture and an extra silky texture. Quinoa cooks to quite a soft consistency and so is ideal for adding bulk to the dish. Serve with a spiced tomato sauce or a cold yoghurt dip and cucumber relish, or a green vegetable, such as okra.

serves 4

preparation: 10 minutes

cooking: 50–55 minutes

suitable for freezing

(Fe) 𝒱

2 tbsp sunflower oil, plus 1 tsp for toasting the quinoa
100g (3½oz) quinoa, rinsed
450ml (¾ pint) boiling water
1 onion, finely chopped
2 tbsp sesame seeds
2 tsp cumin seeds
½ tsp ground turmeric
1cm (½in) piece of fresh root ginger, grated
150g (5oz) hazelnuts, finely ground
150ml (¼ pint) coconut milk
salt and freshly ground black pepper

1 Heat the 1 teaspoon of oil in a saucepan and gently toast the quinoa for 1 minute. Add the boiling water and bring to the boil, stirring a few times. Cover the pan and simmer for 15 minutes, or until quite soft. Drain if necessary and set aside.

2 Meanwhile, heat the remaining oil in a large frying pan and gently fry the onion. When soft, add the seeds and spices and cook for 3–4 minutes. Then stir in the ground hazelnuts and cook for 2–3 minutes. Leave to cool.

3 Mix the cooked quinoa with the nuts and spices, and stir in the coconut milk. Season to taste.

4 Spoon the mixture into a lined, greased 1.2 litre (2 pint) loaf tin. Cook in a preheated oven, 190°C (375°F), Gas Mark 5, for 30–35 minutes, or until just firm to the touch.

nutritional breakdown per serving: kcal 408, kJ 1697, protein 10g, fat 33g (saturated fat 3g), carbohydrate 20g

almond croustade with chard

A classic croustade is made with very thin slices of bread baked to form a crisp shell. This version is easier as it is made with a mixture of breadcrumbs enriched with almonds and cheese, which is then pressed into the base of a dish and baked until crisp. This recipe has many variations as the base can be flavoured with different nuts and cheeses. Alternatively, the cheese can be left out altogether for those wanting a dairy-free recipe.

This topping comprises a well-flavoured cream sauce combined with a colourful assortment of vegetables. It is good as a supper dish, but quite elegant enough to serve at a special meal.

serves 4
preparation: 15 minutes
cooking: 45 minutes
suitable for freezing

Cal Fe

For the croustade:
125g (4oz) ground almonds
125g (4oz) strongly flavoured hard cheese, grated
175g (6oz) fresh breadcrumbs
1 tsp dried thyme
2–3 tbsp sunflower oil

For the topping:
25g (1oz) butter
2 leeks, finely chopped
1 red pepper, cored, deseeded and diced
400g (13oz) chard
2 tbsp plain flour
400ml (14fl oz) milk (semi-skimmed)
1 tsp paprika
50g (2oz) cheese, grated
salt and freshly ground black pepper

1 To make the croustade, mix the ground almonds, grated cheese and breadcrumbs in a large bowl or food processor. Add the dried thyme and 2 tablespoons of the oil. If the mixture seems dry, add extra oil.

2 Press the mixture into a shallow ovenproof dish and bake in a preheated oven, 200°C (400°F), Gas Mark 6, for 15 minutes.

3 To make the topping, melt the butter in a saucepan and gently fry the leeks until soft. Add the red pepper and chard and cook for a few minutes until beginning to soften.

4 Sprinkle in the flour, stir and cook for 2 minutes, then pour in the milk and add the paprika. Stir well and bring to the boil, stirring frequently. Season well and simmer for 2–3 minutes.

5 Spoon the filling over the cooked base and cover with grated cheese. Bake at 200°C (400°F), Gas Mark 6, for 15 minutes. Serve hot.

nutritional breakdown per serving: kcal 686, kJ 2860, protein 28g, fat 48g (saturated fat 16g), carbohydrate 39g

fresh sweetcorn cobbler

A soft corn bread-style mixture baked on top of a colourful selection of vegetables makes a straightforward tasty supper dish. Use fresh sweetcorn if you can as it provides an extra springy texture in the filling. Canned sweetcorn is an acceptable alternative, however, and you can also try many other combinations of vegetables.

serves 4

preparation: 15 minutes

cooking: 40 minutes

suitable for freezing

(Ca)

2 tbsp sunflower oil
1 onion, finely chopped
1 green pepper, cored, deseeded and
  finely chopped
3 sweetcorn cobs, stripped
400g (13oz) carrots, finely chopped
2 tbsp plain flour
400ml (14fl oz) milk
1 tsp dried thyme
salt and freshly ground black pepper

For the topping:
75g (3oz) cornmeal or maize flour
75g (3oz) wholemeal or white flour, plus extra
  for dusting
½ tsp salt
1½ tsp baking powder
1 egg
50ml (2fl oz) milk
50g (2oz) cheese, grated

1 Heat the oil in a saucepan and gently cook the onion, then add the green pepper, sweetcorn kernels and carrots and stir well. Cook for 5 minutes, or until beginning to soften.

2 Sprinkle in the flour, stir and cook for 2 minutes, then pour in the milk and add the dried thyme. Bring the mixture to the boil, stirring frequently. Simmer for 2 minutes and season well. Transfer the mixture to lightly oiled ovenproof ramekins.

3 To make the topping, mix the cornmeal in a bowl with the flour, salt and baking powder.

4 Beat the egg with the milk, then pour over the dry ingredients. Mix to a dough. Working on a lightly floured surface, press the dough into a rough round

shape about 20cm (8in) in diameter. Sprinkle with grated cheese.

5 Cut into rounds that are 5cm (2in) in diameter and arrange on top of the sweetcorn mixture. Bake in a preheated oven, 200°C (400°F), Gas Mark 6, for 25 minutes. Serve hot.

nutritional breakdown per serving: kcal 434, kJ 1823, protein 16g, fat 15g (saturated fat 3g), carbohydrate 63g

cottage pie

Classic, homely and heartwarming, this substantial supper takes a little time to prepare but it can all be done in advance. The filling is good made with brown or Puy lentils, or larger green lentils or aduki beans. Serve this pie with a contrasting vegetable such as cauliflower, cabbage or broccoli.

serves 4

preparation: 15 minutes

cooking: about 1½ hours

suitable for freezing

(Fe) 𝒱

175g (6oz) Puy lentils or brown lentils
500g (1lb) potatoes
3–4 tbsp milk or soya milk
2 tbsp olive oil
1 onion, chopped
2 leeks, sliced
2 celery sticks, finely chopped
175g (6oz) carrots, finely chopped
175g (6oz) parsnip or squash, finely chopped
2 tbsp shoyu or soy sauce
2–3 tbsp tomato purée
1 tsp chopped sage
1 tsp chopped thyme
salt and freshly ground black pepper

1 Cook the lentils in a large saucepan of boiling water for about 20–30 minutes, or until quite soft. Drain and reserve the cooking liquid.

2 Meanwhile, boil the potatoes in another saucepan of water for 15 minutes, or until soft, then drain and mash with the milk, and season well.

3 Heat the oil in a large saucepan and cook the onion until soft. Then add the leeks and celery and cook for a further 4–5 minutes until beginning to soften.

4 Add the carrots and parsnips or squash and continue cooking over a low heat for 10 minutes. Cover the pan so that the juices from the vegetables do not evaporate.

5 Stir in the cooked lentils, then add the shoyu or soy sauce, tomato purée, herbs and enough cooking liquid from the lentils to make the mixture moist but not sloppy. Simmer this mixture for 10 minutes, adding more liquid if necessary. Season well.

6 Spoon the lentil mixture into a lightly oiled ovenproof dish. Cover with the mashed potatoes and bake in a preheated oven, 180°C (350°F), Gas Mark 4, for 35–40 minutes, or until the potato is crisp and brown.

nutritional breakdown per serving: kcal 360, kJ 1525, protein 17g, fat 8g (saturated fat 1g), carbohydrate 59g

celeriac and almond crumble

This tasty crumble makes a good nutritious supper dish. It could be served with red cabbage or a green vegetable, such as broccoli.

serves 4

preparation: 15 minutes

cooking: 1 hour

suitable for freezing

(Fe) *v*

2 tbsp sunflower oil
500g (1lb) leeks, chopped
750g (1½lb) celeriac, cubed
1 tsp chopped rosemary
1 tsp chopped thyme
500ml (17fl oz) passata
juice of ½ lemon
12 whole blanched almonds, to garnish
salt and freshly ground black pepper

For the crumble:
2oz (50g) wholemeal flour
2oz (50g) rolled oats
2oz (50g) ground almonds
1 tsp chopped thyme
3oz (75g) sunflower margarine
salt and freshly ground black pepper

1   Heat the oil in a large saucepan and sweat the leeks until just soft. Add the celeriac and cook slowly for 10 minutes.

2   Add the rosemary, thyme, passata, lemon juice and seasoning. Bring to the boil and simmer, covered, for 10 minutes. Adjust the seasoning and transfer the mixture to an oiled, deep ovenproof dish.

3   To make the crumble, place the dry ingredients, including the thyme, in a bowl. Mix together, then rub in the margarine and season the crumble mixture.

4   Sprinkle the crumble mixture over the filling. Arrange the whole almonds on the top, then bake in a preheated oven, 190°C (375°F), Gas Mark 5, for 30 minutes. Serve hot.

nutritional breakdown per serving: kcal 450, kJ 1868, protein 12g, fat 32g (saturated fat 5g), carbohydrate 30g

CRUMBLES

A crumble topping is a very easy way to add texture and substance to a thick sauce or moist vegetable mixture. The plainest crumbles can be made from a simple mixture of oats and flour, bound together with enough oil to coat the dry ingredients, which saves the job of rubbing in. An oil-based crumble mix is quite crisp and dry so only use it in a stew with plenty of spare liquid. More traditional crumble toppings are made with a solid fat rubbed in. You can vary the flavour by adding different nuts, seeds or herbs. Chopped blanched almonds and walnuts work well, as does chopped parsley, thyme or paprika. Grated cheese will ensure that the mixture browns to an appetising golden colour. An uncooked crumble mixture freezes well, and will also keep in the fridge for up to 2 weeks.

moussaka

A traditional Greek recipe, moussaka comprises layers of fried aubergine, rich tomato sauce and slices of potato finished with a creamy topping then baked. It takes some time to prepare, although this can be done in advance, and the end result is certainly worth the time spent. This robust supper dish needs no accompaniment other than a light crisp salad.

serves 4–6

preparation: 15 minutes, plus parboiling, salting and infusing

cooking: about 1½ hours

suitable for freezing

2 aubergines, sliced
250g (8oz) cauliflower florets
6 –8 tbsp olive oil
400g (13oz) potatoes, parboiled and sliced
salt

For the tomato sauce:
2 tbsp olive oil
1 onion, chopped
1 garlic clove, crushed
500ml (17fl oz) passata
1 tsp dried oregano
¼ tsp ground cinnamon
salt and freshly ground black pepper

For the topping:
450ml (¾ pint) milk
½ onion
1 bay leaf
6 black peppercorns
1 sprig thyme
25g (1oz) butter
25g (1oz) plain flour
2 eggs, beaten
50g (2oz) cheese, grated
salt and freshly ground black pepper

1 Put the aubergine slices in a large colander and sprinkle with salt. Leave for 30 minutes, then pat dry with kitchen paper.

2 Prepare the cauliflower by steaming the florets over a saucepan of boiling water until soft. Drain, then chop roughly.

3 Heat 4 tablespoons of oil in a large frying pan and fry the aubergine slices, a few at a time, until brown. Set aside.

4 To make the tomato sauce, heat the oil in a saucepan and cook the onion and garlic until soft. Add the passata, oregano and cinnamon, then bring to the boil, cover the pan and cook for 30–35 minutes. Season well. Stir in the cooked cauliflower.

5 Meanwhile, infuse the milk for the topping by warming it in a small saucepan and adding the onion, bay leaf, peppercorns and thyme. Leave to stand for at least 10 minutes.

6 To make the topping, melt the butter in a small saucepan. Stir in the flour and cook for 2 minutes. Strain the infused milk into the roux and bring the sauce to the boil, stirring constantly. Simmer for 2 minutes, then season to taste. Leave to cool slightly, then stir in the eggs.

7 To assemble the moussaka, put half the tomato sauce in the base of a lightly oiled ovenproof dish. Top with the slices of potato, then cover with the remaining tomato sauce and top with the slices of aubergine. Cover with the white sauce and sprinkle the grated cheese over the top. Bake in a preheated oven, 180°C (350°F), Gas Mark 4, for 35–40 minutes, or until golden brown on top. Serve hot.

nutritional breakdown per serving (4 portions): kcal 572, kJ 2383, protein 18g, fat 40g (saturated fat 12g), carbohydrate 38g

stir-fry vegetables with cashews and chilli

Chilli and ginger add a kick to this simple stir-fry. Serve with rice or noodles.

serves 3–4

preparation: 15 minutes

cooking: 10 minutes

𝑣

1 tbsp sunflower or groundnut oil
3 shallots, finely chopped
1 garlic clove, crushed
1 chilli, finely chopped
1cm (½in) piece of fresh root ginger, grated
125g (4oz) cashew nuts
250g (8oz) carrots, cut into matchsticks
250g (8oz) mangetout
300g (10oz) mushrooms, halved
juice of 1–2 limes
1 tbsp sesame oil

1 Heat the oil in a wok or large frying pan and quickly fry the shallots with the garlic, chilli and ginger. Add the cashew nuts and stir-fry until toasted.

2 Add the carrots and cook for 1 minute, then add the mangetout and cook for 1 minute more. Add the mushrooms and cook for 3 minutes, then add the lime juice and sesame oil and steam the vegetables for 1 minute.

3 Serve immediately with freshly cooked rice or noodles.

nutritional breakdown per serving (4 portions): kcal 387, kJ 1609, protein 13g, fat 28g (saturated fat 5g), carbohydrate 21g

stir-fry vegetables and tofu with sesame marinade

Try to plan ahead with this recipe as it is best to leave the tofu to marinate as long as possible. For the stir-fry, I have suggested a mixture of vegetables, but many combinations are possible. Serve with rice or noodles.

serves 3–4

preparation: 15 minutes, plus marinating

cooking: 10 minutes

250g (8oz) tofu (bean curd), cut into
 bite-sized pieces
1 tbsp sunflower oil
2 spring onions, chopped
1 garlic clove, chopped
125g (4oz) baby sweetcorn cobs,
 roughly chopped
175g (6oz) sugar snap peas
125g (4oz) mushrooms, sliced
salt and freshly ground black pepper

For the marinade:
3 tbsp dark toasted sesame oil
3 tbsp shoyu or soy sauce
1 tbsp concentrated apple juice
juice of ½ lemon
1 chilli, finely chopped
2 spring onions, finely chopped
2 tbsp chopped coriander leaves
freshly ground black pepper

1 Make the marinade by mixing together all the ingredients in a screw-top jar. Place the tofu in a shallow dish. Pour over the marinade, cover and leave for 2–3 hours, turning the pieces over occasionally.

2 Drain the tofu, reserving the marinade.

3 Heat the oil in a wok or large frying pan then quickly fry the spring onions and garlic. Add the remaining ingredients in order, cooking each briefly before adding the next vegetable.

4 When all the ingredients have been added, add the drained marinated tofu and stir well.

5 Add the reserved marinade and cook for 1 minute. Adjust the seasoning and serve immediately with freshly cooked rice or noodles.

nutritional breakdown per serving (4 portions): kcal 190, kJ 794,
protein 10g, fat 14g (saturated fat 2g), carbohydrate 7g

stir-fry vegetables
with golden coconut sauce

Coconut is used extensively in Oriental cuisine. It adds a rich silky quality and this spicy golden sauce is quick to make. Pour over the stir-fry vegetables to finish off the cooking. Serve with rice or noodles.

serves 3–4

preparation: 15 minutes

cooking: 20 minutes

v

1 tbsp sunflower oil
4 spring onions, finely chopped
375g (12oz) asparagus, chopped
2 red peppers, cored, deseeded and thinly sliced
500g (1lb) broccoli, divided into florets

For the sauce:
1 tbsp groundnut or sunflower oil
2.5cm (1in) piece of fresh root ginger, grated
1 shallot, finely chopped
2 garlic cloves, finely chopped
½ tsp ground turmeric
25g (1oz) creamed coconut
300ml (½ pint) warm water
1 lemon grass stalk, chopped into 3 pieces
1 bay leaf
salt and freshly ground black pepper

1 To make the sauce, heat the oil in a saucepan and gently fry the ginger, shallot and garlic. Add the turmeric and cook for 1 minute.

2 Dissolve the creamed coconut in the warm water in a jug, then pour into the pan. Add the lemon grass and bay leaf. Bring the sauce to the boil. Simmer very gently for 5 minutes, then remove from the heat and season to taste.

3 Have ready all the ingredients for the stir-fry. Heat the oil in a wok or large frying pan and quickly fry the spring onions, then add the asparagus, red pepper and broccoli and fry until just soft.

4 Remove the bay leaf and lemon grass from the sauce and pour over the vegetables. Cook for 2 minutes, then serve with freshly cooked rice or noodles.

nutritional breakdown per serving (4 portions): kcal 179, kJ 742, protein 10g, fat 9g (saturated fat 5g), carbohydrate 15g

stir-fry with chinese sauce

The technique in this recipe is slightly different in that the vegetables are briefly stir-fried, then finished off in a sauce thickened with arrowroot. Cornflour could also be used as a thickening agent. Serve with rice or noodles – if using instant noodles, they can be added in step 4.

serves 3–4

preparation: 10 minutes

cooking: 8 minutes

For the sauce:
150ml (¼ pint) Vegetable Stock (see page 144)
1 tbsp shoyu or soy sauce
1 tbsp lemon juice
1 garlic clove, crushed
1 tbsp concentrated apple juice
1 tsp Chinese five-spice powder
1 tbsp arrowroot

For the stir-fry:
1 tbsp groundnut or sunflower oil
3 spring onions, chopped
1 green pepper, cored, deseeded and sliced
200g (7oz) water chestnuts, halved
250g (8oz) oyster mushrooms
250g (8oz) bean sprouts

1 Mix all the ingredients for the sauce together in a jug and set aside.

2 Heat the oil in a wok or large frying pan and quickly fry the spring onions. Add the green pepper and water chestnuts and fry for 1–2 minutes, then add the oyster mushrooms and cook for 1 minute more.

3 Pour in the sauce and bring to the boil, then simmer, stirring frequently, until the sauce thickens and clears.

4 Add the bean sprouts and mix in well. Serve as soon as they are heated through.

nutritional breakdown per serving (4 portions): kcal 120, kJ 509, protein 5g, fat 4g (saturated fat 1g), carbohydrate 19g

stir-fry with japanese sauce

This stir-fry includes classic Japanese ingredients, such as strips of omelette, together with hijiki and wasabi, which add a distinctive character to this nutritious dish.

serves 3–4

preparation: 15 minutes

cooking: 15 minutes

 (Ca) (Fe)

500g (1lb) egg or rice noodles
1 tsp sesame oil
2 tsp sunflower oil
4 spring onions, finely chopped
500g (1lb) pak choi, shredded
2 red peppers, cored, deseeded and sliced
300g (10oz) green beans, chopped

For the omelette:

2 eggs
2 tbsp water
1 tbsp shoyu or soy sauce
1 tbsp sunflower oil

For the sauce:

300ml (½ pint) hot water
1 garlic clove, crushed
2 tbsp miso
4 tbsp rice wine
2 tbsp shoyu or soy sauce
1–2 tsp wasabi or grated fresh root ginger
1–2 tsp hijiki (dried Japanese seaweed)

1 To make the omelette, lightly beat the eggs with the water and season with the shoyu or soy sauce.

2 Heat a little of the oil in a small frying pan and quickly pour in half of the beaten egg mixture. Allow to cook for 2–3 minutes, then remove from the pan. Make a second omelette in the same way. Leave to cool, then cut into shreds.

3 To make the sauce, mix the ingredients together in a jug and set aside.

4 Cook the noodles in a large saucepan of boiling water for 3–4 minutes. Drain and toss in the sesame oil.

5 Heat the sunflower oil in a wok or large frying pan and quickly sauté the spring onions. Add the shredded pak choi, red peppers and beans and stir-fry until just wilted.

6 Turn down the heat, pour in the prepared sauce and toss in the drained noodles and the omelette strips. Heat through and serve immediately.

nutritional breakdown per serving (4 portions): kcal 699, kJ 2947, protein 28g, fat 19g (saturated fat 4g), carbohydrate 111g

sweet and sour sauce

This is a useful sauce for serving with stir-fried vegetables and Tempura Vegetables (see below), and it is very simple to make.

preparation: 5 minutes

cooking: 5 minutes

v

3 tbsp arrowroot
3 tbsp sherry
3 tbsp shoyu or soy sauce
3 tbsp sugar
250ml (8fl oz) apple juice
12 cardamom pods, crushed and husks removed
1cm (½in) piece of fresh root ginger, grated
1 garlic clove, crushed
3 tbsp cider vinegar
salt and freshly ground black pepper

1 Mix all the ingredients together in a bowl, making sure that the arrowroot is properly dissolved.

2 Tip the mixture into a saucepan and bring to the boil, then simmer, stirring constantly, until the sauce thickens and clears.

3 Adjust the seasoning and serve hot or at room temperature.

nutritional breakdown per total recipe: kcal 594, kJ 2529, protein 5g, fat 0g (saturated fat 0g), carbohydrate 140g

tempura vegetables

Tempura vegetables are chunks of vegetable coated in a light batter and fried until crisp then served with an Oriental dipping sauce. They are best eaten within a few minutes of making so treat this as a very informal meal and cook and eat in batches. For other Japanese recipes, see pages 277 and 280–81.

serves 4

preparation: 20 minutes

cooking: 5–10 minutes

vegetable oil for deep-frying
1kg (2lb) vegetables of your choice (the following work well – green beans, asparagus cauliflower, carrots and mushrooms), chopped or trimmed into manageable pieces
Sweet and Sour Sauce (see above) or wedges of lemon and salt, to serve

For the batter:

1 egg
250ml (8fl oz) ice-cold water
125g (4oz) plain flour
½ tsp salt, optional

1 To make the batter, beat the egg and water together in a bowl, using a balloon whisk, then whisk in the flour and salt, if desired. Do not beat more than necessary since, surprisingly, a slightly lumpy batter works well.

2 Pour oil to a depth of 2.5cm (1in) in a small deep frying pan and heat until a piece of onion dropped in sizzles immediately.

3 Coat a few pieces of prepared vegetables in the batter, then drop into the hot oil. Cook until golden brown.

4 Drain and serve with sweet and sour dipping sauce or with wedges of lemon and salt.

nutritional breakdown per serving: kcal 275, kJ 1149, protein 10g, fat 12g (saturated fat 2g), carbohydrate 34g

sweet and sour sauce top, **tempura vegetables**

satay sauce

This easy sauce is delicious served with Tempura Vegetables (see page 278) or with a stir-fry of vegetables. Its use need not be confined only to Oriental dishes since the sauce also goes well with vegetable or nut burgers and barbecue kebabs. As a variation, you can use clear honey instead of the concentrated apple juice.

preparation: 10 minutes

cooking: 10 minutes

v

1 tbsp sunflower oil
1 small onion, finely chopped
1 garlic clove, crushed
½ chilli, deseeded and finely chopped
300ml (½ pint) water
4 tbsp smooth peanut butter
1–2 tbsp lemon juice
1 tbsp concentrated apple juice

1 tbsp shoyu or soy sauce
salt and freshly ground black pepper

1 Heat the oil in a small frying pan and gently fry the onion, garlic and chilli until soft but not coloured. Remove from the heat.

2 Using a blender or food processor, blend together the water with the peanut butter, lemon juice, concentrated apple juice and shoyu or soy sauce until smooth.

3 Add the cooled onion mixture and blend again. Season to taste.

nutritional breakdown per total recipe: kcal 793, kJ 3288, protein 25g, fat 65g (saturated fat 13g), carbohydrate 29g

sushi

This delicious vegetarian sushi comprises piquant rice topped with vegetables, which are then rolled up in seaweed. Smaller versions are perfect for canapés or picnics. Other fillings for sushi could be chopped egg, cooked asparagus, spinach or broccoli.

makes 20–24

preparation time: 15 minutes, plus chilling time

cooking time: 20 minutes

v

250g (8oz) Japanese sushi rice
400ml (14fl oz) boiling water
½–1 tsp salt
½–1 tsp sugar
2 tsp rice wine vinegar
4 sheets of nori
50–75g (2–3oz) cucumber, cut in strips
50–75g (2–3oz) red pepper, cored, deseeded and cut into strips
50–75g (2–3oz) green beans or mangetout, cooked
salt and freshly ground black pepper
shoyu or soy sauce, or pickled ginger, to serve

1 Place the rice and the water in a large saucepan and cook for 20 minutes or until quite soft. Allow to cool, then mix in the salt, sugar and rice wine vinegar to taste. Season well.

2 Spread each sheet of nori with a portion of the rice mixture. Cover with a selection of the prepared vegetables and roll up.

3 Leave to rest in the refrigerator for 30 minutes, then slice each roll to make 5 or 6 small rolls.

4 Serve with shoyu or soy sauce, or pickled ginger.

nutritional breakdown per 20 sushi: kcal 47, kJ 198, protein 1g, fat 0g (saturated fat 0g), carbohydrate 10g

sushi opposite

Side Dishes, Sauces and Relishes

Many main courses need little more than simple vegetable or salad accompaniments. If you turn to the descriptions of vegetable families on pages 33–57 in the reference section, you'll find plenty of tips on how to cook and serve a wide range of vegetables.

The recipes on the following pages are designed to highlight some of the best cooking techniques and to show off vegetables in a more elaborate fashion creating accompaniments that complement the colour, flavour and texture of a main course. There are some easy sauté ideas, such as aromatic Cabbage and Cumin and fragrant Lemon-glazed Celeriac, and stir-frying, as seen in Stir-fry Shredded Leeks with Tarragon, is also a good way of preparing a single vegetable for an accompaniment. Once in the oven, roasted vegetables need little attention but make a delicious side dish.

Freshly made sauces are often very versatile and this section includes a classic white sauce and a very useful tomato sauce. If you feel more adventurous, try the tasty, dairy-free Leek and Cashew Sauce as well as the quick and spicy Pinto Bean and Red Onion Salsa with Cumin and Roasted Red Pepper Coulis. A selection of mouthwatering, sweet and sour relishes to complement a range of savouries completes the section.

roasted root vegetables with caraway

Roasting vegetables accentuates their mellow flavours and, once in the oven, they require little or no attention, leaving you free to do other things. The beetroots do 'bleed' a little, so try to keep them apart from the other vegetables while they are cooking.

serves 4
preparation: 10 minutes
cooking: 30 minutes

25g (1oz) butter
1 tbsp sunflower oil
400g (13oz) raw beetroots, peeled and
  thinly sliced
400g (13oz) sweet potato, peeled and thinly sliced
400g (13oz) potato, peeled and thinly sliced
1 tsp salt
1 tsp caraway seeds
freshly grated nutmeg
freshly ground black pepper

1 Heat the butter and oil together in a large roasting tin. Mix in the vegetables and spread out in the tin. Sprinkle with the salt, caraway seeds, nutmeg and black pepper.

2 Bake in a preheated oven, 200°C (400°F), Gas Mark 6, for 30 minutes, turning the vegetables a few times during cooking.

3 Once cooked, they should be crisp and browned. Serve hot.

nutritional breakdown per serving: kcal 270, kJ 1146, protein 5g, fat 9g (saturated fat 4g), carbohydrate 46g

cabbage and cumin

Cooked cabbage should retain its crisp texture and nutty flavour. This method is part stir-fry and part steaming, and is simple and quick, keeping both the texture and flavour of the cabbage.

serves 4

preparation: 5 minutes

cooking: 10 minutes

25g (1oz) butter
1 onion, finely chopped
1 garlic clove, crushed
2 tbsp cumin seeds
400g (13oz) cabbage, finely shredded
2–3 tbsp water
salt and freshly ground black pepper

1 Melt the butter in a large saucepan and fry the onion and garlic gently until translucent.

2 Add the cumin seeds and cook for 1 minute, or until just toasted.

3 Add the cabbage with the water and cook for 5 minutes, stirring frequently.

4 Season well and serve immediately.

nutritional breakdown per serving: kcal 87, kJ 359, protein 2g, fat 6g (saturated fat 4g), carbohydrate 7g

VARIATION

This recipe is also great with caraway seeds instead of the cumin seeds.

lemon-glazed celeriac

Fragrant and nutty, this recipe is good hot or cold. Use the same idea for other root vegetables or use orange juice as a flavouring instead of the lemon for a variation. This is good served with egg or grain dishes as well as bakes.

serves 4

preparation: 5 minutes

cooking: 15 minutes

500g (1lb) celeriac, roughly chopped
25g (1oz) butter
2 tbsp soft brown sugar
2 tbsp lemon juice
25g (1oz) pecan nuts, chopped
salt and freshly ground black pepper

1 Steam or cook the celeriac in a saucepan of boiling salted water for 8–10 minutes until just soft. Drain.

2 Heat the butter, sugar and lemon juice in a large frying pan.

3 When melted and mixed, add the celeriac pieces and the pecans. Fry over a medium to high heat until brown. Season well and serve hot or at room temperature.

nutritional breakdown per serving: kcal 203, kJ 839, protein 2g, fat 15g (saturated fat 7g), carbohydrate 15g

stir-fry shredded leeks with tarragon

This is a very easy way of serving leeks and is a combination of stir-fry and braising.

serves 4

preparation: 5 minutes

cooking: 7 minutes

v

4 leeks
2 tbsp sunflower oil
2–3 tbsp white wine
1 tsp tarragon vinegar
2 tsp chopped tarragon
salt and freshly ground black pepper

1 Shred the leeks in a food processor or cut them thinly by hand.

2 Heat the oil in a large frying pan or wok, and quickly stir-fry the leeks until just soft.

3 Add the wine, tarragon vinegar and chopped tarragon and simmer for 3 minutes. Season well and serve immediately.

nutritional breakdown per serving: kcal 77, kJ 318, protein 2g, fat 6g (saturated fat 1g), carbohydrate 3g

pan-fried cauliflower

Crisp fried breadcrumbs and a hint of mustard are a great way of livening up plain cauliflower, providing a pleasing mixture of textures and flavours.

serves 4

preparation: 5 minutes
cooking: 10 minutes

25g (1oz) butter, softened
1 tbsp Dijon mustard
1 cauliflower, divided into florets
2 tbsp olive oil
25g (1oz) fresh breadcrumbs
salt and freshly ground black pepper

1 Combine the softened butter with the mustard in a small bowl and chill.

2 Steam the cauliflower florets over a saucepan of boiling water for 10 minutes, until just tender.

3 Meanwhile, heat the olive oil in a frying pan and fry the breadcrumbs until very crisp.

4 Toss the cooked cauliflower into the mustard butter, season well, immediately stir in the crisp breadcrumbs and serve.

nutritional breakdown per serving: kcal 150, kJ 627, protein 5g, fat 12g (saturated fat 4g), carbohydrate 2g

butternut squash and carrot purée with nutmeg and mascarpone

FILO PARCELS

This purée is also great in filo parcels. Leave the purée to cool, then brush individual sheets of filo pastry with melted butter or oil. Place a spoonful of purée on each sheet and roll up into a parcel. Brush with more butter, place on a baking sheet and bake in a preheated oven, 200°C (400°F), Gas Mark 6, for 15–18 minutes.

Rich and colourful, this purée is excellent with savoury bakes and casseroles. It could also be used as a filling for savoury pancakes. It can be made with other vegetables, such as pumpkin, sweet potato, parsnip or swede.

serves 4

preparation: 10 minutes
cooking: 20 minutes
suitable for freezing
𝒱

300ml (½ pint) water
25g (1oz) butter
2 tsp sugar
375g (12oz) carrots, chopped
375g (12oz) butternut squash, chopped
freshly grated nutmeg
2 tbsp mascarpone cheese
salt and freshly ground black pepper

1 Bring the water to the boil in a large saucepan with the butter and sugar. Add the vegetables and simmer, uncovered, until the water has all evaporated.

2 Using a blender or food processor, purée the cooked vegetables with a generous grating of nutmeg and the mascarpone.

3 Season well and serve immediately.

nutritional breakdown per serving: kcal 162, kJ 674, protein 2g, fat 10g (saturated fat 7g), carbohydrate 17g

pan-fried cauliflower top **butternut squash and carrot purée with nutmeg and mascarpone** bottom

rosti

This originated as a breakfast dish for hungry Swiss farmers who had generally done a morning's work before sitting down to eat. The meal was made from potatoes leftover from the night before.

If you boil the potatoes especially for this dish, cook them until firm but not soft. Choose a waxy textured potato, in other words one more suitable for a potato salad than mashed potato. Rosti can also be made from leftover baked potatoes. This is a robust accompaniment but could also make a meal on its own, served with Red Onion Marmalade with Coriander (see page 295) and a contrasting salad, vegetable or light cheese or egg dish.

serves 4
preparation: 10 minutes
cooking: 35 minutes

1kg (2lb) cooked potatoes
75g (3oz) clarified butter or ghee
salt

1 Grate or thinly slice the cooked potatoes into slices 2–3mm (⅛in) thick.

2 Heat half the fat in a large, flat-bottomed frying pan. Add the grated or sliced potatoes and a little salt, and mix gently over a high heat for 1 minute.

3 Reduce the heat and press the potatoes into a flat cake, no more than 2.5cm (1in) deep using a wooden spoon.

4 Melt a little of the remaining fat around the sides of the pan, letting it run under the rosti cake so that it does not stick to the pan.

5 Cook gently for about 20 minutes, shaking the pan from time to time.

6 Turn the rosti over, either by inverting it into a second pan or by sliding it out on to a plate, turning it over and then sliding it back. Add the rest of the fat and let it run under the rosti as before, then cook for 10 minutes.

7 Serve hot.

nutritional breakdown per serving: kcal 326, kJ 1363, protein 5g, fat 16g (saturated fat 10g), carbohydrate 43g

VARIATION
Add onion, chopped parsley or chard at step 2.

mushroom ragoût

This dish is a good accompaniment that works well with savoury pastries and bakes. It is a little more substantial than a sauce and the dark colours intensify other brown colours or work well with contrasting greens or orange hues.

serves 4

preparation: 5 minutes, plus soaking

cooking: 35 minutes

20g (¾oz) dried ceps or other dried mushrooms
500ml (17fl oz) boiling water
15g (½oz) butter
1 leek, finely chopped
150g (5oz) chestnut or cremini mushrooms, sliced
1 tbsp brandy
1–2 tbsp shoyu or soy sauce
salt and freshly ground black pepper

1 Place the ceps or other dried mushrooms in a bowl, cover with the boiling water and leave for 15 minutes. Strain, reserving the soaking liquid, and chop the mushrooms roughly.

2 Melt the butter in a saucepan and gently cook the leek until quite soft.

3 Add the fresh mushrooms and cook for 2–3 minutes over a high heat to soften and brown. Stir in the chopped dried mushrooms.

4 Add the brandy and cook for 1 minute, then add the reserved mushroom stock and shoyu or soy sauce and bring to the boil.

5 Reduce the heat to a simmer, partially cover the pan and cook for 25 minutes, or until most of the liquid has been absorbed and the mushrooms are very soft. Season to taste and serve hot.

nutritional breakdown per serving: kcal 64, kJ 264, protein 2g, fat 3g (saturated fat 2g), carbohydrate 5g

classic white sauce

*White sauce is often used in vegetarian cookery as a
coating for vegetables, a filling for pancakes or as a
topping on traditional dishes such as lasagne or
moussaka. White sauce can be made with either
wholemeal or white flour. If you are using wholemeal
flour, you may need a little extra butter or margarine in
the recipe to make a smoother roux. Make sure that the
roux is properly cooked and the finished sauce simmered
or the sauce will taste floury.*

serves 4

preparation: 5 minutes, plus infusing

cooking: 10 minutes

suitable for freezing

(Ca)

300ml (½ pint) milk
½ onion
1 bay leaf
6 black peppercorns
1 sprig thyme
freshly grated nutmeg
25g (1oz) butter
25g (1oz) plain or wholemeal flour
salt and freshly ground black pepper

1 Heat the milk in a small saucepan with the onion,
   bay leaf, peppercorns, thyme and a generous
   grating of nutmeg until just warm, then leave to
   stand for 15 minutes. Strain through a sieve.

2 Melt the butter in a small saucepan and, when it is
   foaming, sprinkle over the flour. Mix well and cook
   over a gentle heat for 2–3 minutes to make a roux.

3 Add the milk to the roux – about a quarter at a time
   – stirring very well.

4 Bring the sauce to boiling point, then simmer over
   a very gentle heat for 3–4 minutes.

5 Season well and use as required.

nutritional breakdown per total recipe: kcal 493, kJ 2050,
protein 13g, fat 33g (saturated fat 21g), carbohydrate 39g
nutritional breakdown per serving: kcal 123, kJ 513, protein 3g,
fat 8g (saturated fat 5g), carbohydrate 10g

VARIATIONS

Substitute a little cream or vegetable stock for the milk
to make richer or lighter sauces. For a parsley sauce,
add 3 tablespoons chopped parsley once the sauce is
cooked. For a cheese sauce, add 50–125g (2–4oz) grated
cheese when the sauce is cooked and stir over a gentle
heat until melted.

buttered shallot and wine sauce

*This rich sauce can be served with a simple pasta dish,
with savoury pancakes or with pastry. Try it with
Chestnut and Cep Single Crust Pie (see page 257) or
Roasted Pecan and Cashew Loaf (see page 264).*

serves 4

preparation: 10 minutes

cooking: 20 minutes

25g (1oz) butter
3 shallots, very finely chopped
100ml (3½fl oz) white wine
1 tsp grainy mustard
200ml (7fl oz) double cream
salt and freshly ground black pepper

1 Melt the butter in a saucepan and cook the shallots
   gently until very soft – this takes at least 10 minutes.

2 Pour in the white wine and bring to the boil, then
   cook over a medium heat until the liquid has
   reduced by about half.

3 Stir in the mustard and cream, season well and
   bring to the boil, then remove from the heat.
   Serve hot.

nutritional breakdown per total recipe: kcal 1192, kJ 4915,
protein 5g, fat 117g (saturated fat 74g), carbohydrate 14g
nutritional breakdown per serving: kcal 298, kJ 1229, protein 1g,
fat 29g (saturated fat 18g), carbohydrate 4g

mushroom sauce

This is a delicious dark sauce with complex woody flavours. It is very important to use a mushroom stock and to sweat the vegetable base until very soft, in order to bring out the flavours.

serves 4

preparation: 5 minutes, plus stock making

cooking: 25 minutes

suitable for freezing

𝒱 (using margarine)

25g (1oz) butter or margarine
1 shallot, finely chopped
1 garlic clove, crushed
25g (1oz) plain flour
300ml (½ pint) Dark Mushroom Stock
  (see page 145)
1 tbsp tomato purée
1 tsp dried thyme
1 tbsp miso, dissolved in a little stock
salt and freshly ground black pepper

1 Melt the butter or margarine in a saucepan and very gently fry the shallot and garlic until soft and browned.

2 Sprinkle in the flour and cook, stirring constantly, for 2 minutes. Then add the mushroom stock and bring to the boil, stirring constantly. Add the tomato purée, thyme and miso. Simmer the sauce for 5 minutes, then add seasoning to taste.

3 Cook for a further 10 minutes, partially covered, so that the sauce reduces slightly.

nutritional breakdown per total recipe: kcal 350, kJ 1464, protein 8g, fat 22g (saturated fat 14g), carbohydrate 31g
nutritional breakdown per serving: kcal 88, kJ 366, protein 2g, fat 6g (saturated fat 3g), carbohydrate 8g

from the left **buttered shallot and wine sauce, classic white sauce, mushroom sauce**

QUICK VERSION

For a quick version of this sauce, use the soaking water from 25g (1oz) dried mushrooms in place of the mushroom stock. The flavours are not so intense. A richer version of the sauce can be made by adding a mixture of very finely shredded or sliced vegetables, such as carrots, celery or mushrooms. Cook these with the shallot and garlic at the end of step 1.

very easy tomato sauce

This is an essential recipe to have in your repertoire since it is not only easy to make but can be used in so many different ways. Smother freshly cooked pasta with it, serve it with a bake, such as Lentil Bake with Red Pepper (see page 266), use it sparingly as a pizza topping or spoon it over a plain risotto.

serves 4

preparation: 5 minutes

cooking: 35 minutes

suitable for freezing

(Fe) *v*

2 tbsp olive oil
1 onion, finely chopped
2 x 400g (13oz) cans chopped tomatoes
1 tsp sugar
1 tsp salt
1 bay leaf
1 tsp dried thyme or oregano
freshly ground black pepper

1 Heat the oil in a large saucepan and gently fry the onion until translucent.

2 Add the canned tomatoes, sugar, salt, bay leaf and thyme or oregano. Bring to the boil, then cover the pan and cook slowly for 30 minutes.

3 Leave to cool slightly, remove the bay leaf and then purée the tomato mixture until very smooth, using a blender or food processor. Season with black pepper to taste, and use the sauce as required.

nutritional breakdown per total recipe: kcal 396, kJ 1657, protein 10g, fat 23g (saturated fat 3g), carbohydrate 40g [per serving: kcal 99, kJ 414, protein 2g, fat 6g (saturated fat 1g), carbohydrate 10g]

VARIATIONS

For a garlic finish, add 1–2 crushed garlic cloves at step 3. For a creamy finish, add 1–2 tablespoons olive oil at step 3. For a mushroom sauce, add 400g (13oz) thinly sliced mushrooms once the sauce has been puréed. Return the mixture to the pan, bring to the boil and simmer for about 15–20 minutes. Season to taste.

pinto bean and red onion salsa with cumin

This is a pretty pink-beige salsa with a creamy texture and aromatic spicing. It could also be made with black-eye beans, black beans or red kidney beans, and is delicious served with taco shells and soured cream plus a crisp salad.

serves 4

preparation: 5 minutes

cooking: 15 minutes

suitable for freezing

v

4 tbsp olive oil
1 tsp cumin seeds
1 red onion, very finely chopped
2 garlic cloves, crushed with salt
250g (8oz) pinto beans (cooked weight)
freshly ground black pepper

1 Heat 2 tablespoons of the oil in a medium frying pan and fry the cumin seed gently until just beginning to brown. Add the red onion and garlic and cook very gently until very soft.

2 Add the beans and stir well. Mash in the pan with a potato masher or fork to get a well-textured mixture. Add the remaining 2 tablespoons of oil and pepper.

nutritional breakdown per serving: kcal 202, kJ 845, protein 6g, fat 12g (saturated fat 2g), carbohydrate 19g

leek and cashew sauce

This is an easy, high-protein, dairy-free and wheat-free sauce, which goes well with a wide range of savoury pastries and bakes.

serves 4
preparation: 5 minutes
cooking: 10 minutes
v

2 tbsp sunflower oil
100g (3½oz) cashew nuts
2 leeks, finely chopped
400ml (14fl oz) water
2 tbsp shoyu or soy sauce
salt and freshly ground black pepper

1 Heat the oil in a saucepan and fry the cashew nuts until lightly browned. Remove from the pan using a slotted spoon and set aside.

2 Add the leeks to the pan and fry until soft.

3 Using a blender or food processor, blend the leeks with the cashew nuts, water and shoyu or soy sauce until completely smooth.

4 Season to taste and heat gently before serving.

nutritional breakdown per total recipe: kcal 830, kJ 3434, protein 23g, fat 71g (saturated fat 12g), carbohydrate 26g
nutritional breakdown per serving: kcal 208, kJ 859, protein 6g, fat 18g (saturated fat 3g), carbohydrate 6g

leek and cashew sauce back **pinto bean and red onion salsa** front left **very easy tomato sauce** front right

cucumber relish with
chilli and lemon left
roasted red pepper
coulis centre **red onion
marmalade with
coriander** right

roasted red pepper coulis

This delicious, sweet, smoky dipping sauce is great for barbecue food or as a sauce for pasta. Try spooning some into scrambled eggs or pouring over stir-fry vegetables.

serves 4

preparation: 5 minutes

cooking: 25 minutes

𝑣

4 red peppers, lightly oiled
150ml (¼ pint) olive oil
2 garlic cloves, crushed
2–3 tbsp chopped basil
1–2 tbsp balsamic vinegar
salt and freshly ground black pepper

1 Place the peppers on a baking sheet or in a roasting tin and cook in a preheated oven, 200°C (400°F), Gas Mark 6, for 25 minutes, or until well charred.

2 Leave the peppers until cool enough to handle, then remove the skins and seeds. Do not wash them; roughly chop the flesh.

3 Using a food processor, purée the peppers with the olive oil until very smooth, then add the garlic, basil and balsamic vinegar and blend again. Season well.

4 Store in the fridge and use as required.

nutritional breakdown per total recipe: kcal 1172, kJ 4834, protein 6g, fat 112g (saturated fat 16g), carbohydrate 36g
nutritional breakdown per serving: kcal 293, kJ 1209, protein 2g, fat 28g (saturated fat 4g), carbohydrate 9g

cucumber relish with chilli and lemon

This lively relish is quick to make and great served with grain dishes, barbecue food, with Tempura Vegetables (see page 278) or with Spiced Vegetable Fritters (see page 168).

serves 4
preparation: 5 minutes, plus chilling
cooking: none
v

1 cucumber
2 tbsp snipped chives or chopped spring onions, to garnish

For the dressing:
1 tsp finely chopped green chilli
1 tbsp shoyu or soy sauce
1–2 tbsp lemon juice
salt and freshly ground black pepper

1 Make the dressing by mixing together the chilli, shoyu or soy sauce, lemon juice and seasoning.

2 Cut the cucumber into thirds, then cut into very thin strips using a potato peeler. Add to the dressing and chill for up to 30 minutes.

3 Serve garnished with snipped chives or chopped spring onions.

> nutritional breakdown per total recipe: kcal 44, kJ 178, protein 3g, fat 0g (saturated fat 0g), carbohydrate 7g
> nutritional breakdown per serving: kcal 11, kJ 45, protein 1g, fat 0g (saturated fat 0g), carbohydrate 2g

red onion marmalade with coriander

This moist, dark relish is delicious served with cheese or egg dishes. Use it on bruschetta or savoury toasts, or to give sandwiches an extra kick. It is also great with Rosti (see page 288). It is worth making a large amount since it will store for several weeks in the fridge.

makes about 300g (10oz); serves 4
preparation: 10 minutes
cooking: 45–50 minutes
suitable for freezing
v

3 tbsp olive oil
875g (1¾lb) red onions, roughly chopped
1 tbsp ground coriander
1 tbsp dark brown sugar
2 tbsp balsamic vinegar
salt and freshly ground black pepper

1 Heat the oil in a large saucepan and fry the onions gently so that they start to soften.

2 Sprinkle over the ground coriander and cook for a further 2–3 minutes, then sprinkle in the brown sugar and stir well.

3 Add enough water to cover the onions, then bring to the boil. Simmer very gently for 35–40 minutes until the liquid has virtually evaporated, stirring occasionally at first and more frequently as the water evaporates.

4 Add the balsamic vinegar, stir well and cook for another 5 minutes. Season to taste and leave to cool.

> nutritional breakdown per total recipe: kcal 716, kJ 2973, protein 12g, fat 36g (saturated fat 5g), carbohydrate 92g
> nutritional breakdown per serving: kcal 179, kJ 743, protein 3g, fat 9g (saturated fat 1g), carbohydrate 23g

Salads

Salads suits a modern, lighter style of eating and they certainly needn't be confined to side dishes or eaten only in hot weather. They have a great deal to offer as they are highly nutritious, extremely colourful and simple to put together.

The salads included range from quite substantial meals with ingredients such as rice, bulgar wheat or pulses, to light vegetable concoctions that make good accompaniments or snacks. Choose from more robust salads such as Avocado and Pistachio Salad or the lighter, refreshing Carrot Kohlrabi with Pumpkin Seeds or simple Green Garden Salad.

In a lot of countries, the cuisine includes traditional salads that highlight a particular flavouring or seasoning. Many of these recipes have enormous worldwide appeal, such as Classic Tabbouleh from the Middle East, which has inspired many variations, and crunchy Gado Gado, an Indonesian bean sprout and vegetable salad with a rich dressing made from coconut and peanuts. Also included is a mellow Greek Potato Salad and a Smoked Tofu and Water Chestnut Salad with Oriental Dressing from the Far East. A salad would not be complete without a dressing, and the recipes here include classic vinaigrette with several variations, as well as mayonnaise and lower-fat or lower-calorie suggestions.

chicory and beetroot with mustard dressing

This robustly coloured salad is great as a cool weather dish. Beetroot goes well with the strong flavour of chicory and contrasts with the white leaves. For extra protein, add some toasted hazelnuts and a little hazelnut oil to the dressing.

serves 4
preparation: 5 minutes
cooking: none
𝑣

2–3 heads chicory, sliced
150g (5oz) raw beetroot, finely grated
75g (3oz) watercress or mixed salad leaves

For the dressing:
6 tbsp olive oil
2 tbsp white wine vinegar
2 tsp Dijon mustard
1 garlic clove, crushed
salt and freshly ground black pepper

1 Combine the prepared salad ingredients in a large bowl.

2 Mix the dressing ingredients together in a jug and season to taste.

3 Toss the dressing into the salad and serve immediately.

nutritional breakdown per serving: kcal 176, kJ 727, protein 2g, fat 17g (saturated fat 3g), carbohydrate 4g

marinated bean salad

VARIATIONS

You can add lots of other vegetables, such as tomatoes, bean sprouts, yellow or red peppers and cauliflower.

It is best to make this salad from freshly cooked beans since they soak up the marinade much better when they are warm. If you want to use canned beans or beans that you have cooked and frozen, heat the marinade ingredients gently so that the flavours infuse together, then pour over the beans.

serves 4

preparation: 10 minutes, plus marinating

cooking: about 1–1½ hours

(Fe) ℣

125g (4oz) chickpeas (raw weight), soaked overnight
125g (4oz) red kidney beans (raw weight), soaked overnight
1 green pepper, cored, deseeded and chopped
3 celery sticks, chopped
½ cucumber, chopped

For the marinade:
150ml (¼ pint) olive oil
50ml (2fl oz) red wine vinegar or balsamic vinegar
½ tsp salt
2 bay leaves
1 red onion, chopped
4 tbsp chopped parsley
1 tsp dried thyme
salt and freshly ground black pepper

1 Keeping them separate, drain the soaking chickpeas and kidney beans. Discard the soaking water and bring them to the boil in 2 large saucepans of fresh water. Boil fast for 10 minutes, then cook for 60–90 minutes, or until tender. (Keeping the red kidney beans and chickpeas separate when cooking preserves their colours.)

2 Meanwhile, mix all the marinade ingredients together in a bowl.

3 Drain the cooked pulses and mix together in a large bowl. Pour the marinade over the top and leave to cool.

4 When the beans are cold, add the remaining salad ingredients and mix well. Adjust the seasoning and serve the salad at room temperature.

nutritional breakdown per serving: kcal 453, kJ 1890, protein 15g, fat 30g (saturated fat 4g), carbohydrate 33g

MEZZE

There is a strong tradition of informal meals, or mezze, throughout the Middle East. At these meals, a large assortment of dishes is put on the table at the same time, leaving everyone to make their own selection. Tabbouleh is good served on these occasions, as are roasted vegetables (see Roast Peppers with Basil Vinaigrette, page 313), Hummus (see page 167), Falafel (see page 174), a bowl of cubed feta cheese, olives, marinated chillies and roasted nuts. You could also serve some filo parcels or slices of Kuku with Spinach (see page 181). All of these make a colourful memorable meal.

classic tabbouleh

This salad comes in many guises throughout the Middle East. It can be an equal balance of bulgar and herbs, or it can be vivid green with just a hint of grain. It is, however, invariably doused in a fragrant lemon and olive oil dressing. Additional extras for this salad could include chopped tomatoes, finely chopped cucumber and toasted pine nuts.

serves 4

preparation: 5 minutes, plus soaking

cooking: none

𝑣

125g (4oz) bulgar
½ tsp salt
200ml (7fl oz) boiling water
2 tbsp lemon juice   .
2 tbsp olive oil

2–3 tbsp finely chopped mint
2–3 tbsp chopped parsley
3 spring onions, finely chopped
salt and freshly ground black pepper

1 Place the bulgar and salt in a large bowl. Pour over the boiling water and leave to soak for 30 minutes. The water should be absorbed but drain the bulgar if necessary.

2 Pour in the lemon juice and olive oil and mix in the chopped herbs and spring onions.

3 Season to taste and serve at room temperature.

nutritional breakdown per serving: kcal 187, kJ 780, protein 4g, fat 6g (saturated fat 1g), carbohydrate 30g

beetroot and green bean salad with couscous

With its bold colours and a good combination of flavours, this salad is useful when you want something robust but not heavy. It is great with gratin dishes, such as Sweet Potato and Courgette Gratin (see page 263), as well as with Frittata (see page 179) or savoury quiches. The couscous is useful for absorbing some of the water that leaches out of the vegetables.

serves 4

preparation: 15 minutes, plus standing

cooking: 4–5 minutes

40g (1½oz) couscous
4 tbsp boiling water
125g (4oz) green beans
2 raw or cooked beetroot, diced
⅓ cucumber, diced
4 spring onions, diced
1 red pepper, cored, deseeded and diced
2 tbsp finely chopped coriander
4 tbsp olive oil
juice of 1 lemon
salt and freshly ground black pepper

1 Place the couscous in a small bowl. Add the boiling water and leave to soak.

2 Meanwhile, cook the green beans in a saucepan of boiling water for 4–5 minutes. Drain and chop finely.

3 Toss the beetroot, cucumber and spring onions in a bowl with the red pepper, coriander, cooked beans and couscous.

4 Mix the olive oil with the lemon juice and season well. Pour over the salad and leave to stand for about 30 minutes.

5 Adjust the seasoning to taste and serve at room temperature.

nutritional breakdown per serving: kcal 168, kJ 698, protein 3g, fat 12g (saturated fat 2g), carbohydrate 14g

greek potato salad

Potatoes make splendid robust salads. There are two points to bear in mind. First, choose a suitable variety – don't try and make a salad with a floury overcooked potato, which will easily disintegrate. Second, potatoes thirst for dressings. These can be based on mayonnaise or soured cream. For a less rich result, I prefer a light vinaigrette mixed with natural yoghurt.

serves 4

preparation: 15 minutes

cooking: 15 minutes

500g (1lb) waxy potatoes
125g (4oz) broad beans (shelled weight)
3 spring onions, chopped
2 hard-boiled eggs, chopped
3 artichoke hearts, cooked and sliced or
  4 canned artichoke hearts, sliced

For the dressing:
4 tbsp olive oil
2 tbsp lemon juice
1 garlic clove, crushed
1 tsp dried marjoram
75g (3oz) natural yoghurt
salt and freshly ground black pepper

To serve, optional:
sliced large tomatoes
crisp lettuce (such as cos)
black olives

1 Cook the potatoes in a large saucepan of boiling salted water until just tender. Drain, peel if preferred, then roughly chop.

2 Meanwhile, cook the broad beans in another saucepan of boiling salted water for 5 minutes, or until tender. Drain and refresh in cold water.

3 Mix the cooked potato and broad beans in a large bowl with the remaining salad ingredients.

4 To make the dressing, whisk the olive oil in a jug with the lemon juice, garlic and marjoram. Stir in the yoghurt and season well.

5 Stir the dressing into the potato salad and adjust the seasoning to taste. Serve with additional contrasting salad ingredients if desired.

nutritional breakdown per serving: kcal 296, kJ 1235, protein 11g, fat 15g (saturated fat 3g), carbohydrate 33g

pasta salad

Cook the pasta until just al dente so that it still has some bite when you serve it. Chunky shapes, such as spirals and shells, hold the dressing better.

serves 4

preparation: 15 minutes, plus salting

cooking: 25–30 minutes

2 aubergines, cubed
3–4 tbsp olive oil
250g (8oz) dried wholewheat pasta spirals or shells
8 sun-dried tomatoes, snipped
3 tbsp chopped parsley
salt

For the dressing:
150ml (¼ pint) soured cream
50g (2oz) Roquefort
1–2 tbsp lemon juice
salt and freshly ground black pepper
dark or red salad leaves (such as radicchio, lollo rosso, feuille de chêne), to serve

1 Put the cubes of aubergine in a colander and sprinkle with salt. Leave for 30 minutes, then pat dry with kitchen paper.

2 Spread out on a baking sheet or in a roasting tin, sprinkle over the olive oil and roast in a preheated oven, 200°C (400°F), Gas Mark 6, for 25–30 minutes, until browned. Leave to cool.

3 Meanwhile, cook the pasta spirals in a large saucepan of boiling salted water until just tender. Drain and leave to cool.

4 Tip the pasta into a large bowl and toss in the roasted aubergines, sun-dried tomatoes and parsley.

5 To make the dressing, place the soured cream in a small bowl. Mash in the Roquefort and add lemon juice and seasoning to taste.

6 Toss the dressing into the pasta and vegetables and adjust the seasoning. Serve on a bed of colourful salad leaves.

nutritional breakdown per serving: kcal 713, kJ 2967, protein 15g, fat 53g (saturated fat 13g), carbohydrate 48g

smoked tofu and water chestnut salad with oriental dressing

Colourful and flavoursome, this distinctive salad is prepared in just a few minutes. It can be served as a starter to an Oriental meal, or as a side salad with a grain dish, such as Sesame Millet (see page 228). You could also add bean sprouts or bean shoots as well as mangetout or sugar snap peas.

nutritional breakdown per serving: kcal 260, kJ 1083, protein 12g, fat 18g (saturated fat 4g), carbohydrate 14g

serves 4

preparation: 10 minutes

cooking: 15 minutes

v

2 tbsp sunflower oil
200g (7oz) smoked tofu (bean curd), drained and
  thinly sliced
200g (7oz) water chestnuts
1 tbsp shoyu or soy sauce
200g (7oz) asparagus
1 yellow pepper, cored, deseeded and sliced
4 spring onions, finely chopped
125g (4oz) baby spinach

For the dressing:
3 tbsp sunflower oil
1 tbsp rice wine
1 tbsp shoyu or soy sauce
1 garlic clove, crushed
1 tsp grated fresh root ginger
salt and freshly ground black pepper

1 Heat the oil in a frying pan and fry the tofu
   and water chestnuts for 5 minutes, or until
   lightly browned.

2 Sprinkle over the shoyu or soy sauce and cook for
   a further 2–3 minutes. Remove from the pan.

3 Griddle or grill the asparagus for 3–4 minutes, until
   just softened and browned.

4 Mix the fried tofu, water chestnuts and asparagus
   in a large bowl with the yellow pepper, spring
   onions and baby spinach.

5 To make the dressing, mix all the ingredients
   together well and toss into the bowl of salad.
   Serve straightaway.

spiced rice salad with mango and cashews

Golden rice, flavoured with aromatic spices, makes a wonderful base for a substantial salad. Add fruit, nuts and vegetables for extra colour and texture. For a party special, press this salad into a lightly oiled mould and serve surrounded by extra fruit and nuts.

serves 4

preparation: 10 minutes

cooking: 35 minutes

𝒱

2 tbsp sunflower oil
3 shallots, finely chopped
1 chilli, deseeded and finely chopped
1 tbsp black mustard seeds
2 tsp cumin seeds
2 tsp ground coriander
1 tsp ground turmeric
250g (8oz) long-grain brown rice
600ml (1 pint) boiling water
2–3 tbsp lime juice
1 mango, diced
50g (2oz) cashew nut pieces
1 red pepper, cored, deseeded and finely chopped
salt and freshly ground black pepper

1 Heat the oil in a large saucepan and gently fry the shallots until soft. Add the spices and cook for 2–3 minutes, or until slightly toasted.

2 Stir in the rice, then pour in the boiling water and add ½ teaspoon salt. Bring back to the boil, cover the pan and cook for 30 minutes. All the water should have been absorbed. If necessary, drain the rice or cook it for a few minutes longer without the lid. Stir in the lime juice and leave to cool.

3 While the rice is cooking, roast the cashews by placing them on a baking sheet; roast in a preheated oven, 200°C (400°F), Gas Mark 6, for 5 minutes, or until lightly browned.

4 When the rice is cold, stir in the mango, roasted cashew nuts and red pepper, and season well.

5 If the salad is a little dry, stir in 1 extra tablespoon of sunflower oil or a flavoured oil, such as chilli oil, to give an extra kick.

nutritional breakdown per serving: kcal 403, kJ 1696, protein 8g, fat 14g (saturated fat 2g), carbohydrate 64g

griddled vegetables with brie

Griddled vegetables are delicious in salads as they keep their freshness and colour but develop a different flavour. Other vegetables that are suitable for griddling for salad include asparagus, artichokes, fennel, shallots, leeks and cauliflower. Keep the pieces chunky or they will disappear to nothing. Toss the Brie into this salad at the last minute so that it melts with the warmth of the vegetables.

serves 4

preparation: 10 minutes

cooking: 10 minutes

 (Ca) (Fe)

1 red onion, cut into thick pieces
2 yellow peppers, cored, deseeded and cut into
   thick pieces
3 red peppers, cored, deseeded and cut into
   thick pieces
4 courgettes, thickly sliced
200g (7oz) broccoli florets
250g (8oz) Brie, roughly sliced
3–4 tbsp Fruity Vinaigrette (see page 314)
salt and freshly ground black pepper
salad leaves, to serve

1 Heat a griddle pan or sturdy frying pan until very hot. Toss in the vegetables and cook for several minutes until they start to blister and brown. Turn them over quite frequently.

2 When cooked, season well, remove the pan from the heat and and toss the Brie into the vegetables.

3 Pile the cheese and griddled vegetables on to a bed of salad leaves. Serve immediately with the fruity vinaigrette handed out separately.

nutritional breakdown per serving: kcal 360, kJ 1503, protein 18g, fat 25g (saturated fat 12g), carbohydrate 18g

gado gado

This is a marvellous peanut and bean sprout salad from Indonesia. It is a dish of contrasts – crunchy nuts smothered in a creamy coconut dressing, cool bean sprouts and hot spices, all bound to set your taste buds alight.

serves **4**

preparation: 15 minutes

cooking: 12 minutes

(Fe)

For the salad:

125g (4oz) green beans or mangetout

75g (3oz) peanuts (shelled weight)

1 yellow pepper, cored, deseeded and sliced

150g (5oz) bean sprouts

150g (5oz) Chinese leaves or green cabbage, shredded

2 spring onions, finely chopped

For the dressing:

1 tbsp sunflower oil

2 shallots, finely chopped

1 garlic clove, crushed

½ hot chilli, deseeded and finely chopped

1cm (½in) piece of fresh root ginger, grated

50g (2oz) creamed coconut

100ml (3½fl oz) warm water

2 tbsp lemon juice

100g (3½oz) smooth peanut butter

2 tbsp shoyu or soy sauce

salt and freshly ground black pepper

1   Boil or steam the green beans or mangetout in or over a saucepan of boiling water for 5–6 minutes, or until just tender. Drain and refresh in cold water.

2   Meanwhile, place the peanuts on a baking sheet and cook in a preheated oven, 200°C (400°F), Gas Mark 6, for 5 minutes, or until lightly browned. Cool slightly, then rub off the skins in your hands or using a clean tea towel.

3   Arrange all the salad vegetable ingredients on a large serving platter. Scatter over the roasted peanuts.

4   To make the dressing, heat the oil in a saucepan and gently cook the shallots, garlic, chilli and ginger until quite soft.

5   Dissolve the creamed coconut in a jug containing the warm water, then blend with the cooked shallot mixture in a blender or food processor. Add the lemon juice, peanut butter and shoyu or soy sauce and mix to a smooth sauce.

6   Season to taste and serve the salad with the sauce separate or poured over the top.

nutritional breakdown per serving: kcal 425, kJ 1765, protein 16g, fat 34g (saturated fat 12g), carbohydrate 15g

avocado and pistachio salad

This salad is richly endowed with a cool mixture of colours and exotic flavours. It is a very simple dish to prepare and works well as a main course, served with a bowl of feta cheese, black olives and cherry tomatoes; or serve it as an accompaniment to Griddled Courgette Quiche with Pine Nuts (see page 255) or Mediterranean Galette (see page 358).

serves 4

preparation: 5 minutes, plus soaking

cooking: 5–7 minutes

Fe *v*

125g (4oz) bulgar
½ tsp salt
200ml (7fl oz) boiling water
75g (3oz) unsalted pistachio nuts (shelled weight)
1 avocado, cubed
2 spring onions, finely chopped
3–4 tbsp chopped coriander
4 tbsp olive oil
juice of 1 lime
salt and freshly ground black pepper

1   Place the bulgar and salt in a large bowl. Pour over the boiling water and leave to soak for 30 minutes, then drain if necessary.

2   Meanwhile, place the pistachio nuts on a baking sheet and roast in a preheated oven, 200°C (400°F), Gas Mark 6, for 5–7 minutes, until lightly browned. Cool and chop roughly.

3   Stir the pistachios, avocado, spring onions and chopped coriander into the bulgar.

4   Combine the olive oil and lime juice and season well. Stir into the bulgar salad and serve.

nutritional breakdown per serving: kcal 413, kJ 1718, protein 8g, fat 29g (saturated fat 3g), carbohydrate 31g

robust tomato salad
left **green garden
salad** centre **fennel
and red pepper salad
with lemon and
oregano dressing** right

fennel and red pepper salad with lemon and oregano dressing

The fresh tang of lemon permeates this dressing and complements the crisp fruity salad ingredients. If you require a dairy-free dressing, you can use a soya yoghurt instead of the mayonnaise.

serves 4
preparation: 5 minutes
cooking: 5 minutes

50g (2oz) pecan nuts
200g (7oz) fennel, sliced
1 red pepper, cored, deseeded and sliced
½ cucumber, sliced
75g (3oz) mixed salad leaves (such as cos
lettuce, endive, radicchio)

nutritional breakdown per serving: kcal 316, kJ 1300,
protein 3g, fat 32g (saturated fat 4g), carbohydrate 5g

For the dressing:
1 tbsp mayonnaise
2 tbsp lemon juice
1–2 tsp chopped oregano
6 tbsp olive oil
salt and freshly ground black pepper

1 Spread the pecans on a baking sheet and roast in
   a preheated oven, 200°C (400°F), Gas Mark 6, for 5
   minutes, or until lightly browned.

2 Allow the nuts to cool before tossing with the
   prepared vegetables. Arrange the salad leaves on
   a serving plate and place the vegetables on top.

3 To make the dressing, mix all the ingredients
   together in a jug. Just before serving, toss a little
   dressing into the salad; serve the rest separately.

green garden salad

serves 2–4

preparation: 5 minutes

cooking: none

v

4 tbsp olive oil or flavoured oil
½ tsp coarse mustard
1 tbsp lemon juice
4 tbsp mixed chopped herbs (such as marjoram, oregano, thyme, parsley)
1 tbsp capers, chopped
75g (3oz) mixed green salad leaves (pick the more strongly flavoured leaves, such as watercress, lollo rosso and rocket)
salt and freshly ground black pepper

1 Place the oil in a small bowl and beat in the mustard. Stir in the lemon juice, herbs and capers and season to taste.

2 Just before serving, toss the dressing into the salad leaves.

nutritional breakdown per serving (4 portions): kcal 107, kJ 440, protein 1g, fat 11g (saturated fat 2g), carbohydrate 1g

robust tomato salad

Rich colours and aromatic flavours abound in this salad. It goes perfectly with creamy main course salads, such as pasta or potato, and works well with pastry or egg dishes, such as Frittata (see page 179). Always try to find the best flavoured tomatoes; cherry tomatoes work well, too.

serves 2–4

preparation: 10 minutes, plus standing

cooking: none

v

4 tomatoes, roughly chopped
¼ cucumber, finely chopped
8 small gherkins, chopped
1 small sweet onion, finely chopped
2–3 artichoke hearts, quartered
50g (2oz) pitted black olives

For the dressing:
75ml (3fl oz) olive oil
1–2 tbsp red wine vinegar
1 tbsp chopped parsley
1 tbsp capers
2 tsp grainy mustard
1 tsp chopped oregano
salt and freshly ground black pepper

1 Mix all the vegetables in a large bowl.

2 To make the dressing, mix all the ingredients together in a jug and season to taste.

3 Pour the dressing over the salad and leave to stand for 30 minutes before serving.

nutritional breakdown per serving (4 portions): kcal 212, kJ 880, protein 4g, fat 16g (saturated fat 2g), carbohydrate 13g

red cabbage and black grape salad with orange vinaigrette

This cheerful crunchy salad adds colour on cold days. It benefits from being prepared a little in advance so that the flavours have time to develop. The ingredients, once tossed in the vinaigrette, don't lose their crisp character.

serves 4

preparation: 15 minutes

cooking: 5 minutes

not suitable for freezing

v

50g (2oz) walnut halves
400g (13oz) red cabbage, shredded
125g (4oz) black grapes, halved and deseeded
2–3 celery sticks, finely chopped

For the vinaigrette:
50ml (2fl oz) olive oil
50ml (2fl oz) walnut oil
2–3 tbsp fresh orange juice
1 tbsp cider apple vinegar
1 tsp grainy mustard
2 tbsp chopped parsley
salt and freshly ground black pepper

1 Spread the walnut halves on a baking sheet and roast in a preheated oven, 200°C (400°F), Gas Mark 6, for 5 minutes, or until lightly browned.

2 Allow the nuts to cool before placing in a large bowl with the other salad ingredients.

3 Mix all the vinaigrette ingredients together in a jug and season well. Toss into the salad and adjust the seasoning to taste.

nutritional breakdown per serving: kcal 293, kJ 1215, protein 3g, fat 27g (saturated fat 3g), carbohydrate 10g

carrot and kohlrabi with pumpkin seeds

This refreshing salad can be made with baby turnips instead of the kohlrabi. The combination of mayonnaise and yoghurt in the dressing keeps the mixture creamy but light – for a vegan alternative use the Silken Tofu Dressing (see page 317).

serves 4

preparation: 15 minutes

cooking: 3–4 minutes

50g (2oz) pumpkin seeds
250g (8oz) carrots, coarsely grated
250g (8oz) kohlrabi or baby turnips, roughly grated
4 tbsp mayonnaise
4 tbsp natural yoghurt
2 tbsp chopped parsley
salt and freshly ground black pepper

1 Spread the pumpkin seeds on a baking sheet and roast in a preheated oven, 200°C (400°F), Gas Mark 6, for 3–4 minutes. Allow to cool.

2 Mix the grated carrot and kohlrabi or baby turnips together in a large bowl. Then add the roasted pumpkin seeds.

3 To make the dressing, mix the mayonnaise in a small bowl with the yoghurt, then mix thoroughly into the grated vegetables and pumpkin seeds with the parsley.

4 Season well and keep chilled until ready to serve.

nutritional breakdown per serving: kcal 359, kJ 1482, protein 7g, fat 31g (saturated fat 5g), carbohydrate 13g

red cabbage and black grape salad with orange vinaigrette left, **carrot and kohlrabi with pumpkin seeds** right

roasted peppers with basil vinaigrette

Colourful and succulent, roasted peppers make splendid salads. This type of salad is also useful for a buffet or picnic because it won't spoil on standing and can be easily transported. Peppers can be roasted in large batches as they will keep for several days. Aubergines, onions, shallots and courgettes are also good roasted and used for salads.

serves 4
preparation: 10 minutes
cooking: 35–40 minutes
v

2 large red peppers, lightly oiled
2 yellow peppers, lightly oiled
50g (2oz) walnut pieces, toasted and chopped
sprigs of basil, to garnish

For the dressing:
3–4 tbsp olive oil
1–2 tbsp white wine vinegar
1 garlic clove, crushed
3 tbsp chopped basil
salt and freshly ground black pepper

1 Place the 4 peppers on a baking sheet and roast in a preheated oven, 200°C (400°F), Gas Mark 6, for 35–40 minutes, or until the skins are well charred and seem to be lifting away from the flesh of the peppers.

2 Leave until cool enough to handle, then peel the skin off each pepper. It should come away easily but use a sharp knife for any stubborn patches. Remove the seeds and core. Reserve any juices.

3 Slice the peppers into thick pieces and arrange on a serving plate.

4 To make the dressing, mix the olive oil, vinegar, garlic and chopped basil together in a small jug. Add some of the juices from the roasted peppers. Season well.

5 Drizzle the dressing over the peppers and scatter over the walnut pieces. Serve at room temperature, garnished with fresh basil.

nutritional breakdown per serving: kcal 203, kJ 840, protein 4g, fat 17g (saturated fat 2g), carbohydrate 9g

dressings

These can range from a simple drizzle of olive oil to a luscious creamy mayonnaise or an aromatic vinaigrette. As well as adding flavour, a dressing helps preserve nutrients by protecting the cut ingredients from oxidation.

There are no hard and fast rules about which dressing goes with which salad combination. In general, lighter leafier salads are usually better dressed in a vinaigrette or vinaigrette-style mixture. More robust salad ingredients, such as shredded cabbage, roasted Mediterranean vegetables or chunky carrots, can take sturdier, thicker dressings, based on cream or mayonnaise.

A classic vinaigrette is usually in the ratio of 3 parts oil to 1 part vinegar. You can vary both the type of vinegar used and the type of oil. Obviously, the ratio can be changed if you prefer a sharper or, conversely, a smoother finish. Acidity can also be introduced by adding lemon or lime juice. Garlic, mustard and herbs add flavour to vinaigrette; sugar, honey or concentrated fruit juice sweeten the mixture.

fruity vinaigrette

makes 125ml (4fl oz)

preparation: 5 minutes

cooking: none

v

75ml (3fl oz) olive oil
2 tbsp wine vinegar
1–2 garlic cloves, crushed
1 tsp Dijon mustard
1 tbsp concentrated apple juice
salt and freshly ground black pepper

1 Whisk all the ingredients together in a small bowl or jug, or shake well in a screw-top jar. Season well.

nutritional breakdown per total recipe: kcal 542, kJ 2234, protein 1g, fat 56g (saturated fat 8g), carbohydrate 10g

roasted walnut dressing

This robust dressing is great with griddled courgettes or fennel, as well as with roasted peppers and aubergine. The roasted walnuts will permeate the other ingredients but you can intensify the walnut flavour by substituting some walnut oil for the olive oil.

makes about 200ml (7fl oz)

preparation: 10 minutes

cooking: 5 minutes

v

50g (2oz) walnut pieces
½ tsp grainy mustard
1–2 tbsp red wine vinegar or balsamic vinegar
1 garlic clove, crushed
150ml (¼ pint) olive oil or a mixture of olive and walnut oil
salt and freshly ground black pepper

1 Spread the walnut pieces on a baking sheet and roast in a preheated oven, 200°C (400°F), Gas Mark 6, for 5 minutes, or until lightly browned. Leave to cool.

2 Using a blender or food processor, grind the walnuts finely. Add the mustard, 1 tablespoon of the wine vinegar and the garlic and process again.

3 With the motor running, gradually pour in the oil in a thin steady stream. Season to taste, adding more vinegar if required.

nutritional breakdown per total recipe: kcal 1345, kJ 5535, protein 8g, fat 145g (saturated fat 18g), carbohydrate 3g

lemon and sunflower vinaigrette

makes about 150ml (¼ pint)

preparation: 5 minutes

cooking: none

1 tbsp clear honey
3 tbsp lemon juice
75ml (3fl oz) sunflower oil
1 spring onion, very finely chopped
1 tsp paprika
salt and freshly ground black pepper

1 Whisk all the ingredients together in a small bowl or jug, or shake well in a screw-top jar. Season to taste.

2 Leave to stand 10 minutes before serving.

nutritional breakdown per total recipe: kcal 580, kJ 2400, protein 1g, fat 55g (saturated fat 7g), carbohydrate 21g

green vinaigrette

This is good with tomatoes and chicory.

makes about 175ml (6fl oz)

preparation: 5 minutes

cooking: none

𝑣

125ml (4fl oz) olive oil
1–2 tbsp lemon juice
50g (2oz) chopped herbs (such as chives and parsley)
2 spring onions, finely chopped
1 garlic clove, crushed
salt and freshly ground black pepper

1 Mix the olive oil and lemon juice together in a small bowl or jug.

2 Stir in the herbs, spring onions and garlic. Season to taste.

nutritional breakdown per total recipe: kcal 819, kJ 3370, protein 2g, fat 89g (saturated fat 12g), carbohydrate 4g

mayonnaise

Making mayonnaise used to be a hit-or-miss affair as there was always the possibility of the eggs curdling. Thanks to modern electrical gadgets it is now much easier and virtually foolproof. Do remember, though, to have all the ingredients at room temperature before you start.

makes 300ml (½ pint)

preparation: 10 minutes

cooking: none

2 egg yolks
300ml (½ pint) olive oil
2 tbsp white wine vinegar or lemon juice
salt and freshly ground black pepper

1 Beat the egg yolks thoroughly in a large bowl. Then, using an electric whisk, beat in the olive oil a drop or two at a time.

2 When you have added about half the oil, whisk in 1 tablespoon of the vinegar.

3 Add the rest of the oil in a steady stream. Season well and thin down with more vinegar.

4 Alternatively, make the mayonnaise using a blender or food processor. Place the egg yolks and vinegar in the goblet or bowl. With the motor running, gradually pour in the oil in a thin steady stream until thick and creamy. Season to taste.

nutritional breakdown per total recipe: kcal 2100, kJ 8640, protein 6g, fat 231g (saturated fat 34g), carbohydrate 0g

VARIATIONS

You might prefer to mix the mayonnaise with equal quantities of natural yoghurt, crème fraîche or soured cream. Flavour the mayonnaise by adding chopped herbs, such as parsley, basil, chives or tarragon. Alternatively, add chopped roasted peppers and paprika to make a russet-coloured dressing, or chopped chilli, dried chilli flakes or crushed peppercorns for a hotter finish.

Electric blenders or electric whisks mean the process of making mayonnaise is much speedier and more reliable.

warning

If you fall into the category of those who should be cautious about eating raw egg (see page 82), it is best to buy mayonnaise rather than make your own. Manufactured mayonnaise is made with pasteurised egg, which avoids the problem of salmonella.

tahini dressing

This smooth thick dressing goes well with stir-fry vegetables and substantial salads of grains or potatoes. Use the dressing as a topping rather than stirring it in, so that the colours of the salad remain fresh. This dressing is also good as a dip for crudités.

makes about 175ml (6fl oz)

preparation: 5 minutes

cooking: none

(Ca) (Fe) *v*

4 tbsp tahini
4 tbsp water
juice of 1 lemon
1–2 tbsp olive oil
1 tbsp shoyu or soy sauce
salt and freshly ground black pepper

1 Place the tahini in a small bowl and mix with the water until well blended.

2 Add the lemon juice, olive oil and shoyu or soy sauce and mix well. Season to taste.

nutritional breakdown per total recipe: kcal 1360, kJ 5623, protein 38g, fat 133g (saturated fat 19g), carbohydrate 4g

VARIATIONS

For an aromatic mixture, add 1 teaspoon dry-roasted ground cumin. For a sharper, yet creamy version, add 50g (2oz) natural yoghurt or more to taste.

low-calorie creamy dressing

makes 300ml (½ pint)

preparation: 10 minutes

cooking: none

250g (8oz) cottage cheese
1–2 tsp lemon juice
2 tsp sunflower oil
1 tsp chopped tarragon
50g (2oz) natural yoghurt
1 tsp white wine vinegar or apple cider vinegar
salt and freshly ground black pepper

1 Using a blender or food processor, blend everything together until smooth. Season to taste.

nutritional breakdown per total recipe: kcal 330, kJ 1390, protein 37g, fat 16g (saturated fat 7g), carbohydrate 10g

silken tofu dressing

Silken tofu makes a very good base for a dairy-free cream dressing, and lends itself to all sorts of flavouring variations. You can add ginger, lime, shallots, dry-roasted sesame seeds, or shoyu or soy sauce, as well as herbs and a variety of other spices.

makes 300ml (½ pint)

preparation: 5 minutes

cooking: none

(Ca)

200–250g (7–8oz) silken tofu (bean curd)
2 tbsp lemon juice

2 tbsp sunflower oil
1 garlic clove, crushed
1 spring onion, finely chopped
salt and freshly ground black pepper

1 Mix all the ingredients together until smooth, using a blender or food processor.

2 Season and use as required.

nutritional breakdown per total recipe: kcal 345, kJ 1426, protein 14g, fat 29g (saturated fat 3g), carbohydrate 9g

Cakes, Puddings and Bread

The smell, wafting through the house, of freshly baked bread, cakes or biscuits hot from the oven is something that no one can resist and is guaranteed to boost your popularity ratings. This section shows you how to make basic wholemeal and white bread easily, with variations on these recipes, and you'll find recipes for a mouthwatering variety of international breads including focaccia, corn bread, griddle breads, and a bread made without wheat or other ingredients that contain gluten.

The cake recipes include a deliciously moist Upside-down Apple Cake with Maple Syrup and Lemon, made by the batter method, and a Classic Rich Fruit Cake. As well as tea-time classics there is also an unusual Middle Eastern Pistachio Cake, and a tempting Carrot Cake with a tangy Orange Cream Icing.

Everyone enjoys something sweet to round off a meal, and it does no harm to indulge now and again. The pudding recipes include irresistible treats such as sweet and sticky Layered Fruit Pavlova and mellow Ricotta Cheesecake. There are also some simple suggestions for light fruit desserts, such as Grilled Peaches with Ginger Cream, and a Quick Berry Brûlée. On colder days, you could treat yourself to the warm and fruity Plum Crisp.

plum crisp

This attractive pudding is straightforward to make. If you can't buy a fruit bread, buy a sweet plain bread and add some raisins or sultanas when cooking the plums.

serves 6
preparation: 10 minutes
cooking: 30–35 minutes
suitable for freezing

1 kg (2lb) plums or apricots, stones removed and sliced
125g (4oz) butter or sunflower margarine
4–6 tbsp dark sugar
zest of ½ lemon
1 tsp ground cinnamon
8–10 slices fruit bread

1 Place the plums or apricots in a large saucepan and simmer with 25g (1oz) of the butter or margarine and the sugar and cook for about 5 minutes until just soft. Stir in the lemon zest and ground cinnamon and adjust the sweetening if necessary.

2 Spoon the plums into a buttered or greased shallow ovenproof dish.

3 Spread the remaining butter or margarine over the fruit bread and cut the slices into triangles. Arrange the triangles over the cooked fruit.

4 Bake in a preheated oven, 180°C (350°F), Gas Mark 4, for 25–30 minutes. Serve hot.

CRUMBLES

Fruit stewed in this way can also be topped with a crumble topping. Sweet crumbles are made in a similar way to savoury crumbles (see page 271) except that sugar or other sweeteners are added. You could also add sweet spices, such as ground cinnamon, nutmeg or allspice, as well as seeds, such as sunflower seeds.

nutritional breakdown per serving: kcal 385, kJ 1616, protein 4g, fat 20g (saturated fat 12g), carbohydrate 52g

carrot cake with orange cream icing

This colourful, moist wholemeal cake is straightforward to make. It can be left plain for a dairy-free version or decorated with a cream cheese icing. Do not ice the cake if you intend to keep it for more than a day or so.

serves 12
preparation: 15 minutes
cooking: 1–1¼ hours
suitable for freezing

250g (8oz) self-raising wholemeal flour
1 tsp baking powder
2 tsp ground cinnamon
125g (4oz) sunflower margarine or butter
125g (4oz) clear honey
125g (4oz) soft brown sugar
250g (8oz) carrots, grated
50g (2oz) walnut pieces, chopped
50g (2oz) sultanas
zest of 1 orange

For the icing:
175g (6oz) cream cheese
50g (2oz) icing sugar
1–2 tbsp orange juice

1 Mix the flour, baking powder and ground cinnamon in a large bowl.

2 Gently melt the margarine or butter in a small saucepan with the honey and sugar. Stir into the flour.

3 Add the grated carrot, chopped walnuts, sultanas and orange zest and mix well.

4 Spoon the mixture into a lined medium 1kg (2lb) loaf tin and bake in a preheated oven, 180°C (350°F), Gas Mark 4, for 1–1¼ hours. Turn out and leave to cool on a wire rack.

5 To make the icing, cream the ingredients together in a bowl and spread thickly over the cooled cake.

nutritional breakdown per serving: kcal 342, kJ 1433, protein 4g, fat 19g (saturated fat 6g), carbohydrate 42g

classic rich fruit cake

*This is a useful cake as it keeps extremely well and cuts
cleanly. It is great for taking on hikes and picnics, but also
for serving as a festive treat.*

serves 12–16

preparation time: 10 minutes

cooking time: 3–3½ hours

suitable for freezing

175g (6oz) unsalted butter
175g (6oz) muscovado sugar
4 eggs
200g (7oz) wholemeal self-raising flour
2 tsp mixed spice
175g (6oz) currants
175g (6oz) sultanas
175g (6oz) raisins
150g (5oz) chopped glacé cherries
10–12 whole almonds, to decorate

1 Place the butter and sugar in a large bowl and
cream together.

2 Add the eggs, 1 at a time, and beat each very well,
adding a little of the flour in between each addition
of egg to prevent the mixture curdling.

3 Add the remaining flour, the mixed spice and all
the dried fruit and mix together very well. Spoon
the mixture into a greased and lined 20cm (8in)
round cake tin.

4 Smooth the top of the mixture and arrange the
whole almonds in a circular pattern. Bake in a
preheated oven, 150°C (300°F), Gas Mark 2, for
3–3½ hours. Leave to cool in the tin.

nutritional breakdown per serving (12 slices): kcal 407,
kJ 1714, protein 6g, fat 16g (saturated fat 9g), carbohydrate 65g

upside down apple cake with maple syrup and lemon

serves 8
preparation: 20 minutes
cooking: 30 minutes
suitable for freezing

150g (5oz) butter
2 tbsp maple syrup
juice and zest of ½ lemon
3 tart dessert apples (such as Granny Smith),
  cored, peeled, quartered and thinly sliced
125g (4oz) soft brown sugar
125g (4oz) self-raising flour
2 eggs
demerara sugar for sprinkling

1 Melt 25g (1oz) of the butter and pour into a 20cm (8in) loose-bottomed round cake tin. Add the maple syrup and sprinkle in the lemon zest.

2 Arrange the slices of apple, slightly overlapping each other, around the base of the tin. Squeeze over the juice of half a lemon.

3 Using a food processor or electric hand-held beater, mix together the remaining butter, the soft brown sugar, flour and eggs and pour or spoon this over the apple slices. Smooth the top of the cake mixture.

4 Bake in a preheated oven, 180°C (350°F), Gas Mark 4, for 30 minutes.

5 Leave to stand in the tin for 5 minutes, then turn out. Sprinkle with demerara sugar and serve warm or cold.

nutritional breakdown per serving: kcal 309, kJ 1295, protein 3g, fat 17g (saturated fat 11g), carbohydrate 38g

deluxe chocolate and prune refrigerator cake

This is rich, irresistible and extremely easy to make. It is good for parties as it can be served in very small quantities. Do not take it out of the fridge until just before serving since it is at its best when cold and crisp. Use ready-to-eat prunes as they will be softer. If these are unavailable, soak ordinary prunes in fruit juice or alcohol for 30 minutes or so before starting the recipe.

makes 16–20
preparation: 10 minutes, plus chilling
cooking: 6 minutes
suitable for freezing

200g (7oz) dark chocolate, broken into small
  pieces
200g (7oz) butter
150g (5oz) ready-to-eat prunes, chopped
100g (3½oz) pecan nuts, roasted and roughly
  chopped
250g (8oz) digestive biscuits, roughly crushed
50ml (2fl oz) rum or brandy

1 Melt the chocolate with the butter in a large bowl set over a saucepan of hot but not boiling water.

2 Remove from the heat and stir in all the other ingredients.

3 Spoon the mixture into a deep, lined 20 x 30cm (8 x 12in) tray. Leave to set in the fridge for at least 2 hours.

4 Cut into small squares to serve.

nutritional breakdown per square (16 portions): kcal 294,
kJ 1223, protein 2g, fat 22g (saturated fat 11g), carbohydrate 22g

pistachio cake

*This is a traditional cake made in the Middle East. It is
sometimes known as 1-2-3-4 because, when measured in
cups, the starting point is 1 cup of oil, 2 of sugar, 3 of flour
and then 4 eggs. In this version I have used less sugar and
added pistachio nuts and raisins.*

serves 12
preparation: 10 minutes
cooking: 1–1¼ hours
suitable for freezing
(Fr)

250g (8oz) soft brown sugar
4 eggs
250ml (8fl oz) light olive oil
375g (12oz) plain flour
3 tsp baking powder
250g (8oz) raisins
250g (8oz) unsalted pistachio nuts (shelled
  weight)
3 tbsp milk, optional

1 Place the sugar and eggs in a large bowl and whisk
together. Whisk in the oil, then the flour and
baking powder.

2 Stir in the raisins and pistachio nuts, reserving
a few nuts for decoration. Add the milk if the
mixture seems a little dry.

3 Spoon the mixture into a lined, 20cm (8in) square
cake tin. Bake in a preheated oven, 180°C (350°F),
Gas Mark 4, for 1–1¼ hours.

4 Remove from the oven and allow to cool in the tin
for 10 minutes, then turn out and decorate with the
remaining pistachios, roughly chopped. Cover the
cake with a tea towel until cold.

nutritional breakdown per serving: kcal 543, kJ 2279,
protein 10g, fat 29g (saturated fat 3g), carbohydrate 64g

all-in-one banana loaf

Moist and dense, this all-in-one banana loaf is good served plain or buttered.

serves 12

preparation: 10 minutes

cooking: 30–40 minutes

suitable for freezing

125g (4oz) pecan nuts
3 ripe bananas, chopped
125g (4oz) butter, melted
125g (4oz) brown sugar
3 eggs
250g (8oz) self-raising flour
75g (3oz) dried apricots, slivered

1   Set aside half the pecans for decoration.

2   Put all the remaining ingredients in a food processor and mix together until well combined.

3   Spoon the mixture into a greased and lined 20cm (8in) round cake tin or medium 1kg (2lb) loaf tin, decorate with the reserved nuts, and bake in a preheated oven, 160°C (325°F), Gas Mark 3, for 30–40 minutes.

4   Leave to cool in the tin.

nutritional breakdown per serving: kcal 312, kJ 1307, protein 5g, fat 18g (saturated fat 7g), carbohydrate 36g

very lemon wedges

This is a refreshing bite of lemon on a simple base. It makes a good mid-morning snack or could be cut into very tiny pieces to serve at a party.

makes 12
preparation: 10 minutes
cooking: 30–35 minutes
suitable for freezing

For the base:
50g (2oz) butter, softened
50g (2oz) golden caster sugar
75g (3oz) plain or wholemeal flour

For the topping:
250g (8oz) cream cheese
150g (5oz) golden caster sugar
1 egg
juice and zest of 1 lemon
½ tsp vanilla extract

1 To make the base, mix the ingredients to a dough, using a blender or food processor. Press into an 18cm (7in) round ovenproof dish.

2 Bake in a preheated oven, 180°C (350°F), Gas Mark 4, for 15–20 minutes, or until just golden.

3 To make the topping, blend the ingredients together until smooth, using a blender or food processor. Spoon the filling over the cooked base and bake at 180°C (350°F), Gas Mark 4, for 15–20 minutes, or until just set.

4 Leave to cool then cut into 12 pieces.

nutritional breakdown per square: kcal 215, kJ 898, protein 2g, fat 14g (saturated fat 9g), carbohydrate 22g

raisin and almond flapjack

There are many variations on this flapjack recipe. You can vary the type of flakes used – try barley or millet instead of oats. You could also use different dried fruits, such as chopped dates, slivered mango, apricot or sultanas.

makes 12–16
preparation: 10 minutes
cooking: 30–35 minutes
suitable for freezing
𝒱 (using syrup)

250g (8oz) vegetable margarine
50g (2oz) soft brown sugar
125g (4oz) clear honey or golden syrup
250g (8oz) rolled oats
250g (8oz) wholemeal flour
125g (4oz) raisins
50g (2oz) almonds, chopped

1 Put the margarine, sugar and honey or syrup in a small saucepan and melt together.

2 Mix the oats, flour, raisins and almonds together in a large bowl.

3 When the margarine mixture is boiling, pour it over the dry ingredients and stir very well. Spoon the mixture into a lightly greased ovenproof tray, approximately 18 x 28cm (7 x 11in), and bake in a preheated oven, 180°C (350°F), Gas Mark 4, for 20–25 minutes.

4 Mark into 12–16 pieces and leave to cool in the tray before cutting.

nutritional breakdown per flapjack (12 pieces): kcal 402, kJ 1686, protein 6g, fat 22g (saturated fat 8g), carbohydrate 49g

apricot lattice

A cross between a cake and a tart, this colourful latticed pudding is easy to make. If you are in a hurry, you could use an apricot jam or jelly for the filling instead of the purée used here.

serves 12
preparation: 15 minutes
cooking: 1–1¼ hours
suitable for freezing

250g (8oz) dried apricots
300ml (½ pint) water, plus 1 tbsp
250g (8oz) self-raising flour
125g (4oz) caster sugar
125g (4oz) vegetable margarine
1 egg, lightly beaten
flour for dusting

1　Place the apricots in a saucepan with the water. Bring to the boil, then simmer for 30–40 minutes, or until quite tender. Allow to cool, then purée with the cooking liquid, using a blender or food processor, until smooth. Set aside.

2　Using the blender or food processor again, mix the flour, caster sugar, margarine and egg together to a soft dough. Add up to 1 tablespoon of cold water if the mixture seems dry.

3　Using two-thirds of the dough, press it into a 23cm (9in) flan dish. Spread the apricot purée on top.

4　Roll out the remaining dough on a lightly floured surface and cut into thin strips. Arrange the strips on top of the purée in a lattice pattern.

5　Bake in a preheated oven, 180°C (350°F), Gas Mark 4, for 30–35 minutes, or until golden brown. Serve at room temperature.

nutritional breakdown per serving: kcal 232, kJ 977, protein 3g, fat 9g (saturated fat 4g), carbohydrate 36g

ricotta cheesecake

This light cheesecake is simple to make. The dried fruit can be varied – raisins or slivers of dried pear work very well. The fruit can be soaked in fruit juice but a little alcohol does add a special flavour.

serves 8

preparation: 10 minutes, plus soaking

cooking: 45–50 minutes

suitable for freezing

50g (2oz) sultanas
3 tbsp Marsala
3 eggs, separated
50g (2oz) caster sugar
500g (1lb) ricotta cheese
2 tbsp plain flour
juice and zest of 1 lemon
whipped cream, to serve

1 Place the sultanas in a bowl. Add the Marsala and leave to soak for at least 30 minutes.

2 Place the egg yolks in a bowl and beat with the sugar until thick. Add the ricotta cheese, flour, lemon zest and juice and stir well. Mix in the soaked sultanas.

3 Whisk the egg whites in a large bowl until standing in soft peaks. Fold into the ricotta cheese mixture. Spoon the mixture into a buttered and floured 20cm (8in) ring. Bake in a preheated oven, 180°C (350°F), Gas Mark 4, for 45–50 minutes.

4 Leave to cool before turning out. Serve with whipped cream.

nutritional breakdown per serving: kcal 187, kJ 782, protein 9g, fat 9g (saturated fat 5g), carbohydrate 17g

layered fruit pavlova

This fruit pavlova has a sticky marshmallow-type base, which is made by adding cold water to the egg white mixture. Choose colourful fruit for the topping. In this recipe I have used mango and nectarines, but you could try soft fruits, such as raspberries and strawberries, as well as other tropical fruits.

serves 8

preparation: 10 minutes, plus cooling

cooking: 45 minutes

suitable for freezing (base only)

3 egg whites
2 tbsp cold water
250g (8oz) caster sugar
1 tsp wine or cider vinegar
1 tsp vanilla extract
3 tsp cornflour
pinch of salt
300ml (½ pint) double cream
2 mangoes, peeled, stones removed and sliced
2 nectarines, stones removed and sliced
icing sugar for dusting

1 Beat the egg whites in a large bowl, until they form stiff peaks but are not dry.

2 Add the water and beat again, then add the sugar, a little at a time, beating thoroughly until the sugar is dissolved.

3 Sprinkle in the vinegar, vanilla extract, cornflour and salt and beat again. Spoon the mixture on to a baking sheet lined with baking parchment.

4 Bake the pavlova base in a preheated oven, 150°C (300°F), Gas Mark 2, for 45 minutes. Then turn off the oven and leave the meringue in the oven to cool completely.

5 To make the topping, whip the cream in a bowl until standing in peaks. Spread over the base and cover with sliced mango and nectarines. Dust with icing sugar.

nutritional breakdown per serving: kcal 347, kJ 1457, protein 3g, fat 18g (saturated fat 11g), carbohydrate 46g

CAKES, PUDDINGS AND BREAD

strawberry yoghurt ice

For special occasions, add a liqueur to the fruit; for a richer version, replace some of the yoghurt with cream.

serves 4–6

preparation: 10 minutes, plus freezing

cooking:

suitable for freezing

375g (12oz) strawberries
125g (4oz) caster sugar
200g (7oz) natural yoghurt

1 Blend the strawberries and sugar together until smooth, using a blender or food processor. Pass the mixture through a sieve to remove the pips.

2 Stir the yoghurt into the mixture. Pour into a freezerproof container and freeze for 2 hours.

3 Remove from the freezer and beat until smooth with an electric whisk. Return to the freezer for a further 2 hours.

4 To serve, remove from the freezer 10 minutes before serving.

nutritional breakdown per serving: kcal 175, kJ 742, protein 3g, fat 1g (saturated fat 0g), carbohydrate 42g

carob or chocolate mousse

serves 4

preparation: 5 minutes

cooking: none

(Ca) (Fe) 𝒱 (using syrup)

200–250g (7–8oz) silken tofu (bean curd)
3 tbsp tahini
1 banana, roughly chopped
1–2 tbsp clear honey or syrup
25g (1oz) carob or chocolate

1 Blend together the silken tofu, tahini, banana and sweetening in a blender or food processor.

2 Grate in the carob or chocolate and blend again for a few seconds. Spoon into 4 attractive glasses and chill before serving.

nutritional breakdown per serving: kcal 353, kJ 1468, protein 12g, fat 27g (saturated fat 4g), carbohydrate 17g

strawberry yoghurt ice back **carob mousse** front

water ices

For refreshing dairy-free ices, make a light sugar syrup (see page 59) and stir into a fruit purée, such as strawberries, or combine with a well-flavoured juice, such as orange or lemon juice. Pour into a freezerproof container. Beat once or twice during the initial freezing process to break up the ice crystals. For children, freeze the mixture in small quantities in moulds and add lollipop sticks.

quick berry brûlée

BAKED FRUIT

For a simple cooked fruit dish using a mixture of fruits, slice a selection of fruit, such as pear, apple and dried date, and wrap in a buttered square of greaseproof paper. Sweeten with a little sugar and bake in a preheated oven, 200°C (400°F), Gas Mark 6, for 15 minutes. This also works well with apricots, plums or a scattering of berries, such as blackberries.

This recipe works well with fruit that doesn't need cooking, such as strawberries and other soft fruit, or with apricots, peaches or plums.

serves 4
preparation: 5 minutes
cooking: 5 minutes

250g (8oz) strawberries, halved
250g (8oz) mascarpone cheese or thick
  natural yoghurt
50–75g (2–3oz) caster sugar

1 Place the strawberries in a flameproof dish and cover with mascarpone cheese or thick yoghurt. (The mascarpone is quite hard to spoon over but it will even out as it melts under the grill.)

2 Sprinkle over the caster sugar. Place under a preheated very hot grill and cook until the sugar caramelises. Serve hot.

nutritional breakdown per serving: kcal 328, kJ 1364, protein 4g, fat 25g (saturated fat 19g), carbohydrate 23g

grilled peaches with ginger cream

You could also grill nectarines, apricots and plums, as well as pears and apples, in the same way as the peaches used here.

serves 4

preparation: 5 minutes

cooking: 2–3 minutes

For the ginger cream:

250g (8oz) ricotta cheese

2 tbsp double cream

1 tbsp ginger syrup

1 tbsp finely chopped stem ginger

For the fruit:

4 ripe peaches, halved and stones removed

15g (½oz) butter, softened

1 To make the ginger cream, place the ricotta in a bowl with the double cream and ginger syrup and blend until smooth. Stir in the finely chopped stem ginger.

2 Brush the peach halves with the softened butter. Place under a preheated grill and cook for 2–3 minutes.

3 Serve hot with the ginger cream.

nutritional breakdown per serving: kcal 259, kJ 1080, protein 8g, fat 19g (saturated fat 12g), carbohydrate 16g

low-fat cream

This is a useful low-fat accompaniment to baked or grilled fruits or to serve with fruit salad.

serves 6

preparation time: 5 minutes, plus chilling

cooking: none

250g (8oz) natural fromage frais

up to 150ml (¼ pint) fruit juice

1 tsp vanilla extract

1 Using a blender or food processor, process the fromage frais until smooth, adding sufficient fruit juice to give a pouring or spooning consistency.

2 Flavour with vanilla extract to taste, then chill.

nutritional breakdown per serving: kcal 55, kJ 232, protein 6g, fat 3g (saturated fat 1g), carbohydrate 2g

VANILLA CREAM

To make a vanilla cream follow the ginger cream recipe but use 2–3 drops vanilla extract, or to taste, instead of the ginger and syrup, and add 1 tablespoon honey or icing sugar, or to taste.

wholemeal bread

This recipe is suitable for wholemeal loaves, rolls and plaits. Many different savoury flavourings can be added to the basic dough, for example 1 teaspoon dried thyme, 50g (2oz) grated cheese, 1 teaspoon dried chilli flakes or 1–2 tablespoons sunflower or sesame seeds.

makes 2 loaves, each makes 12 slices

preparation: 15 minutes, plus rising and proving

cooking: 35–40 minutes

suitable for freezing

Step 1 Add the oil to the mixture.
Step 2 Use a wooden spoon to draw to a dough.
Step 3 Knead well until the dough is smooth.
Step 4 Leave to rise in a clean bowl.
Step 5 Knock the air out of the dough.
Step 6 Leave to rise in greased or oiled tins.

750g (1½lb) strong wholemeal flour, plus extra for dusting
1 tsp salt
7g (¼oz) sachet easy-blend yeast
400ml (14fl oz) water (⅔ cold, ⅓ boiling)
1 tbsp olive oil

1 Mix the flour, salt and yeast together in a large bowl. Pour in the water and add the olive oil. Work the ingredients into a dough and knead on a lightly floured surface for 5 minutes, or until the dough is smooth and elastic but not sticky.

2 Return the dough to a clean bowl and cover with clingfilm or a damp tea towel. Leave to rise in a warm place for about 1 hour – the dough should have doubled in size.

3 Again working on a lightly floured surface, knock the air out of the dough and knead again briefly.

4 Shape into 2 loaves. Place in small, oiled 500g (1lb) loaf tins and leave to prove for up to 30 minutes.

5 Bake in a preheated oven, 220°C (425°F), Gas Mark 7, for 35–40 minutes. Test that the loaf is cooked by tapping the base – it should sound hollow. If it is not cooked, replace in the tin and cook for another 5 minutes.

6 Turn out and leave to cool on a wire rack.

nutritional breakdown per slice: kcal 102, kJ 432, protein 4g, fat 1g (saturated fat 0g), carbohydrate 20g

VARIATIONS

Rolls – a good-sized uncooked roll weighs about 75g (3oz). If you are making rolls for a party, make them smaller – about 50g (2oz).

To make rolls, follow steps 1–3 for bread making. Divide your dough into equal-sized pieces. Knead each lightly to make a ball shape, then shape into rounds or crescents. Set on an oiled baking sheet and leave to prove for 10 minutes. Bake in a preheated oven, 220°C (425°F), Gas Mark 7, for 15–20 minutes, depending on the size of the rolls. Leave to cool on a wire rack.

troubleshooting

- dense or heavy loaves may mean that the initial dough was too dry. If you notice cracks in the dough as you knead, this is definitely the case

- soggy bread is either undercooked or has been left too long to prove in the tin and it has collapsed

- lopsided loaves mean there is uneven heat in the oven. Try turning the loaf round during cooking

enriched white bread

Adding milk and egg to a dough gives a softer crust and a richer texture. Use a strong, preferably unbleached, white flour for the best flavour.

makes 12 slices
preparation: 15 minutes, plus rising and proving
cooking: 35–40 minutes
suitable for freezing

500g (1lb) strong white flour, plus extra for dusting
7g (¼oz) sachet easy-blend yeast
1 tsp salt
250ml (8fl oz) warm milk
25g (1oz) butter, melted

Step 1 To make a perfect plait, roll out three even strips.
Step 2 Line them up and start plaiting in the middle towards one end.
Step 3 Continue plaiting to the end of the first half.
Step 4 Turn the plait around and plait the other half.
Step 5 Tuck in the ends firmly.

1 Place the flour, yeast and salt in a large bowl.

2 Add the warm milk and melted butter and draw the ingredients into a dough. Knead on a lightly floured surface for 5 minutes, or until the dough is smooth and elastic but not sticky.

3 Return the dough to a clean bowl and cover with clingfilm or a damp tea towel. Leave to rise in a warm place for about 1 hour – the dough should have doubled in size.

4 Again working on a lightly floured surface, knock the air out of the dough and knead again briefly.

5 To make a plait, divide the dough into 3 equal pieces and roll each one into a 'rope', about 30cm (12 in) long. Lay the 3 lengths side by side. To get an even plait, begin plaiting from the middle towards one end, then turn the whole thing round and plait the other end. Pinch the pieces together at each end of the plait.

6 Place the plait on a baking sheet and leave to prove until roughly doubled in size.

7 Bake in a preheated oven, 220° (425°F), Gas Mark 7, for 35–40 minutes, or until cooked – it should sound hollow when tapped on the base. Turn the loaf over and cook for a further 3 minutes to crisp the base.

8 Leave to cool on a wire rack.

nutritional breakdown per slice: kcal 176, kJ 747, protein 6g, fat 4g (saturated fat 2g), carbohydrate 32g

focaccia

This is a flat bread, enriched with olive oil and flavoured with herbs or typical Mediterranean ingredients, such as olives, sun-dried tomatoes and oregano. You can also use this dough as a pizza base.

makes 2 rounds, each cuts into 12 wedges

preparation: 15 minutes, plus standing, rising and proving

cooking: 20–25 minutes

suitable for freezing

7g (¼oz) sachet yeast
450ml (¾ pint) water
750g (1½lb) strong white flour, plus extra for dusting
1½ tsp salt
5 tbsp olive oil
125g (4oz) olives
1 tsp dried oregano
coarse sea salt

1 Mix the yeast with the water and about one-quarter of the flour in a large bowl. Stir to make a batter and leave to stand in a warm place for about 10 minutes.

2 Add the remaining flour, the salt and 4 tablespoons of the olive oil. Draw the ingredients into a dough. Knead on a lightly floured surface for 5 minutes, or until the dough is smooth and elastic but not sticky.

3 Place the dough in an oiled bowl, cover with clingfilm or a damp tea towel and leave to rise in a warm place for 1 hour.

4 Again working on a lightly floured surface, knock the air out of the dough, then work in the olives and dried oregano. Shape the dough into 2 rounds, each about 2.5cm (1in) thick. Place on a baking sheet and leave to prove for up to 30 minutes.

5 Using the end of a wooden spoon, make indentations in the dough, dipping the end of the spoon in flour each time you put it in the dough. Brush the focaccia with the remaining olive oil and bake in a preheated oven, 220°C (425°F), Gas Mark 7, for 20–25 minutes.

6 Once cooked, sprinkle with coarse salt and leave to cool on a wire rack.

nutritional breakdown per wedge: kcal 134, kJ 565, protein 4g, fat 3g (saturated fat 1g), carbohydrate 24g

glazing and decorating

A glaze on a loaf looks very attractive and is easy to do. Beat 1 egg yolk with a little salt and brush this over the risen loaf just before it goes in the oven. Then scatter over some sesame or poppy seeds. A light sugar syrup or warmed honey can be used to glaze a loaf after it has been baked.

gluten-free bread

This is a dense loaf, which slices well and can be toasted if necessary. The buckwheat flour adds an intense flavour – use potato flour if you prefer. Gluten-free breads will not rise in the same way as wheat loaves but they need not be heavy. This loaf is lightened with a mash of cooked squash – you could vary this by using carrots or pumpkin. You could give the bread extra texture by adding linseeds or sesame seeds at step 2 if you wish.

makes 20 slices
preparation: 20 minutes
cooking: 30–40 minutes
suitable for freezing
v

7g (¼oz) sachet easy-blend yeast
250ml (8fl oz) lukewarm water
125g (4oz) brown rice flour
1 tsp sugar
125g (4oz) buckwheat flour
25g (1oz) soya flour
200g (7oz) butternut squash, cooked and mashed
1 tsp salt
1 tbsp sunflower oil

1 Combine the yeast with the warm water, rice flour and sugar in a large bowl. Mix well and leave for 10 minutes.

2 Stir in the buckwheat and soya flour, the mashed squash, salt and oil. Mix very well, then spoon into a greased medium 1kg (2lb) loaf tin.

3 Bake in a preheated oven, 180°C (350°F), Gas Mark 4, for 30–40 minutes. Turn out and leave to cool on a wire rack.

nutritional breakdown per slice: kcal 62, kJ 259, protein 2g, fat 1g (saturated fat 0g), carbohydrate 12g

soda bread

Soda bread is a yeast-free bread, which does not need to rise and therefore can be made, baked and eaten in less than an hour. For a richer dough you can add melted butter; if you want a sweet, almost cake-like bread add some sugar and dried fruit.

makes 8–12 wedges

preparation: 10 minutes

cooking: 35–40 minutes

suitable for freezing

375g (12oz) plain wholemeal flour, plus extra
   for dusting
125g (4oz) plain white flour
1 tsp baking powder
½ tsp salt
300ml (½ pint) milk
1 egg

1   Place the flours, baking powder and salt in a large bowl. Beat the milk and egg together in a jug and pour over the flour. Mix until you have a soft dough.

2   Turn on to a lightly floured surface and knead very lightly to shape into a rough ball.

3   Place on a floured baking sheet and flatten to a round, about 3.5cm (1½in) thick. Using a floured sharp knife, mark the dough into quarters with deep cuts that go almost through the dough round. Make shallower cuts in between so that you have 8 even divisions marked.

4   Bake in a preheated oven, 190°C (375°F), Gas Mark 5, for 35–40 minutes, or until the crust is well browned.

5   Leave to cool on a wire rack.

nutritional breakdown per wedge (8 portions): kcal 224, kJ 948, protein 9g, fat 3g (saturated fat 1g), carbohydrate 42g

griddle bread

These quick breads have a distinctive chewy texture and can be made with either white or wholemeal flour, although the wholemeal versions do not puff up in the same way. Eat them hot with a dip, or brush with a little butter and serve with dhal and spicy dishes.

makes 12
preparation: 15 minutes
cooking: 20 minutes
suitable for freezing

375g (12oz) plain flour, plus extra for dusting
¾ tsp baking powder
pinch of salt
1–2 tsp dry-roasted coriander or cumin seeds
200g (7oz) natural yoghurt

1 Place the flour, baking powder, salt and coriander or cumin seeds in a large bowl. Stir in the yoghurt to make a soft dough. Add a little more yoghurt if necessary but the dough should be pliable not sticky.

2 Knead briefly on a lightly floured surface, then divide the dough into 12. Roll or flatten each piece of dough into a round, about 10cm (4in) in diameter. The dough should be quite thin.

3 Heat a large frying pan and dry-fry each round for 2–3 minutes, or until it has puffed up slightly and the surface looks brown and blistered. Turn over and cook the other side for 2 minutes.

4 Once cooked, keep warm wrapped in a clean tea towel, while you cook the remainder. Serve hot.

nutritional breakdown per serving: kcal 110, kJ 468, protein 4g, fat 1g (saturated fat 0g), carbohydrate 24g

savoury cheese corn bread

makes 8 slices
preparation: 10 minutes
cooking: 20 minutes
suitable for freezing

125g (4oz) wholemeal flour
125g (4oz) cornflour
50g (2oz) cheese, grated
1 tbsp sugar
2 tsp baking powder
½ tsp salt
1 tsp dried chilli flakes
2 eggs
250ml (8fl oz) milk
2 tbsp sunflower oil

1 Place the flours, grated cheese, sugar, baking powder, salt and dried chilli flakes in a large bowl.

2 Beat the eggs with the milk in a jug, then add the oil. Add this to the dry ingredients and mix quickly.

3 Pour the mixture into a greased 20 x 20cm (8 x 8in) ovenproof dish and bake in a preheated oven, 200°C (400°F), Gas Mark 6, for 20 minutes, or until golden brown and firm to the touch.

4 Serve hot or warm, cut into slices or wedges.

nutritional breakdown per slice: kcal 200, kJ 844, protein 6g, fat 8g (saturated fat 2g), carbohydrate 28g

savoury cheese corn
bread left griddle
bread right

Entertaining

If you love food, it often follows that you enjoy making and sharing meals with other people. This is certainly one of the pleasures in my life. Entertaining can range from the simplest, casual supper of a plate of pasta and a glass of wine, to a full-blown formal meal with all the trimmings. This part of the book looks at a number of different special occasions, namely barbecues, picnics, buffets, and summer and winter dinner parties. Along with the recipes is a timetable that shows you what to prepare in advance. Although particular recipes have been highlighted here, there are numerous other recipes in the book that can be used for entertaining.

PLANNING AHEAD

Many meals, especially soups, stews and sauces, are better cooked the day before and reheated. Alternatively, use the freezer to get things prepared in advance. Don't forget that often, at least part of a recipe can be cooked ahead of time. For example, you could make the dressing for a salad, cook the rice, or make a filling for a pastry. When planning a menu, try to make sure you always offer a variety of ingredients, a choice of textures and a good range of colours, so that every part of the meal looks different.

FORMAL MEALS

At a formal dinner party, there is bound to be a fair amount of attention on the food, so it is worth planning the menu carefully. Apart from looking for variety, spend time thinking about how to present each part of the meal, and whether to have individually plated meals or a centrepiece. Both can look equally good. It is also necessary to leave yourself enough time for putting together small details such as garnishes and appropriate serving dishes.

INFORMAL MEALS

Don't feel that you have to stick to conventional ways of serving meals – a starter, main course and dessert. There is no reason why you cannot have a meal comprising several small dishes. The Middle Eastern mezze are a classic example of this – a large assortment of dishes are offered at once and everybody helps themselves. Alternatively, you can serve small dishes separately, so that each course becomes a taster in itself.

IMPROMPTU MEALS

Keep a well-stocked storecupboard for impromptu meals. Dishes based on grains or pasta are very easy to throw together. Or you could offer two or three tasty snacks supplemented with cheese, breads and bought-in pâté, such as hummus. During the summer, a barbecue, where you can cook to order, can also be fun.

wines

Matching wine and food should be fun, and if a food and wine combination you choose doesn't quite work as you expect, you can always eat and drink separately!

Before trying to link food with a suitable wine, spend time tasting wines on their own and learning to identify different characters and flavours. It may take years of experience and lots of tasting to absorb the complexities, but there are some basic things to look for. When tasting, pour a little wine into a large glass and swill it round. This will release the bouquet which may indicate the flavour. Does the wine smell spicy or flowery? Is it earthy or aromatic? When you sip it, take a mouthful and concentrate on both the initial flavour and the aftertaste. Is it powerful or light? Is it sweet or acidic? Zingy or lingering?

Look at the colour too. Is it a deep red or almost rose? Is it a clear white or a honey hue? Whilst colour and flavour have a more subtle relationship, getting to know the look of a wine may help you build up terms of reference as you start to work out what you like.

Once you have a vocabulary of flavour in your mind, try to think of wine as an ingredient that you are putting with your dish in just the same way that you have a cook's instinct for balancing texture or richness, or matching flavours, such as putting basil with tomato. When you discover a few wines that you like, you can start linking them with food.

First, consider the character of the dish. If your meal is robust and full of flavour, it will need a wine to match. Wines with plenty of flavour are described as full-bodied. This applies whether they are red or white. When looking for a full-bodied wine, remember that reds tend to have more body than whites, and wines from warmer climates such as Australia, South Africa, California, South America, Italy and Spain tend to have more colour, body and alcohol – in other words more weight. Labels on the wine bottles can also be very helpful. If your main dish is light and delicate, it should be partnered with wine of a similar character. Wines from cooler climates, such as New Zealand, Germany, much of France and the US Pacific Northwest, tend to have less colour, body and alcohol. The flavours of these wines are more subtle.

Secondly, think about the flavour influences in your dish. Is it redolent with herbs, hotly spiced, or aromatic? Is it characterised by earthy flavours, sweetness or acidity? Use your choice of wine to echo these qualities or act as a balancing ingredient. Spicy dishes can be matched with spicy wines such as Gewurztraminer from Alsace. Similarly, you could complement robust aromas by choosing an equally weighty wine such as Australian Shiraz or Californian Zinfandel. Flavours can also be used as a counter-balance, for example a crisp, acidic wine such as a Sauvignon Blanc from New Zealand will act as a foil for a rich, creamy dish.

Another good starting point is to serve wines from the region that inspired the dish. For example, the flavours of a Mediterranean tomato and herb dish would work well with a Hermitage from southern France.

Finally, consider the season and the time of day. Light wines are more suitable in the middle of the day (unless you plan a lengthy siesta) and your choice of wine will probably be different on hot, sunny days as opposed to icy cold winter days. Naturally, the food you choose to serve at these times is likely to vary as well. Cold food and light summery meals are good with crisp, light wines that are delicious chilled, for example a Riesling or a delicate Chardonnay from a cool climate. If you are expecting to be thirsty, it is probably wise to go for a wine with a lower alcohol content.

Red wine

Examples of full-bodied red wines include most New World Shiraz and Cabernet Sauvignon reds, southern French reds and many southern Spanish and Italian wines. Less weighty, but still substantial, reds embrace most red wines from Bordeaux, Burgundy and Chianti. Light-bodied reds feature Beaujolais and many from the Loire, as well as most reds from Alsace, Germany and the US Northwest. Spicy reds wines include Syrrah, South American Maalbec and Zinfandel.

White wine

For a full-bodied white, try an oak-aged Chardonnay or Semillon from the New World. For a medium-bodied white wine, try Australian Riesling, Pinot Blanc from Alsace, or Soave or Frascati from Italy. Light white wines that are made from Sauvignon Blanc, Riesling or local grape varieties can be found in the Loire, northern Italy, Switzerland, Germany, New Zealand, Washington State and England. New Zealand and the countries of northern Europe produce a number of delicate whites.

It is very helpful to go to informal wine-tastings offered by specialist wine merchants, because it gives you the opportunity to sample different varieties. It isn't true that vegetarian food automatically has to be paired with white wine! If you have personal favourites, that is fine, but if you want to branch out, give your palate time to develop. Above all, enjoy!

fruit punches

It is useful to have some tantalising non-alcoholic drinks to serve at parties and on special occasions. These drinks can be made from bought or freshly extracted juices. They are less intense than the pure fruit and vegetable juice recipes on page 138 as they use a significant amount of water.

cucumber and orange cooler with mint

cucumber and orange cooler with mint right pineapple punch left

serves 6
preparation: 5 minutes
cooking: none
v

1 cucumber
300ml (½ pint) orange juice
sprigs of mint
still or sparkling mineral water to taste
crushed ice, to serve

1 Set aside one-quarter of the cucumber. Peel the rest and place in a blender or food processor with the orange juice and blend until smooth.

2 Slice the remaining cucumber thinly and stir in. Add the sprigs of mint, then dilute to taste with mineral water. Chill well and serve poured over crushed ice.

nutritional breakdown per serving: kcal 20, kJ 90, protein 1g, fat 0g (saturated fat 0g), carbohydrate 5g

pineapple punch

This is delicious made with freshly extracted juices if you have a juicer, otherwise buy ready-made fruit juice and make the passion fruit juice by pressing the flesh through a sieve. You need only a small quantity but it does make a big difference to the overall flavour.

serves 6
preparation: 5 minutes, plus chilling
cooking: none
v

250ml (8fl oz) pineapple juice
250ml (8fl oz) apple juice
juice of 2 passion fruit
juice of 1 lemon
2 oranges
125g (4oz) raspberries

300ml (½ pint) sparkling mineral water or to taste
edible flowers or sprigs of mint or lemon balm

1 Mix together the pineapple, apple, passion fruit and lemon juices. Peel the oranges, then slice them thinly on a plate so that you retain all the juice. Add to the fruit juice with the raspberries and chill well.

2 Just before serving, stir in chilled sparkling mineral water to taste and garnish with edible flowers or sprigs of mint or lemon balm.

nutritional breakdown per serving: kcal 63, kJ 270, protein 1g, fat 0g (saturated fat 0g), carbohydrate 15g

barbecues

A barbecue is a lovely way to enjoy food and, if well organised, it should be a leisurely affair. When planning a barbecue menu, bear in mind that it is good to have either a couple of contrasting kebabs, or a kebab and a vegetable, such as the stuffed mushrooms on page 348.

If you intend serving platters of barbecued vegetables, have ready slices of baguette or warm pitta bread to add substance. Use ready-made vegetarian sausages and burgers to supplement the meal, as well as interesting breads and a variety of cheeses.

It is a good idea to have a choice of nibbles and snacks to keep your guests or family happy while the food is being cooked. Keep salads in a cool bag or the fridge until ready to serve.

preparation and equipment

Light a charcoal barbecue about 45 minutes before you want to start cooking. Don't start cooking until the flames have died down and the coals are glowing with a powdery grey surface. Make sure you have plenty of fuel; if you do need to top up the coals during the barbecue, put fresh coals around the sides rather than on top.

Vegetables that take up a fair amount of space will need to be cooked in batches unless you have an enormous cooking area. Wipe metal skewers with oil so that the food does not stick; soak wooden skewers in water for up to 30 minutes before use so that they don't scorch. Hand-held grills and hinged wire baskets are useful for holding odd-shaped vegetable pieces, as well as being an easy way to turn over batches of food. Long-handled tongs are also useful items. After your barbecue, leave everything to cool down before disposing of ashes and cleaning the grill.

barbecue safety

- Wear a thick protective apron and oven glove
- Do not use petrol, paraffin or white spirit to light the barbecue
- Do not leave a barbecue unattended
- Have ready a bucket of sand or soil in case of fire
- Do not leave picnic food in the sun
- All food that has been out of the fridge for several hours is best thrown away at the end of the party

menu

Tofu Kebabs

Haloumi, Sweet Onion and Apple Kebabs

Sweetcorn with Herb, Shallot and Olive Butter

Stuffed Mushrooms with Walnuts
and Sun-Dried Tomatoes

Sliced Aubergine with Yoghurt Dip

Mixed Vegetable Platter

tofu kebabs

Tofu is an excellent ingredient for a kebab. It provides a contrast to the vegetables, as well as adding nutrients. Here it is marinated in an Orient-inspired marinade.

makes 8

preparation: 15 minutes, plus marinating

cooking: 10 minutes

v

For the marinade:

juice of 1 lemon

2 tbsp dry sherry

2 tbsp shoyu or soy sauce

2 tbsp concentrated apple juice

1 tbsp sesame oil

2 garlic cloves, crushed

2.5cm (1in) piece of fresh root ginger, peeled and grated

1 chilli, deseeded and chopped

For the kebabs:

250g (8oz) tofu (bean curd), cut into bite-sized pieces

1kg (2lb) mixed vegetables (such as peppers, baby onions, mushrooms, cherry tomatoes, courgettes), chopped into bite sized pieces

1 Mix all the ingredients for the marinade together in a large bowl.

2 Mix the tofu and the vegetables carefully into the marinade and leave for at least 2 hours, and longer if possible.

3 Thread the pieces on to oiled metal or presoaked wooden skewers, alternating the tofu with pieces of vegetable.

4 Barbecue for several minutes so that the vegetables char and the tofu is heated right through. Brush on a little of the marinade residue while the kebabs are cooking.

nutritional breakdown per kebab: kcal 76, kJ 320, protein 5g, fat 3g (saturated fat 0g), carbohydrate 7g

haloumi, sweet onion and apple kebabs

Haloumi is a great cheese for barbecuing since it softens, rather than melts, and the heat of the cooking brings out its full flavour. It partners well with most vegetables and is mixed here with a sweet variety of onion and slices of apple.

makes 8

preparation: 10 minutes, plus marinating

cooking: 10 minutes

For the marinade:

4 tbsp olive oil

1 tbsp cider vinegar

1 garlic clove, crushed

1 tbsp wholegrain mustard

salt and freshly ground black pepper

For the kebabs:

500g (1lb) haloumi, cubed

3 sweet onions, each cut into 8 wedges

2 apples, each cut into 8 wedges

1 Whisk the marinade ingredients together in a bowl and season to taste. Add the cubes of haloumi and pieces of onion and apple. Leave for at least 1 hour.

2 Thread alternate pieces of cheese, onion and apple on to oiled metal or presoaked wooden skewers and barbecue until the vegetables brown slightly and the cheese is hot. Baste with a little more marinade and serve hot.

nutritional breakdown per kebab: kcal 270, kJ 1124, protein 14g, fat 21g (saturated fat 10g), carbohydrate 8g

sweetcorn with herb, shallot and olive butter

makes 4

preparation: 10 minutes

cooking: 15–20 minutes

125g (4oz) butter, softened
1 shallot, very finely chopped
25g (1oz) pitted olives, finely chopped
1 tbsp chopped thyme
juice of ½ lemon
4 corn on the cob
salt and freshly ground black pepper

1 Combine the softened butter with the shallot, olives and thyme in a small bowl, then mix in the lemon juice and chill well.

2 To cook the sweetcorn, either wrap the cobs in foil or roast in their husks on the barbecue for 15–20 minutes.

3 To serve, dot with the flavoured butter and a little seasoning.

nutritional breakdown per ½ cob: kcal 162, kJ 670, protein 2g, fat 14g (saturated fat 9g), carbohydrate 8g

stuffed mushrooms with walnuts and sun-dried tomatoes

Choose large flat mushrooms for this easy recipe.

serves 6–8

preparation: 10 minutes

cooking: 10–15 minutes

6–8 large flat mushrooms

For the filling:
75g (3oz) walnuts, roasted
8 large sun-dried tomatoes
1 tsp fennel seeds
3 spring onions, finely chopped
1 garlic clove, crushed
1–2 tbsp olive oil
salt and freshly ground black pepper

1 Place all the filling ingredients in a blender or food processor, reserving a little oil to coat the mushrooms, and blend to a coarse paste. Season well.

2 Wipe each mushroom with oil, then cover with the filling.

3 Place the mushrooms on the barbecue and cook for 10–15 minutes, or until really well done.

nutritional breakdown per serving (6 portions): kcal 246, kJ 1014, protein 3g, fat 25g (saturated fat 3g), carbohydrate 2g

sliced aubergine with yoghurt dip

Remove the seeds from the chilli unless you want a particularly fiery dip.

serves 4

preparation: 10 minutes

cooking: 10 minutes

250g (8oz) natural yoghurt
2 spring onions, finely chopped
1 mild green chilli, very finely chopped
½ tsp cardamom seeds, crushed
2 tbsp olive oil
1 large or 2 medium aubergines, thinly sliced
salt and freshly ground black pepper

1 Tip the yoghurt into a bowl and stir in the spring onions and chilli. Add the cardamom, season well and chill before serving.

2 Season the olive oil and use it to brush the slices of aubergine. Place under a preheated grill for 10 minutes, turning once, until well cooked.

3 Serve the aubergine slices garnished with spring onions, if desired, and hand the dip out separately.

nutritional breakdown per serving: kcal 114, kJ 475, protein 5g, fat 7g (saturated fat 1g), carbohydrate 10g

sliced aubergines with yoghurt dip above back **stuffed mushrooms with walnuts and sun-dried tomatoes** front

mixed vegetable platter

Huge platters of barbecued vegetables, redolent with colour and flavour, make a stunning presentation. Peppers and onions work particularly well, but many other vegetables are worth a try. Cook a contrasting mixture of vegetables each time so that there is a choice while waiting for the next batch. Before barbecuing vegetables, toss them in a well-seasoned oil or a special oil, such as walnut or chilli oil, which adds a lively flavour. Serve platters of vegetables with hot pitta bread or split barbecued baguettes, creamy cheese or roasted nuts.

Below are ways to prepare some of the most suitable vegetables for a barbecue.

Courgettes – look for sweet baby courgettes that you can simply trim and leave whole. Turn while cooking. Larger courgettes can be sliced into ovals or chunky sticks – don't cut them too fine or they shrivel to nothing.

Celery – this is best marinated before cooking (see below) as it can be rather dry. Trim individual sticks, then split them lengthways or cut diagonally.

Baby corn cobs – trim and leave whole if cooking for a platter with dips; otherwise cut across them in half for threading on to skewers, making it easier to turn.

Fennel – this can be quite dry, so marinate first (see below) or brush well with a good oil. Trim off the feathery tops and slice lengthways thinly or leave in quarters.

Mushrooms – button mushroom and small cup varieties can be left whole and are good for kebabs. Alternatively, field mushrooms can also be thickly sliced and cooked and added to vegetable platters or served with dips. They are very good stuffed (see page 348).

Onion – use both the red and the sweet onion as they are milder and delicious when barbecued. Trim away the root leaving enough so that the layers of the onion do not fall apart. Then cut into 8 wedges.

Peppers – The three sweeter peppers – red, orange and yellow – work very well, while the green variety can be bitter. Remove the seeds, then cut into halves or quarters. For kebabs it is best to use chunks or slices.

Potatoes – these don't barbecue as such, but if you have a decent supply of charcoal, you can wrap them in foil and bake among the coals. My tip is always cook one extra since inevitably one seems to get lost in the fire!

Corn on the cob – like potatoes, corn cobs can also be roasted very successfully among the coals. They take about 20 minutes and taste great – even the burnt bits!

Squash and sweet potato – these can be barbecued but need to be cut into quite small chunks and cooked over a slow fire if possible. They are particularly good for adding colour contrast to kebabs.

FOIL WRAPPED

Some vegetables are best barbecued in foil. For large tomatoes, halve them, season with salt and pepper, a little balsamic vinegar and basil. Wrap in foil and cook for about 10 minutes. New potatoes can be wrapped in foil with butter and garlic cloves. Cook for about 20 minutes and sprinkle with snipped chives to serve.

BARBECUED FRUIT

Barbecued fruit can be served as a separate course or mixed with vegetables and served as kebabs or on a platter. Brush fruit with lemon juice or lemon and honey, or add to a savoury marinade before barbecuing. Serve with yoghurt, cream or silken tofu for a sweet course. The following fruits barbecue well: apricots, nectarines, peaches, pineapples, apples and pears.

vegetable marinade

Use this marinade with barbecued vegetables (see above).

Sufficient for about 1kg (2lb) vegetables; serves 8

preparation: 5 minutes

cooking: none

v

150ml (¼ pint) olive oil
50ml (2fl oz) red wine vinegar
1–2 tbsp balsamic vinegar
juice of ½ lemon
1 tsp grated lemon zest
1 tbsp chopped rosemary
1 tbsp chopped oregano
4 garlic cloves, thinly sliced
salt and freshly ground black pepper

1 Mix all the ingredients for the marinade together in a bowl. Season well.

To marinate vegetables, stir in the chosen vegetable pieces, cover and leave for 1–2 hours. Spread out on the barbecue and cook well, turning during the cooking.

To serve with hot pitta bread, split open the pitta, brush with a little marinade and sprinkle with some crumbled cheese or freshly grated Parmesan. Warm the bread through on the grill then fill with vegetables, adding extra grated cheese.

nutritional breakdown per serving (not including vegetables):
kcal 126, k 517, protein 0g, fat 14g (saturated fat 2g),
carbohydrate 7g

picnics

Picnics can range from the elegant to the robust, depending on the circumstances and what is required. In this section you'll find a variety of ideas for dishes that will travel well and benefit from standing, from classic Cheese and Potato Pasties to more exotic fare such as Stuffed Vine Leaves with Spiced Bulgar. For an ideal picnic dessert try the juicy Blueberry Summer Pudding.

menu

Onion Plait with Mustard Seeds

Watercress Roulade with Asparagus and Crème Fraîche

Cheese and Potato Pasties

Blueberry Summer Pudding

Other recipes that make good picnic fare:

Avocado Gazpacho
(see page 143)

Poached Vegetables
with Herbs and Wine
(see page 162)

Roasted Aubergine
and Garlic Dip
(see page 167)

Hummus
(see page 167)

Kuku with Spinach
(see page 181)

Leek and Feta Parcels
(see page 260)

Beetroot and Green
Bean Salad with
Couscous
(see page 300)

Greek Potato Salad
(see page 301)

Red Cabbage and
Black Grape Salad
with Orange
(see page 311)

Vinaigrette
(see page 311)

Classic Rich Fruit
Cake (see page 321)

Pistachio Cake
(see page 324)

onion plait with mustard seeds

This lightly textured bread has a gorgeous aroma and is delicious with a soft or semi-soft cheese, such as goat's cheese or Brie.

. makes 10–12 slices

preparation: 15 minutes, plus rising and proving

cooking: 35–40 minutes

suitable for freezing

𝑣

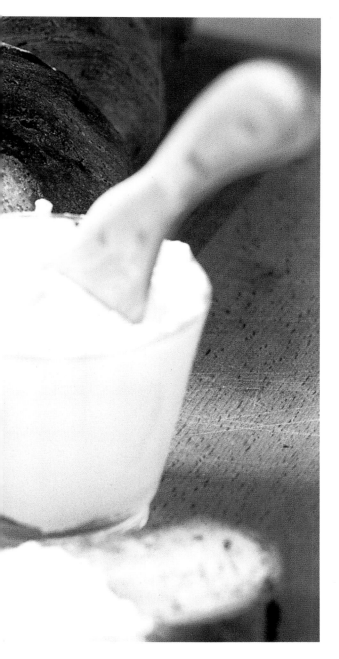

2 tbsp olive oil

1 tbsp black mustard seeds

200g (7oz) onion, finely chopped

400g (13oz) strong white flour, plus extra for dusting

100g (3½oz) wholemeal flour

7g (¼oz) sachet easy-blend yeast

1 tbsp muscovado sugar

1 tsp salt

300ml (½ pint) warm water

1 Heat the oil in a frying pan and gently fry the mustard seeds for 1 minute. Add the onion and fry until well cooked and coloured. Leave to cool.

2 Place the flours, yeast, sugar and salt in a large bowl and pour in the warm water.

3 Add the onion mixture and draw the ingredients into a dough. Add more water if necessary. Knead on a lightly floured surface for at least 5 minutes, so that the dough becomes smooth and elastic.

4 Return the dough to a clean bowl and cover with clingfilm or a damp tea towel. Leave to rise in a warm place until the dough has doubled in size.

5 Again working on a lightly floured surface, knock the air out of the dough and knead again briefly, then divide into 3 equal pieces. Roll out each piece into a sausage shape, roughly 25cm (10in) long. Lay the lengths side by side and plait together, pinching the pieces together at each end of the plait.

6 Place the plait on a baking sheet and cover with clingfilm. Leave to prove until roughly doubled in size.

7 Bake in a preheated oven, 220° (425°F), Gas Mark 7, for 30–35 minutes, or until cooked – it should sound hollow when tapped on the base.

8 Turn the loaf over and cook for a further 3 minutes to crisp the base. Leave to cool on a wire rack.

> ### PLAITING A LOAF
>
> When plaiting a loaf it is best to start the plait in the middle and then plait towards either end as this will make the plait more even, and avoids stretching the dough too much (see page 336).

nutritional breakdown per slice: kcal 206, kJ 874, protein 7g, fat 3g (saturated fat 0g), carbohydrate 40g

watercress roulade with asparagus and crème fraîche

This impressive dish makes a welcome alternative to pastry-based savouries and will travel well if properly wrapped. It will keep in the fridge for 24 hours.

serves 4
preparation: 20 minutes
cooking: 12–15 minutes
Ⓒₐ

200g (7oz) watercress or 100g (3½oz)
  watercress and 100g (3½oz) rocket
5 eggs, separated
50g (2oz) fresh Parmesan, grated
freshly grated nutmeg
125g (4oz) asparagus
3 spring onions, finely chopped

125g (4oz) crème fraîche
salt and freshly ground black pepper
fresh watercress and Parmesan shavings,
  to garnish, optional

1   Place the watercress, and rocket if using a combination of both, in a bowl and cover with boiling water. Leave for 30 seconds then drain. Squeeze dry and chop very finely.

2   Beat the egg yolks in a bowl with the watercress and grated Parmesan. Grate over some nutmeg and season well.

3   Whisk the egg whites in another bowl until they stand in soft peaks.

4 Stir 1 tablespoon of egg white into the egg yolk mixture, then gently fold in the remaining egg whites.

5 Spoon the mixture into a lined, 23 x 33cm (9 x 13in) Swiss roll tin. Shake slightly to even out the mixture.

6 Bake in a preheated oven, 200°C (400°F), Gas Mark 6, for 12–15 minutes, or until just firm. Turn out on to a sheet of baking parchment and leave to cool.

7 Meanwhile, to make the filling, steam the asparagus over a saucepan of boiling water for 5 minutes, or until just tender. Drain and chop finely. Place in a bowl.

8 Stir in the spring onions, then the crème fraîche. Season well.

9 Spread the filling over the roulade. To roll it up, start by folding in one short edge of the roulade, then use the baking parchment to help you ease it into a roll.

10 Wrap the roulade in clingfilm for travelling. Serve garnished with watercress and shavings of Parmesan, if desired.

nutritional breakdown per serving: kcal 310, kJ 1288, protein 16g, fat 24g (saturated fat 13g), carbohydrate 7g

cheese and potato pasties

GLAZING

To give the pasties a glaze, use an egg wash. Beat 1 egg yolk with 1 tablespoon water and a little salt. Brush over the pasties before baking.

These are great for a picnic or outdoor meal, full of flavour and very satisfying – perhaps a reward for a long distance walk! Serve on their own or, if you have plates and cutlery, add a salad or two to provide colour.

makes 6

preparation: 20 minutes, plus pastry making

cooking: 30–35 minutes

suitable for freezing

250g (8oz) potato, roughly chopped
250g (8oz) squash or swede, roughly chopped
25g (1oz) butter
1 onion, finely chopped
3 tbsp chopped parsley
100g (3½oz) cheese, grated
1 tsp Dijon mustard
1 quantity Quick Flaky Pastry (see page 256)
flour for dusting
salt and freshly ground black pepper

1 Cook the potato and squash or swede in a saucepan of boiling salted water for 10–15 minutes until soft. Drain and set aside.

2 Meanwhile, melt the butter in a large saucepan and fry the onion for 10 minutes until soft and lightly browned. Remove from the heat.

3 Mash the cooked vegetables with the onion and all the residue of butter. Add the parsley, grated cheese and mustard and mix well. Season to taste.

4 Roll out the pastry on a lightly floured surface and cut into 6 rounds that are 18cm (7in) in diameter.

5 Put a portion of the cheesy vegetable filling on each round. Moisten the edges with cold water, then fold over each piece to make a semi-circle and crimp the edges together.

6 Place the pasties on a baking sheet and prick with a fork. Bake in a preheated oven, 220°C (425°F), Gas Mark 7, for 20 minutes, or until golden brown.

nutritional breakdown per serving: kcal 480, kJ 2000, protein 10g, fat 31g (saturated fat 15g), carbohydrate 42g

VARIATION

Other vegetables can be added to pasties, for example carrots, parsnips or beetroot. You could also add a few cooked beans or lentils to make a very hearty filling.

blueberry summer pudding

Ideal for using soft summer fruits, this easy colourful pudding makes a good picnic or buffet dish. All manner of berries can be used but blueberries add a light clean flavour. Make this recipe in a glass bowl so that you can check on how well the juices are soaking into the bread. Turn out the pudding only when you arrive at the picnic.

serves 6

preparation: 20 minutes, plus standing

cooking: 3–4 minutes

400g (13oz) blueberries
400g (13oz) raspberries or strawberries
200g (7oz) redcurrants
150g (5oz) caster sugar
1 medium loaf (white or soft brown bread)
extra fruit and cream, to serve, optional

1 Place the fruit in a large saucepan and sprinkle with the sugar.

2 Heat the fruit for 3–4 minutes until the juices begin to run, then leave to cool.

3 Cut the loaf into slices and remove the crusts. Cut a small disc of bread to fit the bottom of a 1.2 litre (2 pint) pudding basin. Line the sides of the basin with more slices of bread, reserving a few slices to cover the top.

4 Pile all the fruit into the centre of the bread-lined basin and pour the juices over the top.

5 Place the reserved bread on top of the fruit, trimming to fit. Cover with a plate that just fits inside the basin and put a 1kg (2lb) weight on top so that the fruit is pressed down and the juices are pressed into the bread. Leave to stand overnight in a cool place – it is best to stand the basin on a tray to collect any juice that may ooze out.

6 Turn the pudding out just before serving and serve with extra fruit and cream, if desired.

nutritional breakdown per serving: kcal 348, kJ 1484, protein 9g, fat 2g (saturated fat 0g), carbohydrate 79g

buffet for 12

This is a cold buffet with plenty of variety in terms of texture, colour and flavour. You can add extra savouries according to the number of people for whom you are catering. For dairy-free savoury alternatives, serve a Saffron Onion Pizza (see page 198) and Spiced Hazelnut and Quinoa Bake (see page 267). Substantial salads, such as Marinated Bean Salad (see page 298) and Spiced Rice Salad (see page 304) are also good for buffets and have the advantage that they can be prepared well ahead.

suggested timetable

One or two days before:
Make the filling for the vine leaves and store in a container in the refrigerator. Make the filling for the filo triangles and store in a container in the refrigerator.

The day before:
Fill and cook the vine leaves.
Make the vegetable terrine and chill.

On the day:
Make the galette.
Assemble the filo triangles and cook.

menu

Stuffed Vine Leaves with Spiced Bulgar

Mediterranean Galette

Layered Vegetable Terrine

Red Pepper and Parmesan Filo Triangles

Choice of salads

---

mediterranean galette opposite back
stuffed vine leaves with spiced bulgar opposite front

mediterranean galette

This tasty galette is baked in the oven rather than fried and flipped over in the classic manner. It is certainly more foolproof when prepared in this way. As with all egg dishes, be bold with the flavouring so that the finished dish is not bland. The galette can be served hot but I think the flavours are more evident once the dish is cool.

serves 12
preparation: 10 minutes
cooking: 40 minutes

2 tbsp olive oil
1 onion, finely chopped
1 garlic clove, crushed
3 courgettes, sliced
1 red pepper, cored, deseeded and chopped
300g (10oz) broad beans (shelled weight), steamed or boiled until just tender
6 eggs
150g (5oz) cream cheese
1 tsp dried thyme
2 tbsp chopped basil
2 tbsp freshly grated Parmesan
salt and freshly ground black pepper

1 Heat the oil in a saucepan and fry the onion and garlic until soft. Add the courgettes and red pepper and cook for 4–5 minutes, then add the cooked broad beans and stir well. Remove the pan from the heat.

2 Lightly mix the eggs in a large bowl with the cream cheese and herbs. Season well. Stir in the cooked vegetables, then pour the mixture into a lightly buttered ovenproof dish.

3 Dust with the freshly grated Parmesan and bake in a preheated oven, 190°C (375°F), Gas Mark 5, for 30 minutes, or until well browned and firm in the centre. Leave to cool.

4 Cut the galette into wedges or slices and serve at room temperature.

nutritional breakdown per serving: kcal 148, kJ 616, protein 7g, fat 11g (saturated fat 5g), carbohydrate 5g

stuffed vine leaves with spiced bulgar

Vine leaves stuffed with bulgar or rice make pretty packages that look good as part of a buffet spread. This filling is lightly fruited with apricot. Tiny currants are good, too, as well as versions that use just herbs. Make a meal of these by serving them with a bowl of natural yoghurt and a crisp salad.

makes 50
preparation: 25 minutes
cooking: 45–50 minutes
𝓋

50 vine leaves
juice of 1 lemon
2 tbsp olive oil
2 tbsp chopped mint, to garnish
natural yoghurt and wedges of lemon, to serve

For the filling:
1 tbsp olive oil
1 onion, very finely chopped
½ tsp ground cinnamon
½ tsp ground turmeric
50g (2oz) dried apricots, sliced
75g (3oz) pine nuts
125g (4oz) bulgar
450ml (¾ pint) Vegetable Stock (see page 144)
  or water
2 tbsp chopped mint
salt and freshly ground black pepper

1 To make the filling, heat the olive oil in a saucepan and cook the onion for 10 minutes over a very gentle heat until it is really soft. Add the ground spices and cook for 2–3 minutes, then add the apricots, pine nuts and bulgar and mix well.

2 Pour in 300ml (½ pint) of the stock, bring to the boil and simmer for 5 minutes. The bulgar will still be firm at this stage. There may also be some liquid left in the pan but this will probably be absorbed on standing. Stir in the mint and season well.

3 Rinse the vine leaves if using brine-packed ones and cut off the stalks. Put a dessertspoonful of filling on each leaf, tuck in the sides and roll up.

4 Arrange the stuffed leaves in the base of a deep ovenproof dish, seam sides down. When the first layer of vine leaf parcels is completed, cover with more layers of parcels until all the leaves and filling

are used. Pour over the remaining stock with the lemon juice and olive oil.

5 Cover and bake in a preheated oven, 180°C (350°F), Gas Mark 4, for 30 minutes. Leave to cool.

6 Remove the parcels from the dish using a slotted spoon and serve at room temperature, garnished with mint and accompanied by natural yoghurt and wedges of lemon.

nutritional breakdown per stuffed vine leaf: kcal 29, kJ 120, protein 1g, fat 2g (saturated fat 0g), carbohydrate 3g

USING FRESH VINE LEAVES

If using fresh vine leaves, blanch them in boiling water for 1 minute, then refresh in cold water and drain. This process makes them pliable.

layered vegetable terrine

A beautiful concoction of layered vegetable purées, which is baked until set, then served, thinly sliced, for an elegant addition to a buffet. Although there is much work involved in the preparation, it can all be done well ahead of time, leaving a simple assembly. This recipe will also serve 6–8 people as a starter for a special meal.

serves 12

preparation: 30 minutes

cooking: about 1 hour

suitable for freezing

500g (1lb) carrots, chopped
500g (1lb) fennel, chopped
500g (1lb) spinach, chopped
6 eggs
6–8 tbsp double cream
salt and freshly ground black pepper

1 Cook the carrots in a saucepan of boiling water for 15–20 minutes, or until soft. Drain well and leave to cool.

2 Meanwhile, cook the fennel in another saucepan of boiling water for 15–20 minutes, or until soft. Drain well and leave to cool.

3 Steam the spinach in its own juices for 3–4 minutes, or until the leaves have wilted. Drain well and then leave to cool.

4 Place the cooked carrots in a blender or food processor and purée until smooth, adding 2 eggs and 3 tablespoons cream. Season well, remove from the blender and set aside.

5 In the same way, purée the fennel in the rinsed blender or food processor until smooth, again adding 2 eggs and 3 tablespoons cream. Season well and set aside.

6 Lastly, again using the rinsed blender or food processor, purée the spinach until smooth, adding 2 eggs. Season well.

7 Prepare a deep 900–1200ml (1½–2 pint) loaf tin by lining it with baking parchment. Place one-third of the carrot purée in the base, cover with one-third of fennel purée, then one-third of spinach purée. Repeat the layering to give 3 layers of each purée, finishing with the spinach.

8 Bake in a preheated oven, 180°C (350°F), Gas Mark 4, for 35–45 minutes, or until the terrine feels firm to the touch. Leave to cool in the tin, then lift out and transfer to a serving plate. For a buffet it is preferable to serve the terrine already sliced as it can be tricky for your guests to do – use a very sharp knife.

nutritional breakdown per serving: kcal 146, kJ 604, protein 5g, fat 11g (saturated fat 6g), carbohydrate 6g

red pepper and parmesan filo triangles

Savoury parcels and packages make simple, quick meals and filo pastry is an ideal wrapping. Be liberal with the brushed oil and butter or the end result will be papery and dry. As for fillings, almost any vegetable, nut or cheese combination can be used – especially tasty leftovers – just choose something that is not too sloppy.

makes 24 small triangles
preparation: 15 minutes
cooking: 40–45 minutes
suitable for freezing

For the filling:
4 large red peppers, lightly oiled
200g (7oz) sun-dried tomatoes
4–6 tbsp freshly grated Parmesan
salt and freshly ground black pepper

For the triangles:
24 sheets filo pastry
50–75g (2–3oz) butter, melted
3–4 tbsp olive oil

1 To make the filling, place the peppers in a roasting tin and place in a preheated oven, 200°C (400°F), Gas Mark 6, for 20–25 minutes, or until well charred.

2 Leave the peppers until cool enough to handle, then remove the skins and seeds. Do not wash them.

3 Chop the peppers roughly and place in a blender or food processor with the tomatoes and Parmesan. Blend to make a coarse paste. Season well.

4 To make the triangles, work with 1 sheet of filo pastry at a time. Take a sheet and brush well with a mixture of melted butter and olive oil. Fold lengthways to make a strip and brush again with the melted butter and oil mixture.

5 Place a dessertspoonful of filling on one end of the strip. Fold the end over at an angle to cover the filling and make a triangular shape. Continue folding the pastry over the filling, always keeping the triangle shape, until the pastry strip is rolled up. Brush well with more melted butter and oil.

6 Repeat the process with the remaining sheets of pastry and filling.

7 Place the triangles on a lightly greased baking sheet and bake in a preheated oven, 200°C (400°F), Gas Mark 6, for 20 minutes, or until crisp. Serve warm or at room temperature.

nutritional breakdown per 'triangle': kcal 190, kJ 798, protein 5g, fat 9g (saturated fat 3g), carbohydrate 24g

VARIATION

For a dairy-free option, substitute pitted black olives for the Parmesan cheese in the filling and use olive oil only to brush the filo pastry. It gives the pastry a slightly drier finish but is still very appetising.

finger food buffet for 16

Finger food is great for entertaining. Plan a selection of ideas, some of which you can make in advance. Choose a range of textures and lay the savouries on large trays and garnish with fresh fruit and vegetables. For 16 people allow about 6–8 different items. Double quantities as necessary and supplement with some of the additional suggestions, right.

suggested timetable

One or two days before:
Make the bruschetta bases and store in an airtight container.
Roast the almonds and store in an airtight container.

The day before:
Make spiced new potatoes and dip; cover and refrigerate.

Prepare toppings for bruschetta and store in an airtight container in the refrigerator.

On the day:
Assemble the bruschetta.
Make the tartlets.

menu

Asparagus Tartlets

Spiced New Potatoes with Sharp Cream Dip

Roasted Almonds with Shoyu

Bruschetta with Fresh Tomato and Basil

Bruschetta with Roasted Walnuts and Black Olives

Other finger food savouries could include:
Savoury Choux with Avocado and Pesto
(see page 164)
Dips with Crudités (see page 166–67)
Falafel (vegan) (see page 174)
Baked Tofu and Button Mushrooms (vegan)
(see page 175)

asparagus tartlets

These little tartlets with their rich pastry base make mouthwatering savouries.

makes 36

preparation: 15 minutes, plus pastry making

cooking: 25–30 minutes

suitable for freezing

2 x quantity Enriched Shortcrust Pastry (see page 254)
flour for dusting

For the filling:
50g (2oz) butter
4 shallots, finely chopped
500g (1lb) asparagus, roughly chopped
4 tbsp white wine
250ml (8fl oz) double cream
4 eggs, beaten
2 tbsp chopped tarragon
salt and freshly ground black pepper

1 To make the filling, melt the butter in a saucepan and cook the shallots over a gentle heat until translucent. Add the asparagus and cook for several minutes until beginning to soften.

2 Add the wine to the pan, increase the heat and cook until the liquid has reduced, then remove the pan from the heat.

3 Mix the cream, eggs and tarragon together in a bowl, and season well.

4 Roll out the chilled pastry on a lightly floured surface to fill 36 individual tartlet tins. Arrange pieces of cooked asparagus and shallot in each case. Pour over the cream and egg mixture.

5 Bake the tartlets in a preheated oven, 200°C (400°F), Gas Mark 6, for 15–20 minutes, or until firm to touch. Serve warm or at room temperature.

nutritional breakdown per tartlet: kcal 138, kJ 573, protein 3g, fat 10g (saturated fat 6g), carbohydrate 9g

spiced new potatoes with sharp cream dip
opposite top and right

asparagus tartlets
opposite bottom

spiced new potatoes with sharp cream dip

These flavoursome potatoes make a substantial appetiser for a finger food party. As they cook they take on a gorgeous rusty glow from the mixture of tomato purée and red wine vinegar, as well as absorbing the spices and herbs. Prepare well ahead so that the flavours develop.

serves 16

preparation: 10 minutes

cooking: about 1 hour

𝒱 (excluding dip)

50ml (2fl oz) sunflower or olive oil
750g (1½lb) baby new potatoes
1 tbsp red wine vinegar
2 garlic cloves, crushed
1 tbsp tomato purée
150ml (¼ pint) Vegetable Stock (see page 144)
  or water
1 medium hot chilli, chopped
1 tsp ground cumin
1 sprig thyme
salt and freshly ground black pepper

For the dip:
200g (7oz) soured cream
3 tbsp chopped herbs (chives, parsley or tarragon)
1 spring onion, finely chopped
1 garlic clove, crushed
1 tsp cider vinegar
salt and freshly ground black pepper

1 Heat the oil in a large frying pan and fry the potatoes, in batches if necessary, until lightly browned. Use more oil if required. Remove from the pan and place in an ovenproof dish.

2 Mix together in a jug the red wine vinegar, garlic, tomato purée, stock, chilli, cumin and thyme. Season well and pour over the potatoes. Add a little water if necessary.

3 Bake in a preheated oven, 190°C (375°F), Gas Mark 5, for 35–40 minutes until tender. Turn the potatoes once or twice during the cooking. Leave to cool in the dish.

4 To make the dip, blend everything together in a small blender or food processor until you have a very smooth consistency. Season to taste. Serve the potatoes at room temperature with the soured cream dip in a separate bowl.

VARIATION

For a dairy-free version of this recipe, replace the soured cream with tofu. Blend the tofu with 6–8 tablespoons water so that it has the consistency of natural yoghurt. Then add 1–2 tablespoons sunflower or olive oil to the dip to give it a creamy texture.

nutritional breakdown per serving: kcal 84, kJ 350, protein 1g, fat 5g (saturated fat 2g), carbohydrate 8g

OUT OF SEASON

When new potatoes are not in season, make this recipe using larger potatoes, cut into bite-sized wedges.

roasted almonds with shoyu

Roasted almonds make a delicious nibble. They can also be tossed in spices, such as cumin or paprika, as well as coarse rock salt and ground pepper, straight after cooking.

serves 16
preparation: 2 minutes
cooking: 40 minutes

500g (1lb) whole blanched almonds
2–3 tbsp shoyu or soy sauce

1 Roast the almonds in a preheated oven, 150°C (300°F), Gas Mark 2, for 30 minutes or until they are light brown.

2 Sprinkle with the shoyu or soy sauce and roast again for 10 minutes more.

3 Leave to cool. Keep in airtight jars.

nutritional breakdown per serving: kcal 193, kJ 799, protein 7g, fat 17g (saturated fat 2g), carbohydrate 2g

bruschetta

Bruschetta are toasted slices of ciabatta or focaccia topped with a variety of flavourings. They make very simple snacks and great nibbles prior to a meal. You can obviously vary the toppings to fit in with whatever else you are serving. Wholemeal bruschetta take longer to bake.

makes 16
preparation: 5 minutes
cooking: 10 minutes
𝓋

1 ciabatta loaf or baguette, cut into 16 slices
2–3 tbsp olive oil and 1–2 garlic cloves, peeled and halved, or 2–3 tbsp Garlic Oil (see page 196)
2–3 tbsp freshly grated Parmesan, optional

1 Arrange the slices of bread in a single layer on a baking sheet and bake in a preheated oven, 200°C (400°F), Gas Mark 6, for 5–7 minutes.

2 Rub the surfaces with garlic, then brush with olive oil. Alternatively, brush liberally with garlic oil.

3 If using Parmesan, sprinkle the bruschetta with a little cheese and bake again briefly. Serve as they are or topped with one of the toppings given below.

nutritional breakdown per bruschetta with tomato and basil topping (without Parmesan): kcal 90, kJ 380, protein 3g, fat 3g (saturated fat 1g), carbohydrate 13g

fresh tomato and basil topping

This topping is good on toast baked with Parmesan cheese.

sufficient for 16 bruschetta
preparation: 15 minutes
cooking: none
𝓋

1kg (2lb) tomatoes, skinned and finely chopped
2 garlic cloves, crushed
1 shallot, finely chopped
3–4 tbsp chopped basil leaves
1–2 tbsp olive oil
salt and freshly ground black pepper

1 Mix the finely chopped tomatoes with the crushed garlic, shallot and basil leaves. Season well and sprinkle over the olive oil.

2 Pile the topping on top of the bruschetta toasts just before serving.

nutritional breakdown for whole recipe: kcal 339, kJ 1426, protein 8g, fat 19g (saturated fat 3g), carbohydrate 37g

roasted walnut and black olive topping

For a lively extra to this nibble, you can add some flakes of dried chilli to the topping.

sufficient for 16 bruschetta

preparation: 10 minutes

cooking: 5 minutes

125g (4oz) walnut pieces
2 tbsp white wine vinegar
1 garlic clove
4–6 tbsp olive oil
2 tbsp chopped parsley
1 green pepper, cored, deseeded and
  finely chopped
300g (10oz) pitted black olives, finely chopped
salt and freshly ground black pepper

1 Roast the walnuts in a preheated oven, 200°C (400°F), Gas Mark 6, for 4–5 minutes, or until well browned. Leave to cool, then chop finely and place in a blender or food processor.

2 Add the wine vinegar and garlic to the nuts and grind the ingredients to a paste. With the motor running, pour in the oil in a thin steady stream.

3 When thoroughly blended, scrape the walnut mixture into a clean bowl. Mix in the parsley, chopped green pepper and 250g (8oz) of the finely chopped olives. Season to taste.

4 Pile the topping on top of bruschetta toasts just before serving. Garnish with the remaining black olives.

nutritional breakdown per serving: kcal 106, kJ 436, protein 1g, fat 11g (saturated fat 1g), carbohydrate 1g

bruschetta with fresh tomato and basil topping left **walnut and black olive topping** right

QUICK AVOCADO TOPPING

Avocado also makes a great topping for bruschetta. Mash the flesh of one avocado with some crème fraîche, chopped coriander leaves and lime juice. Season well and pile it on bruschetta just before serving.

summer dinner party for 8

This pretty meal, bursting with colour, captures the essence of summer. Start with a light but tangy goat's cheese soufflé, impress with a glossy tarte tatin full of roasted Mediterranean vegetables and end with glistening nectarines and refreshing raspberry coulis. An added bonus is that this dinner party really is stress-free entertaining – most of the preparation for the meal can be done in advance, and all you need to do on the evening is relax and enjoy yourself.

suggested timetable

Several days before:
Make the Mascarpone and Amaretti Ice
Make the pesto
Roast the almonds (optional)
Make the Falafel and freeze (optional)

Two days before:
Make the tomato sauce for the soufflés
Prepare the raspberry coulis
Make the vinaigrette

The day before:
Make the soufflés and chill
Make the flaky pastry and chill

On the day:
Finish the tarte tatin
Assemble the soufflés ready for reheating
Prepare the nectarines
Make the salad
Make sure the cheese has time to come to room temperature
Fry the falafel (optional)

menu

Appetizers (optional) – Roasted Almonds with Shoyu
(see page 364) or miniature Falafel with yoghurt
(see page 174)

Twice-Baked Goat's Cheese Soufflés with Tomato Sauce and
Walnuts

Tarte Tatin with Roasted Mediterranean Vegetables

New Potatoes with Pesto
(or Avocado and Pistachio Salad, see page 307)

Garden Salad with Green Olive Dressing

Bowl of cherry tomatoes

Grilled Nectarines with Fresh Raspberry Coulis

Mascarpone and Amaretti Ice

Cheese and biscuits (I suggest a blue and a hard cheese
with a good tang)

twice baked goat's cheese soufflés with tomato sauce and walnuts

Choose a well-flavoured goat's cheese so that the tang comes through. You could also use Gruyère or fontina instead. Twice-baked soufflés are prepared in the same way as regular soufflés, except they are baked in small dishes such as ramekins or tea cups. Leave them to cool completely in the dish, then chill them. Don't worry that they collapse at this stage. When required, heat them in the chosen sauce. They will puff up a little and make a tasty light starter.

serves 8

preparation: 25 minutes

cooking: about 1 hour

suitable for freezing (tomato sauce only)

50g (2oz) butter
50g (2oz) plain flour
250ml (8fl oz) milk
200g (7oz) well-flavoured soft goat's
 cheese, crumbled
4 large eggs, separated
2 tbsp chopped walnut pieces
2 tbsp freshly grated Parmesan
salt and freshly ground black pepper
garnish of green salad leaves, to serve

For the tomato sauce:
1 tbsp olive oil
1 onion, chopped
1 garlic clove, chopped
800g (1lb 10oz) canned chopped tomatoes
 or passata
1 bay leaf
1 tsp dried thyme
½ tsp granulated sugar
1–2 tbsp walnut oil
salt and freshly ground black pepper

1 Lightly grease 8 ramekin dishes or tea cups. Line the base of each with a small piece of baking parchment.

2 Melt the butter in a small saucepan. Stir in the flour to make a roux and cook for 1 minute. Add the milk gradually and, stirring constantly, bring the sauce to the boil and simmer for 2–3 minutes – it should be very thick. Season well and add the goat's cheese.

3 Stir the egg yolks into the goat's cheese sauce.

4 Whisk the egg whites in a large bowl until stiff. Stir 1 tablespoon of egg white into the cheese sauce. Then fold in the remaining egg white, using a metal spoon.

5 Spoon the mixture into the prepared ramekins and bake in a preheated oven, 200°C (400°F), Gas Mark 6, for 15 minutes. Leave to cool completely, then remove from the moulds and chill until required.

6 To make the tomato sauce, heat the oil in a saucepan and gently cook the onion and garlic until translucent.

7 Pour in the canned chopped tomatoes or passata and add the bay leaf, thyme, sugar and ½ teaspoon salt. Bring to the boil and simmer, covered, for 20 minutes.

8 Meanwhile, spread the walnut pieces on a baking sheet and roast at 200°C (400°F), Gas Mark 6, for 4–5 minutes. Set aside.

9 Leave the tomato sauce to cool, remove the bay leaf and then, using a blender or food processor, blend until smooth, adding the walnut oil and a little seasoning.

10 To assemble, place the soufflés in a greased ovenproof dish and cover with tomato sauce, reserving about 200ml (7fl oz). Sprinkle with grated Parmesan, then bake at 200°C (400°F), Gas Mark 6, for 15 minutes.

11 To serve, heat the reserved tomato sauce gently. Spoon a couple of tablespoons of sauce on each plate and place a soufflé in the centre. Sprinkle over a few roasted walnuts and serve hot with a garnish of green salad leaves.

nutritional breakdown per serving: kcal 293, kJ 1219, protein 11g, fat 23g (saturated fat 8g), carbohydrate 11g

tarte tatin with roasted mediterranean vegetables

This classic pie is baked with the crust on top, then turned upside down to serve. The end result is a light base topped with a mouthwatering selection of dark glazed vegetables. Use either flaky pastry or shortcrust for the base. You can simply lay the pastry straight over the roasted vegetables but I think it is safer to line a clean dish with baking parchment so that you can be sure the pie will turn out. This pie is also great as a picnic dish; vary the vegetables to suit and serve it with Avocado and Pistachio Salad (see page 307). For more information on making pastry, see pages 252–58.

serves 8

preparation: 45 minutes, plus chilling and standing

cooking: about 1 hour

𝑣

For the pastry:
250g (8oz) plain flour, plus extra for dusting
½ tsp salt
150g (5oz) butter, solid vegetable fat or a
  mixture, frozen for 30 minutes before using
1 tbsp lemon juice
8–9 tbsp ice-cold water

For the filling:
1 large red pepper, cored, deseeded and
  sliced lengthways
1 large yellow pepper, cored, deseeded and
  sliced lengthways
1 aubergine, cubed
1 red onion, sliced
3–4 tbsp olive oil
1 tbsp balsamic vinegar
salt and freshly ground black pepper

1 To make the pastry, sift the flour and salt into
   a large bowl.

2 Grate in the frozen fat, then add the lemon juice
   and just enough water to draw the mixture into
   a dough, using a rounded knife. Draw up to a ball
   and knead very lightly.

3 Wrap the dough in greaseproof paper and chill for
   30 minutes.

4 Roll out the dough on a lightly floured surface to
   a long oblong. Lightly mark the pastry into thirds.
   Fold in one end third on top of the middle third,

then fold the remaining third over the top. Seal the edges of the folded pastry and give it a quarter turn on the work surface. Repeat this rolling and folding process once more – done to trap air in the pastry – and chill again for 30 minutes.

5 Meanwhile, to make the filling, toss the vegetables in the olive oil and season well.

6 Spread them out in a large roasting tin or flameproof dish. Bake in a preheated oven, 200°C (400°F), Gas Mark 6, for 30 minutes, or until well browned.

7 Remove the vegetables from the roasting tin with a slotted spoon. Add the balsamic vinegar to the roasting tin and place the tin on the hob to deglaze, then scrape out the juices and reserve.

8 Line a shallow baking dish or ovenproof plate with baking parchment and spoon over the juices from the roasting tin. Spread the roasted vegetables over the base, arranging them in an attractive pattern.

9 Roll out the pastry on a lightly floured surface to a size to fit over the vegetables. Place the pastry on top of the vegetables and tuck in the sides.

10 Bake at 220°C (425°F), Gas Mark 7, for 30 minutes. Leave to stand for about 10 minutes, then turn out. Serve warm or at room temperature.

nutritional breakdown per serving: kcal 306, kJ 1277, protein 4g, fat 21g (saturated fat 8g), carbohydrate 28g

new potatoes with pesto

serves 8

preparation: 5 minutes

cooking: 15 minutes

1kg (2lb) new potatoes
2–3 tablespoons pesto (see page 211)
salt and freshly ground black pepper

1 Boil the new potatoes in a large saucepan of boiling water for 15 minutes, until just tender.

2 Drain and toss in the pesto while still warm. Season to taste and serve warm or at room temperature.

nutritional breakdown per serving: kcal 126, kJ 533, protein 4g, fat 4g (saturated fat 2g), carbohydrate 20g

garden salad with green olive dressing

serves 8

preparation: 5 minutes

cooking: 3–4 minutes

𝓋

50g (2oz) pumpkin seeds
125g (4oz) mixed green leaves

For the dressing:
4 tbsp olive oil or flavoured oil
juice and zest of 1 lemon
10 pitted green olives, finely chopped
1 tsp chopped thyme
1 tsp chopped oregano
1 garlic clove, crushed
salt and freshly ground black pepper

1 Mix the oil, lemon juice and zest together in a jug and stir in the chopped olives, thyme, oregano and crushed garlic. Season well.

2 Spread the pumpkin seeds on a baking sheet and roast in a preheated oven, 200°C (400°F), Gas Mark 6, for 3–4 minutes.

3 Just before serving, toss the dressing into the salad leaves. Sprinkle the roasted pumpkin seeds over the top.

nutritional breakdown per serving: kcal 95, kJ 390, protein 2g, fat 9g (saturated fat 1g), carbohydrate 1g

tarte tatin with roasted mediterranean vegetables opposite

mascarpone and amaretti ice

If you prefer not to use alcohol in this dessert, soak the sultanas in fruit juice instead.

serves 8

preparation: 10 minutes, plus soaking and freezing

cooking: none

suitable for freezing

250g (8oz) mascarpone cheese
500ml (17fl oz) natural yoghurt
50g (2oz) caster sugar
50ml (2fl oz) milk
4 amaretti biscuits, crumbled
50g (2oz) sultanas, soaked for at least 30 minutes in 2–3 tbsp brandy or Marsala

1 Mix all the ingredients together in a large bowl.

2 Pour the mixture into a freezer container and freeze for 2 hours, then beat vigorously for 2–3 minutes and freeze again for a further 2 hours. Alternatively, use an ice-cream maker and follow the manufacturer's instructions.

3 Remove from the freezer and place in the fridge 15 minutes before serving. However, if you have made the ice some time in advance, it will need longer than 15 minutes in the fridge to soften before serving.

nutritional breakdown per serving: kcal 247, kJ 1030, protein 6g, fat 15g (saturated fat 10g), carbohydrate 22g

grilled nectarines with raspberry coulis

It is important to have very ripe, good-quality nectarines for this dish. If nectarines are not in season, then use peaches, which can be grilled in the same way. Alternatively, you could make a fresh berry compôte with redcurrants, blueberries and strawberries. Dust with icing sugar and serve in a pool of coulis.

serves 8

preparation: 10 minutes

cooking: 3–4 minutes

8 ripe nectarines, halved and stones removed
juice of ½ lemon
15–25g (½–1oz) butter, melted

For the coulis:

375g (12oz) fresh or frozen raspberries, thawed
75g (3oz) white caster sugar
1–2 tablespoons kirsch

1 To make the coulis, purée the raspberries with the sugar using a blender or food processor, then press the mixture through a sturdy, preferably conical sieve. Add the kirsch to taste.

2 Place the nectarine halves, cut side up, on a large baking sheet and sprinkle with lemon juice.

3 Brush with melted butter and place under a preheated grill. Cook for 3–4 minutes, or until just soft. Leave to cool.

4 To serve, arrange the nectarines on serving plates, drizzled with the raspberry coulis.

nutritional breakdown per serving: kcal 158, kJ 672, protein 3g, fat 3g (saturated fat 2g), carbohydrate 30g

grilled nectarines with raspberry coulis bottom left
mascarpone and amaretti ice top right

winter dinner party for 6

This is a sumptuous menu, suitable for special meals and festive occasions. It is easy to double the quantities if you are entertaining on a grander scale. I have chosen two moist vegetables to accompany the brioche. However, you could make a sauce instead, such as the Buttered Shallot and Wine Sauce (see page 290) or the dairy-free Leek and Cashew Sauce (see page 293).

A dairy-free brioche is not possible since the eggs and butter give the dough its distinct character. Instead make Quick Flaky Pastry (see page 256) and use smoked tofu in place of the mozzarella, which works very well. A suitable dairy-free alternative to the soup would be Carrot and Parsnip Soup with Coconut and Tamarind (see page 151).

suggested timetable

Two days before:
Prepare the Chestnut and Chocolate Petits Fours

Make the brûlée base
Slice and chill the citrus fruits to accompany the brûlée

The day before:
Prepare the soup
Prepare the brioche and the filling, but do not assemble

On the day:
Assemble the brioche
Prepare the side vegetable dishes
Finish the brûlée

menu

Cream of Fennel Soup with Saffron

Wild Rice and Mushroom Brioche

Roast Shallots with Almonds

Hot Red Cabbage with Beets

Lemon Brûlée and sliced citrus fruits

Chestnut and Chocolate Petits Fours

cream of fennel soup with saffron

This is an attractive, delicately flavoured soup.

serves 6
preparation: 40 minutes
cooking: 20 minutes
suitable for freezing

25g (1oz) butter
1 onion, finely chopped
425g (14oz) fennel, finely chopped
125ml (4fl oz) white wine
pinch of saffron strands
1 litre (1¾ pints) Vegetable Stock (see page 144)
175g (6oz) crème fraîche
salt and freshly ground black pepper

1   Melt the butter in a large saucepan and gently cook the onion until soft. Add the fennel, cover the pan and cook very gently for about 10 minutes, or until tender. Stir occasionally.

2   Pour in the wine and increase the heat, then reduce until the liquid has mostly evaporated.

3   Grind the saffron using a pestle and mortar, then infuse a little of the vegetable stock.

4   Mix the infused saffron and remaining vegetable stock together and pour over the fennel. Bring to the boil, stirring well.

5   Cover the pan and simmer for 15–20 minutes, or until the fennel is very soft.

6   Cool slightly then, using a blender or food processor, purée the soup to a smooth cream, working in batches. Sieve for a very smooth finish, if preferred. Stir in the crème fraîche and season to taste.

7   Return the soup to a clean pan and heat through before serving.

nutritional breakdown per serving: kcal 173, kJ 713, protein 1g, fat 15g (saturated fat 10g), carbohydrate 4g

hot red cabbage with beets

Beetroot and red cabbage are a happy partnership, intensifying each other's colour. When beetroot is out of season use dessert apples instead.

serves 6

preparation: 10 minutes

cooking: 40 minutes

suitable for freezing

v

2 tbsp sunflower oil

1 red onion, finely chopped

750g (1½lb) red cabbage, shredded

250g (8oz) raw beetroot, grated

2 tbsp concentrated apple juice

2 tbsp red wine vinegar

2–3 tbsp water

salt and freshly ground black pepper

1 Heat the oil in a large saucepan and gently fry the onion until quite soft.

2 Add the cabbage and beetroot and stir well. Cook over a slow heat for 5 minutes, then add the concentrated apple juice and wine vinegar. Season well.

3 Add the water and cover the pan. Cook over a low heat, stirring occasionally for 30 minutes, or until the cabbage is very well cooked.

4 Adjust the seasoning and serve hot or cold.

nutritional breakdown per serving: kcal 95, kJ 397, protein 2g, fat 4g (saturated fat 0g), carbohydrate 13g

wild rice and
mushroom brioche
served with **roast
shallots with
almonds**

wild rice and mushroom brioche

serves 6

preparation: 25 minutes, plus rising and chilling

cooking: 1 hour–1 hour 10 minutes

suitable for freezing

For the pastry:
250g (8oz) plain flour, plus extra for dusting
1 tsp golden caster sugar
7g (¼oz) sachet easy-blend yeast
pinch of salt
3 tbsp milk at room temperature
2 eggs, beaten
100g (3½oz) butter, softened

For the filling:
75g (3oz) wild rice
50g (2oz) butter
4 shallots, chopped
425g (14oz) mushrooms, chopped
3 tbsp chopped parsley
125g (4oz) mozzarella, cubed
salt and freshly ground black pepper

1 Using a food processor or electric mixer, put the flour, sugar, yeast and salt into the bowl, then mix in the milk and eggs. Process until evenly combined.

2 Beat in the softened butter, a piece at a time, to give a smooth glossy dough. Add a little more flour if the dough is very slack. Transfer to a clean bowl and cover with clingfilm. Leave to rise for 1½ hours.

3 Knock the air out of the dough, add a little more flour if necessary, then return it to the bowl. Cover with clingfilm and chill thoroughly, preferably overnight.

4 To make the filling, put the rice in a saucepan. Add twice its volume of water and cook for 35–40 minutes. Drain if necessary.

5 Meanwhile, melt the butter in a saucepan and gently cook the shallots until soft. Add the chopped mushrooms and cook for 10 minutes until well softened, then remove from the heat. Stir in the parsley, season well and leave to cool.

6 Stir the cooked rice into the mushroom mixture and add the mozzarella. Adjust the seasoning.

7 Roll out the brioche dough on a lightly floured surface to a large oblong to cover a baking sheet. Pile the mushroom filling along the centre, then fold the 2 long edges of the pastry oblong over the filling so they meet in the middle. Moisten the edges and press together. Make diagonal cuts in the dough along either side, using a sharp knife. Bake the brioche in a preheated oven, 200°C (400°F), Gas Mark 6, for 25–30 minutes, or until golden brown and crisp.

8 Serve hot with vegetables.

nutritional breakdown per serving: kcal 479, kJ 2000, protein 15g, fat 28g (saturated fat 17g), carbohydrate 44g

roast shallots with almonds

This is an easy dish to make and the moist shallots complement the brioche.

serves 6

preparation: 5 minutes

cooking: 45 minutes

25 g (1oz) butter, melted
2 tbsp olive oil
25g (1oz) blanched almonds, roughly chopped
1 tbsp dark sugar
pinch of cayenne pepper
30–36 shallots or baby onions, peeled
salt and freshly ground black pepper

1 Melt the butter and oil together, pour into a gratin dish and stir in the almonds, sugar, cayenne and season. Stir in the shallots.

2 Cover with a lid or sheet of foil and bake in a preheated oven, 180°C (350°F), Gas Mark 4, for 20 minutes.

3 Remove the lid and bake for a further 20–25 minutes. Serve hot.

nutritional breakdown per serving: kcal 160 kJ, 662, protein 2g, fat 13g (saturated fat 5g), carbohydrate 10g

lemon brûlée

serves 6

preparation: 15 minutes, plus chilling

cooking: 20 minutes

6 egg yolks
40g (1½oz) caster sugar
zest of ½ lemon
600ml (1 pint) double cream
1 vanilla pod
125–150g (4–5oz) granulated sugar

For the citrus platter:
selection of contrasting citrus fruits, such as pink
and white grapefruit, orange, Ugli fruit

1 Place the egg yolks, caster sugar and lemon zest in a bowl and beat until light and fluffy.

2 Heat the cream in a small saucepan with the vanilla pod until hot but not boiling.

3 Remove the vanilla pod and pour the cream over the egg mixture, beating continuously.

4 Pour the mixture into a double saucepan or a bowl set over a pan of hot but not boiling water, and cook very gently until the mixture thickens. This takes about 10–15 minutes – if you try to rush it the eggs will scramble.

5 Once thick, pour into 6 ramekins or 1 shallow gratin dish. Cover with clingfilm and leave to set in the fridge.

6 Meanwhile, to prepare the citrus platter, peel and segment the fruit and arrange on a serving plate. Chill well.

7 Two hours before serving, sprinkle granulated sugar over each ramekin. Place under a preheated hot grill and brown until caramelized. Leave to cool before serving with the platter of citrus fruit.

nutritional breakdown per serving: kcal 663, kJ 2753, protein 6g, fat 54g (saturated fat 32g), carbohydrate 42g

chestnut and chocolate petits fours

Exquisitely rich and so simple to create, these petits fours make the perfect indulgent finish to this meal. You may find that there are enough here for two meals – but that will depend entirely on the appetite of your guests.

makes 36

preparation: 10 minutes, plus chilling

cooking: 2 minutes

suitable for freezing

100g (3½oz) dark chocolate, broken into
  small pieces
100g (3½oz) crème fraîche
400g (13oz) chestnuts (cooked weight – see
  page 257)
100g (3½oz) caster sugar
1–2 tbsp Grand Marnier
1 tsp orange zest

1 Melt the chocolate carefully with the crème fraîche in a bowl set over a saucepan of hot but not boiling water. Remove from the heat and beat until smooth.

2 Using a blender or food processor, purée the chestnuts finely, then add the remaining ingredients and blend again.

3 Spoon the chocolaty chestnut mixture into a lined, lightly buttered 15cm (6in) tin. Leave in the fridge for at least 4 hours, preferably overnight. Cut into small squares before serving.

nutritional breakdown per square: kcal 46, kJ 195, protein 0g,
fat 1g (saturated fat 1g), carbohydrate 9g

Index

An italic page reference indicates an illustration.

A

Additives 31

Adolescence 23

Aduki bean 94, *94*

Adulthood 23

Alcohol 25

Allspice 109, *109*

Almonds 102, *102*
  Almond Croustade with
    Chard 268, *268*
  Almond and Lemon Pilaf
    234, *234*
  Oyster Mushroom and
    Roast Almond Pâté 165,
    165
  Roasted Almonds with
    Shoyu 364

Antioxidants 15

Apples 60, *60*
  cider vinegar 117
  dried 73
  Upside Down Apple Cake
    with Maple Syrup and
    Lemon 322, *322*

Apricots 61
  Apricot Lattice 328, *328*
  dried 73

Artichokes, globe 40, *40*

Artichokes, Jerusalem 53

Asparagus 41, *41*
  Asparagus and Pea Fricassee
    with Eggs 185, *185*
  Asparagus Tartlets 362, *363*

Aubergines (eggplant) 55
  Caponata of Roasted
    Vegetables 176
  Moussaka 272, *272*
  Pasta Salad 302, *302*
  Roasted Aubergine and
    Garlic Dip 166, *167*
  Rosemary Polenta with
    Aubergine and Dolcelatte
    224
  Sliced Aubergine with
    Yoghurt Dip 349, *349*

Avocadoes 43, *43*
  Avocado Gazpacho *142*,
    143
  Avocado and Pistachio
    Salad 307, *307*
  Savoury Choux with
    Avocado and Pesto 164,
    164

B

Babies and toddlers 22

Baby corn cobs 47

Banana 68, *68*

All-in-One Banana Loaf 325,
  325
Banana and Almond Milk 140

Barbecue dishes
  Haloumi, Sweet Onion and
    Apple Kebabs 346, *347*
  Stuffed Mushrooms with
    Walnuts and Sun-Dried
    Tomatoes 348, *349*
  Sweetcorn with Herb,
    Shallot and Olive Butter
    348
  Tofu Kebabs 346, *347*

Barley 86, *86*
  Country Vegetable Broth
    with Barley 156

Basil 106, *106*

Bay 105, *105*

Beans 46, *46* (see also individual
    references)
  cooking time of 91
  freezing 92
  Marinated Bean Salad 298

Bean sprouts 93
  Gado Gado 306, *306*
  growing 93

Beetroot 52
  Beetroot and Green Salad
    with Couscous 300, *300*

Belgian endive see chicory

Bell pepper see sweet pepper

Bhindi see okra

Black beans 95, *95*
  Black Beans 190
  Refried Black Beans 191

Blackberry 64, *64*

Blackcurrants see red, white
  and blackcurrants

Black-eye beans 94, *94*

Blueberries 64
  Blueberry Muffins, 135, *135*

Blue cheeses 80

Borlotti beans 94, *94*

Bouillon powder 112

Bouquet garni 107

Bran 88, *88*

Brassicas 36–38

Brazil nuts 101, *101*

Bread
  Bruschetta 364, *365*
  Enriched White Bread
    336, *336*
  Focaccia 337, *337*
  Gluten-Free Bread 338,
    338
  Griddle Bread 340, *341*
  Savoury Cheese Corn
    Bread 340, *341*

Soda Bread 339, *339*
Wholemeal Bread 334,
  334–35

Brie 80, *80*

Broad beans 47
  Broad Bean and Chickpea
    Tagine 242, *242*

Broccoli 37
  Broccoli and Mushroom
    Lasagne with Almonds
    220
  Broccoli and Stilton Roulade
    183, *183*

Brussels sprouts 37, *37*

Buckwheat 86, *86*
  Buckwheat with Leeks and
    Wild Mushrooms 238,
    238
  flour 89

Buffet dishes 358–65
  Bruschetta 364
  Fresh Tomato and Basil
    Topping 364
  Layered Vegetable Terrine
    360
  Mediterranean Galette 358
  Red Pepper and Parmesan
    Filo Triangles 361
  Roasted Almonds with
    Shoyu 364
  Roasted Walnut and Black
    Olive Topping 365
  Spiced New Potatoes with
    Sharp Cream Dip 363
  Stuffed Vine Leaves with
    Spiced Bulgar 359

Bulgar 88, *88*
  Bulgar with Roasted
    Aubergine, Yellow Pepper
    and Red Onion 230, *230*
  Classic Tabbouleh 299, *299*
  Layered Bulgar with
    Tomatoes and Feta 231,
    231
  Stuffed Vine Leaves with
    Spiced Bulgar 359, *359*

Business life, eating out 24

Butter 75

Butter beans 95, *95*

Buttermilk 74, *75*

Button mushrooms 45

Buying and storing spices 108

Buying and storing vegetables 43

C

Cabbage 36–37
  Brussels sprouts 37
  Cabbage and Cumin 284,
    284

Chinese leaves 38, 42
  green 36, *36*
  kale 36
  red 37
  white (Dutch) 37, *37*

Caffeine 25

Cakes and sweet snacks
  All-in-One Banana Loaf
    325, *325*
  Carrot Cake with Orange
    Cream Icing 320, *320*
  Chestnut and Chocolate
    Petits Fours 377, *377*
  Classic Rich Fruit Cake
    321, *321*
  Deluxe Chocolate and
    Prune Refrigerator Cake
    323, *323*
  Pistachio cake 324, *324*
  Raisin and Almond Flapjack
    327, *327*
  Upside Down Apple Cake
    with Maple Syrup and
    Lemon 322, *322*
  Very Lemon Wedges
    326, *326*

Calabrese see purple sprouting
  broccoli

Camembert 80, *80*

Cancer 27

Cannellini beans 95, *95*

Cape gooseberries see physalis

Capers 112

Carambola see star fruit

Caraway 109, *109*

Carbohydrate and fibre 14

Cardamom 111, *111*

Carob powder 119

Carrots 50, *50*
  Carrot Cake 320, *320*
  Carrot and Kohlrabi with
    Pumpkin seeds *310*, *311*
  Carrot and Parsnip Soup
    with Coconut and
    Tamarind 151, *151*

Cashew nuts 102, *102*
  cashew nut milk or cream 99

Cauliflower 38, *38*
  Pan-Fried Cauliflower 286,
    287
  Spiced Cauliflower and
    Green Beans 251

Cayenne pepper 109, *109*

Celeriac 53, *53*
  Celeriac and Almond
    Crumble 271, *271*
  Celeriac and Emmental
    Soup 154, *154*
  Lemon-Glazed Celeriac
    285, *285*

Celery 41, *41*
  Chickpea and Celery Soup with Gremolada 152
Cep mushrooms 45
Cereals
  Toasted Muesli 134
Chanterelle mushrooms (Girolle) 45
Chard *see* spinach and chard
Cheddar 78, *78*
Cheese 76–81, *76–81* (*see also* individual entries)
  buying 76
  cooking with 77
  rennet 76
  storing 77
Cheese Dishes
  Cheese and Potato Pasties 356, *356*
  Cheese and Tomato Pizza 198
  Leek and Feta Parcels 260
  Twice Baked Goat's Cheese Soufflés with Tomato Sauce and Walnuts 366, *367*
Cherries 62
Chervil 107, *107*
Chestnut (Paris) mushrooms 45
Chestnuts 102, *102*
  Chestnut and Cep Single Crust Pie 257, *257*
Chèvre, fresh 80
Chicory (Belgian endive) 41, *41*, 42
  Chicory and Beetroot with Mustard Dressing *296*, 297
  Grilled Chicory with Two Cheeses 161, *161*
Chickpeas 94, *94*
  Chickpea and Celery Soup with Gremolada 152, *152*
  Chickpea Curry 247, *247*
  Falafel 174, *174*
  Hummus *166*, 167
Children 22
Chilli 57, *57*
  chilli oil 116
  Cooked Salsa with Chilli 190
Chilli powder 109
Chinese leaves (Chinese cabbage) 38, *38*, 42
Chives 106, *106*
Chocolate 119, *119*
  Carob or Chocolate Mousse 331, *331*

Deluxe Chocolate and Prune Refrigerator Cake 323, *323*
Cinnamon 109, *109*
Citrus fruit 66–67
Clarified butter *see* ghee
Clotted cream 75
Cloves 109, *109*
Coconut 102, *102*
Coconut milk or cream 95
Concentrated fruit juice 119
Continental lentils 95
Convalescence 25
Cooking with spices 108
Cooking wholegrains 84–85
Coriander 106, *106*, 110, *110*
Corn (sweetcorn) *46*, 47, *47*
  Fresh Sweetcorn Cobbler 269, *269*
  Sweetcorn with Herb, Shallot and Olive Butter 348
Cornflour (maize) 89
Corn oil 115
Coronary heart disease 26
Cottage cheese 81, *81*
  Low-Calorie Creamy Dressing 317
Courgette *54*, 55
  Griddled Courgette Quiche with Pine Nuts 255, *255*
  Sweet Potato and Courgette Gratin 263
Couscous 88, *88*
  Couscous with Spiced Tofu and Mixed Pepper Sauce 237, *237*
Cracked wheat 88, *88*
Cranberries 65
Cream 74
  clotted cream 75
  crème fraîche 74–75
  Low-Fat Cream 333
  soured cream 75
Cremini mushrooms 45
Cucumber 43, *43*
  Cucumber and Orange Cooler with Mint 345, *345*
  Cucumber Relish with Chilli and Lemon *294*, 295
Cumin 109, *109*
Currants 73

D
Dairy products 28
Dates 71, *71*
  dried 73
Desserts *see* puddings
Diet
  and adolescence 23
  and adulthood 23
  approaches to 29
  and babies and toddlers 22
  and business life 24
  and children 22
  and food allergies 28
  and health 20, 26, 27, 28
  and lifestyle and nutritional needs 24
  and old age 23
  and pregnancy 21
  and raw food 29
  and sport 24
  vegan 29
  and wholefood 29
Dill 107, *107*
Dinner party dishes, summer 366–71
  Garden Salad with Green Olive Dressing 369
  Grilled Nectarines with Raspberry Coulis 371
  Mascarpone and Amaretti Ice 370
  New Potatoes with Pesto 369
  Tarte Tatin with Roasted Mediterranean Vegetables 368
  Twice Baked Goat's Cheese Soufflé with Tomato Sauce and Walnuts 367
Dinner party dishes, winter 372–77
  Chestnut and Chocolate Petits Fours 377
  Cream of Fennel Soup with Saffron 372
  Hot Red Cabbage with Beets 373
  Lemon Brûlée 376
  Roast Shallots with Almonds 374
  Wild Rice and Mushroom Brioche 374
Dips
  Roasted Aubergine and Garlic Dip 167
  Sliced Aubergine with Yoghurt Dip 349
  see also relishes, sauces and marinades
Dressings
  Fruity Vinaigrette 314
  Green Vinaigrette 315, *315*

Lemon and Sunflower Vinaigrette 315
Low-Calorie Creamy Dressing 317
Mayonnaise 316, *316*
Roasted Walnut Dressing 314
Sherry 163
Silken Tofu Dressing 317
Tahini Dressing 317
Dried fruit 72–73, *72–73*
  Classic Rich Fruit Cake 321, *321*
Drinking habits 25
Dry-roasted spices 108
Dwarf sweetcorn *see* baby corn cobs

E
Eggplant *see* aubergines
Eggs 82, *82*
  alternatives to 83
  Baked Eggs with Mozzarella and Fresh Tomatoes 182, *182*
  boiled 178
  Eggah or Kuku 179
  folded 179
  fried 178
  frittata 179
  Huevos Rancheros 193
  Japanese Omelette 179
  Omelette 179
  Poached Egg 179
  Scrambled Egg 178
  tortilla 179
Emmental 79, *79*
Endive 42
Enoki mushrooms 45

F
Fats 8, 13
Fennel 41, *41*
  Cream of Fennel Soup with Saffron 372, *373*
  Fennel and Red Pepper Salad with Lemon and Oregano Dressing 308, *308*
  Leek and Fennel Frittata 180
  Pasta with Roasted Fennel and Patty Pans 216
  Tagliatelle with Fennel and Fresh Herbs 207
Fennel seeds 109, *109*
Fenugreek 111, *111*

Feta 79, 79

Figs 71, 71
   dried 73

Fines herbes 107

Flageolet beans 94, 95

Flavourings 112–13

Flour and pasta 89

Fontina 79, 79
   Polenta Cheese Squares
     222

Food additives 31

Food allergies 28

Food, choosing 30

Fragrant rice *see* jasmine rice

Fresh chèvre 81, 81

Fresh mushrooms 44

Fresh soft cheeses 80–81

Fromage frais 81, 81

Fruit 58–73 (*see also individual
   entries*)
   buying and preparation of
     58–59
   cooking and serving 59
   Layered Fruit Pavlova
     330, 330
   storing 58

Fruit juice, concentrated 119

Fruit vegetables 54–57 (*see also
   individual entries*)

Ful (or foul) medames 95, 95

G

Galangal 110, 110

Garlic 49, 49
   garlic oil 116

Genetically modified organisms
   (GMOs) 31

Ghee 75

Ginger 110, 110

Girolle mushrooms *see*
   chanterelles

Globe artichoke 40

Gluten 28

Glutinous rice 87

Gomasio (Gomashio) 112

Gooseberries 65

Gorgonzola 80, 80

Grains 84–88 (*see also
   individual entries*)
   wholegrains and flakes 86

Granadilla 69

Grapefruit 67

Grapes 62, 62
   Red Cabbage and Black
     Grape Salad with Orange
     Vinaigrette 311

Green cabbage 36

Groundnuts *see* peanuts
   groundnut (peanut) oil
     115

Gruyère 79, 79

Guava 69, 69

Gumbo *see* okra

H

Haloumi 79, 79

Hard and semi-hard cheeses
   78–79

Haricot beans 95
   Quick Baked Beans 202,
     202

Hazelnuts 101, 101
   hazelnut oil 116
   Spiced Hazelnut and
     Quinoa Bake 267, 267
   Wild Rice with Hazelnuts,
     Carrots and Artichokes
     236

Healthy diet 20

Herbs 104–107
   buying and storing 104
   de Provence 107
   freezing 104
   Green Vinaigrette 315
   Herb Soufflé 170, 171
   home-dried 105
   mixtures 107
   oil 104, 116
   vinegar 105

High blood pressure 26

Hijiki 113

Honey 118, 118

Horseradish 110

I

Infused oils 116

Infused vinegars 117

Ingredients 33–119

J

Jaggery *see* palm sugar

Jasmine rice 87

Jerusalem artichokes 53

Juices
   Carrot, Apple and Celery
     138
   of citrus fruit 66
   Spiced Mango 138
   Tomato, Cucumber and
     Watercress 138

Junipers 110, 110

K

Kaki fruit *see* persimmon

Kebabs
   Haloumi, Sweet Onion and
     Apple Kebabs 346, 347
   Tofu Kebabs 346, 347

Kiwi fruit 69, 69

Kohlrabi 38, 38

Kombu 113

Kumquat 67, 67

L

Ladies' fingers *see* okra

Leafy beets *see* spinach and
   chard

Leafy greens 39

Leeks 49

Leek dishes
   Buckwheat with Leeks and
     Wild Mushrooms 238
   Griddled Leeks and
     Asparagus with Cream
     Cheese Dressing 160,
     160
   Leek and Cashew Sauce
     293, 293
   Leek and Fennel Frittata
     180, 180
   Leek and Feta Parcels
     260, 260
   Leek and Potato Cakes with
     Gruyère 177, 177
   Potato and Leek Boulangère
     262
   Stir-Fry Shredded Leeks
     with Tarragon 285, 285

Lemons 66
   Lemon and Sunflower
     Vinaigrette 315
   Very Lemon Wedges 326,
     326

Lemon grass 110, 110

Lentils 95
   brown 95, 95
   continental 95, 95
   cooking of 92
   Puy 95
   split red 95, 95

Lentil dishes
   Cottage Pie 270, 270
   Lentil Bake with Red Pepper
     266, 266
   Lentil Lasagne 218
   Mixed Lentil Dhal 250, 250
   Puy Lentil and Mushroom
     Soup 148, 148
   Red Bean and Lentil Chilli
     240
   Red Lentil Soup with
     Cumin 146, 146
   Spinach and Lentil Turnovers
     253, 253

Lentilles vertes 95

Lettuce 42

Lifestyle and nutritional needs
   24–25

Lima beans 95, 95

Limes 66

Lime leaves 110, 110

Long-grain rice 87

Lychee, rambutan and
   mangosteen 70

M

Mace 111

Malt extract 119

Mangetout 46, 46

Mango 68, 68
   dried 73
   Spiced Mango Juice 138
   Spiced Rice Salad with
     Mango and Cashews 304

Mangosteen *see* lychee,
   rambutan and mangosteen

Maple syrup 119

Margarine 116

Marjoram 105, 105

Mascarpone 81, 81
   Mascarpone and Amaretti
     Ice 371

Melon 70, 70
   Chilled Melon Soup with
     Wine and Honey 158

Mexican dishes 90
   Enchiladas 191
   Huevos Rancheros 193
   Quesadillas 192

Milk 28
   allergies to 28
   and cream products 74–75,
     74–75
   soya 83

Millet 86, 86
   Millet Pilaf with Pine Nuts
     239
   Sesame Millet with Pan-fried
     Courgettes, Asparagus and
     Avocado Cream 228, 228

Minerals 18–19

Mint 106, 106

Miso 97

Morel mushrooms 45

Mozzarella 81, 81

Muesli, Toasted 134

Mung beans 94, 94

Mushrooms 44–45
   Baked Tofu and Button
     Mushrooms 175
   Dried mushrooms 44
   Filo Pie with Double
     Mushrooms and Goat's
     Cheese 261, 261

Giant Mushrooms Stuffed with Wild Rice and Roasted Onions 173, *173*
Layered Mushroom and Olive Bake 137, *137*
Mushroom and Olive Ravioli 213, *213*
Mushroom Pizza 198
Mushroom Ragoût 289, *289*
Mushroom Risotto with Tarragon 226
Mushroom Sauce 291, *291*
Oriental Mushroom Soup with Chilli and Ginger 153, *153*
Spiced Mushroom Rice 235, *235*
Stuffed Mushrooms with Walnuts and Sun-Dried Tomatoes 348, *349*
Mustard 111, *111*

N

Nectarine 62
Glazed Nectarines with Dolcelatte 159, *159*
Grilled Nectarines with Raspberry Coulis 370, *371*
Non-dairy alternatives 83
Noodles *see* pasta and noodles
Nutmeg 111, *111*
Nutrition 11–17
Nutritional needs 24–25
Nutritional values
of chees· 76
of dairy products 34
of eggs 82
of grains 84
of milk and cream products 74
of nuts and seeds 98
of oils 114
of pulses 90
of sea vegetables 113
of vegetables 34
of vinegars 117
Nuts
creams and milks 99
oils 115–16
Quick Nut Nuggets 205, *205*
Nuts and seeds 28, 99–103 (*see also individual references*)
buying and storing 94
chopping and grating 95
roasting 95
Nut dishes
Almond Croustade with Chard 268
Roasted Pecan and Cashew Loaf 264

Roasted Walnut Dressing 314
Spiced Hazelnut and Quinoa Bake 267, *267*

O

Oats 86, *86*
Obesity 27
Oils 114–16, *114–16* (*see under individual entries*)
Okra (ladies' fingers, gumbo, bhindi) 47, *47*
Spiced Gumbo Soup 150, *150*
Old age 23
Olives
Green Olive Tapenade 166, *166*
Olive oil 114–15
Mayonnaise 316, *316*
Olive paste 112
Onion family 48–49
Onions 48, *48*
Caramelised Onion Soup with Brandy 155, *155*
Onion Plait with Mustard seeds 353, *353*
Red Onion Marmalade with Coriander 294, 295
Saffron Onion Pizza 198
Open, flat (Portobello) mushrooms 45
Oral contraceptive 25
Oranges 67, *67*
Oranges with Red Onion and Black Olives in Sherry Dressing 163, *163*
Orchard, stone and vine fruit 60–62
oregano 105
Organic dairy products 74
Organic foods 30
Oriental greens 39
Osteoporosis 27

P

Palm sugar (jaggery) 119
Pancakes 186
American Pancakes 136, *136*
Buckwheat Pancakes 187
Crespelles 189, *189*
Mushrooms and Goat's Cheese Pancakes 188, *188*
Roquefort and Celeriac Pancakes 187
Wholemeal Pancakes 186, *186*
Papaya (pawpaw) 68

Paprika 110, *110*
Parmesan 78, *78*
Parsley 105, *105*
Parsnips 50, 52, *52*
Passion fruit 69, *69*
Pasta and noodles 89
Baked Pasta Gratin with Fresh Sweetcorn 203, *203*
Basic Pasta 208–9, *208–9*
Broccoli and Mushroom Lasagne with Almonds 220, *221*
Lentil Lasagne 218, *219*
Mushroom and Olive Ravioli 213, *213*
Pasta with Roasted Fennel and Patty Pans 216, *216*
Pasta Salad 302, *302*
Pasta with Sauté Vegetables and Mascarpone 214, *214*
Pasta with Spinach, Shiitake Mushrooms and Tofu 217, *217*
Ricotta, Pesto and Herb Ravioli 215
Tagliatelle with Fennel and Fresh Herbs 206, 207
Pastry
choux 258, *258*
Enriched Shortcrust Pastry (pâté brisée) 254, *254*
Quick Flaky Pastry 256, *256*
Wholemeal Shortcrust Pastry 252, *252*
Pawpaw *see* papaya
Peaches 62, *62*
Grilled Peaches with Ginger Cream 333, *333*
Peanuts
Peanut butter 100, *100*
Peanut (groundnut) oil 100, *100*
Roasted Peanut and Coriander Sambal 168, *169*
Satay Sauce 281
Pears 61, *61*
Fresh Pear Compote with Apricots and Prunes *132*, 133
Peas 46
yellow split 95
Pecans 102, *102*
Roasted Pecan and Cashew Loaf 264, *265*
Peppercorns 111, *111*
Peppers
Artichoke and Red Pepper Gougère 259, *259*
Green Rice with Chilli 232
Red Pepper and Parmesan Filo Triangles 361, *361*
Roasted Peppers with Basil Vinaigrette *312*, 313

Roasted Red Pepper Coulis 294, *294*
Roasted Yellow Pepper Soup 149, *149*
Strata 184, *184*
Persimmon (kaki fruit) 70, *70*
Physalis (Cape gooseberry) 71, *71*
Pimento *see* sweet pepper
Pineapples 70
Pineapple Punch 345, *345*
Pine nuts 101, *101*
Pinto beans 94, *94*
Pinto Bean and Red Onion Salsa 292, *293*
Pistachio 100, *100*
Pistachio Cake 324, *324*
Pizza Dishes
Basic Pizza Bases 194, *194–95*
Cheese and Tomato Pizza 198, *199*
Classic Tomato Pizza Topping 196, *196*
Mushroom Pizza 198, *199*
Pesto, Plum Tomato and Black Olive Pizza 197, *197*
Quick Scone Pizza with Grilled Vegetables and Gruyère 201, *201*
Saffron Onion Pizza 198, *199*
Spinach and Chilli Calzone 200, *200*
Three-Flour Pizza Bases 195
Plums 62, *62*
Plum Crisp *318*, 319
Pods and sweetcorn 47
Polenta dishes
Baked Polenta with Rich Tomato and Mascarpone Sauce 223, *223*
Rosemary Polenta with Aubergine and Dolcelatte 224
Pomegranates 71, *71*
Poppy seeds 111, *111*
Porcini mushrooms 45
Portobello mushrooms *see* open, flat mushrooms
Potatoes 51, *51*
Baked Potatoes 202
Greek Potato Salad 301, *301*
New Potatoes with Pesto 369
Potato Gnocchi 225, *225*
Potato and Leek Boulangère 262, *262*
Rosti 288, *288*
Spiced New Potatoes with Sharp Cream Dip 363, *363*

Pregnancy, and diet 21

Pre-menstrual tension, and diet 27

Protein 12

Prunes 73

Puddings
Apricot Lattice 328, *328*
Blueberry Summer Pudding 357, *357*
Carob or Chocolate Mousse 331, *331*
Grilled Peaches with Ginger Cream 333, *333*
Layered Fruit Pavlova 330, *330*
Lemon Brûlée 376, *376*
Plum Crisp *318, 319*
Quick Berry Brûlée 332, *332*
Ricotta Cheesecake 329, *329*
Strawberry Yoghurt Ice 331, *331*

Pulses 90–95
cooking beans 91
cooking lentils 92
freezing beans 92
growing bean sprouts 93
preparing dried 91

Pumpkin 56, *56*

Pumpkin seeds 103, *103*

Purées, soft fruit 63

Purple sprouting broccoli 36

Puy lentils 95

Q

Quark 81, *81*

Quinoa 86, *86*
flour 89

R

Radishes 43, *43*

Raisins 73
Raisin and Almond Flapjack 327, *327*

Rambutan *see* lychee, rambutan and mangosteen

Raspberries 63

Raspberry vinegar 117

Raw food diet 29

Red cabbage 37
Hot Red Cabbage with Beets 373, *373*
Polenta Cheese Squares 222
Red Cabbage and Black Grape Salad with Orange Vinaigrette *310, 311*

Red kidney beans 94, *94*
Marinated Bean Salad 298, *298*

Red Bean and Lentil Chilli 240, *240*

Red wine vinegar 117

Red, white and blackcurrants 64

Relishes
Cucumber Relish with Chilli and Lemon 294, *295*
Pinto Bean and Red Onion Salsa with Cumin 292
Red Onion Marmalade with Coriander 294, *295*
see also sauces and marinades

Rennet 76

Rice 87, *87*
flour 89
wine vinegar 117

Rice dishes
Green Rice with Chilli 232, *232*
Mushroom Risotto with Tarragon 226, *226*
Paella with Many Vegetables 233, *233*
Red Rice with Pan-Fried Squash, Mushrooms and Pecan Nuts 229, *229*
Risotto with Roasted Squash 227, *227*
Spiced Mushroom Rice 235
Spiced Rice Salad with Mango and Cashews 304, *304*
Sushi 280, *281*
Wild Rice and Mushroom Brioche 374, *375*

Ricotta 81, *81*
Ravioli 215, *215*
Ricotta Cheesecake 329, *329*
Ricotta, Pesto and Herb Ravioli 215

Ripened soft cheeses 80

Root vegetables and tubers 50–53

Roquefort 80, *80*

Rosemary 105, *105*

Rutabaga *see* swede

Rye flour 89

S

Safflower oil 115

Saffron 109, *109*

Sage 105, *105*

Salad leaves 42
Garden Salad with Green Olive Dressing 369
Green Garden Salad 308, 309

Salads
Avocado and Pistachio Salad 307, *307*

Beetroot and Green Bean Salad with Couscous 300, *300*
Carrot and Kohlrabi with Pumpkin seeds *310, 311*
Chicory and Beetroot with Mustard Dressing 296, 297
Classic Tabbouleh 299, *299*
Fennel and Red Pepper Salad with Lemon and Oregano Dressing 308, *308*
Gado Gado 306, *306*
Greek Potato Salad 301, *301*
Green Garden Salad *308, 309*
Griddled Vegetables with Brie 305, *305*
Marinated Bean Salad 298, *298*
Pasta Salad 302, *302*
Red Cabbage and Black Grape Salad with Orange Vinaigrette *310, 311*
Roasted Peppers with Basil Vinaigrette *313, 312*
Robust Tomato Salad 308, 309
Smoked Tofu and Water Chestnuts with Oriental Dressing 303, *303*
Spiced Rice Salad with Mango and Cashews 304, *304*

Salad onions *see* spring onions

Salad vegetables 43

Salmonella 82

Salsa *see* relishes

Sauces and marinades
Buttered Shallot and Wine sauce 290, *291*
Classic White Sauce 290, *291*
Gorgonzola Sauce with Walnuts 212
Leek and Cashew Sauce 293, *293*
Lightly Spiced Tomato Sauce 210
Mushroom Sauce 291, *291*
Mushroom Sauce with Wine and Herbs 212
Pesto 211
Roasted Red Pepper Coulis 294, *294*
Satay Sauce 281
Sweet and Sour Sauce 278, *279*
Vegetable Marinade 351
Very Easy Tomato Sauce 292, *293*
see also dressings and relishes

Savoury Butters
Roast Garlic Butter 210
Sage Butter 211

Scallions *see* spring onions

Sea vegetables 113
agar agar 113
arame 113
dulse 113
hijiki 113
kombu 113
nori 113
wakami 113

Semolina 88, *88*

Sesame seeds 103, *103*

Shallots 49, *49*
Buttered Shallot and Wine sauce 290, *291*
Roasted Shallots with Almonds 374, *375*

Sharon fruit 70

Sherry vinegar 117

Shiitake mushrooms 45

Short-grain rice 87

Shoyu Sauce 97

Smoothies
Banana and Almond Milk 140, *141*
Savoury Smoothie 140, *141*
Tofu and Strawberry with Vanilla 140, *141*

Snow peas *see* mangetout

Soft fruits 63–65

Soft fruit purées 63

Solid vegetable fat 116

Soups
Avocado Gazpacho *142, 143*
Caramelised Onion with Brandy 155, *155*
Carrot and Parsnip with Coconut and Tamarind 151, *151*
Celeriac and Emmental 154, *154*
Chickpea and Celery Soup with Gremolada 152, *152*
Chilled Bean 157, *157*
Chilled Melon with Wine and Brandy 158, *158*
Chowder with Sweet Potato 147, *147*
Country Vegetable Broth with Barley 156, *156*
Cream of Fennel Soup with Saffron 372, *373*
Oriental Mushroom with Chilli and Ginger 153, *153*
Puy Lentil and Mushroom 148, *148*
Red Lentil with Cumin 146, *146*
Roasted Yellow Pepper 149, *149*
Spiced Gumbo 150, *150*

Soured cream 75

Soya products 96–97
beans 83, 95, *95*

cheese and yoghurt 83
flour 83
milk 97
miso 97
shoyu sauce 97
soy sauce 97
tamari sauce 97
tempeh 97
textured vegetable protein
(TVP) 97
tofu 96
Soy sauce, 97
Spices 108–11 (see also
individual entries)
Spinach and chard (leafy beets)
39, 39
Kuku with Spinach 181, 181
Pasta with Spinach, Shiitake
Mushrooms and Tofu 217
Spinach and Chilli Calzone
200
Spinach and Lentil Turnovers
253, 253
Spinach and New Potato
Curry with Coconut 248,
249
Split red lentils 95
Spring onions 49
Squash, butternut 56
Butternut Squash and
Carrot Purée with
Nutmeg and
Mascarpone 286, 287
Red Rice with Pan-Fried
Squash, Mushrooms and
Pecan Nuts 229
Squash blossoms 56
Squash, summer 55
Squash, onion, 227
Risotto with Roasted
Squash 227
Stalks and buds 40–41 (see also
individual entries)
Star anise 111, 111
Star fruit (carambola) 71, 71
Sticky rice see glutinous rice
Stilton 80, 80
Stir-fry dishes
Stir-Fry with Chinese Sauce
276, 276
Stir-Fry with Japanese Sauce
277, 277
Stir-Fry Shredded Leeks
with Tarragon 285, 285
Stir-Fry Vegetables with
Cashew Nuts and Chilli
273, 273
Stir-Fry Vegetables with
Golden Coconut Sauce
275, 275
Stir-Fry Vegetables and Tofu
with Sesame Marinade
274, 274
Stock
Basic Vegetable Stock 144

cubes 112
Dark Mushroom Stock 145
Strawberries 63
Strawberry Yoghurt Ice
331, 331
Quick Berry Brûlée 332,
332
Straw mushrooms 45
Stress, and vitamins 24
Sugar 118
Sugar-free jams and spreads 119
Sugar snaps see mangetout
Sultanas 73
Summer savory 107, 107
Summer squash 55
Sun-dried tomatoes 113, 113
sun-dried tomato purée 113
Sunflower oil 115
Sunflower seeds 103, 103
Swede (rutabaga) 53
Sweetcorn see corn
Sweeteners 118–19
Sweet pepper 54
Sweet Potatoes 51, 51
Chowder with Sweet
Potato 147, 147
Sweet Potato and
Courgette Gratin 263,
263
Sweet Potato Stew 241, 241
Sweet rice see glutinous rice

T
Tahini 83, 103, 103
Tahini Dressing 317
Tamarind 111, 111
Tamari sauce 97
Tarragon 106, 106
vinegar 117
Tempeh 97, 97
Textured vegetable protein
(TVP) 97
Thyme 105, 105
Tofu 83, 83, 96, 96
Baked Tofu and Button
Mushrooms 175, 175
Silken Tofu Dressing 317
Smoked Tofu and Water
Chestnut Salad with
Oriental Dressing 303, 303
Tofu Fritters 204, 204
Tofu Goulash with
Aubergines and
Mushrooms 246, 246
Tofu and Strawberry with
Vanilla 141
Tomatoes 56–57, 57
Classic Tomato Pizza
Topping 196

Fresh Tomato and Basil
Topping 364, 365
Layered Bulgar with
Tomatoes and Feta 231
Robust Tomato Salad
308, 309
Stuffed Italian Tomatoes
with Red Pesto and
Mozzarella 172, 172
sun-dried 113
Tomato, Cucumber and
Watercress Juice 138
Very Easy Tomato Sauce
292, 293
Tomato purée, sun-dried 113
Tree fruit, dried 73
Tropical fruits 68–71
Truffles 113
Turmeric 111
Turnips 52–53

V
Vanilla 111
Vegan diet 29
Vegetables 34–57
buying and storing 34
freezing of 34
nutritional value of 34
preparation and cooking
of 35
and stress 29
Vine fruit 72–73
Vinegars 117, 117
Vinegar, herb 105
Vitamins 16, 17

W
Wakami 113
Walnuts 100, 100
Roasted Walnut and Black
Olive Topping 365, 365
walnut oil 116
Watercress 42
Watercress Roulade with
Asparagus and Crème
Fraîche 354–55, 354–55
Wheat 88, 88
Wheat flakes 88, 88
Wheat flour 89
Wheatgerm, 88 88
White cabbage (Dutch) 37
White wine vinegar 117
Wholefood diet 29
Wholegrains and flakes 86
Wild rice 87
Wild Rice with Hazelnuts,
Carrots and Artichokes
236

Wild Rice and Mushroom
Brioche 374, 375
Winter squash 56

Y
Yeast extract 112
Yellow split peas 95
Yoghurt 75
Savoury Smoothie 140

Acknowledgements

This book took up a good chunk of my life and involved a large number of people. I am very pleased with the end result and so to all those who played a part, however small, I would like to say thank you.

There are also some key people who deserve a special mention. A huge thank you to Rachel Anderson for making all the testing of the recipes so enjoyable with her enthusiasm and generous spirit. My thanks also go to Ann Halsey, Antonia Halse, Marco and Monica Bonafini, Cherry Wilson, Kay Denny, Caroline Moran, Ann-Marie Kjof and Amal Rashid for contributing recipe ideas.

I would also like to thank Shirley Patton who was mainly responsible for managing this project and who drew together the many threads of this book in a highly focused and very supportive manner.

At Ivy Press I would like to thank Peter Bridgewater, Terry Jeavons and Sophie Collins for keeping this book alive; Caroline Earle, for picking up the final editing; Alistair Plumb whose design really brought the text to life; and Jacqueline Clark and Marie Louise Avery, who respectively made and photographed my recipes.

Picture Credits

The publishers wish to thank the following for the use of pictures:

Cephas: 45 bottom left, 117 top.
Bruce Coleman Collection: 24 bottom, 87 top right.
Corbis UK Ltd: 24 top, 27 top, 62 bottom right, 76 bottom left, 108 top right, 118 bottom.
Garden Picture Library: 13 bottom, 30 bottom, 64 bottom right, 73 bottom left, 115 top, 119 bottom right.
Science Photo Library: 18 top, 28 bottom, 30 top, 88 top right, 90 left, 112.